S0-AEP-771

Android Programming for Beginners

Learn all the Java and Android skills you need to start making powerful mobile applications

John Horton

BIRMINGHAM - MUMBAI

Android Programming for Beginners

Copyright © 2015 Packt Publishing

All rights reserved. No part of this book may be reproduced, stored in a retrieval system, or transmitted in any form or by any means, without the prior written permission of the publisher, except in the case of brief quotations embedded in critical articles or reviews.

Every effort has been made in the preparation of this book to ensure the accuracy of the information presented. However, the information contained in this book is sold without warranty, either express or implied. Neither the author, nor Packt Publishing, and its dealers and distributors will be held liable for any damages caused or alleged to be caused directly or indirectly by this book.

Packt Publishing has endeavored to provide trademark information about all of the companies and products mentioned in this book by the appropriate use of capitals. However, Packt Publishing cannot guarantee the accuracy of this information.

First published: December 2015

Production reference: 3050416

Published by Packt Publishing Ltd.
Livery Place
35 Livery Street
Birmingham B3 2PB, UK.

ISBN 978-1-78588-326-2

www.packtpub.com

Credits

Author
John Horton

Reviewers
Nayanesh Ramchandra Gupte
Klaas Kabini
Márton Kodok
Paresh Mayani

Commissioning Editor
Edward Gordon

Acquisition Editor
Nadeem Bagban

Content Development Editor
Divij Kotian

Technical Editor
Mrunmayee Patil

Copy Editor
Neha Vyas

Project Coordinator
Nikhil Nair

Proofreader
Safis Editing

Indexer
Monica Ajmera Mehta

Graphics
Kirk D'Penha

Production Coordinator
Nilesh Mohite

Cover Work
Nilesh Mohite

About the Author

John Horton is a coding and gaming enthusiast based in the UK. He has a passion for writing apps, games, books, and blog articles about coding, especially for beginners.

He is the founder of Game Code School, `http://www.gamecodeschool.com`, which is dedicated to helping complete beginners to get started with coding, using the language and platform that suits them best.

John sincerely believes that anyone can learn to code and that everybody has a game or an app inside them, but they just need to do enough work to bring it out.

He has authored around a dozen technology books, most recently, the following:

- *Android Game Programming by Example* (`https://www.packtpub.com/game-development/android-game-programming-example`)
- *Learning Java Building Android Games* (`https://www.packtpub.com/game-development/learning-java-building-android-games`)

Thanks to Jo, Jack, James, Ray, and Rita.

Also to everybody at Packt Publishing who lent a hand with this book: Edward Gordon, Divij Kotian, and Mrunmayee Patil. Thank you for your continuous support throughout this journey.

About the Reviewers

Nayanesh Ramchandra Gupte is an enthusiastic Android professional based in Bangalore — the Silicon Valley of India. He is a full-stack engineer and has been exploring Android for more than 5 years. Until now, he has worked with different organizations and developed more than 40 Android applications. Some of these apps are featured with the Top Developer badge on Google Play. Programming, especially in Java and Android, is not just a part of his career, but his passion as well.

Besides being a software engineer, he works as an Android consultant and is associated with the Google Developers Group based in Bangalore. Writing personal blogs and articles on Java and Android remain a couple of his interests. He works as a professional Android trainer and pursues teaching and illustration as his hobbies.

Associated with one of the e-commerce giants in India, Nayanesh is a part of the core engineering team. He also works closely with the Product and UX team to build a next-generation platform for e-commerce.

You can know more about him at `https://about.me/NayaneshGupte`, and you can find him on LinkedIn at `http://in.linkedin.com/in/nayaneshgupte/`.

To begin with, I credit my parents who have always nurtured my dreams and constantly supported me to make them happen. I want to thank my fiancée, Aakanksha, and my in-laws who trusted my dynamic decisions while I was hopping cities and organizations with the aim of improving my career graph. I sincerely want to thank Sudarshan Shetty, my guide, because of whom I got engrossed in Java and Android. His teachings have brought me a long way. I am sure there is much more to explore. I owe a lot to my best buddies, Saurabh and Rahul, since it was all because of them that I decided to get into this field of programming. Lastly, the journey would have been incomplete without my colleagues and mentors, Rishi and Vishal, from whom I learned what passion for programming really is!

Márton Kodok has extensive experience as a web, mobile, and desktop software engineer. He has also been a backend programmer and team leader, where he mostly concluded projects for various U.S. companies. He is a lead developer in various scalable projects and an active contributor to scalable solutions such as Beanstalkd Console and Riak-admin interface. He is an expert in databases and search systems such as Google, BigQuery, and Elasticsearch. He is also an active member of Stack Overflow, has spoken at many conferences, and has mentored many young, talented enthusiasts. You can find him at `ro.linkedin.com/in/pentium10` and `http://stackoverflow.com/users/243782/pentium10`.

Paresh Mayani is a software engineer who has been exploring the horizon of Android development since Cupcake (Android 1.5). He has hands-on experience of designing, building, and publishing Android Apps. His skills range from technical documentation, UX/UI design, code and performance optimization, to writing extensive testing for applications.

He's actively involved in the Android community too—writing blog posts, helping fellow Android developers by posting answers on Stack Overflow, and giving talks around the world. He is among top 0.25% with and manages more than 60,000 reputation points. He is one of the top 10 highest contributors to the Android tag on Stack Overflow.

He is the founder/organizer of the Google Developers Group, Ahmedabad, India. By looking at his experience and his contribution to the Android community, he was recently nominated for the Google Developers Expert program led by Google. You can find more about him at his blog, `http://www.technotalkative.com/`.

www.PacktPub.com

Support files, eBooks, discount offers, and more

For support files and downloads related to your book, please visit www.PacktPub.com.

Did you know that Packt offers eBook versions of every book published, with PDF and ePub files available? You can upgrade to the eBook version at www.PacktPub.com and as a print book customer, you are entitled to a discount on the eBook copy. Get in touch with us at service@packtpub.com for more details.

At www.PacktPub.com, you can also read a collection of free technical articles, sign up for a range of free newsletters and receive exclusive discounts and offers on Packt books and eBooks.

https://www2.packtpub.com/books/subscription/packtlib

Do you need instant solutions to your IT questions? PacktLib is Packt's online digital book library. Here, you can search, access, and read Packt's entire library of books.

Why subscribe?

- Fully searchable across every book published by Packt
- Copy and paste, print, and bookmark content
- On demand and accessible via a web browser

Free access for Packt account holders

If you have an account with Packt at www.PacktPub.com, you can use this to access PacktLib today and view 9 entirely free books. Simply use your login credentials for immediate access.

Dedicated to everyone who has no place to stay or insufficient strength to want to live,
especially those who used up all their strength serving someone else.

Table of Contents

Preface

Do you have a great idea for an app, but don't know how to make it a reality? Are you trying to start a career in programming, but haven't found the right way in? Or maybe you're just frustrated that all the so-called "beginner's guides" to learn Android require you to know Java. If so, *Android Programming for Beginners* is for you. But why choose Android?

Learn by example and build three real-world apps and over 40 mini apps throughout the book!

Why Android?

When Android first arrived in 2008, it was almost seen as a poor relation to the much more stylish iOS on Apple iPhone. But, quite quickly, through diverse handset offers that struck a chord with both the practical price-conscious as well as the fashion-conscious and tech-hungry consumers, Android user numbers exploded. Now, after seven major releases, the annual sales of Android devices is increasing almost every year.

For many, myself included, developing Android apps is the most rewarding thing (apart from our friends and family) in the world.

Quickly putting together a prototype of an idea, refining it, and then deciding to run with it as well wiring it up into a fully-fledged app is an exciting and rewarding process. Any programming can be fun, and I have been programming all my life, but creating for Android is somehow extraordinarily rewarding.

Defining exactly why this is so is quite difficult. Perhaps it is the fact that the platform is free and open. You can distribute your apps without requiring the permission of a big controlling corporation—nobody can stop you. And at the same time, you have the well-established, corporate-controlled mass markets such as Amazon App Store, Google Play, Samsung Galaxy Apps, as well as other smaller marketplaces.

More likely, the reason developing for Android gives such a buzz is the nature of the devices. They are deeply personal. You can create apps that actually interact with people's lives. You can educate, entertain, organize, and so on. But it is there in their pocket ready to serve them in the home, workplace, or on holiday. Everyone uses them, from infants to seniors.

This is no longer considered geeky, nerdy, or reclusive; developing Android apps is considered highly skillful and really successful developers are hugely admired, even revered.

If all this fluffy kind of spiritual stuff doesn't mean anything to you, then that's fine too; developing for Android can make you a good living or even make you wealthy. With the continued growth of device ownership, the ongoing increase in CPU and GPU power and the non-stop evolution of the Android operating system (OS) itself, the need for professional app developers is only going to grow.

In short, the best Android developers—and perhaps more importantly, Android developers with the best ideas—are in greater demand than ever. Nobody knows who these future Android coding heroes are and they might not even have written their first line of Java yet.

But is this book for me?

So why isn't everybody an Android developer? Obviously, not everybody will share my enthusiasm for the thrill of creating software that can help people make their lives better, but I'm guessing that because you are reading this, you might.

Unfortunately, for those who do, there is a kind of glass wall on the path of progress that frustrates many aspiring Android developers.

Android uses Java to make its apps respond, think, and communicate with users. Every Android book, even those aimed at so-called beginners, assumes at least an intermediate level of Java and most (if not all), a fairly advanced level. So, good to excellent Java knowledge is a prerequisite for learning Android.

Unfortunately, learning Java in a completely different context to Android can sometimes be a little dull, and some of what you learn is not directly transferable into the world of Android either.

I think it makes more sense, is vastly more enjoyable, and is significantly quicker and more rewarding, to teach Java in a purely Android environment—to teach Java with the single overriding goal of learning to develop professional standard Android apps. And that's what this book is about.

What this book covers

Chapter 1, The First App, sets up your Android development environment, and then it helps you build and deploy your first simple app to an emulator and a real Android device.

Chapter 2, Java – First Contact, teaches some absolute beginner Java coding as well as shows you how to implement your first user interface design.

Chapter 3, Exploring Android Studio, gets to grips with the tools of the trade of professional Android developers with a fast tour around Android Studio.

Chapter 4, Designing Layouts, focuses on building user interfaces by exploring the layouts and widgets that make up an Android app as well as builds some apps that demo our new skills.

Chapter 5, Real-World Layouts, takes user interfaces a step further by designing and implementing some apps with layouts more like what you would see on professional Android apps.

Chapter 6, The Life and Times of an Android App, explores how the Android operating system works under the surface by building apps that demonstrate the Android lifecycle and how we make it work for us.

Chapter 7, Coding in Java Part 1 – Variables, Decisions, and Loops, gives you the first major glimpse of Java, the native language of Android, and the way we will be bringing our apps to life. Zero previous coding experience is assumed.

Chapter 8, Coding in Java Part 2 – Methods, discusses that methods are one of the key building blocks of all the apps we will make in this book. In this chapter, we will build a few working mini apps to explore how to use methods.

Chapter 9, Object-Oriented Programming, states that OOP is the way that all modern programming is done, especially Java. This chapter holds the key to using all the advanced and exciting features contained in Android.

Chapter 10, Everything's a Class, will bring together everything we have seen in all the other chapters so far. By the end of this chapter, our design and Java skills will be as one and we will be well placed to start building apps with more advanced features.

Chapter 11, Widget Mania, covers the use of our new OOP, Java, and UI knowledge that we will be able to use and interact with many of the user interface features available in Android.

Chapter 12, Having a Dialogue with the User, starts ramping up what we can do now. In this chapter, we will build apps that use pop-up windows to get input from the user as well as start the first major app of the book, Note To Self.

Chapter 13, Handling and Displaying Arrays of Data, will discuss Java arrays and then show you how to use them in some apps, as almost any app that we build will need to be able to handle significant amounts of data.

Chapter 14, Handling and Displaying Notes in Note To Self, will use the skills you learned and practiced in the previous chapter and will enhance our Note To Self app in order for the user to be able to view and access all their data.

Chapter 15, Android Intent and Persistence, covers how to build multiscreen apps, how to let the user seamlessly navigate between them, and how to implement a settings screen that remembers user's preferences.

Chapter 16, UI Animations, teaches how to use the really useful Android SeekBar widget and how to animate our UI to make it spin, bounce, flash, and more.

Chapter 17, Sound FX and Supporting Different Versions of Android, finds out how to bring our apps to life with sound effects. In this chapter, you will explore the SoundPool class to add beeps, buzzes, clicks, or even explosions.

Chapter 18, Design Patterns, Fragments, and the Real World, sets the scene for the most advanced part of the book. In this chapter, you will learn how professionals organize their code with patterns and see exactly how to use this knowledge to build Android apps.

Chapter 19, Using Multiple Fragments, shows you how to use the Android Fragment to make our apps modular so they can run on multiple different device types, such as phones and tablets, and appear differently on each but run from exactly the same code that we write.

Chapter 20, Paging and Swiping, builds some apps that use the really cool swiping effect. In this chapter, you will learn how to swipe left and right between pages, menus, and images in an app.

Chapter 21, Navigation Drawer and Where It's Snap, explains how to use the navigation drawer UI in your apps, how to swipe from the edge of the screen to reveal the user's navigation choices, and how to get started on the most advanced app we will build using navigation drawer.

Chapter 22, Capturing Images, builds a mini app to use the device camera in order to capture and store images and then enhance our main app as well.

Chapter 23, Using SQLite Databases in Our Apps, teaches you how databases work with a focus on the Android database of choice, SQLite. In this chapter, we will build a database mini app.

Chapter 24, Adding a Database to Where It's Snap, shows you how to code an advanced database to store user data, photos, and even GPS coordinates.

Chapter 25, Integrating Google Maps and GPS Locations, shows you how to connect live to the Google Maps service to add real global mapping data to your apps.

Chapter 26, Upgrading SQLite – Adding Locations and Maps, teaches you how to upgrade the database from *Chapter 24, Adding a Database to the Where It's Snap App* and add the ability to capture and show a map and GPS locations along with the user's photos in the Where it's snap app.

Chapter 27, Going Local – Hola!, will help you understand how to easily add multiple different languages to make apps with a truly global reach.

Chapter 28, Threads, Touches, Drawing, and a Simple Game, discusses how to build a simple but working retro Pong game to explore the important topics of drawing, screen touches, and multithreaded computing.

Chapter 29, Publishing Apps, shows you how to build deployable apps and publish them on the Google Play global marketplace.

Chapter 30, Before You Go, discusses briefly how you might like to take your Android and Java skills further.

What you need for this book

Android Studio running on any of the major operating systems can use the code in this book. Android Studio is a free software and full setup instructions for Windows are in the opening chapter.

Android Studio is the recommended development tool, and at the time of publication, the minimum system requirements were as follows:

Windows
- Microsoft® Windows® 8/7/Vista/2003 (32 or 64 bit)
- 2 GB RAM minimum; however, 4 GB RAM is recommended
- 400 MB hard disk space
- At least 1 GB for Android SDK, emulator system images, and caches

- 1280 x 800 minimum screen resolution
- Java Development Kit (JDK) 7
- Optional for accelerated emulator: Intel® processor with support for Intel® VT-x, Intel® EM64T (Intel® 64), and Execute Disable (XD) Bit functionality

Mac OS X

- Mac® OS X® 10.8.5 or a higher version, up to 10.9 (Mavericks)
- 2 GB RAM minimum; however, 4 GB RAM is recommended
- 400 MB hard disk space
- At least 1 GB for the Android SDK, emulator system images, and caches
- 1280 x 800 minimum screen resolution
- Java Runtime Environment (JRE) 6
- Java Development Kit (JDK) 7
- Optional for accelerated emulator: Intel® processor with support for Intel® VT-x, Intel® EM64T (Intel® 64), and Execute Disable (XD) Bit functionality

On a Mac OS, run Android Studio with Java Runtime Environment (JRE) 6 for optimized font rendering. You can then configure your project to use Java Development Kit (JDK) 6 or JDK 7.

Linux

- A GNOME or KDE desktop
- GNU C Library (glibc) 2.15 or later
- 2 GB RAM minimum; however, 4 GB RAM is recommended
- 400 MB hard disk space
- At least 1 GB for the Android SDK, emulator system images, and caches
- 1280 x 800 minimum screen resolution
- Oracle® Java Development Kit (JDK) 7

Tested on Ubuntu® 14.04, Trusty Tahr (64-bit distribution capable of running 32-bit applications).

Who this book is for

Are you trying to start a career in programming, but haven't found the right way in? Do you have a great idea for an app, but don't know how to make it a reality? Or maybe you're just frustrated that "to learn Android, you must know Java." If so, this book is for you. You don't need any programming experience to follow along with this book, just a computer and a sense of adventure.

Conventions

In this book, you will find a number of text styles that distinguish between different kinds of information. Here are some examples of these styles and an explanation of their meaning.

Code words in text, database table names, folder names, filenames, file extensions, pathnames, dummy URLs, user input, and Twitter handles are shown as follows: "We will see this, perhaps most distinctly, when we look at `RelativeLayout` later in the chapter."

A block of code is set as follows:

```
android:layout_below="@+id/textView"
```

When we wish to draw your attention to a particular part of a code block, the relevant lines or items are set in bold:

```
<RelativeLayout xmlns:
  android="http://schemas.android.com/apk/res/android"
    xmlns:tools="http://schemas.android.com/tools"
      android:layout_width="match_parent"
    android:layout_height="match_parent"
      android:paddingLeft="@dimen/activity_horizontal_margin"
    android:paddingRight="@dimen/activity_horizontal_margin"
    android:paddingTop="@dimen/activity_vertical_margin"
    android:paddingBottom="@dimen/activity_vertical_margin"
      tools:context=".LayoutExperiments">


</RelativeLayout>
```

Any command-line input or output is written as follows:

```
Rambo's health =: 150
Vassily's health =: 50
Wellington's health =: 100
Green Beret: is shooting
Sniper: is shooting
Sailor: is shooting
```

New terms and **important words** are shown in bold. Words that you see on the screen, for example, in menus or dialog boxes, appear in the text like this: "As we have already seen, widgets have properties that we can either set in XML or through the **Properties** window."

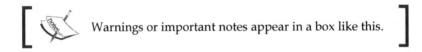

Warnings or important notes appear in a box like this.

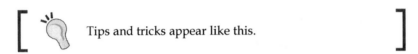

Tips and tricks appear like this.

Reader feedback

Feedback from our readers is always welcome. Let us know what you think about this book—what you liked or disliked. Reader feedback is important for us as it helps us develop titles that you will really get the most out of.

To send us general feedback, simply e-mail feedback@packtpub.com, and mention the book's title in the subject of your message.

If there is a topic that you have expertise in and you are interested in either writing or contributing to a book, see our author guide at www.packtpub.com/authors.

Customer support

Now that you are the proud owner of a Packt book, we have a number of things to help you to get the most from your purchase.

Downloading the example code

You can download the example code files from your account at http://www.packtpub.com for all the Packt Publishing books you have purchased. If you purchased this book elsewhere, you can visit http://www.packtpub.com/support and register to have the files e-mailed directly to you.

All the finished code and resources for every one of the projects in this book can be found in the download bundle in a folder named after the chapter number for example Chapter 1, Chapter 2, and so on. Furthermore inside each of these folders you will find a sub-folder with the name of the app. Then as you would expect, within this folder will be the code files and the resources for that app. And finally, the resources and code files are further sub divided into folder names that correspond to their correct place within a project. So for example, to explore the completed files for the project in *Chapter 2, Java – First Contact* you would look in Chapter 2/Hello Android. In there you will find code files and resources in folders named java and layout. As we learn about and use more resource types, so the number of subfolders within the application folder in the download bundle will grow. Our Android Studio projects actually contain dozens of files and folders. The download bundle will only contain the files and folders we need to edit, or that are being discussed. We will take a closer look at the structure of an Android project in the second chapter.

Downloading the color images of this book

We also provide you with a PDF file that has color images of the screenshots/diagrams used in this book. The color images will help you better understand the changes in the output. You can download this file from https://www.packtpub.com/sites/default/files/downloads/AndroidProgrammingforBeginners_ColoredImages.pdf.

Errata

Although we have taken every care to ensure the accuracy of our content, mistakes do happen. If you find a mistake in one of our books—maybe a mistake in the text or the code—we would be grateful if you could report this to us. By doing so, you can save other readers from frustration and help us improve subsequent versions of this book. If you find any errata, please report them by visiting http://www.packtpub.com/submit-errata, selecting your book, clicking on the **Errata Submission Form** link, and entering the details of your errata. Once your errata are verified, your submission will be accepted and the errata will be uploaded to our website or added to any list of existing errata under the Errata section of that title.

To view the previously submitted errata, go to `https://www.packtpub.com/books/content/support` and enter the name of the book in the search field. The required information will appear under the **Errata** section.

Piracy

Piracy of copyrighted material on the Internet is an ongoing problem across all media. At Packt, we take the protection of our copyright and licenses very seriously. If you come across any illegal copies of our works in any form on the Internet, please provide us with the location address or website name immediately so that we can pursue a remedy.

Please contact us at `copyright@packtpub.com` with a link to the suspected pirated material.

We appreciate your help in protecting our authors and our ability to bring you valuable content.

Questions

If you have a problem with any aspect of this book, you can contact us at `questions@packtpub.com`, and we will do our best to address the problem.

1
The First App

Welcome! In this chapter, we won't waste any time in getting started with developing Android apps.

We will look at what is so great about Android, what Android and Java are exactly, how they work and complement each other, and what this means to us as future developers.

After this, we will spend a little time setting up our development environment and then get straight to building and deploying our first app.

By the end of this chapter, we will have done the following:

- Set up the **Java Development Kit (JDK)**, part of the required Android development environment
- Installed Android Studio, the final part of our Android development environment
- Built our very first Android app
- Deployed an Android emulator
- Run our app on an Android emulator and a real device

How Java and Android work together

After we write a program in Java for Android, we click on a button to change our code into another form that is understood by Android. This other form is called **Dalvik EXecutable (DEX)** code, and the transformation process is called **compiling**. Compiling takes place on the development machine after we click on that button. We will see this work right after we set up our development environment.

Android is a fairly complex system, but you do not need to understand it in depth to be able to make amazing apps. The part of the Android system that **executes** (runs) our compiled DEX code is called the **Dalvik Virtual Machine (DVM)**. The DVM itself is a piece of software written in another language that runs on a specially adapted version of the Linux operating system. So what the user sees of Android, is itself just an app running on another operating system.

The purpose of the DVM is to hide the complexity and diversity of the hardware and software that Android runs on but, at the same time, its purpose is to expose all of its useful features. This exposing of features generally works in two ways. The DVM itself must have access to the hardware, which it does, but this access must be programmer friendly and easy to use. The way the DVM allows us access is indeed easy to use because of the Android **Application Programming Interface (API)**.

The Android API

The Android API is the code that makes it really easy to do exceptional things. A simple analogy could be drawn with a machine, perhaps a car. When you step on the accelerator, a whole bunch of things happen under the hood. We don't need to understand about combustion or fuel pumps because a smart engineer has provided an **interface** for us. In this case, a mechanical interface — the accelerator pedal.

Take the following line of Java code as an example; it will probably look a little intimidating if you are completely new to Android:

```
locationManager.getLastKnownLocation
    (LocationManager.GPS_PROVIDER);
```

However, once you learn that this single line of code searches for the available satellites and then communicates with them in orbit around the Earth while retrieving your precise latitude and longitude on the planet, it is easy to begin to glimpse the power and depth of the Android API in conjunction with the DVM. Even if that code does look a little challenging at the moment, imagine talking to a satellite in some other way!

The Android API is mainly a whole bunch of Java code. So, how do we use all this code to do cool stuff without getting swamped by its complexity? How do we find and manipulate the pedals, steering wheel, and sunroof of the Android API?

 There are many different estimates to the number of lines of code that have gone into Android. Some estimates are as low as 1 million, some as high as 20 million. What might seem surprising is that, despite this vast amount of code, Android is known in programming circles for being "lightweight".

Java is object-oriented

Java is a programming language that has been around a lot longer than Android. It is an object-oriented language. This means that it uses the concept of reusable programming objects. If this sounds like technical jargon, another analogy will help. Java enables us and others (such as the Android development team) to write Java code that can be structured based on real-world "things" and, here is the important part, it can be **reused**.

So, using the car analogy, we could ask the question: if a manufacturer makes more than one car in a day, do they redesign each and every part for each and every car?

The answer, of course, is no. They get highly skilled engineers to develop exactly the right components that are honed, refined, and improved over years. Then, that same component is reused again and again, as well as occasionally improved. Now, if you are going to be picky about my analogy, then you can argue that each of the car's components still have to be built from raw materials using real-life engineers, or robots, and so on.

This is true. What the software engineers actually do when they write their code is build a blueprint for an object. We then create an object from their blueprint using Java code and, once we have that object, we can configure it, use it, combine it with other objects, and more. Furthermore, we can design blueprints and make objects from them as well. The compiler then translates (manufactures) our custom-built creation into DEX code.

In Java, a blueprint is called a **class.** When a class is transformed into a real working thing, we call it an **object**.

Objects in a nutshell

We could go on making analogies all day long. As far as we care at this point:

- Java is a language that allows us to write code once that can be used over and over again.
- This is very useful because it saves us time and allows us to use other people's code to perform tasks we might otherwise not have the time or knowledge to write for ourselves.
- Most of the time, we do not even need to see this code or even know how it does its work!

One last analogy. We just need to know how to use that code, just as we only need to learn to drive the car.

So, a smart software engineer up at Google HQ writes a desperately complex Java program that can talk to satellites. He then considers how he can make this code useful to all the Android programmers out there. One of the things he does is he makes features such as getting the device's location in the world a simple one-line task. So the one line of code we saw previously sets many more lines of code in action that we don't see. This is an example of using somebody else's code to make our code infinitely simpler.

What exactly is Android?

We know that to get things done on Android, we write Java code of our own, which also uses the Java code of the Android API. This is then compiled into DEX code and run by the DVM, which in turn has connections to an underlying operating system called Linux.

Then the manufacturers of the Android devices and individual hardware components write advanced software called **drivers**, which ensure that their hardware (CPU, GPU, GPS receivers, and so on) can run on the underlying Linux operating system.

Our compiled Java code, along with some other resources, is placed in a bundle of files called an **Android application package (APK)**, and this is what the DVM needs to run our app. This process is explained in the following figure:

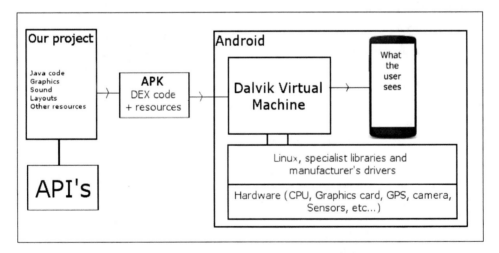

In summary, all we need to do is learn how to read and code Java, so we can begin to learn and take advantage of the Android API.

All these tools are free, so let's take a look at the development environment we will be using.

The development environment

A **development environment** is a term that refers to having everything you need in order to develop, set up, and be ready to go in one place. We need the following two things to get started:

- We talked a fair bit about compiling our Java code, as well as other people's Java code, into DEX code that will run on the DVM, on people's Android devices. In order to use Java code, we need a free software called the JDK. The JDK also includes other people's code, which is separate from the Android API.

- There is a whole range of tools that are required to develop for Android, and we also need the Android API, of course. This whole suite of requirements is collectively known as the Android **software development kit (SDK)**. Fortunately, downloading and installing a single application will give us these things all bundled together. This single application is called Android Studio.

Android Studio is an **integrated development environment** (IDE) that takes care of all the complexities of compiling our code and linking with the JDK and the Android API. Once we have installed the JDK and Android Studio, we can do everything we need inside this application.

What could possibly go wrong?

I got a lot of feedback via my website `http://gamecodeschool.com` about a previous book of mine that showed how to install an Android development environment. People said that setting this up can be the hardest part. So I've written this section to be as thorough as possible because not everybody has a smooth setup experience.

Hopefully, you won't need all the extra tips and detailed figures, but there are a few vagaries that can trip us up while setting up the development environment.

 Most likely, these instructions will get you up and running quickly and cover all your issues. If there is an issue that I haven't managed to anticipate, don't let it beat you! I guarantee that you are not the first to have that exact issue. Perform a web search (use Google), be really specific in your search criteria, and I am confident you will be coding in no time at all.

This guide will get around 99% of the Windows user's setup in a couple of hours. All the coding and development information you need will be covered 100% step by step.

For Mac and Linux users, most of these instructions can be easily interpreted as the key points of the tutorial are more about what we do inside of the setup programs and less about the specific environment we are using. My apologies for not providing comprehensive instructions for every operating system.

A note to the existing developers who use Eclipse

There are multiple options regarding which software to use when developing Android apps. In the early days of developing Android, an IDE called Eclipse was most commonly used. A few years ago, a new "official" contender for the best Android IDE was released. This was Android Studio. The problem after its first release was that it was still in the beta (not finished) stage. It had numerous bugs, including some quite awkward ones. However, even then it was the preferred IDE for many because of its smooth operation, cool looks, official status, and prestigious heritage.

Now that Android Studio has exceeded version 1, there is virtually no reason to use anything else, especially if you are just getting started with Android. If you already have Eclipse set up for Android development and really don't want to change, that's fine, the code in this book will work. However, there will be significant differences in the instructions, especially regarding the **user interface (UI)** designer. Also, the code in this book has been thoroughly tested by others and me in Android Studio.

The sections that follow will set up a development environment with the JDK and Android Studio as our IDE of choice.

The JDK

This can be as simple as downloading, double-clicking on the downloaded file, and following the installation instructions. However, sometimes it isn't. So, it is probably worth running through the installation process step by step and pointing out along the way a few options that can make things easier.

What if I already have Java?

Most PC/Mac computers already have Java installed. Many modern apps require Java, and a classic example of this is the game *Minecraft*. Java is subtly, but significantly, different from the JDK. Java on its own just runs programs that have been written in Java for PC. This is the PC equivalent to the DVM. Java on its own, however, will not compile our code or make other people's code that we need available. This more common version of Java is called the **Java Runtime Environment (JRE)**. When we install the JDK, it will also install the JRE, whether you already have it or not. So, if you are conscientious about keeping your hard drive in order, you could uninstall the JRE using the Windows Control Panel in the usual way before proceeding. Then find and delete your existing Java folder.

This tutorial will then reinstall the latest version of the JRE as well as the JDK. If, however, you know that you have a program that uses Java and you don't want to mess with its configuration, then go ahead with this tutorial, but just be aware that there will be a JRE and an associated Java folder in two places on your hard drive.

To summarize the preceding in case anything is unclear: this tutorial assumes that you don't have an existing folder named Java, but will work just fine even if you do.

Installing the JDK

As a little bit of preparation before we install the JDK, you need to know which operating system you have and whether it is 32 or 64 bit. If you are unsure, use this little tip to find out.

Do I have a 32-bit or 64-bit Windows system?

To find out, right-click on My Computer (This PC on Windows 8) icon, left-click on the **Properties** option, and look under the **System** heading of the **System type** entry like this:

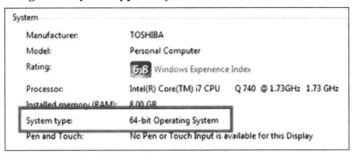

Now we are ready to install the JDK. This fairly simple set of steps will set up the JDK quickly. The only slight delay is the download itself, which could take a while on slower Internet connections. The actual installation process should be fast and trouble free:

1. Visit the Java JDK downloads page at `http://www.oracle.com/technetwork/java/javase/downloads/jdk8-downloads-2133151.html`.

2. If the link has changed, conduct a web search for Java JDK download. The only potential stumbling block at this stage is that you click on a link for the JRE instead. JDK is what we need. The following is a screenshot of the important part of this page:

Java SE Development Kit 8u51

You must accept the Oracle Binary Code License Agreement for Java SE to download this software.

○ Accept License Agreement ● Decline License Agreement

Product / File Description	File Size	Download
Linux x86	146.9 MB	jdk-8u51-linux-i586.rpm
Linux x86	166.95 MB	jdk-8u51-linux-i586.tar.gz
Linux x64	145.19 MB	jdk-8u51-linux-x64.rpm
Linux x64	165.25 MB	jdk-8u51-linux-x64.tar.gz
Mac OS X x64	222.09 MB	jdk-8u51-macosx-x64.dmg
Solaris SPARC 64-bit (SVR4 package)	139.36 MB	jdk-8u51-solaris-sparcv9.tar.Z
Solaris SPARC 64-bit	98.8 MB	jdk-8u51-solaris-sparcv9.tar.gz
Solaris x64 (SVR4 package)	139.79 MB	jdk-8u51-solaris-x64.tar.Z
Solaris x64	96.45 MB	jdk-8u51-solaris-x64.tar.gz
Windows x86	176.02 MB	jdk-8u51-windows-i586.exe
Windows x64	180.51 MB	jdk-8u51-windows-x64.exe

3. Your download page will most likely be slightly different. There will be a newer version of the JDK by the time you read these words, so the 8u51 will be different. That's OK, we just need whichever is the newest version. Simply click on the **Accept License Agreement** radio button that is highlighted in the previous screenshot and then click on the download link, which is on the right-hand side column corresponding to your operating system in the **Product/File Description** column. If you are not sure whether you have 32-bit or 64-bit Windows, refer to the tip before this section.

4. Wait while the JDK is downloaded to your hard drive.

5. In the folder where you've downloaded the JDK, right-click on the `jdk-8u51-windows-x64.exe` file and select **Run as administrator**. The precise name of the file you have will vary based on whether you have 32-bit or 64-bit Windows and what the current version of the JDK happens to be at the time.

6. There will be a series of windows that will guide us through the installation process. The most we have to do is just click on **Next** to proceed. As promised, I will guide you through them one at a time and point out when you might like to make changes or make a note of things. The following is a screenshot of the first window that you will see during the installation:

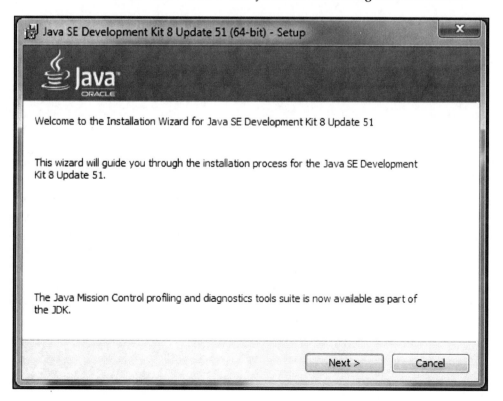

7. Now, click on **Next** and you will see this window:

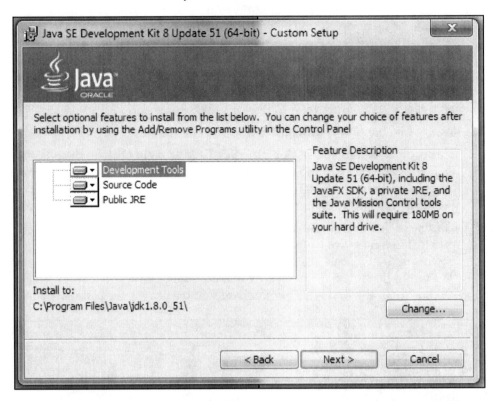

8. On the window pictured in the previous screenshot, we can leave all the options at their default values. They are just what we need. The **Install to** setting is worth considering, however. By the time we install the JDK, Android Studio, and all the extra tools and files that come with it, we will have around 6 gigabytes of files and folders. Now, consider that we will also be making lots of projects throughout the course of this book. Ideally, we want all of these files, folders, and projects to be on the same hard drive. They don't have to be, but we might avoid some problems later on if they are. So, do you have at least 6 gigabytes of space on the hard drive that you've chosen by default? If not, you might like to browse to another folder. In addition to this, as we will see later on in this tutorial, it will be handy (but not essential) to simplify the folder names used to install the JDK. So, click on the **Change** button and you will see this window:

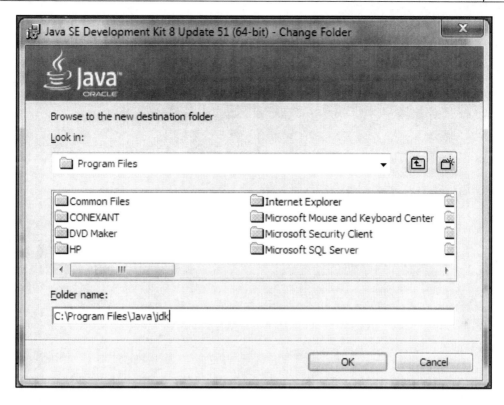

9. Browse to the hard drive where you will be installing all of your development tools. Then simplify the names of the folders in which you will install the JDK to just `Java\JDK\`. As you can see in the next screenshot, I have also switched to my `D:\` drive, as I have more space there:

10. It actually doesn't matter what you call these folders as long as you remember where they are and what they are called, including whether they are uppercase or lowercase letters. Perhaps you can jot down a note or copy and paste them to a file on your desktop. When you are happy with the chosen installation location and folder names, go ahead and click on **Next**.

11. The next window will not appear on every installation. If you don't see the window pictured as follows, its fine, you can skip to step 13. If you do see the window, proceed to step 12.

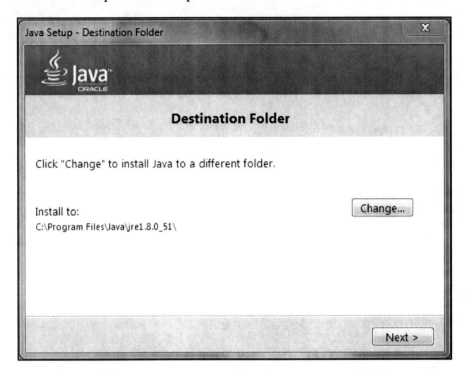

12. Understandably, this window could cause confusion if you have never done any Java development before. You might be thinking that we had already chosen the destination folder for Java. We chose the location for the JDK. This window refers to the bog-standard Java—the JRE. This is what runs Java programs on your PC and, since we are developing for Android, we don't need it. However, we still need to choose a location in order to proceed. Accept the default and just click on **Next**. If you are a tidiness obsessive like me, you can change to the same Java folder from step 8 and then click on **Next**.

13. Next, you will see the window that says **3 Billion Devices Run Java**. Android has over 1.1 billion devices alone at the time of writing this despite a slow start in 2015. You might also like to know that there are more than 18,000 different distinct devices. Seriously, Google it if you think it sounds crazy. You can do this while you wait for the installation to complete.

14. Now, you will see the final screen. Click on **Next Steps** if you are curious, but there is no need because we will be covering Android-specific next steps without delay.

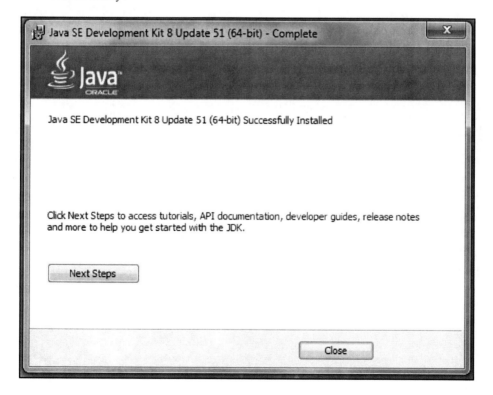

15. Click on **Close**, and we are almost done installing the JDK, with just a few more precautionary steps left.

16. Now, we will make sure that Windows (and all its applications) know where to find the JDK. Right-click on your My Computer (This PC on Windows 8) icon and **Properties | Advanced system settings | Environment Variables | New** (under **System variables** and not under **User variables**). Now you can see the **New System Variable** dialog as follows:

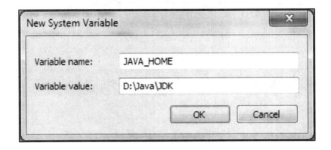

17. As shown in the previous screenshot, type JAVA_HOME in **Variable name** and enter D:\Java\JDK in the **Variable value** field. If you've installed the JDK somewhere else, then the file path you enter in the **Variable value** field will need to point to where you've placed it. Be sure to type it correctly, make sure that the slashes \ are the right way around, and don't add any extra slashes.

18. Click on **OK** to save your new settings. Now, click on **OK** again to clear the **Advanced system settings** window.

We have successfully installed the JDK, which we need to develop Android apps with Android Studio, and we have also installed the JRE, if it wasn't installed already, which we won't be using, but this won't cause us any problems either.

Setting up Android Studio

Now that the JDK is installed and ready to go, we are only one step away from building our first Android app. Installing Android Studio can take a bit longer than the JDK and is a little more nuanced, but it is nothing a determined, aspiring, developer won't be able to handle with ease.

What could possibly go wrong?

This whole process could take an hour or two. Not because there is lots of work for us to do, but because we need to initiate some fairly large downloads. Also, at several different stages in the process, Android Studio will connect to the internet and update itself. If you have a fast internet connection, then you can probably knock a good percentage off of my rough estimate of the time required.

Now that we know what to expect, we can get on with the installation of Android Studio. Follow the given steps to do so. There is nothing especially tricky about this, and the few aspects that might need some consideration will be discussed as they arise:

1. Visit `https://developer.android.com/sdk/index.html` and click on the **Download Android Studio for Windows** button. If at the time of reading this the link has changed, simply Google `Download Android Studio`.

2. Next, you will see the **Terms and Conditions** page as shown in the following screenshot:

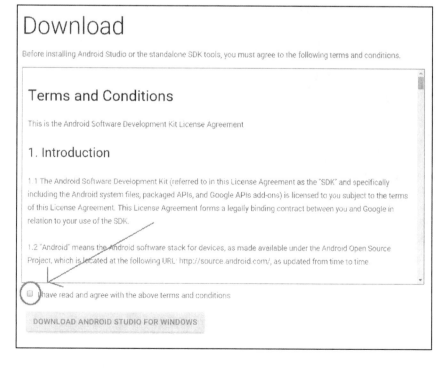

3. Click on the **I have read and agree with the above terms and conditions** checkbox as highlighted in the previous screenshot.

4. Now, click on the **DOWNLOAD ANDROID STUDIO FOR WINDOWS** button. Wait for the download to complete.

5. Open the folder where you have downloaded Android Studio. Right-click on the `android-studio-bundle-141.1980579-windows.exe` file and select **Run as administrator**. Your file will most likely have a different name based on whichever is the current version of Android Studio at the time.

6. When you get the **Do you want the following program to be allowed to make changes to this computer** message, click on **Yes**. You will see the first window of the installation process.

7. Let's step through the setup process a window at a time. Pictured next is the first window that you will see when you start the setup process:

8. Click on **Next**. Now we can see a few options, as in this next screenshot:

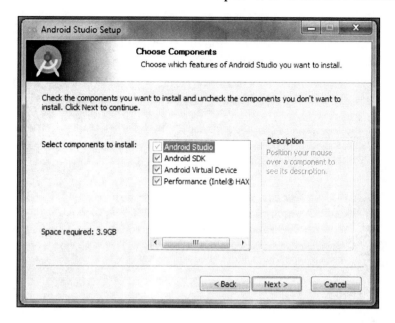

9. Make sure that all the options have a tick next to them, and then click on **Next**.

10. The next window is the license agreement. Click on **I Agree** and you will see some settings that warrant a short discussion. Take a look at the next screenshot that shows you the **Install Locations** window:

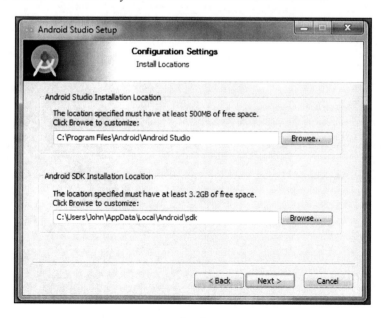

11. In this step, we want to install the Android Studio IDE and Android SDK to the same hard drive where we installed the JDK. So you might just be able to click on **Next** at this point. However, if you've installed the JDK to another drive, then we need to change the drive and the folders we use at this step too. This isn't strictly essential, but it can avoid problems for some users.

12. For **Android Studio Installation Location**, choose the root of the drive where you've installed the JDK followed by \Android Studio. So in my case, this will be D:\Android Studio. For **Android SDK Installation Location**, choose the same hard drive and simply add Android\sdk as the location. So if, like me, you've installed the JDK on D:, then choose D:\Android\sdk. The next screenshot makes this clear:

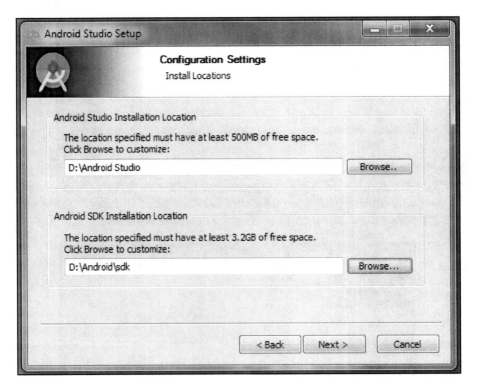

13. Click on **Next** when you have selected your installation locations.

14. Next, you might see the **Emulator Setup** window as pictured in the next figure. If you do, then accept the default settings and click on **Next**; otherwise, you can skip to step 15. Don't worry if you don't see this screen, it is a minor issue to do with running the Android emulators a bit more smoothly. Most of the time, you will probably want to use a real device anyway.

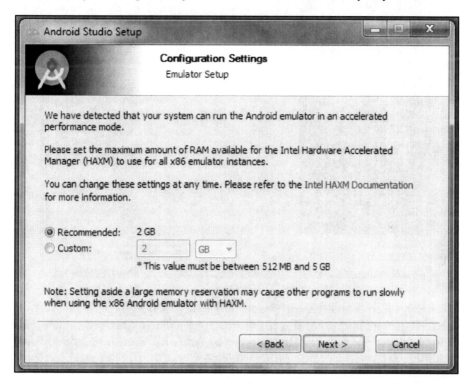

15. We are nearly there now. The next window asks you to choose a start menu folder, just as when we install any new Windows app. You might want to make a note of this location. Click on **Install** to accept the default settings, and Android Studio will begin to install itself and extract the SDK to the appropriate folder that we selected earlier. This might take some time.

16. When you see the **Installation Complete** window, click on **Next**. Now, you will see the following window:

17. Click on **Finish** to bring up the second to last window of the installation process. Assuming that this is your first time using Android Studio, click on the **I do not have a previous version of Android Studio or I do not want to import my settings** radio button and click on **OK**.

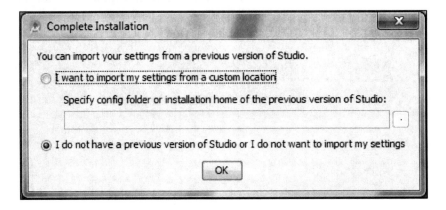

18. Now, in the next figure, you get to choose the theme that Android Studio will use. If you like a conventional black text on white background appearance, then choose **IntelliJ**, and if you want a cool dark style, choose **Darcula**. You can alter any of these schemes from within Android Studio if you change your mind later.

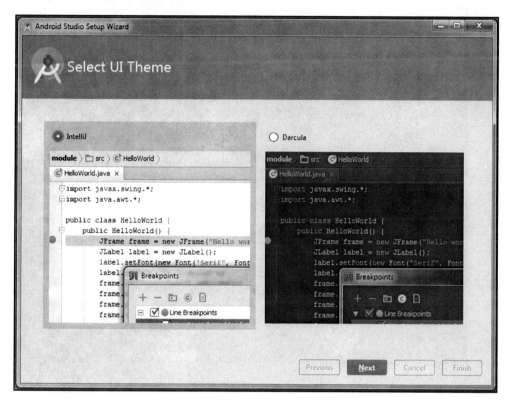

19. Click on **Next** when you have chosen your theme.

20. Now Android Studio will connect to the Internet and download some of the Android tools that we will be using soon. Again, this could take a while.

21. When the **Downloading Components** window has done its work, it will present you with a **Finish** button. Click on it.

22. Finally, we are presented with the **Welcome to Android Studio** screen. This screen, among other things, allows us to start a new project or open an existing project. Take a look at the next screenshot:

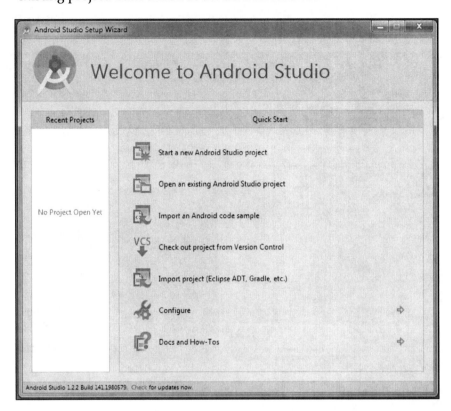

23. You can close this window and take a break or leave it open and read on because we will be back here really soon.

This was a fairly lengthy tutorial but, hopefully, it wasn't too tough. Android Studio and the supporting tools that we need are installed and ready to go. We are really close now to building our first app.

First, let's look at the composition of an Android app a little.

What makes an Android app

We already know that we will write Java code that will itself use other people's Java code and will be compiled into DEX code that runs on the DVM. In addition to this, we will also be adding and editing other files as well. These files are known as **Android resources**.

Android resources

Our app will include resources such as images, sounds, and user interface layouts that are kept in separate files from the Java code. We will slowly introduce ourselves to them over the course of this book.

They will also include files that contain the textual content of our app. It is a convention to refer to the text in our app through separate files because it makes them easy to change, and this makes it easy to create apps that work for multiple different languages.

Furthermore, the actual UI layouts of our apps, despite the option to implement them with a visual designer, are actually read from text-based files by Android.

Android (or any computer), of course, cannot read and recognize text in the same way that a human can. Therefore, we must present our resources in a highly organized and predefined manner. To do so, we will use **Extensible Markup Language** (**XML**). XML is a huge topic but, fortunately, its whole purpose is to be both human and machine readable. We do not need to learn this language, we just need to observe (and then conform to) a few rules. Furthermore, most of the time when we interact with XML, we will do so through a neat visual editor provided by Android Studio. We can tell when we are dealing with an XML resource because the filename will end with the .xml extension.

You do not need to memorize this, as we will constantly be returning to this concept throughout the book.

The structure of Android's Java code

In addition to these resources, it is worth noting that Java, as used in Android, has a structure to its code. There are many millions of lines of code that we can take advantage of. This code will obviously need to be organized in a way that makes it easy to find and refer to. It is organized under predefined packages that are specific to Android.

Android packages

Whenever we create a new Android app, we will choose a unique name known as a **package**. We will see how to do this in the *Our first Android app* section. Packages are often separated into **subpackages**, so they can be grouped together with other similar packages. We can simply think of these as folders and subfolders.

We can also think of all the packages that the Android API makes available to us as books that contain code, from a library. Some common Android packages we will use include the following:

- `android.graphics`
- `android.database`
- `android.view.animation`

As you can see, they are arranged and named to make what is contained in them as obvious as possible.

 If you want to get an idea for the sheer depth and breadth of the Android API, then take a look at the Android package index at http://developer.android.com/reference/packages.html.

Earlier, we learned that reusable code blueprints that we can transform into objects are called **classes**. Classes are contained in these packages. We will see in our very first app how to easily **import** other people's packages along with specific classes from those packages for use in our projects. A class will almost always be contained in its own file, with the same name as the class, and have the `.java` file extension.

In Java, we further break up our classes into sections that perform the different actions for our class. We call these sections **methods**. These are, most often, the methods of the class that we will use to access the functionality provided within all those millions of lines of code. We do not need to read the code. We just need to know which class does what we need, which package it is in, and which methods from within the class give us precisely the results we are after.

The next diagram shows a representation of the Android API. We can think about the structure of the code that we will write in exactly the same way, although we will most likely have just one package per app. Of course, because of the object-oriented nature of Java, we will only be using selective parts from this API. Also note that each class has its own distinct **data**. Typically, if you want access to the data in a class, you need to have an object of that class.

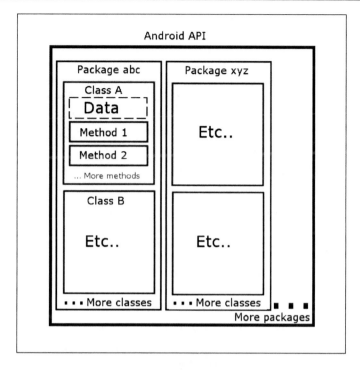

You do not need to memorize this, as we will constantly be returning to this concept throughout the book.

By the end of this chapter, we will have imported multiple packages and some classes from them and we will have used other people's methods. By the end of *Chapter 2, Java – First Contact*, we will have even written our very own methods as well.

Our first Android app

In programming, it is a tradition for the first app of a new student to use whichever language/OS they are using to say hello to the world. We will quickly build an app that does just that, and in *Chapter 2, Java – First Contact*, we will go beyond this and add some buttons that actually respond to the user.

Creating the project

We will start with the creation of this project. What follows here are the steps to create a new project. My instructions at each step might seem a little verbose, but that is just because this is the first time we are running through them. After a few chapters, when we create new projects, I will be able to describe the instructions in a sentence and you will be able to create the project in 30 seconds. As this is the first one, let's do this step by step and learn it all along the way:

1. Start Android Studio by clicking on its icon in the start menu folder that you chose in step 15 of the previous tutorial.

> If you can't find the icon, you can find the file directly in the bin folder at the location where you installed Android Studio. Find the studio64.exe file on a 64-bit PC or the studio.exe file on a 32-bit PC and double-click on it in the same way that you start any other Windows app.

2. If you get the **Windows Firewall has blocked some features of this program** message, as pictured in the next screenshot, click on **Allow access**:

3. Now, you will see the **Welcome to Android Studio** start menu that we saw at the end of the previous tutorial. Go ahead and click on **Start a new Android Studio project**. You will see the **New Project** screen pictured next. Starting a new project is very easy and mainly involves accepting the default settings on a few different screens. Let's take a closer look at some of the options, however, because they will increase our understanding of Android and Android Studio:

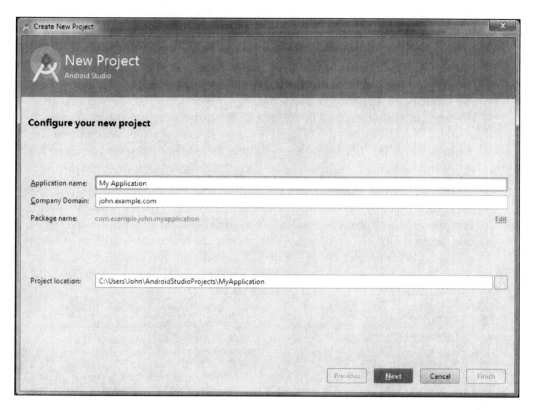

4. First, note that we can name our application in the **Application name** field. You can choose any name you like for your first application, but just be aware that Android Studio will soon generate a whole bunch of code and files for us and that the name you choose will be reflected in them. If you want your code and files to be identical to those that we will be examining shortly, call your application `Hello Android`.

5. Next, note the **Company Domain** field. This is where you will enter the details of your company. It is a convention and very practical (because it is unique) to use the domain name of your company website. If you don't have a company or domain name, enter the domain name I am using: gamecodeschool.com. Unlike the application name, using a different company domain will have almost zero effect on the code and files that we will examine later. Although if you are using your own domain name, do refer to the tip *Using your own domain name or application name*, after this tutorial. Choose and enter a company domain name.

6. Now, look at the **Package name** field. It has been automatically derived from the previous two fields. If you used the same two values as suggested in the previous two steps, your package name will be com.gamecodeschool. helloandroid. Remember that a package is a collection of the Java classes that are our code files, and our apps can comprise one or more packages if we wish them to, but they must comprise at least one package. We can edit the package name by clicking on the edit link, but we have no need to do so here.

7. Finally, in the **Project location** field, you can accept the default settings or browse to the location where you would like to store all your Android projects. You have the option to change this for each project that you create. I've put personal projects in my Dropbox folder so, if my PC breaks down mid project, I know my files are safe. Android Studio can also work from an online code repository, such as GitHub, but we are not covering that in this book. Here is a screenshot of the **New project** window after steps 5, 6, and 7:

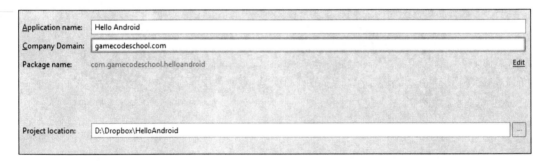

8. Click on the **Next** button to continue and you will see the **Target Android Devices** window:

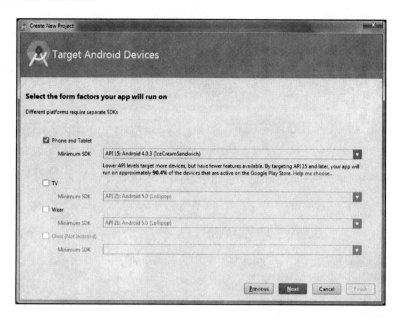

9. Here, we can see that we have the option of developing an application for a phone, tablet, TV, and wear. Wear is the range of Android-enabled smartwatches. In the preceding screenshot, in the grayed-out part at the bottom of the window, we can also see that we can develop for Glass, Google's trendy Android-enabled glasses, although we would need to install additional files to do this. In this book, we will be developing for phones and tablets, so the already selected option is just what we need. The only other thing we need to choose on this screen is the **Minimum SDK**. We already know that the Android SDK is a collection of packages of code that we will be using to develop our apps. Like any good SDK, the Android SDK is regularly updated, and each time it gets a significant update, the version number is increased. Simply put, the higher the version number, the newer the features you get to use; the lower the version number, the more devices our app will work on. For now, the default setting **API 15: Android 4.0.3 (IceCreamSandwich)** will give us lots of great features and at least 90% compatibility with the Android devices that are currently in use. If, at the time of reading this, Android Studio is suggesting a newer API, then go with it.

10. Click on the **Next** button. Now we can see the **Add an activity to Mobile** window:

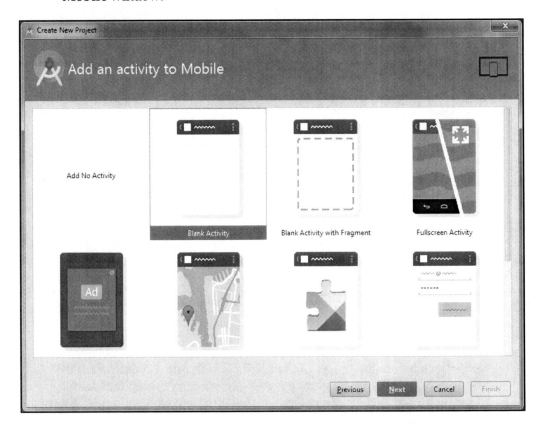

11. In the previous sections, we discussed Java classes in brief. An `Activity` class is a special Java class and every Android app must have at least one. It is the part of the code where our app will start when it is launched by the user, and this also handles any interaction with the user. The options on this screen provide different ready-made templates of the `Activity` class code in order to give programmers a fast start when creating various types of apps. As we are starting from scratch, the most appropriate option for us is **Blank Activity**. Make sure that **Blank Activity** is selected by clicking on it and then clicking on **Next**. Now, take a look at the **Customize the Activity** window:

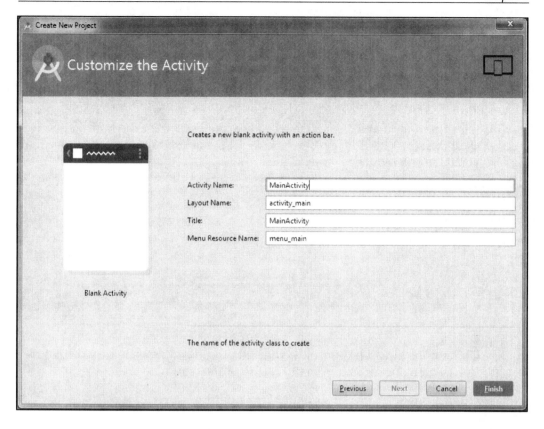

12. The **Customize the Activity** window gives us four things that we can play with. It is perfectly possible to leave them all at their default settings, but let's change them to make them more meaningful and discuss what each one is. **Activity Name** is the name of the class that will contain our code. If this sounds odd, to be more specific, we will have a class that *is an* activity *called* whatever we name it here. Name the activity `MyActivity`.

13. The next field is **Layout Name**. We discussed earlier in this chapter that Android UI layouts are usually defined in a separate XML text file, not with our Java code. The layout name is what this file will be called. Name the layout `my_layout`.

14. The next field is **Title**. This is different than the **Activity Name** field and will be used by Android on the device's screen as the name of the app. Name the title `My App`.

15. Finally for this screen, we have **Menu Resource Name**. Menus are the pop-up options that you get on Android when (perhaps unsurprisingly) you click on the menu button. They might also be shown on the topmost bar of the app known as the **action bar**. This varies depending on the version of Android a device is running. These are considered to be part of the UI as well and are usually defined in this separate XML file. Name our menu file my_menu.

16. It is important that the exact case and spacing is used for the information we enter in steps 12, 13, 14, and 15. Check out the next close-up figure to see that you have entered the text just right:

Activity Name:	MyActivity
Layout Name:	my_layout
Title:	My App
Menu Resource Name:	my_menu

17. Click on the **Finish** button, and Android Studio will now create a project for us based on our choices from the previous 16 steps.

We now have a project ready for us to deploy or modify.

Using your own domain name and application name

Using your own domain and application name is absolutely fine. The only thing to be aware of is that the first line of code that we will see when we look at our Java code (in *Chapter 2, Java – First Contact*), will be, and needs to be, different. This is the package name. In the context of this book, we won't ever need to change the package name or do anything with it, so it doesn't matter what you call your apps or whether you use your own domain name.

The only time this could cause a problem is when you create a project (with a different name or package name) and then copy and paste the code from the download bundle. The reason for this is that this code will have a different package name. All you need to do to overcome this problem is either create your project with the same package name as the code files you are copying and pasting from or change the very first line of code, after you have copied and pasted it, to reflect the package name of the project you've created.

A note on version controlling

In this book, we will be covering everything you need to know to publish professional apps. One thing we will not be discussing is working collaboratively as part of a team or any backup strategies for your code. If you only intend to build apps on your own, then you don't need to know any more. However, Android Studio works almost seamlessly with a number of different **Version Control Systems (VCS)** and code repositories. VCS and their related code repositories have a number of advantages, which are as follows:

- You can allow multiple programmers to contribute to the same project and even the same file

- You can click on a button to roll back your work to a specified position if you realize you have gone wrong

- You can store your code seamlessly in a repository on the cloud/Web and work on your project from any development machine without any concern about backing up the files

Achieving all these benefits is not complicated and, in some cases, it is even free. The problem with introducing VCS in a book like this is that there are an awful lot of options and there is no simple, universally best option that will suit everybody. In addition, it introduces yet another hurdle before we can get down to the business of making apps.

 If the topic of version control sounds interesting, try exploring these two providers:
- http://www.bitbucket.org
- https://www.github.com

Now, you might be surprised to know that we can actually deploy our app to an emulator or a real Android device. Throughout this book, all the code for each project is supplied in the download bundle in a folder that reflects the chapter number. There is no code, however, in the Chapter 1 folder because all the code in this project has been automatically generated by Android Studio and we don't need to type anything for this project. We will, however, examine, modify, and add to this autogenerated code in the next chapter.

Deploying and testing the app

We need to test our apps frequently throughout development to check for any errors, crashes, or anything else unintended. It is also important to make sure that the app looks good and runs correctly on every device type/size that you want to target. Clearly, we do not own each of the many thousands of Android devices. This is where emulators come in.

Emulators, however, are sometimes a bit slow and cumbersome, although they have improved a lot recently. If we want to get a genuine feel of the experience that our user will get, then nothing beats deploying an app to a real device. So we will probably want to use both real devices and emulators while developing our apps.

First, we will deploy to an emulator and then on a real device.

Deploying to an emulator

Deploying to an emulator is a matter of a few mouse clicks. There is a ready-made emulator that is included with Android Studio. At the time of writing this, it is Nexus 5. This may well be updated to a newer device by the time you read this. The basic functionality described here will likely be identical, but the device name and screenshots might vary slightly from your experience:

1. Just below the menu bar is a row of neat-looking buttons that we will explore as the book progresses. The button we want right now is the green triangle that represents play. Identify the button using the next screenshot and click on it:

2. Next, you will see the **Choose Device** window. Click on the **Launch emulator** option as shown in the next screenshot:

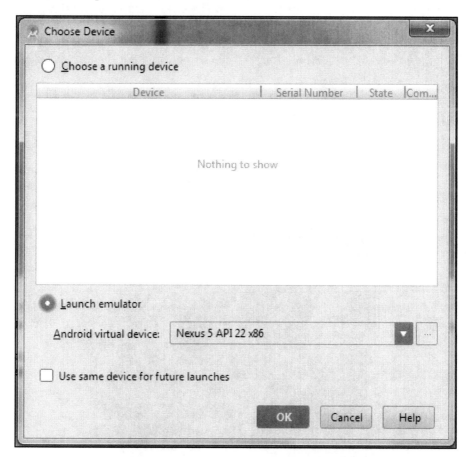

3. Click on **OK** to launch the emulator. Nexus 5 comes preconfigured when you install Android Studio, but you can also choose and customize emulators yourself. Refer to the tip *Creating a new emulator* after this tutorial.

4. The emulator might take some time to start! Sometimes, it might even take 5 minutes or more. This is partly dependent on whether Android Studio has detected whether your PC can run **HAXM (Hardware Acceleration Execution Manager)** during the setup phase or not. Either way, all the tutorials in this book will work just fine. Wait for the emulator to start. When your emulator has loaded, you will see something like the next screenshot:

5. We need to simulate swiping a finger up on the screen to unlock. So click and drag up from somewhere near the bottom on the emulator screen. You can now see your first app in action, as shown in the following screenshot:

6. Let's play a little bit with the emulator. Click on the back button to quit the app, as shown in the next screenshot:

7. Note that you can see the launcher icon for your app with the name you gave it when we created the project. Obviously, we will need to replace the default Android icon before we release our app into the world. This will do for now though.

8. You can click on the launcher icon to run the app again or try running any of the other apps. Play with the emulator for a bit.

Congratulations, you have now run and played with your first app. In addition to this, we have seen that we can do many things on an emulator that we previously could only do on a real device.

 Emulators take time to start up

If you are planning to use the emulator again soon, then leave it running in order to avoid having to wait for it to start again.

If you want to try out your app on a tablet, TV, or even a watch, you're going to need a different emulator.

Creating a new emulator

If you want to create an emulator for a different Android device, this is really simple. From the main menu, navigate to **Tools | Android | AVD Manager**. On the **AVD Manager** window, click on **Create New Virtual Device**. Now click on the type of device you want to create: **TV**, **Phone**, **Wear**, or **Tablet**. Now simply click on **Next** and follow the instructions to create your new AVD. The next time you run your app, the new AVD will appear as an option to run the app on.

Now we can take a look at how to get our app onto a real device.

Deploying to a real Android device

The first thing to do is to visit your device manufacturer's website and obtain and install any drivers that are required for your device and operating system.

Many of the more recent Android devices don't need any drivers at all. You could try simply plugging it in!

The next few steps will set up the Android device for debugging. Note that different manufacturers structure the menu options slightly differently to others. However, the following sequence is probably very close, if not exact, to enable debugging on most devices:

1. Click on the **Settings** menu option or the **Settings** app.

2. Click on **Developer options**.

3. Tick the checkbox for **USB Debugging**.

4. Connect your Android device to the USB port of your development system. You can see in the following figure that on the **Devices | Logcat** subtab of the **Android** tab, at the bottom of the Android Studio window, my **Samsung GT I9100** has been detected:

5. Click on the Play icon from the Android Studio toolbar, just as we did when running the app on the emulator.

6. When the **Choose Device** window appears, click on **Choose running device** and then on your device; in my case, this would be **Samsung GT I9100**.

7. Finally, click on **OK** to debug the app on your chosen device.

You can now see your app in all its glory on your device and show it to your friends and admirers alike.

Note that although the app is running on a real device, this is still running in the debug mode so we can get feedback about what is happening to our app. In *Chapter 29, Publishing Apps*, we will see how to generate a signed, distributable app that can be uploaded to Google Play.

FAQ

1. So is Android not really an operating system, but just a virtual machine? And are all phones and tablets really Linux machines?

   No, all the different subsystems of an Android device, which includes Linux, the DVM, and the libraries and drivers together, are what make up the Android operating system.

2. I still don't understand all of these technical terms, such as DVM, object-oriented, APK, and so on. Should I reread this chapter?

    No, that isn't necessary, as we just need to introduce this jargon, and we will be revisiting them all as well as clarifying them as the book progresses. You just need to understand the following:

    - ° We will be writing Java code and creating other resources
    - ° Android Studio, with the help of the JDK, will turn this code and these resources into real Android apps

Now, you are good to go and can move on to *Chapter 2, Java – First Contact.*

Summary

So far, we have set up an Android development environment and created and deployed an app on both an emulator and a real device. If you still have unanswered questions (and you probably have more than at the start of this chapter), don't worry because as we dig deeper into the world of Android and Java, things will become clearer. As the chapters progress, you will build a very rounded understanding of how everything fits together, and then success will just be a matter of practice and digging deeper into the Android API.

In the next chapter, we will edit the UI using the visual designer and raw XML code, write our first Java methods, and get to use some methods provided to us by the Android API.

2

Java – First Contact

We now have a working Android development environment, and we have built and deployed our first app. It is obvious, however, that autogenerated code by Android Studio is not going to make the next top-selling app on Google Play. We need to explore this autogenerated code in order to understand Android and then begin to build on this useful template. With this aim in mind, in this chapter, we will do the following:

- See how to get technical feedback from our apps
- Examine the Java code and UI XML code from our first app
- Get the first taste of using the Android UI designer
- Write our first Java code
- Learn a few core Java fundamentals and how they relate to Android

First, let's see how to find out whether things are going wrong.

Examining the log output

In the previous chapter, we mentioned that our app was running in a debug mode so we could monitor it and get feedback when things go wrong. So, where is all this feedback then?

You might have noticed a whole load of scrolling text at the bottom of the Android Studio window. If not, click on the **Android** tab at the bottom-left corner of the screen and then make sure that the **logcat** tab is selected as well, as indicated by the areas highlighted in solid red in the next figure (the dashed red areas will be discussed in a moment):

You can drag the window to make it taller, just like you can in most other Windows applications.

This is called the logcat or sometimes, it is referred to as the **console**. It is our app's way of telling us what is going on underneath what the user sees. If the app crashes, the reason or clues about the reason will appear here. If we need to output debugging information, we can do so here as well.

> If you just cannot work out why your app is crashing, copy and pasting a bit of text from logcat in to Google will often reveal the reason.

You might have noticed that most, if not all, of the contents is fairly unintelligible. That's OK. At the moment, we are only interested in the errors that will be highlighted in red and the debugging information, which you will learn about next. If we want to see less unneeded text in our logcat window, we can turn on a filter.

In the previous figure, I highlighted two areas with dashed red lines. One of them is the drop-down list that controls this filter. Click on it now and change it from **Verbose** to **Info**. We have cut down the text output significantly. We will see how this is useful when we have made some changes to our app and redeployed it. We will do this after we have explored the code and the assets that make up our project. Also, double-check the second red-dashed highlighted area if it says **Show only the selected application**. If it doesn't, click on it and change it to this now.

Now, we can take a look at what Android Studio automatically generated for us, and then, we can set about changing it to personalize it beyond what we got from the project creation phase.

Exploring the project assets and code

We are going to take a look at the resource files that contain the code that defines our simple UI layout, and the file that contains our Java code. At this stage, we will not attempt to understand it all, as you need to learn more before it makes sense to do so. What we will see, however, is the basic content and structure of both the files so that we can reconcile it with what we already know about Android resources and Java.

Let's look at the Java code first. You can see this code for real by clicking on the **MyActivity.java** tab, which is shown in the next figure:

As we are not looking at the details of the code, an annotated screenshot is probably more useful than reproducing the actual code in the text form. Refer to the next figure while reading on. I've labeled key parts of the code here to explain it further:

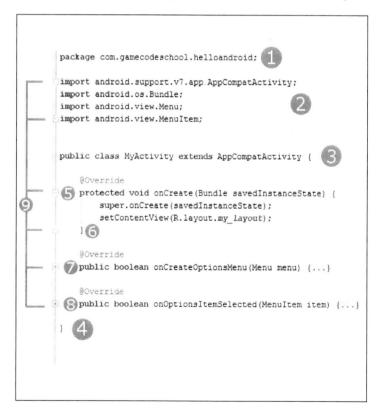

Let's get to understand this code a bit better. The first thing to point out is the part labeled as **9**. This points to all the little **+** and **-** buttons in the editor that can collapse and expand parts of the code. I have indeed collapsed two parts of the code: parts **7** and **8**. I have done so because they are not of interest to us at the moment and provide none of the functionality we are discussing. So, what you can see here is probably slightly different than what you will see when you look at the code in Android Studio directly.

The part labeled as **1** is called the **package declaration**, and as you can see, it contains the package name that we chose when we created the project. Every Java file will have a package declaration at the top of the code.

The part labeled as **2** is four lines of code that all begin with the word `import`. After the word import, we can see that there are various dot-separated words. The last word of each line is the name of the class that the line imports into our project, and all the previous words are the packages and subpackages that contain these classes. This means that in our project, we will have access to `AppCompatActivity`, `Bundle`, `Menu`, and `MenuItem`. We will not discuss all of these classes immediately, just the concept of importing, which is important right now. Note that we can add extra classes from any package at any time, and we will when we improve upon our app shortly.

The part labeled as **3** of our code is called the **class declaration**. Here is that line in full. I have highlighted one part of it here:

```
public class MyActivity extends AppCompatActivity {
```

The class declaration is the start of a class. Take a note of the highlighted part. Here, `MyActivity` is the name we've chosen when we created the project, and it is also the same as the `MyActivity.java` filename, as we would expect it to be, having discussed Java classes previously. The `extends` keyword means that our class called `MyActivity` will be of the type `AppCompatActivity`. We can, and will, use some classes without this `extends` part.

We use extends here because we want to use all the code that went into the AppCompatActivity class as well as add our own code to it as well. So we **extend** it. All this and more will become clear in *Chapter 9, Object-Oriented Programming*.

Finally, for the part labeled as **2**, look at the opening curly brace at the end of the line: {. Now look at the bottom of the figure at the part labeled as **4** of our code. This closing curly brace } denotes the end of the class. Everything in between the opening and closing curly braces, { . . . }, is part of the class.

Now look at the part labeled as **5** of the code. Here is that line of code in full, including the key part for our discussion at the moment, which is highlighted as shown:

```
protected void onCreate(Bundle savedInstanceState) {
```

This is a **method signature**. The highlighted part, onCreate, is the **method name**. We make a method execute its code by using its name. We say we are **calling** a method when we do this. Although we will not concern ourselves at the moment with the parts of the code on either side of the method name, you might have noticed Bundle, one of the classes we import at the part labeled as **2** of our code. If we remove this import line, Android Studio would not know what Bundle was, and it would be unusable and indicated in a red underline as an error. Our code would not compile and run. Note that the very last thing in the line of the preceding code is an opening curly brace {. This denotes the start of the code that is contained within the onCreate method. Now, jump to the part labeled as **6** of our code and you will see a closing curly brace }. You can probably guess this is the end of the method.

The parts labeled as **7** and **8** are also methods that I have collapsed to make the figure and this discussion more straightforward. Their names are onCreateOptionsMenu and onOptionsItemSelected.

We know enough about our Java code to make some progress. We will see this code for real and change it in the *Improving our app and deploying again* section.

Examining the layout file

Now we will look at just one of the many .xml files. The following is the my_layout.
xml file that contains the XML code that defines the UI design of our app. If you
want to view this code for real, just click on the my_layout.xml tab next to the
MyActivity.java tab that we clicked on to find the Java code:

If we first look at the part of the code labeled as **1**, we can see that the very first thing
is <RelativeLayout.... A RelativeLayout tag is a UI element that is used to wrap
other parts of the UI.

When we add a new element to a UI in Android, we always start with < followed by
the element's name. The code that follows defines the properties that this element
will have. This can include dozens of different things depending upon the type
of UI element it is. Here, among a bit of other XML code, we can see properties
such as layout_height, paddingRight, paddingTop, and paddingBottom. All
these **properties** define how RelativeLayout will appear on the user's screen. The
properties for RelativeLayout end at the first > symbol.

If we look at the bottom of our XML figure, we will see the code labeled as **2**.
This code, </RelativeLayout>, marks the end of RelativeLayout. Anything in
between the closing > symbol of the element's properties and </RelativeLayout>,
which defines its end, is considered a **child** of the element. So, we can see that
RelativeLayout has/contains a child. Let's look at that child now.

Using what you just learned, we can devise that the UI element that starts at the position labeled as **3** in the figure is called **TextView**. Just like its parent, the tag starts with < and its name is <TextView. . . . If we look further at TextView, we can see that it has a number of properties. It has a text property that is set to "Hello world!". This, of course, is the exact text that our app shows to the user. It also has the layout_width and layout_height properties that are both set to "wrap_content". This tells TextView that it can take up as much space as the content it contains needs. As we will see throughout the book, there are many more properties available for this and other UI elements. The final property in TextView is id, and we will see how we and Android use the id property in the next section when we improve our first app.

Note that the code at the part labeled as **4** in our XML figure is />. This marks the end of the TextView element. This is slightly different to how the end of RelativeLayout was written. When an element in XML contains no children, we can just end it like this />. When the element contains children and its end comes further on in the code from where its properties are defined, it is much clearer to end the element by repeating its name, as </RelativeLayout>.

We will see this code for real in the next section and learn more about the properties, as well as see a totally new type of UI element: Button.

Improving our app and deploying again

We will take a more thorough and structured look at Android Studio, in particular the visual designer in the next chapter. For now, I thought it would be good to make a small addition to our UI, as well as write our first few lines of Java code.

 You can get the completed code files for this project in the Chapter 2 folder of the download bundle.

In Android, there are often multiple ways to get the same thing done. Here, we will see how we can refer to a method in our Java code directly from the UI designer or XML code. Then, once we have done this, we will jump to the Java code and write our very own methods that our new UI refers to. Not only that, but we will write code within our methods that both gives an output on the logcat/console and uses a really cool Android feature that pops up a message to the user.

Modifying the UI

Here, we will add a couple of buttons to the screen and we will then see a really fast way to make them actually do something. We will add a button in two different ways. First, using the visual designer, and second, by adding and editing XML code directly. Follow these right here in the UI designer steps:

1. Let's make our view of Android Studio as clear and straightforward as possible. Click on the **Android** tab to hide the logcat. The window will automatically reveal itself again next time it has a new output.

2. Make sure that the `my_layout.xml` file is selected by clicking on its tab above the main editing window, as shown in the following figure:

3. When the file is selected, you have two choices in the way you want to view it. Either **Design** or **Text** can be selected from the two tabs underneath the main editing window. Make sure that **Design** is selected, as shown in the following figure:

4. You will know that the previous steps have been successful when you see a nice big representation of your app in a smartphone template in the editor window, as shown in the next figure:

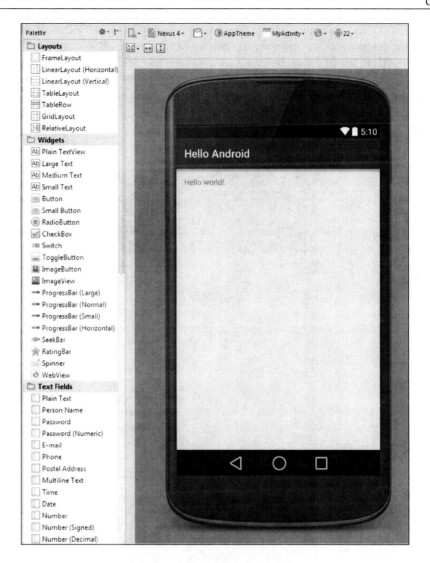

5. Also, in the previous figure, note the tall thin area to the immediate left-hand side of the smartphone in the editor window. It is called **Palette** and is labeled accordingly.

6. In the **Palette** window, under the **Widgets** heading, find the **Button** widget, as shown in the next figure. Depending on the size and resolution of your monitor, you might need to scroll the **Palette** window a little:

7. Click on and hold the **Button** widget and then drag it onto the smartphone somewhere near the top and the center of the layout. It doesn't matter if the widget is not exact. In fact, it doesn't matter at all where it goes as long as it is on the smartphone somewhere. It is good to practice to get it right, however. So, if you are not happy with the position of your button, then you can click on it to select it on the smartphone and then press the *Delete* key on the keyboard to get rid of it. Now you can repeat this step until you have one neatly placed button that you are happy with. Perhaps, like in this next figure:

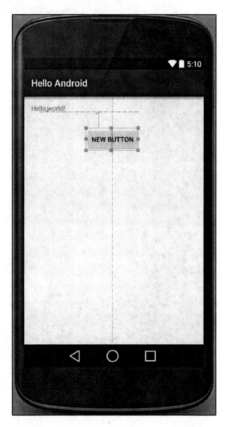

8. At this point, we could run the app on the emulator or a real device and the button would be there. If we clicked on it, there would even be a simple animation to represent that the button is being pressed and released. Feel free to try this now if you like. However, the next best-selling app on Google Play will need to do more than this. We are going to edit the properties of our widget using the **Properties** window. Make sure that the button is selected by clicking on it. Now, find the **Properties** window on the right-hand side of the editing window, as shown in the next figure:

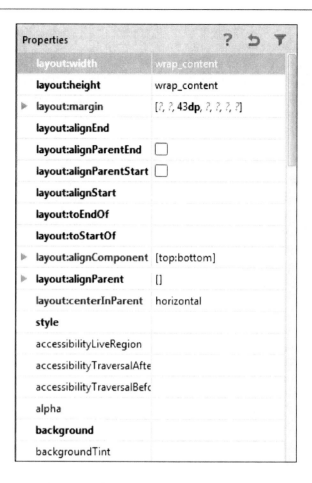

9. As you can see, there is a large array of different properties that we can edit right here in the UI designer. In *Chapter 10, Everything's a Class*, we will also edit and manipulate these properties in our Java code. For now, we will edit just one property. Scroll the **Properties** window until you see the **onClick** property and then click on it to select it for editing, as shown in the following figure:

10. Type `topClick` in the available field and press *Enter* on the keyboard. Be sure to use the same case, including the slightly counterintuitive lowercase `t` and uppercase `c`. What we have done here is we've named the Java method in the code that we want to **call** when this button is clicked by the user. The name is arbitrary, but as this button is on the top part of the screen, the name seems meaningful and easy to remember. The odd casing that we've used is a convention that will help us keep our code clear and easy to read. We will see the benefits of this as our code gets longer and more complicated. Of course, at the moment we don't have a method called `topClick`. We will write this method using Java code after we have looked at another way to add widgets to our UI. You could run the app at this point and it would still work. But if you click on the button, it will crash and the user will get an error because the method does not exist. For more such information, refer to the *Common errors* info box at the end of these steps.

11. Now we will add our final button for this project. Click on the **Text** tab below the editor to see the XML code that makes our UI:

12. You will see a button as well as the XML code through which we can still see our design in a slightly smaller window on the right-hand side of the code. Click on the button on the UI design and you will note that the code that represents the start and end of our button is highlighted, albeit, quite subtly:

```
<RelativeLayout xmlns:android="http://schemas.android.com/apk/res/android"
    xmlns:tools="http://schemas.android.com/tools" android:layout_width="match_parent"
    android:layout_height="match_parent" android:paddingLeft="16dp"
    android:paddingRight="16dp"
    android:paddingTop="16dp"
    android:paddingBottom="16dp" tools:context=".MyActivity">

    <TextView android:text="Hello world!" android:layout_width="wrap_content"
        android:layout_height="wrap_content"
        android:id="@+id/textView" />

    <Button
        android:layout_width="wrap_content"
        android:layout_height="wrap_content"
        android:text="New Button"
        android:id="@+id/button"
        android:layout_below="@+id/textView"
        android:layout_centerHorizontal="true"
        android:layout_marginTop="43dp"
        android:onClick="topClick" />



</RelativeLayout>
```

13. Very carefully and accurately, click the cursor before the opening < of our button code. Now, click and drag the first < symbol from before, to just after the last > symbol of the code that represents our button. This will highlight the code that we are after, as in this next figure:

```
<Button
    android:layout_width="wrap_content"
    android:layout_height="wrap_content"
    android:text="New Button"
    android:id="@+id/button"
    android:layout_below="@+id/textView"
    android:layout_centerHorizontal="true"
    android:layout_marginTop="43dp"
    android:onClick="topClick" />
```

14. Now, use the keyboard shortcut *Ctrl + c* to copy the code. Leave just one empty line of space below our button code and click on it to place the cursor. Then, use the keyboard shortcut *Ctrl + v* to paste the copied code. This figure is what you will see when you do so:

```xml
<Button
    android:layout_width="wrap_content"
    android:layout_height="wrap_content"
    android:text="New Button"
    android:id="@+id/button"
    android:layout_below="@+id/textView"
    android:layout_centerHorizontal="true"
    android:layout_marginTop="43dp"
    android:onClick="topClick" />

<Button
    android:layout_width="wrap_content"
    android:layout_height="wrap_content"
    android:text="New Button"
    android:id="@+id/button"
    android:layout_below="@+id/textView"
    android:layout_centerHorizontal="true"
    android:layout_marginTop="43dp"
    android:onClick="topClick" />
```

15. If you look at the editor, you will see that our code has one line in each of our buttons underlined in red, indicating two apparent errors. This is because Android Studio cannot tell the difference between our two buttons. Or more specifically, both buttons claim to be the same button. A button is distinguished from other buttons by its **ID**. We can set a button's id property in XML code directly or via the **Properties** window. Let's fix our two errors by making the two buttons have a different ID to each other. On the second button, simply change the following line:

```xml
android:id="@+id/button"
```

Change the preceding line of code to this:

```xml
android:id="@+id/button2"
```

16. Now we have two distinct buttons with unique IDs. We will see in *Chapter 9, Object-Oriented Programming* how to use these IDs to manipulate buttons in our UI by referring to these IDs in our Java code. Take a look at the visual design. Here, we can still see only one button. Look at the following line of XML code that is present in both our buttons:

```xml
android:layout_below="@+id/textView"
```

17. This is the line of code that describes *where* the button should go in the layout to Android. As with our IDs, until we changed them, this line of code is identical in both the buttons. So, it is not surprising that the buttons are in the exact same place, and this is the reason we can only see one of them. Again, in the second button, change the line of code in question to the following:

```
android:layout_below="@+id/button"
```

18. Now, the second button is below the first. We will examine what has happened a little more closely when we have edited just one more property. Here is a close-up figure of our two buttons on our UI design:

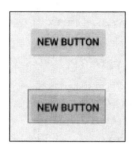

19. Let's change one more thing about our second button before we consider our UI for this project complete. Identify the following line of code at the end of the code for the second button:

```
android:onClick="topClick" />
```

Note that it has the name of our soon-to-be-written method, topClick, within double quotation marks "".

20. Be sure that you have identified the code in the **second** button and then change the word top to bottom. Now, we must create two Java methods (topClick and bottomClick) to avoid crashes when our user starts clicking on buttons.

21. Run the app and see that everything looks good, unless you click on a button and the app crashes.

We have achieved a lot through this simple exercise. It is true that much of the XML code is most likely still generally incomprehensible. That's OK, because in the next two chapters we will be really getting to grips with the visual designer and the XML code.

We have seen how when we drag a button onto our design, the XML code is generated for us. Also, if we change a property in the **Properties** window, the XML code is edited for us. Furthermore, we can type (or in our case, copy and paste) the XML code directly to create new buttons on our UI, or edit the existing ones.

Despite not having explained anything about the actual makeup of the XML code, you have probably deduced a few things from it. If you have not taken a minute to read through the XML, it might help to take a glance over it now. Perhaps, the following are among your deductions:

- The line that starts with `android:onClick=...` allows us to define a Java method that will handle what happens when that button is clicked.

- The line that starts with `android:layout_below=...` allows us to specify the ID of another UI element below which we wish to display this current element.

- The line that starts with `android:text=...` allows us to specify the text that will appear on the button.

- We can probably also take a guess that the line `android:layout_centerHorizontal="true"` will center the button (or other UI elements) horizontally.

- And anyone who has done some basic web programming will be able to guess that the line `android:layout_marginTop="43dp"` will give the element a margin at the top of `43` of whatever `dp` is referring to.

- In addition to this, each line defines or sets a different property, starts with `android:`, and then states the property that is to be defined. For example, `layout_marginTop=`, and then the value to set this property to: `"43dp"` or `"true"`.

- We can also see that a button starts with the code `<Button` and ends with the code `/>`.

You don't need to remember all these points, as we will keep bumping into them, as well as other similar conventions, throughout the book, especially in the next two chapters.

Common errors

Remember when we clicked on the button, as we had not written the method that it calls, the app crashed? If you call a method that does not exist from the user interface, you will get a long but helpful error message in logcat, which among a lot of other things, will contain the `Caused by: java.lang.NoSuchMethodException: topClick` message. We will slowly get to grips with common errors that we might see in tips like this throughout the book.

If you call a method that does not exist from the user interface, the user will get this message.

In *Chapter 4*, *Designing Layouts*, we will examine much more closely how to control the position and appearance of lots of different widgets and other UI elements from the palette. You will also learn exactly what dp and other useful Android units of measurement are.

Now, let's write our first Java code and wire up our buttons by writing the methods for them.

Meet Java

Take a look at the **MyActivity.java** tab. Here, we can see the code that we briefly discussed.

Before we write our own methods to correspond with the methods that our buttons are already wired up to call, let's take a look at Java **comments**. Java comments are really handy when we are learning to code, as well as for experienced developers too.

Java comments

In programming, it is always a good idea to write messages known as code comments and sprinkle them liberally among your code. This is to remind us what on earth we were thinking at the time we wrote the code. To do this, you simply need to append a double forward slash and then type your comment like this:

```
// This is a comment and it could be useful
```

In addition to this, we can use comments to comment out a line of code. Suppose we have a line of code that we temporarily want to disable, then we can do so by adding two forward slashes, like this:

```
// The code below used to send a message
// Log.i("info","our message here");
// But now it doesn't do anything
// And I am getting ahead of where I should be
```

> Using comments to comment out code should only be a temporary measure. Once you have ascertained the correct code to be used, the commented out code should be deleted in order to keep the code file clean and organized.

Let's look at the two different ways to send messages in Android, and then we can write a few methods that will send messages when our new UI buttons are pressed.

Sending messages

In the introduction section of the previous chapter, we talked a bit about using other people's code. We saw that we could do some quite complex things with a relatively small amount of code (like talk to satellites). To get our coding started, we are going to use two different classes from the Android API that simply allow us to output messages. The first class, Log, allows us to output messages to the logcat window. The second class, Toast, is not a tasty breakfast treat, but it will produce a toast-shaped pop-up message for the user to see.

Here is the code that we need to write to send a message to the logcat:

```
Log.i("info","our message here");
```

Exactly why this works will become clearer in *Chapter 9, Object-Oriented Programming*, but for now, we just need to know that whatever we put between the two sets of quote marks will be the output of the logcat window. We will see where to put this type of code shortly.

Here is the code we need to write in order to send a message to the user's screen:

```
Toast.makeText(this, "our message", Toast.LENGTH_SHORT).show();
```

This is a very convoluted-looking line of code, and exactly how it works, again, will not become clear until *Chapter 9, Object-Oriented Programming*. The important thing here is that whatever we put between the quote marks will appear in a pop-up message to our users.

Let's put some code just like this into a real app.

Writing our first Java code

So we now know the code that will provide an output to logcat or the user's screen. But, where do we put it? For now, we just need to understand that the onCreate method is executed as the app prepares to be shown to the user. So if we put our code at the end of this method, it will run just as the user sees the app. Sounds good.

We know that to execute the code in a method, we need to call it. We have wired our buttons up to call a couple of methods: topClick and bottomClick. Soon, we will write these methods. But who or what is calling onCreate!? The answer to this mystery is that Android itself calls onCreate in response to the user clicking on the app icon to run the app. In *Chapter 6, The Life and Times of an Android App*, we will explore the **Android lifecycle** and it will be really clear exactly which code is executed and when. You don't need to completely comprehend this now. I just wanted to give you an overview of what was going on.

Let's quickly try this out. We know that the onCreate method is called just before the app starts for real. Let's copy and paste the following lines of code into the onCreate method of our Hello Android app and see what happens when we run it:

1. Identify the closing curly brace } of the onCreate method and add the highlighted code, as shown in the next snippet:

```
@Override
    protected void onCreate(Bundle savedInstanceState) {
        super.onCreate(savedInstanceState);
        setContentView(R.layout.my_layout);

        // Let's take a look at Toast and Log in action
        Toast.makeText(this, "Can you see me",
          Toast.LENGTH_SHORT).show();

        Log.i("info", "Done creating the app");
    }
```

2. Note that the two instances of the word `Toast` and the word `Log` are highlighted in red in Android Studio. They are errors. We know that `Toast` and `Log` are classes and that classes are containers for code. Android Studio doesn't know about them until we tell it about them. We must add `import` to each class. Fortunately, this is semi-automatic. Click anywhere in the `onCreate` method.

3. Hold the *Alt* key and then press *Enter*. You need to perform this step twice. Once for `Toast` and once for `Log`. Android Studio adds the import directives at the top of the code with our other imports, and with this, the errors are gone.

4. Scroll to the top of **MyActivity.java** and take a look at the added import directives. Here they are, in case you are following along on a tablet or a paperback and don't have your development machine close by:

```
import android.util.Log;
import android.widget.Toast;
```

5. Now, run the app in the usual way.

The next figure is a screenshot of the output in the logcat window:

```
07-20 15:10:11.329  28669-28669/com.gamecodeschool.helloandroid I/art:  Not late-enabling -Xcheck:jni (already on)
07-20 15:10:11.451  28669-28676/com.gamecodeschool.helloandroid I/art:  Debugger is no longer active
07-20 15:10:11.506  28669-28669/com.gamecodeschool.helloandroid I/info:  Done creating the app
07-20 15:10:11.773  28669-28692/com.gamecodeschool.helloandroid I/OpenGLRenderer:  Initialized EGL, version 1.4
```

Look at the logcat you can see that our message **Done creating the app** was the output. Although it is mixed up among other system messages that we are currently not interested in. If you watch the emulator when the app first starts you will also see the neat pop-up message that the user will see.

It is possible that you might be wondering why the messages were output at the time they were. The simple answer is that the `onCreate` method is called just before the app starts to actually respond to the user. We will often put code in this method to get our apps set up and ready for user input. This is part of the lifecycle of an Android app, and you will learn more about it in *Chapter 6, The Life and Times of an Android App*.

 Alt + *E* is just one of the numerous useful keyboard shortcuts. The following is a keyboard shortcut reference for Android Studio. More specifically, it is for the IntelliJ Idea IDE, on which Android Studio is based. Take a look at it and bookmark this web page as it will be invaluable over the course of this book: http://www.jetbrains.com/idea/docs/IntelliJIDEA_ReferenceCard.pdf

Now, we will go a step further and write our own methods that are called by our UI buttons. We will place similar `Log` and `Toast` messages in them.

Writing our own Java methods

Let's get straight on with writing our first Java methods with a few more `Log` and `Toast` messages inside them. Open up our Hello Android project in Android Studio if it is not open already:

1. Identify the closing curly brace } of the `MyActivity` class, as discussed previously. Inside that curly brace, enter the following code that is highlighted after the `onCreate` method that we just dealt with:

```
@Override
protected void onCreate(Bundle savedInstanceState) {
   super.onCreate(savedInstanceState);
   setContentView(R.layout.my_layout);

   // Let's take a look at Toast and Log in action
   Toast.makeText(this, "Can you see me", Toast.LENGTH_SHORT).
     show();
   Log.i("info", "Done creating the app");
}

public void topClick(View v){
   Toast.makeText(this, "Top button clicked",
     Toast.LENGTH_SHORT).show();
   Log.i("info","The user clicked the top button");
}

public void bottomClick(View v){
   Toast.makeText(this, "Bottom button clicked",
     Toast.LENGTH_SHORT).show();
   Log.i("info","The user clicked the bottom button");
}
```

2. First, note that we appear to have two lines that contain part of our `Toast` code each. This is not strictly true. The problem is that the line of code is quite long and it wraps onto a second line in this book. If you check the code from the download bundle, you will see that it is on one line. The actual ending of a line of code in a method can be determined by the position of the semicolon ;. When you enter the code from step 1, be sure to enter all the `Toast` code on one line.

3. Note that the two instances of the word "View" are in red, indicating an error. Simply use the *Alt + Enter* keyboard combination to import the View class and remove the errors.

4. Deploy the app on a real device or emulator and start tapping away so we can observe the output.

At last, our app does something we told it to do and when we told it to. We can see that the method names we defined in the button properties are indeed called when the buttons are clicked. Admittedly, we still don't understand why Toast and Log really work, and neither do we fully comprehend the public void and (View v) parts of our method's syntax. This will become clear as we progress.

Presenting the code as clearly as possible

Future code will usually not be presented as numbered steps. On this occasion, I have presented the code as part of some numbered steps in a tutorial. Presenting code in a book, especially when it is being read on a mobile device, can be problematic. As soon as a line of code is too long for the width of the medium it is being presented on, the line wraps to the next, causing a lack of clarity. We saw this with our Toast code in the last tutorial. As we will see, to some extent this is unavoidable, but to mitigate this as much as possible, blocks of code will typically not be shown as numbered steps any more. Instead, great effort will be made on my part to make sure that the context of the code and the order it should be entered in is made abundantly clear in other ways.

Examining the log output

If you check the logcat output, you can see that a log entry was made from the onCreate method, just as before, as well as from the two methods that we wrote each time you clicked on a button.

And in the next figure, you can see that the top button has been clicked and the topClick method was called, triggering the Toast pop-up message, which is highlighted in the following figure:

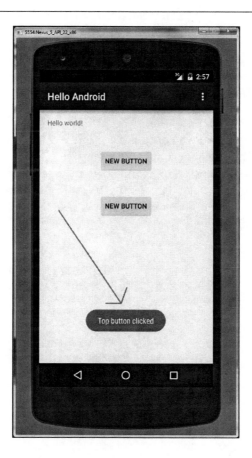

Throughout this book, we will regularly provide an output to the logcat so we can see what is going on behind the UI of our apps. Toast messages are more appropriate for notifying the user that something has occurred, perhaps a download that has completed or a new e-mail has arrived.

FAQ

1. Can you remind me what methods are?

   Methods are containers for our code that can be executed (called) from other parts of our code. Methods are contained within a class.

2. Like the last, I found this chapter really hard. Do I need to reread it?

   No, as long as you've built the app, you have made enough progress to handle the next chapter. All the blanks in our knowledge will be steadily filled in and replaced with glorious moments of realization as the book progresses.

Summary

In this chapter, we achieved quite a bit. We saw and edited our layout XML file using both the UI designer, as well as through tinkering with the raw code. We took a glimpse at our first Java code and even added our own methods in order to output debugging messages to the console, and pop-up Toast messages to the user.

In the next chapter, we will take a complete guided tour of Android Studio to see exactly where different things get done at the same time, to understand how our projects assets, such as files and folders, are structured, and to learn how to manage them. This will prepare us to take a more in-depth look at the UI design in *Chapter 4, Designing Layouts* and *Chapter 5, Real-World Layouts*, and build some significant real-world layouts for our apps.

3
Exploring Android Studio

In this chapter, we will take a guided tour of the most important areas of Android Studio. This is so that we can quickly and easily discuss *where* the different actions that we will perform take place. This is the only chapter in this book where we won't actually build an app or do some coding, but it is nice and short and will set us up for all the apps that we will build.

Here are the key things that we will do:

- We will take a fairly detailed tour of the windows, tabs, and features of Android Studio
- We will get to know the different files and folders involved in an Android project

Let's get started with the Android Studio tour.

The Android Studio guided tour

Android Studio remembers what you were doing just before you shut it down. So it is possible that when you start it up next, it will initially look a little different from how I show and describe it here. Start reading this guided tour, and it shouldn't take more than a couple of clicks to follow along and inspect all the different areas.

I rarely suggest that it is worth memorizing information, as repeated use and practice of concepts is a much better method to make important ideas take hold. However, on this occasion, it is worth remembering the names of the key Android Studio windows; this is so that you can easily follow along with where the action is when we are doing future tutorials. Of course, we have seen a few of these already (such as the editor and the Properties window), and if you can't remember them all, you can easily refer to this section later.

Tip of the day

Each time you start Android Studio, you will be presented with a "**Tip of the day**" message box. It is well worth reading these, as although some of the tips might not make sense at the moment, many of them contain really, valuable information that can either save time or enlighten us in some way.

Parts of the UI

In this next figure, you can see Android Studio open with the `Hello Android` app from the previous chapter. Although we are done with this project, it can serve us one more time here.

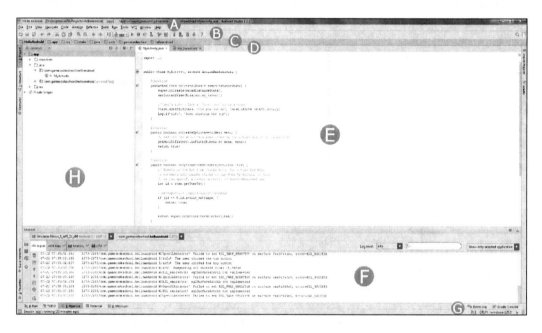

Let's take a quick look at the different areas that are labeled in the preceding screenshot, and then we can focus on the design views that Android Studio offers us:

- **A**: This is the **menu bar**. As with most applications, we can get to almost any option from here.

- **B**: This is the **tool bar**, from which you can access one of the many quick-launch icons. From here, some of the most commonly used options can be accessed with a single click.

- **C**: This is the **navigation bar**. It shows us the location of the file that is currently open in the editor window within our project and allows us to quickly navigate to a file or folder.

- **D**: These are the **editor tabs**. We can click on a tab to see its contents in the editor window. Note that there are more files in our project than are shown in the editor tabs. We can add a file to the editor tabs by double-clicking on them in the **project explorer**. Refer to **H** to see the files and folders.

- **E**: This is the **editor** and this is where we will spend the majority of our time. Note that although the previous screenshot shows a plain old code file in the editor, when we select a layout file to open, the editor window transforms itself into a mini design studio. And, it also performs some other context-sensitive transformations for other file types, as we will see throughout the rest of the book.

The console

The **F** window in the preceding screenshot is labeled **Android**. This is where we have been viewing the **logcat** output. Note, however, that on the top of this window, there are the following tabs:

- **logcat**: This is the place where errors, the Log output, and other useful information will appear.

- **ADB logs**: This is like a virtual console where we can get things done from the command line. There will be no need to do so in this book.

- **Memory**: Click on this tab when your app is running to see a pretty graph of your app's memory usage. We can use this tab to look for unexpected spikes in memory usage and try and make our apps more memory efficient.

- **CPU**: Click on this tab when your app is running to see a pretty graph of your app's CPU usage. We can use this tab to look for unexpected spikes in CPU usage and try and make our apps more efficient.

Including the four tabs we just discussed here, there are another four tabs below the window. If you click on one of the following tabs, the Android window changes the window name or divides the current window in two. Here is what you can do with the four tabs that are below the Android window:

- **TODO**: This shows the TODO comments spread throughout the project's code. This is really useful; try this out: type `// TODO note to self` anywhere in your code. Perhaps like this:

  ```
  // TODO: The flashing pig bug might be caused by the code below!
  ```

And no matter how many code files you have, you will see your note and be able to jump to the precise line in the code directly from your TODO window. Think of it as a code comment on steroids. Why not try it now?

- **Android**: This takes us back to the Android window and the four tabs we discussed previously.
- **Terminal**: You can use this to navigate your OS and do anything you can do from a console (DOS) window.
- **Messages**: As the name suggests, you will get system and error messages in this window.

More console features

At the part labeled **G**, in the corner of the preceding screenshot, we have two more tabs: **Event log** and **Gradle console**. Immediately below the two tabs is the **status bar**. When Android Studio is busy doing something for us, it will let us know here. So if things seem a bit unresponsive or you are not sure whether you actually clicked on the play icon, then check here first before clicking on it again.

Now let's look at the two tabs in detail:

- **Event Log**: Every time Android Studio completes a significant event, it is logged here. So if you can't remember the steps you have taken so far or whether a particular process has been completed successfully, you can check here.
- **Gradle console**: Gradle is a build system. Without us even realizing, Android Studio has been using Gradle to automate the process of turning the files in our project into an app that can be run on a device. This console allows you to give the Gradle tool a few commands and see it's response. We won't need to do this, however.

 If you want to learn more about Gradle and go beyond the knowledge you need to complete this book, you can do so with this exploratory tutorial: http://www.vogella.com/tutorials/AndroidBuild/article.html

The project explorer

The part labeled as **H** is the **project explorer**. This is essentially a file browser. We will explore the file and folder structure of our project in the next section, but just know that you can navigate to a file in this window and double-click on it to open it and add a tab for it to the editor window.

Note that there are a number of tabs down the left-hand side of Android Studio that cause the project explorer window to be replaced. Here is a quick run down of what the main ones do, starting from the top:

- **Project**: Click on this tab to switch back to the project explorer we just discussed.
- **Structure**: Here, we can see the hierarchy of our project broken down into classes, methods, and other components. Then, we can simply click on a part of the hierarchy to be taken to the selected part of the code in the editor window.
- **Build variants**: Android Studio enables us to test multiple different versions — builds — of our app. This isn't something that we need to discuss in this book.
- **Favorites**: Through this, you can see all the places that you have visited the most, bookmark files, or the points in your code that you have been debugging.

Transforming the editor into a design studio

I declined to label all the possible tab options around the edge of the UI because there are so many of them and as we saw, sometimes exactly which tabs you can see depends upon the context and the view that is currently occupying the given window. We gave most of the tabs a mention in this quick tour when we talked about the window that is nearest to them.

One set of tabs that does require further coverage are the tabs that contain the open files (**D**). The reason for this is that the editor window (**E**) completely transforms itself depending upon what file type is open in it. We have already seen the editor window transform itself when we switch between our Java code and our layout file.

As a reminder, click on the **my_layout.xml** tab (**D**). Next, make sure that we have the main design view by clicking on the **Design** tab at the bottom-left corner of the editor window. Here is another labeled screenshot to make sure that we are referring to the right parts of the editor window when in the design view:

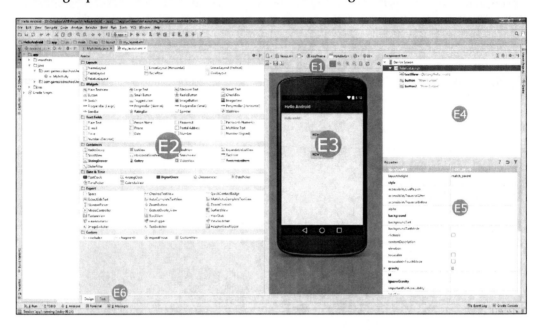

We will spend most of our time, in the next few chapters, in the design view of the editor window. If the previous screenshot looks slightly different than your layout, then you can take the following steps to make your layout more design friendly:

1. Make the editor window larger by making sure that the Android window is closed. Click on the **Android** tab if the window is open, and this will make it disappear.

2. Make the project explorer window smaller by dragging the area between it and the editor to the left.

3. Make the **Palette** area (**E2**) larger by dragging its right-hand side edge to the right.

4. Tweak all the window sizes to suit your preferences.

You will note that all the windows we discussed right from **A** to **H** are still present/available, and it is just the editor window that has been radically transformed. Let's have a look at what the editor window has to offer by following the labels on the previous screenshot.

E1 – the Preview toolbar

This small, but useful, area of Android Studio is certainly worth talking about. I won't cover every button, but here are some of the highlights. If you want to see what your layout will look like on a particular phone or tablet, click on the virtual device drop-down list and select the device of your choice, as shown in the following screenshot:

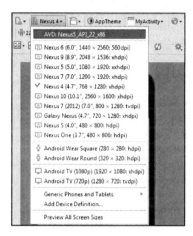

You can also click on the button pictured as follows to rotate the preview to landscape. Click on the button shown here to try this out:

As you might expect, this will make our layouts look significantly different. We will start to see how we can handle this later in the chapter and throughout the book.

We can zoom in and out of our layout design with the buttons shown here:

And the button shown next is the refresh button, which is just like the refresh button in a web browser. It forces the preview of our layout to be updated in case it doesn't happen automatically.

We haven't covered every button or control, but we have seen enough to move on.

E2 – exploring the palette

Next, we have the **Palette** window. The palette contains dozens of different design elements that we can drag onto our layouts. These are divided into categories and are all covered in the following sections. The key categories for this chapter are **widgets** and **layouts**, so we will cover them more thoroughly than the rest. Take a look at this close-up shot of the palette:

Palette		
Layouts		
FrameLayout	LinearLayout (Horizontal)	LinearLayout (Vertical)
TableLayout	TableRow	GridLayout
RelativeLayout		
Widgets		
Plain TextView	Large Text	Medium Text
Small Text	Button	Small Button
RadioButton	CheckBox	Switch
ToggleButton	ImageButton	ImageView
ProgressBar (Large)	ProgressBar (Normal)	ProgressBar (Small)
ProgressBar (Horizontal)	SeekBar	RatingBar
Spinner	WebView	
Text Fields		
Plain Text	Person Name	Password	Password (Numeric)
E-mail	Phone	Postal Address	Multiline Text
Time	Date	Number	Number (Signed)
Number (Decimal)			
Containers			
RadioGroup	ListView	GridView	ExpandableListView
ScrollView	HorizontalScrollView	SearchView	TabHost
SlidingDrawer	Gallery	VideoView	TwoLineListItem
DialerFilter			
Date & Time			
TextClock	AnalogClock	DigitalClock	Chronometer	DatePicker
TimePicker	CalendarView			
Expert		
Space	CheckedTextView	QuickContactBadge
ExtractEditText	AutoCompleteTextView	MultiAutoCompleteTextView
NumberPicker	ZoomButton	ZoomControls
MediaController	GestureOverlayView	SurfaceView
TextureView	StackView	ViewStub
ViewAnimator	ViewFlipper	ViewSwitcher
ImageSwitcher	TextSwitcher	AdapterViewFlipper
Custom		
<include>	<fragment>	requestFocus	CustomView

Let's go through some of the key sections of the palette and later, we will begin to actually use them:

- **Layouts**: Layouts are, as their name suggests, used to lay out all the other elements within them. What is key, however, and will become apparent as we progress, is how different layouts are more suited to different situations. In addition, we can use the same widgets on different types of layouts, and the XML code that will be generated for us will vary quite a lot. This will not be a problem for us because we will look at lots of examples, and as we will see later, we do not need to remember the different syntax for each layout type; we just need to be aware of the different situations suited to each layout type. Also, we will regularly use multiple layouts as part of the same design. That is, there will be layouts within layouts. Just think about putting storage containers of different shapes and sizes within bigger containers. It's the same concept. You will learn through practice about which containers are best for which contents in different situations.

- **Widgets**: Are the most commonly used elements on the palette. Typically, there will be multiple widgets contained within a layout. Widgets are the part of our layout that the user will most often see and interact with. We have already seen the **Button** and **PlainTextView** widgets.

- **Text Fields**: These are like **PlainTextView** from the **Widgets** category, but are very specific to the type of text that they are most suited to and are most often used when the user actually interacts with or changes the values that they hold. Take a look at the names of the elements in the **Text Fields** category and you will see that they all have names that allude to their likely use.

- **Containers**: Containers are like layouts with a specific purpose. For example, the **Radio Group** container will hold multiple **Radio Button** elements from the widget category. The **ScrollView** container will hold a whole bunch of other elements and enable the user to scroll through them. **VideoView** is a fast and easy way to allow the user to have a fully functional video player with little to no coding. We will see some of these containers in action later in the book.

- **Date & Time**: Ever wondered why the pop-up date or calendar selector looks so similar on so many apps? That's because they are using the Date and Time elements.

- **Expert**: These elements are fairly diverse from each other. We will see some of the elements from the expert category throughout the book. For example, in *Chapter 28, Threads, Touches, Drawing, and a Simple Game*, we will see **SurfaceView** in action when we take a whirlwind tour of how to make animated 2D games for Android.

- **Custom**: We can think of these as the building blocks of specialized layout elements. Fragment is probably the most powerful and versatile of all the layout elements, and we will spend the majority of latter part of this book taking advantage of it.

After that fast overview of the palette, let's move on to **E3**.

E3 – the layout preview

This is the layout preview where we will preview our masterpieces. Take a closer look at **E1** to see how we can switch between landscape and portrait, refresh or zoom the preview, and change the virtual device. And here is a close-up view of **E3**, which shows the layout preview just after a new project is started:

As we will see when we take a look at the area labeled **E6**, we can view our layouts/designs visually or as code.

E4 – the Component Tree

This is the **Component Tree**. It can be a UI designer's life saver. As our layouts get more complicated with layout elements nested inside other layout elements and widgets all over the place, the XML code as a whole can become awkward to navigate. The Component Tree allows us to see the structure as well as the individual elements of our design. We can expand and collapse parts of it; jump to specific sections of the XML code; as well as drag, drop, and rearrange parts of our design with it.

E5 – the Properties window

This is the **Properties** window. We have already been here when we were editing the properties of our widgets back in *Chapter 2, Java – First Contact*. We have seen that we can edit properties in both the XML code and the Properties window. There is no right or wrong way to do this and, most likely, you will end up using both. Where the Properties window can be really helpful, when we are just starting to program for Android, is in two areas. One obvious one less so. The obvious advantage is that we don't have to mess around with all that nasty-looking XML code. The other advantage is that, even when we get comfortable with the XML code, it is going to be a long time before we remember the names of all the properties. The Properties window allows us to browse through all the available properties for the selected element. When we add a property, it will, of course, add the full line of XML, negating the need for us to remember what the property was called and the convoluted syntax needed to add it.

E6 – text and design view tabs

Here, we can see the tabs that are used to switch between the **Text** (XML) view and the **Design** view. These tabs are only visible when we are viewing a file that has these views available. For example, when we are viewing our Java code, these tabs will not be present.

Let's talk some more about the project folder and file structure now.

The project folder and file structure

Let's take a closer look at the files and folders that are part of our project. Open up the `Hello Android` app from earlier to follow along. Android is a fussy thing, and it likes all of the different resources (layout files, code, images, sounds, and so on) to go in the correct folders or it will complain and not compile or run correctly.

Android Studio, with the help of Gradle, keeps track of the resources in our project and can advise us when we are trying to use something that doesn't exist or if we've misspelled the name of an image or a sound file, for example. Almost instantly after adding a resource to the project, Android Studio will 'know' about it and make it available to us.

If you expand all of the folders in the project explorer, even from our simple project from *Chapter 1, The First App*, you will see a vast array of files and folders.

If the vastness and depth of some of the files and folders is a bit intimidating, then you will be pleased to learn that we will never need to look at or edit most of them. Most of them are managed by Android Studio. We will focus on the key folders and file types that we will be using as Android developers.

Expand the following folders (if they aren't already) by clicking on the little triangle to the left-hand side of each of them, once each on: app, src, main, java, res, main, and layout folder. You will see something close to this next figure. This figure is a close-up view of the folders we are most interested in. As usual, I have labeled the most useful parts, so we can refer to them and describe them.

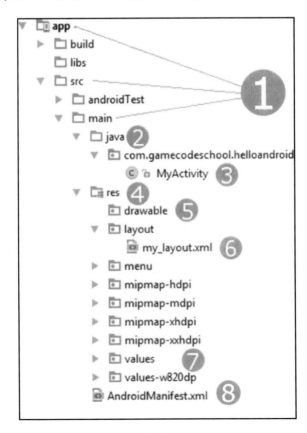

We can find almost every file and folder we will need in the `app/src/main` folder as indicated by (**1**).

Note that in the `java` folder (**2**), inside a subfolder with the same name as the package for this project (`com.gamecodeschool.helloandroid`), we can see our `MyActivity.java` (**3**) code file. Android Studio hides the file extension for `.java` files, but being inside the `java` folder should make it plain what we are dealing with. If we create two or more different packages in a project, then the subfolders with the names of the packages will appear in the `java` folder and, of course, will contain their `.java` files as we might expect.

The other major thing we will be constantly adding to and editing in our Android projects is resources. These are all contained within the **res** folder (**4**). As we saw in *Chapter 1, The First App*, the variety of resources our projects can use is wide. Let's see where some of them go.

The `drawable` folder (**5**) is where all the graphical assets go. If we design a fancy button, background, or icon, then this is the place for it. In addition to this, we will create subfolders within the `res` folder that contain scaled versions of our graphical resources. These subfolders are used by devices with varying screen densities and sizes and have names such as `drawable-hdpi`, `drawable-mdpi`, `drawable-xhdpi`, and `drawable-xxhdpi`.

These folders will contain equivalent graphical resources for devices with high (h), medium (m), extra high (xh), and extra extra high (xxh) dpi screens. This is optional because Android will scale any graphics where a version specific to the current screen type is not provided; however, this often results in a stretched or low-quality appearance.

Inside the `layout` folder, we can find our `my_layout.xml` (**6**) file, which, of course, contains the layout from our project. We can have more than one layout in a project and when we create them, they will appear in this folder. As an example, we might have a project with `home_layout.xml`, `settings_layout.xml`, and `main_layout.xml`. In addition to this, just like with the `drawable` folders, we can have subfolders within `res` for the layouts of devices with different dpi screens. The names are fairly predictable, but for the sake of clarity, they would be `layout-hdpi`, `layout-mdpi`, and so on.

We can also add folders that handle different orientations such as `layout-landscape` and `layout-portait`.

Furthermore, we can add folders that handle the screen size as opposed to density, such as `layout-large`, `layout-xlarge`, and more.

Folders galore

All this talk of folders might be making your brain ache. The first thing to note is that, as we already mentioned with the `drawable` folder, the extra folders are always optional. You can easily build an app with only one set of graphics and layout files. In fact, the techniques we learn in the latter part of this book reduce the need for dozens of different folders in the `res` folder. However, being aware of devices of different sizes/dpi's, testing on the related emulators, and catering for them when necessary will make your app truly versatile with a consistent appearance. Now for the bad news; there are even more screen qualifiers than these main qualifiers that we mentioned here. If you want to take a look, you can do so at `http://developer.android.com/guide/practices/screens_support.html`. We will make some use of these different folders throughout the book and deal with them in a step-by-step manner when we do.

Moving on to number **7** on our folder structure diagram, we have the `values` folder. This contains the `strings.xml` file. Note that the name of our app is not mentioned anywhere in our Java code. The reason for this is that although you can hardcode text into your Java code or a layout file, it is much better to use **string resources** in the `strings.xml` file. Here is why. String resources are the indexed text (words and phrases) that the user sees in our app (such as `Hello world!`) contained in the `strings.xml` file.

Let's say you have a settings screen and on at that settings screen layout, you hardcode the words Settings, Volume, and Theme. No problem so far. Now consider that your app might have multiple different screens and each of them has a button that the user can click on to go to the Settings screen. That's OK, just hardcode the text in the buttons as well. Now imagine that the lead designer decides that the Settings screen should be called Options and not Settings, and the app is also going to be released in the German market, which will require all the strings changed to German, of course. Now consider that your app has more than just a settings screen; perhaps, it has pop-up tips on how to use your app. Even something as apparently straightforward as the app's title might not only be different when translated to other languages but might even be different, perhaps for cultural reasons in some countries.

By using string resources, we can manage this problem simply. Take a look at the `strings.xml` file in the `values` folder by double-clicking on it. Here are the contents for your convenience. Note that I have highlighted one line of code in the following snippet:

```
<resources>
    <string name="app_name">Hello Android</string>
    <string name="hello_world">Hello world!</string>
    <string name="action_settings">Settings</string>
</resources>
```

Now look at this next figure that shows a line of code on `TextView` in the `my_layout.xml` file from the Hello Android project:

```
<TextView android:text="Hello world!" android:layout_width="wrap_content"
<TextView android:text="@string/hello_world" android:layout_width="wrap_content"
```

In the previous figure, I was hovering the mouse cursor over the phrase "Hello world!". Note that the code reads `text="Hello world!"`, but the pop up shows that actually the phrase is not contained directly in the `TextView` tag itself, but is being referenced in the `strings.xml` file via the `@string/hello_world` identifier.

So, string resources allow us to define the text that appears in our app and then refer to its index in the `strings.xml` file. This makes problems such as words and phrases that appear multiple times or translating to new languages more manageable.

Doing things this way does seem longwinded for one simple phrase, but when we consider the previous scenario of the settings screen, then the advantages are plain. Throughout this book, we will hardcode and use string resources depending on which seems most appropriate for the situation. Generally, when implementing a complete project, we will do things properly, and when we are making a simple app just to learn a concept, we will cheat and hardcode our Strings.

All is not as it seems

If you use your operating system's file browser and browse to the project folder, then you will see that things are quite different than how they appear in the project explorer. There are many more subfolders than the project explorer reveals. The project explorer not only gives you access to all the files and folders you need, it also simplifies their location and un-buries them a little. The real file and folder structure is required by Android, so we mustn't try and change it. So performing all the editing, moving, and adding directly through Android Studio is a good idea.

It is not necessary to memorize everything we have said about files and folders. Each time we need to do something with a folder or file, I will be really specific about what to do. It is just helpful to have an overview of the structure that Android needs to work properly. Just think of Android as a fussy (but loving) flatmate who absolutely must have a place for everything and everything in its place.

FAQ

1. How can I possibly keep track of where all the different files and folders go?

    It is true that Android is a filesystem control freak and we need to make sure that every file is named and placed carefully. However, you don't need to remember the details because we will discuss exactly where to put things as we proceed.

2. String resources seem like they are going to be a bit of a burden, are they?

    The right way to add text to our app is using String resources. Throughout the book, when we are just looking at examples, we will not usually bother with String resources, but when we implement the main projects throughout this book, we will use String resources as they were intended. So we will avoid the overhead most of the time and use them when they are of genuine time-saving/practical benefit.

Summary

Now that we know the names and locations of all the key parts of Android Studio, we can make fast progress.

In the next chapter, we are going to start looking in more depth at the UI designer and see how we can control the positioning and appearance of our design at the same time by becoming more familiar with the XML layout code and the UI designer. Let's get on with some UI design.

4
Designing Layouts

In this chapter we will learn some UI basics, such as how we control the size and position of the widgets in our layouts. We will further come to understand the slightly scary XML code and see new ways we can avoid having to edit the code directly by using the UI designer, by covering the following:

- Looking at the code structure underlying a UI design/layout
- Learning how to position widgets precisely
- Building three really simple UI designs from scratch

Exploring Android UI design

We will see with Android UI design that so much of what we learn is context sensitive. The way that a given widget's x property will influence its appearance might depend on a widget's y property. It probably isn't possible to learn this verbatim. It is most likely best to expect to gradually get better and faster results with practice.

For example, if you play with the designer by dragging and dropping widgets onto the design, the XML code that is generated will vary quite extensively depending upon which layout type you are using. This is because different layout types use different means to determine the position of their children. We will see this, perhaps most distinctly, when we look at `RelativeLayout` later in the chapter.

This information might initially seem like a problem, or a bad idea, and it certainly is a little awkward at first. What we will grow to learn, however, is that this apparent abundance of layout options and their individual quirks are actually a good thing because they give us almost unlimited design potential. There are very few layouts you can imagine that are not possible to achieve.

This unlimited potential comes with a bit of complexity however. So, rather than a few step-by-step examples that lack explanation, I thought a three-pronged approach would be worthwhile. A bit of theory, a bit of experimenting, and finally some practical examples. This chapter deals with theory and experimenting, and in the next chapter, we'll deal with the practical examples.

Structure of a UI design

When we create a new project, Android Studio creates a new layout for us. As we have seen, this autogenerated layout is very simple and contains a single TextView widget. The TextView widget is unsurprisingly the standard way of displaying text. On the palette it is labeled as **Plain TextView** but in XML code it just says TextView. I will refer to it in the way that seems most appropriate for the current context.

 It will become apparent as we progress, but it is worth making clear at this point that all our layouts will be designed in XML, not Java. In later chapters, you will learn more Java and then we will see how we write Java code to manipulate these layouts.

What we haven't looked at quite as closely is that the generated activity_main.xml file also contains a layout. Layouts come in a few different types and the one that is provided with our auto-generated layout is called RelativeLayout. Here is the XML that makes this layout:

```
<RelativeLayout xmlns:
  android="http://schemas.android.com/apk/res/android"
  xmlns:tools="http://schemas.android.com/tools"
  android:layout_width="match_parent"
  android:layout_height="match_parent"
  android:paddingLeft="@dimen/activity_horizontal_margin"
  android:paddingRight="@dimen/activity_horizontal_margin"
  android:paddingTop="@dimen/activity_vertical_margin"
  android:paddingBottom="@dimen/activity_vertical_margin"
  tools:context=".LayoutExperiments">
</RelativeLayout>
```

Anything in between the closing > that defines the properties of the layout itself and the `</RelativeLayout>` is a child (like our solitary `TextView`) of the layout. That child will be influenced by the properties of its parent, and also must use properties appropriate to its parent. For example, when we placed a button as a child of the `RelativeLayout` in *Chapter 2*, *Java – First Contact*, it used the following syntax to position itself immediately below the `TextView` that has an ID of `textView`:

```
android:layout_below="@+id/textView"
```

Depending upon the type of layout a child is contained within, it will need to use appropriate syntax to influence its appearance/position. The only way to learn all the different intricacies of the different layout types, and how they affect their child widgets, is to start using them.

 As we add, edit, and delete widgets and views in this section, it is not important to make your project the same as mine. The purpose of this section is not to achieve a meaningful end result, only to explore as many of the widgets, layouts, and their properties as we can in as few pages as possible. **Do** try everything. **Don't** worry about making it the same as the pictures or following the instructions to the letter. If I add a small margin or other property to a widget, feel free to add an enormous one if you want to give it a go. If you want to see exactly what I created then the project files are in the `Chapter 4` folder in the download bundle.

First we will explore the straightforward widgets and their properties, then the layouts, and finally we will use them meaningfully together in a series of mini layout projects.

Configuring and using widgets

Widgets are all the UI elements on the palette under the heading **Widgets**. First let's have a look at some of the properties of a widget. Note that some widgets have properties unique to themselves, but there are a lot of properties that all the widgets share, and they are useful to take a look at. Let's learn about some of the ways we can configure and use widgets before we use them for real.

Widget properties

As we have already seen, widgets have properties that we can either set in XML or through the **Properties** window.

Setting the size

A widget's size can depend on a number of properties and the context in which they are used. Probably the most straightforward is by using actual units of size. We briefly saw this in the last chapter but we didn't look into it in any depth.

Sizing using dp

As we know, there are thousands of different Android devices. In order to try and have a system of measurement that works across different devices, Android uses **density independent pixels** or **dp** as a unit of measurement. The way this works is by first calculating the density of the pixels on the device an app is running on.

 We can calculate density by dividing the horizontal resolution by the horizontal size, in inches, of the screen. This is all done on-the-fly, on the device on which our app is running.

All we have to do is use dp in conjunction with a number when setting the size of the various properties of our widgets. Using density independent measurements we can design layouts that scale to create a uniform appearance on as many different screens as possible.

So, problem solved then? We just use dp everywhere and our layouts will work everywhere? Unfortunately, density independence is only part of the solution. We will see more of how we can make our apps look great on a range of different screens in this chapter and throughout the rest of the book.

As an example we can affect the height and width of a widget directly, by adding the following code to its properties:

```
. . .
android:height="50dp"
android:width="150dp"
. . .
```

Alternatively we can use the properties window and add them through the comfort of the appropriate edit boxes as shown next. Which option you use will depend on your personal preference but sometimes one way will feel more appropriate than another in a given situation. Either way is correct and as we go through the book making mini-apps, I will usually point out if one way is *better* than another.

height	50**dp**

width	150**dp**

Or we can use the same `dp` units to set other properties such as margin and padding. We will look at margin and padding in a minute.

Sizing fonts using sp

Another device dependent unit of measurement, used for sizing Android fonts is **scalable pixels** or **sp**. The `sp` unit of measurement is used for fonts and is pixel density dependent in the exact same way that `dp` is. The extra calculation that an Android device will take into account when deciding how big your font will be, based on the value of `sp` you use, is the user's own font size settings. So, if you test your app on devices and emulators with normal size fonts, then a user who has a sight impairment (or just likes big fonts) and has the font setting on large, will see something different to what you saw during testing.

If you want to try playing with your Android device's font size settings, you can do so by selecting **Settings | Display | Font size**, as shown:

As we can see in the previous image there are quite a number of settings and if you try it on **Huge** the difference is, well, huge!

We can set the size of fonts using `sp` in any widget that contains text. This includes `Button`, `TextView`, and all the UI elements under the **Text Fields** category in the palette, as well as some others. We do so by setting the `textSize` property like so:

```
android:textSize="50sp"
```

As usual we can also use the properties window to achieve the same thing.

Determining size with wrap or match

We can also determine how the size of widgets and many other UI elements behave in relation to the containing/parent element. We can do so by setting the layoutWidth and layoutHeight properties to either wrap_content or match_parent.

For example, if we set the properties of a lone button on a layout to the following:

```
...
android:layout_width="match_parent"
android:layout_height="match_parent"
....
```

Then the button will expand in both height and width to **match** the **parent**. We can see that the button in the next screenshot fills the entire screen:

More common for a button is `wrap_content`, as shown next:

```
. . . .
android:layout_width="wrap_content"
android:layout_height="wrap_content"
. . . .
```

This causes the button to be as big as it needs to be, to **wrap** its **content** (width and height in `dp` and text in `sp`).

Using padding and margin

If you have ever done any web design, then you will be very familiar with the next two properties. **Padding** is the space from the edge of the widget to the start of the content in the widget. **Margin** is the space outside of the widget that is left between other widgets—including the margin of other widgets, should they have any. Here is a visual representation:

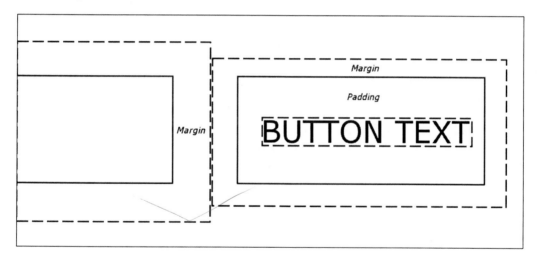

We can set padding and margin in a straightforward way, equally for all sides, like this:

```
. . .
android:layout_margin="43dp"
android:padding="10dp"
. . .
```

Look at the slight difference in the naming convention for the margin and the padding. The padding is just called `padding` but the margin is referred to as `layout_margin`. This reflects the fact that padding only affects the widget itself but margin can affect other widgets in the layout.

Or we can specify different top, bottom, left, and right margins and padding, like this:

```
android:layout_marginTop="43dp"
android:layout_marginBottom="43dp"
android:paddingLeft="5dp"
android:paddingRight="5dp"
```

Specifying margin and padding values for a widget is optional and a value of zero will be assumed if nothing is specified. We can also choose to specify some of the different side's margin and padding but not others, as in the previous example.

It is probably becoming obvious that the way we design our layouts is extremely flexible, but also that it is going to take some practice to achieve precise results with this many options. We can even specify negative margin values to create overlapping widgets.

Let's look at a few more properties and then we will go ahead and play around with a few widgets for real.

Using the layout_weight property

Weight refers to the relative amount compared to other UI elements. So, for `layout_weight` to be useful, we need to assign a value to the `layout_weight` property on two or more elements. We can then assign portions that add up to 100% in total. This is especially useful for dividing up screen space between parts of the UI where we want the relative space they occupy to remain the same regardless of screen size. Using `layout_weight` in conjunction with `sp` and `dp` units can make for a really simple and flexible layout. For example, take a look at this code:

```
<Button
    android:layout_width="match_parent"
    android:layout_height="0dp"
    android:layout_weight=".1"
    android:text="one tenth" />

<Button
    android:layout_width="match_parent"
    android:layout_height="0dp"
    android:layout_weight=".2"
    android:text="two tenths" />

<Button
    android:layout_width="match_parent"
    android:layout_height="0dp"
    android:layout_weight=".3"
```

```
    android:text="three tenths" />

<Button
    android:layout_width="match_parent"
    android:layout_height="0dp"
    android:layout_weight=".4"
    android:text="four tenths" />
```

Here is what this code will do:

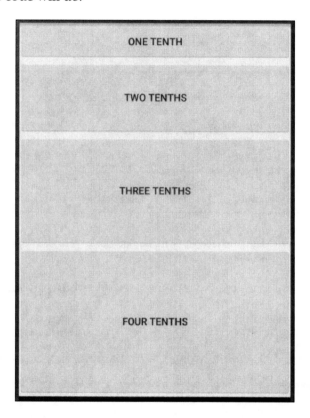

Notice that all the layout_height properties are set to 0dp. Effectively the layout_weight is replacing the layout_height property. The context in which we use layout_weight is important (or it won't work) and we will see this in a real project soon. Also note that we don't have to use fractions of 1, we can use whole numbers, percentages, and any other number, and as long as they are relative to each other they will probably achieve the effect you are after. Note that layout_weight only works in certain contexts and we will get to see where when we build some layouts.

Using gravity

Gravity can be our friend and can be used in so many ways in our layouts. It helps us affect the position of a widget by moving it in a given direction; like it was being acted upon by gravity. The best way to see what gravity can do is to take a look at some example code and pictures.

Setting the `gravity` property on a button (or other widget) to `left|center_vertical` like this:

```
android:gravity="left|center_vertical"
```

Will have an effect that looks like this:

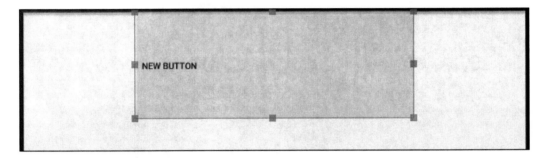

Notice that the contents of the widget (in this case the button's text) are indeed aligned left and centrally vertical.

In addition, a widget can influence its own position within a layout element with the `layout_gravity` element, like this:

```
android:layout_gravity="left"
```

This would set the widget within its layout, probably as expected, like this:

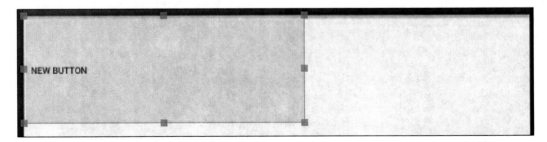

The previous code allows different widgets within the same layout to be effected as if the layout has multiple, different gravities.

The contents of all the widgets in a layout can be affected by the `gravity` property of their parent layout by using the same code as a widget:

```
android:gravity="left"
```

Let's mention a few more properties and then we can go about using some of them.

More properties

There are in fact many more properties than those we have discussed. Some we won't need in this book and some are quite obscure and you might never need them in your entire Android career. But others are quite commonly used such as: `background`, `textColor`, `alignment`, `typeface`, `visibility`, and `shadowColor`; but these are best explored with a practical experiment. So let's do that now.

Experimenting with widgets

If you are unsure on any of the following steps then refer back to *Chapter 1, The First App* for further discussion and images for most of the steps. You can find the completed code files for this tutorial in `Chapter 4/Widget Experiments`:

1. Start the new project wizard by left-clicking on **File | New Project**. If you are on the **Welcome to Android Studio** start menu then left-click **Start a new Android Studio project**.

2. Name the application `Widget Experiments`, enter your preferred domain name and project location, then click on **Next**.

3. On the **Target Android Devices** window accept the default settings by left-clicking on **Next**.

4. On the **Add an Activity to Mobile** window left-click **Blank Activity** then left-click on **Next** to proceed.

5. On the **Customize the Activity** window, name the activity `WidgetExperimentsActivity`, make the title `Widget Experiments`, and leave everything else at default. Now press **Finish**.

6. Wait for Android Studio to create the new project.

7. If you already had a project open at the start of this tutorial you will now have two completely separate instances of Android Studio running. You can close the previous one.

8. Arrange your design view as we did earlier to give extra space to the **Palette**, **Component Tree**, and **Properties** windows.

9. Now we have a new project we will talk about and play with some widgets. Left-click and drag a **Button** from the **Widgets** category of the palette onto the top-left corner of the design preview.

10. In the **Properties** window scroll to find the `text` property and change it to `Left Button`.

11. In the properties window scroll to find the `width` property and change it to `150dp`. Note there is no space between 150 and dp.

12. Scroll to the **layout:margin** property. Note there is a little grey triangle to the left that when clicked will reveal more options to this property. Set the `left` property to `10dp`, the `top` property to `100dp`, the `right` property to `50dp`, and the `bottom` property to `50dp`. The next screenshot should help with this step:

▼ layout:margin	[?, 10**dp**, 100**dp**, 50**dp**, 50**dp**, ?, ?]
all	
left	10**dp**
top	100**dp**
right	50**dp**
bottom	50**dp**

13. Of course if we wanted a consistent margin on all sides of our button we could have entered a value in the `all` property. Observe the design preview after these steps. We can see the effect of the larger `100dp` `top` margin and the smaller `10dp` `left` margin. We can also observe the button text is just as we set it and the button is more elongated because we set the `width` property to `150dp`. The `right` and `bottom` margins are not visually apparent at the moment.

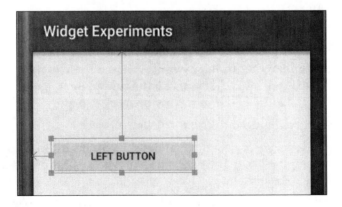

14. Now, drag another **Button** onto the layout and place it vertically in line with the previous button and to the right.

15. Set the `text` property to `Right` and the `width` property to `80dp`. Notice that the button does indeed shrink a little. Let's experiment some more.

16. Drag **Plain TextView** onto the layout and center it horizontally and below the two buttons.

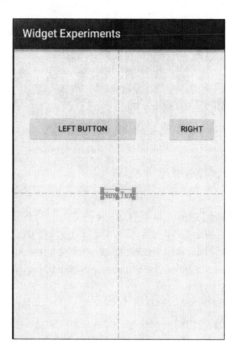

17. Change the `textSize` property to `100sp`. We can see in the next screenshot that the text is too wide to fit onto one line and it wraps onto two. We can also see by the blue rectangle surrounding `TextView` that it is even overlapping the two buttons above:

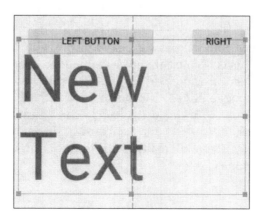

18. Now, change both the `width` and `height` properties to `150dp`. We have now constrained `TextView`, however the `textSize` property we set remains, causing the text to be partially obscured.

19. Let's fix this and add a few enhancements through a few more properties. Change the `textSize` property to `65sp`. Change the `layoutWidth` property to `match_parent`. This will make it as wide as its parent (`RelativeLayout`). Change the `gravity` property to `center`. Set the `alpha` property, which changes the transparency, to `.5`. Notice that the text now fits quite nicely as it is smaller and has the entire width of the device, and is also centered.

20. Now find and click on the `background` property, left-click on the three periods **...**, and now left-click on the **Color** tab. You can now click the color chooser on any color you like. Now our `TextView` has a background color.

21. Find and left-click on the `textColor` property. Left-click the **Color** tab and choose a color for your text that compliments the background color you chose in the previous step.

22. Now change the **typeface** property to `serif` and notice that the font has changed.

23. Add **ImageView** from the palette, below `TextView`. Notice that it is almost unnoticeable. This is because it needs an image to display. Scroll to the `src` property, left-click the three periods **...**, and scroll down the list of possible sources for our image. Right near the end under the **Mip Map** heading, double left-click on `ic_launcher`. We now have the cute Android logo embedded in `ImageView`. The next screenshot shows how my experiment ended. Obviously if you are reading this in print you will be unable to see the precise colors of the text and the background:

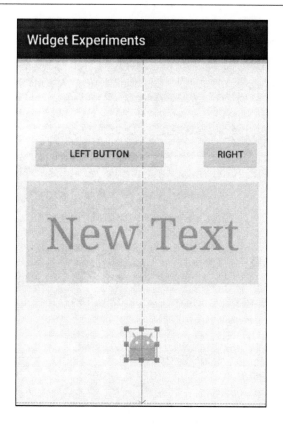

24. Finally, left-click on `TextView` to select it. Find the `visibility` property. By default this is set to `visible`. Try changing it to `invisible`. It disappears. This is probably what you expected and not the highlight of the chapter. But now try changing the `visibility` property to `gone`. Note how `ImageView` jumps up the layout to below the buttons. It does indeed behave as if the text is "gone". You probably remember that we said we can change properties on-the-fly while our app is running, using our Java code. Switching between `visible`, `invisible`, and `gone` can be really useful.

25. You can run this app on an emulator or a real device.

In this widget experiment we could see how many of the properties we have discussed interact with each other. We also saw a few new properties. You probably also noticed that a few of the properties we mentioned in some detail before the experiment haven't been demonstrated yet. Most notably `padding`. These are best showcased using **Layouts** from the palette and will be seen soon.

You only need to glance at the **Palette** window and the **Properties** window to realize we have only scratched the surface of the layout options in Android. But what we have learned will actually allow us to design a surprisingly large variety of layouts.

Let's look at some layouts.

Containing widgets in layouts

We know that layouts are one of the main building blocks of our UI. And in Android we have several types of layout that we can choose from to suit our specific design goals.

We will now do some experimentation with some of the main layout types.

RelativeLayout

This is the type of layout that was automatically included within our `Hello Android` project for us. Let's just play around with it some more.

RelativeLayout in action

If you are unsure on any of the following steps then refer back to *Chapter 1*, *The First App*, for further discussion and images for most of the steps. The code for this mini app can be found in the `Chapter 4/Layout Experiments` folder:

1. Start the new project wizard by left-clicking on **File | New Project** if you already have an existing project open or, if you are on the **Welcome to Android Studio** start menu, then left-click on **Start a new Android Studio project**.

2. Name the application `Layout Experiments`, enter your preferred domain name and project location, then click on **Next**.

3. On the **Target Android Devices** window accept the default settings by left-clicking on **Next**.

4. On the **Add an Activity to Mobile** window left-click **Blank Activity** then left-click **Next** to proceed.

5. On the **Customize the Activity** window name the activity `LayoutExperimentsActivity`, make the app title `Layout Experiments`, and leave everything else at the default. You don't need to change the Activity name for this to work, it just makes this project more distinct from the others we will build. Now press **Finish**.

6. Wait for Android Studio to create the new project.

7. Arrange your design view as we did earlier to give extra space to the **Palette**, **Component tree**, and **Properties** windows.

Now we have a new project we will talk about and play with some layouts.

Notice the top element of the **Component tree** window, after the **Device Screen** element. We already have `RelativeLayout` by default. This type of layout allows its children to use descriptions of positions relative to itself and its other children. Let's explore this:

1. Left-click and drag a **Plain TextView** widget from the palette and drop it just underneath the existing **Plain TextView**.

2. Now do the same with **Button** and drop it below the `TextView` we added in the previous step.

3. Next place a **Switch** widget below the **Button** widget from the last step.

Your layout will probably look something like this next screenshot, which is a close-up view of the top left of the UI designer:

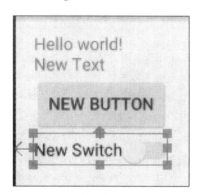

What is more interesting than the appearance, however, is the XML code that has been generated. Let's explore it now. Left-click on the **Text** tab below the editor window to reveal the generated XML.

Here are the entire contents of `activity_layout_experiments.xml` with the code for the parent `RelativeLayout` removed. Take a look at the code and take a close look at the three highlighted lines:

```
<TextView
  android:text="@string/hello_world"
  android:layout_width="wrap_content"
  android:layout_height="wrap_content"
```

```
        android:id="@+id/textView" />

    <TextView
        android:layout_width="wrap_content"
        android:layout_height="wrap_content"
        android:text="New Text"
        android:id="@+id/textView2"
        android:layout_below="@+id/textView"
        android:layout_alignParentLeft="true"
        android:layout_alignParentStart="true" />

    <Button
        android:layout_width="wrap_content"
        android:layout_height="wrap_content"
        android:text="New Button"
        android:id="@+id/button"
        android:layout_below="@+id/textView2"
        android:layout_alignParentLeft="true"
        android:layout_alignParentStart="true" />

    <Switch
        android:layout_width="wrap_content"
        android:layout_height="wrap_content"
        android:text="New Switch"
        android:id="@+id/switch1"
        android:layout_below="@+id/button"
        android:layout_alignParentLeft="true"
        android:layout_alignParentStart="true" />
```

In the code we can identify each of the widgets we added to our layout by the opening word of each code block. So the first <TextView block is the start of the text that reads **Hello world!** in the previous screenshot. The second block that begins with <TextView is therefore our very own TextView that we dragged onto the UI design ourselves. This TextView is the one with the text **New Text** in the previous screenshot.

Furthermore, the block of code that starts with <Button is of course our button labeled **NEW BUTTON** in the previous screenshot. And at this point you can probably guess that the code block that begins with <Switch is the Switch widget.

Also note that the last two lines of code for each widget are the same. Here they are again:

```
android:layout_alignParentLeft="true"
android:layout_alignParentStart="true" />
```

What this is effectively saying is to place this widget on the top left of its parent. So you might expect the widgets to be on top of one another?

Previously I suggested taking a close look at the three highlighted lines in the code. Let's examine the first highlighted line, which is from the first TextView that we added below TextView that was already there (the one with the text **Hello world!**). Here is the highlighted line of code again:

```
android:layout_below="@+id/textView"
```

What this is saying is place me below the widget with the id of textView. If you look at the main code listing again you will indeed see that the id property of TextView containing the text **Hello world!** is set to textView with the following line of XML:

```
android:id="@+id/textView" />
```

This method of describing where the contents of a layout go is for **RelativeLayout** only. It is perfect for some types of practical app designs (perhaps forms) and extremely awkward for others.

Let's explore some other layout types and then we will build some layouts that take advantage of each layout type we have experimented with.

Using LinearLayout

With this layout the clue is in the name. All the widgets contained in LinearLayout will be displayed in the order in which they are added. We can certainly still add margins, padding, and so on, but the order is fixed. It is linear (or sequential). LinearLayouts applies either vertical or horizontal ordering. Let's quickly make a project and combine a few LinearLayouts with some widgets.

The code for this mini app can be found in the Chapter 4/Linear Layout Experiment folder:

1. Create a new project in Android Studio. Call it Linear Layout Experiment, choose a **Blank Activity**, and leave all the other settings at their defaults.

2. Let's start with a completely clean sheet. Right-click on the layout folder in the project explorer. From the menu, choose **New** | **Layout resource file** as shown in the next screenshot:

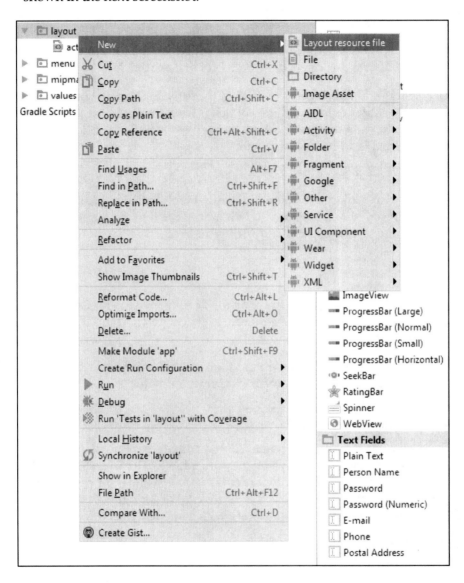

3. Then in the **File name** field enter linear_experiment and then left-click on **OK**.

4. The new file is created and opened in the editor. If the file is not automatically opened in design view then left-click on the **Design** tab at the bottom left of the editor window.

5. Look in the **Component Tree** window and you will see that we have been provided, by default, with LinearLayout as the root of our design. Also notice the word **vertical** in brackets, which indicates this is a *vertical* LinearLayout.

6. From the **Layouts** category of the palette drag a **LinearLayout (Horizontal)** onto the design. Drop it at the top of the layout.

7. Now drag a **LinearLayout (Vertical)** onto the design and confirm in **Component Tree** that it has indeed been added after the previous LinearLayout, as shown next:

8. Now find the layout:weight property in the **Properties** window of the currently selected LinearLayout and set it to .5. Do this for the other LinearLayout that we added by left-clicking it in the **Component Tree**, finding the layout:weight property, and setting it to .5. We can see that the **Component Tree** is especially useful when the design itself is not clear about where exactly the elements that make our layout are situated. We now have two vertically nested LinearLayouts, the top one is a horizontal LinearLayout and the bottom one is a vertical LinearLayout. And they both take up exactly .5 (half) of the screen.

9. Add two **Buttons** from the **Widgets** category of the palette to the top (horizontal) LinearLayout. Notice how they arrange themselves horizontally. But they are rather untidily stuck to the left-hand side of the layout.

10. Select the horizontal (top) `LinearLayout` by left-clicking it in either the design or **Component Tree**. Find the `gravity` property and left-click on the small triangle to the left of the word `gravity` to reveal the options for this property. Now left-click on the `center_horizontal` check box. The next image should make this step clear:

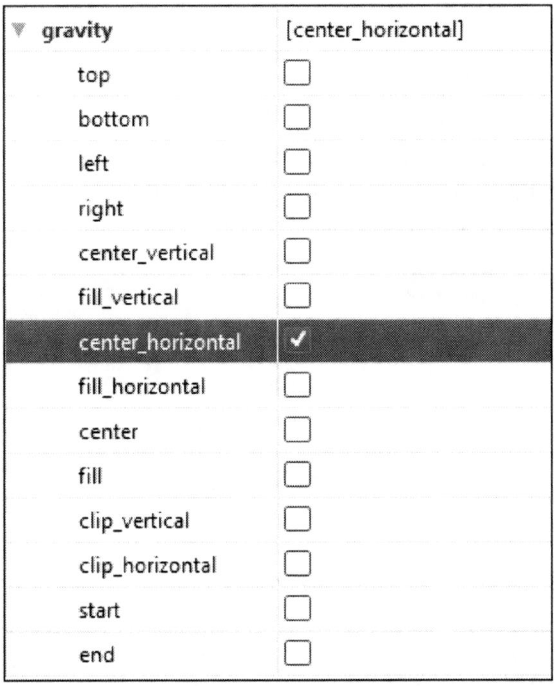

▼ gravity	[center_horizontal]
top	☐
bottom	☐
left	☐
right	☐
center_vertical	☐
fill_vertical	☐
center_horizontal	✓
fill_horizontal	☐
center	☐
fill	☐
clip_vertical	☐
clip_horizontal	☐
start	☐
end	☐

11. Now drag three **Plain TextView** widgets from the palette to the vertical (bottom) `LinearLayout`. Notice how they are nicely ordered from top to bottom but squashed to the top.

12. Select the vertical (bottom) `LinearLayout` either by clicking on it in the layout or the component tree. Find the `gravity` property and click the triangle to reveal the options, just as we did for the other `LinearLayout` in step 8. Left-click the check box for `center_vertical`. Now the `TextViews` are neatly centered but are squashed together.

13. Let's add a margin to each of the `TextView` widgets to solve this problem. Left-click to select the topmost `TextView`. Scroll to find the `layout_margin` property. Left-click the `layout_margin` property then add the value `20dp` next to the **top** option.

14. Repeat the previous step for each `TextView`.

Now we have a nice neat layout of buttons and text, as shown in the following screenshot:

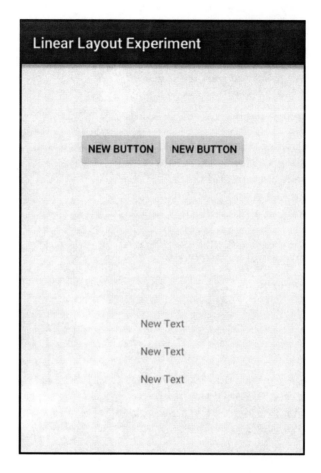

This works because the first vertical LinearLayout wraps the other two on top of each other. We use layout_weight in the wrapped layouts to make them take up half the screen space each. The first wrapped layout lays its buttons out from left to right because it is horizontal, and the second wrapped layout lays its text from top to bottom because it is vertical. In addition both wrapped layouts use the gravity property to center the widgets as well.

The one issue that you will notice if you try and run the app to see it on an emulator or a real device is that the default "Hello world!" layout from the activity_main. xml file is shown to the user, not our linear_experiment.xml layout.

We can fix this with these simple steps:

1. Open up `MainActivity.java` in the editor.

2. Look at the `onCreate` method and find the following line of code:

   `setContentView(R.layout.`**`activity_main`**`);`

3. Change the highlighted part, `activity_main` to the name of the layout we want to display, `linear_experiment`.

4. Run the app again and it will display our neat and tidy experiment.

Here we can see that the `setContentView` method call, within the `onCreate` method, is what displays a layout to the user. We just need to pass in the name of the XML layout as an argument. We append `R.` (for the `res` folder) and `layout.` (for the `layout` folder) and it just works. Don't worry too much about the new terminology, we will look at passing in arguments in *Chapter 8, Coding in Java Part 2 – Methods*.

The new knowledge we have just gained about how to use Java to display a given UI layout in XML will be useful in the next project.

We have probably done enough experimenting. Now let's build some slightly more real-world UI's.

Summary

Although the layout projects from this chapter were not really very realistic in nature, they have served the purpose of introducing many aspects of Android UI design. We know about sizing, positioning, spacing, and gravity. We have also seen some options for layout type as well, such as `Relative` and `LinearLayout`.

In the next chapter we will actually build some UI layouts like you might find in a real-world app.

5
Real-World Layouts

So far, we have only used a single phone emulator. As we will be building some layouts more suited to Android tablets, it is time to look at configuring a tablet emulator. We will then be in a position to be a bit more daring with our UI designs. We will build two different UI designs, however, we will do so in just one mini-app. We will soon see how we can change our Java code to see the layout we are currently interested in. In this chapter we will cover the following:

- Configuring a tablet emulator
- Building a scrolling list-detail layout
- Building a fairly intricate form submission layout

Building a real-world UI

These simple yet practical projects will begin to demonstrate how we can create some designs that might actually make it into a real app.

As usual, you can find all the code for this section in the download bundle in the `Chapter 5/RealUI` folder.

For a bit of variation, we can see the process of creating a new emulator; let's make ourselves a Nexus 7 AVD.

Creating a tablet emulator

So, we can really go to town on our designs and add loads of new widgets and views; let's make an emulator with more screen real estate. Note that the subsequent UI projects will work fine on a phone (although look a bit more squashed) but now seemed like a good time to take a look at making a new emulator:

1. Click the AVD Manager icon in the toolbar.

2. On the **Your Virtual Devices** screen, left-click the **Create Virtual Device...** button.

3. Now we can see the **Select Hardware** window. In the **Category** column left-click **Tablet**. In the **Name** column left-click **Nexus 7 (2012)**. Now left-click **Next**.

4. On the **System Image** screen left-click **Next** to accept the default options.

5. Left-click **Finish** and we have a shiny new Nexus 7 emulator ready to test our future apps on.

You can repeat these steps and choose a different device type and model at step 3, and at step 4 you can further customize the device to your liking.

> **Help, my emulator is stuck**
>
> Some emulators will appear slightly off-screen when you run them. If it is the title bar of their window that is hidden, this can be really awkward to move or close. Press *Alt* + *Space*, then select **Move** from the context menu. You can now move your emulator window with the keyboard arrow (cursor) keys or the mouse. Left-click to place the emulator window in a better position.

Now we will build two real-world UI's. Create a new project and call it **Real UI**. As usual choose a **Blank Activity** and leave all the other settings at their defaults.

Now switch to our new Nexus 7 in design view by left-clicking it from the drop-down list of AVDs we discovered during the Android Studio guided tour. Click on the rotate button to switch the design view to landscape.

All of our practical UI's will be in this one project. However, for each we will create a new layout file. The automatically generated `layout_main.xml` file will not be used. Of course, when we are done building our UI we will need to change the call to `setContentView` in our Java code to choose the UI that we would like to see in action.

Let's start with a `LinearLayout`.

List-detail layout with ScrollView and LinearLayout

A common layout seen in quite a few Android apps is the list-detail layout. That is on one part of the screen there is a list of some item types (perhaps small images and product names), and then on another part of the screen there is the detail of whichever item from the list is currently selected.

Making a fully functional app of this type will take a little more Java practice but we can quickly see how to make a simple layout along these lines:

1. Use the Real UI project we recently created but let's start with a completely clean sheet for the layout. Right-click the `layout` folder in the project explorer. From the pop-up context sensitive options menu, choose **New | Layout resource file**.
2. Make sure **LinearLayout** is selected for the **Root element**.
3. Name the file `list_detail_layout` then left-click **OK**.
4. In the **Properties** window, find the **orientation** property of the `LinearLayout`, which is provided by default, and change it to `horizontal`.
5. Drag a **LinearLayout(vertical)** onto the design.
6. Now drag a **LinearLayout(horizontal)** onto the design.
7. To be able to discern between the two new layouts we have just added you will probably need to look at the component window. Here is an image of the component window after step 6:

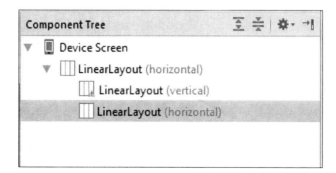

8. Select the first (vertical) `LinearLayout` within the root `LinearLayout`, find its **layout:weight** property, and set it to 40. Set its `background` to a color of your choice by finding and left-clicking the **background** property ellipses ..., then left-clicking the **Color** tab and choosing a color.

9. Select the second (horizontal) `LinearLayout` within the root `LinearLayout`, find its **layout:weight** property, and set it to 60. We now have two clearly discernible areas of the screen: one taking up 40%, the other 60%, as shown next:

10. Now drag a **ScrollView** from the **Containers** section of the palette and drop it on the left-hand smaller (40%) width `LinearLayout`.

11. Now drag another **LinearLayout(vertical)** on top of the `ScrollView`.

12. Now drag around 20 (seriously!) **Large Text** widgets onto the `LinearLayout` you added in the previous step. As the `LinearLayout` is initially squashed flat, it will be easier to start by dragging the **Large Text** widgets onto the `LinearLayout` via the component tree window.

13. Now drag an **ImageView** to the right-hand `LinearLayout`. Make it display the Android icon by finding its **src** property and browsing to **ic_launcher** at the end of the list on the **Projects** tab, as we did while experimenting with `ImageView` earlier. The image serves no purpose here other than to demonstrate that it is completely distinct from the functionality we are about to witness in the left-hand side of our UI.

14. Change the `ImageView` **layout:weight** property to 1 to make the image larger.

15. Change the call to `setContentView` in `MainActivity.java` to the same as the next line of code:

    ```
    setContentView(R.layout.list_detail_layout);
    ```

16. The code will now set our new layout as the layout for our app. Run the app on the Nexus 7 emulator.

When the app is running you can left-click and drag the left-hand pane of the app to scroll the contents up and down. Notice that the Android image in the right-hand pane stays still:

We achieved this by adding two `LinearLayouts` to our root `LinearLayout`. We made one cover 40% and the other 60% of the parent by setting their `layout_weight` properties to `40` and `60` respectively. Then we put a `ScrollView` into the left-hand `LinearLayout` and put another vertical `LinearLayout` into the `ScrollView`. We did this step because `ScrollView` can only have one child (very wise). However, once we have the `LinearLayout` inside the `ScrollView` we can add as many widgets as we like and they will all scroll nicely, as we saw.

Designing a form with RelativeLayout

We have already played around with `RelativeLayout` as it is the default layout when we create a new project. With this project we will lay out a fairly comprehensive form—similar to what you might ask a user to fill out when subscribing to a service.

It will probably help to see the layout before we get started. So here it is with the name and password fields already filled out so we can see what different fields will look like:

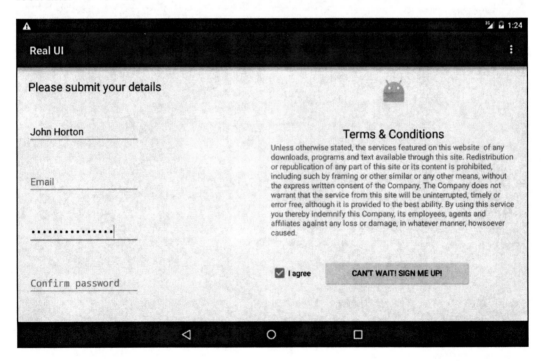

Now we can see the end goal, let's get on with creating it for real:

1. Use the same project as we did for the previous layout but let's start with a completely clean sheet for the layout. Right-click the `layout` folder in the project explorer. From the pop-up context sensitive options menu, choose **New | Layout resource file**.

2. Make sure **LinearLayout** is selected for the **Root element**. Why we use `LinearLayout` when we are supposed to be learning about `RelativeLayout` will soon become apparent.

3. Name the file `form_layout` then left-click **OK**.

4. Select the `LinearLayout` at the root of our design and change its **orientation** property from `vertical` to `horizontal` from the properties window.

5. Drag and drop two `RelativeLayout` elements onto the design. Make sure they are both children of the root `LinearLayout`. If this is awkward, remember you can drag them directly onto the component tree view to make sure they have the intended parent. The end result is as shown in the following component tree image:

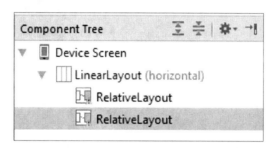

6. Now we will make sure that each of the `RelativeLayout` elements take up exactly half the screen each. Find the `layout:weight` property of each in turn and set them both to `.5`. By doing so each layout will take up half the space. As long as the amounts are relative to each other they will work. So you could use 50 and 50 if you prefer.

7. As a precautionary step, check that there are no values set in the **layout:margin** property for either of the RelativeLayout elements. Sometimes when we drag and drop elements onto the design, Android Studio will add a margin without us realizing. If there are any values for any of the `RelativeLayout` margins, delete them. You should now have two equal-sized layouts filling the design.

8. Drag and drop a **Large Text** widget onto the top-left corner of the design. Put it right in the corner, don't worry about leaving a margin at the moment.

9. Double left-click the widget from the previous step to open up an editing window for its `text` property. Enter the text `Please submit your details`. This has exactly the same effect as editing the `text` property in the **Properties** window.

10. From the **Text Fields** category of the palette, drag a **Person Name** widget onto the design but don't drop it straight away. Position the widget hard to the left of the design and slightly below the previous text we added in step 9. Notice that as you move the **Edit Text** up and down you can see the margin property changing. The next image should make this clear:

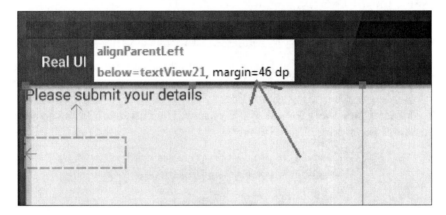

11. Try and get the margin property as close as possible to `46 dp`, then, while still against the left side of the design, drop the **Edit Text**. If you didn't get the margin quite right, in the **Properties** window set **margin:top** to `46dp`.

12. In the properties window find the **hint** property and set it to `Name`. This will put text on our widget but as soon as the user taps it to enter his name the text will disappear.

13. From the **Text Fields** category of the palette, drag an **Email** widget onto the design but don't drop it straight away. Position the widget hard to the left of the design and slightly below the previous text we added in step 9. Notice, as before, that as you move the widget up and down you can see the margin property changing. Drop it when it is `46 dp` exactly or edit **margin:top** in the **Properties** window.

14. Find the **hint** property and change it to `Email`.

15. From the **Text Fields** category of the palette, drag a **Password** widget onto the design but don't drop it straight away. Position the widget hard to the left of the design and slightly below the previous text we added in step 9. Drop it when it is 46 dp exactly or edit **margin:top** in the **Properties** window. The Password widget is simply an editable text field that obscures what the user has entered. You can see this in action in the image showing the completed layout that we saw before this tutorial.

16. Find the **hint** property and change it to Password.

17. From the **Text Fields** category of the palette, drag a **Password** widget onto the design but don't drop it straight away. Position the widget hard to the left of the design and slightly below the previous text we added in step 15. Drop it when it is 46 dp exactly or edit **margin:top** in the **Properties** window.

18. Find the **hint** property and change it to Confirm password. At this point your layout should look like this next image:

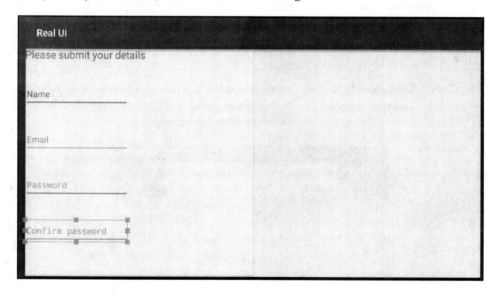

19. Moving on to the right-hand side of the form, drag an **ImageView** and drop it on the hard left and top of the right-hand RelativeLayout.

20. Set its **src** property to ic_launcher by browsing to it on the **Projects** tab after left-clicking the **...** link, as we have done before.

21. Set the **layout:width** property to match_parent. This doesn't make the actual image larger but it prevents it being wrapped so that the next step will work.

22. Find the **layout:centerInParent** property and set it to horizontal. The Android robot image should now be in the center-top of the right-hand RelativeLayout.

23. Drag a **Large Text** widget from the palette onto the right-hand `RelativeLayout`. You should be able to center it and set the margin between the `ImageView` to `46 dp` before letting go of it. If your mouse doesn't have quite the right sensitivity to achieve this, you can set **margin:top** in the **Properties** window. You can also use the **Properties** window to set the **layout:centerInParent** property to `horizontal` if necessary.

24. Now we will add the actual terms and conditions. Obviously, following in the long tradition of all terms and conditions, we want to make this text smaller than the rest of the text on the form. Drag a **Small Text** widget to `10 dp` below and exactly central to the previous `Large Text` widget. You can achieve this using exactly the same techniques that we used in the previous step.

25. Find the **text** property in the **Properties** window. Copy and paste some random text, sufficient to fill about the same amount of space as the terms and conditions takes up in the completed layout image we looked at before this tutorial. Leave just enough space for a button and some margin below.

26. Drag a **Check Box** widget onto the layout and position it on the hard left of the right-hand `RelativeLayout` and 46 dp below the terms and conditions.

27. Edit the **text** property to `I agree`.

28. Drag a **Button** onto the layout and line it up with the bottom edge of the `Check Box` and around `85 dp` from the right. This next image should make this clear, as well as show all our progress to date:

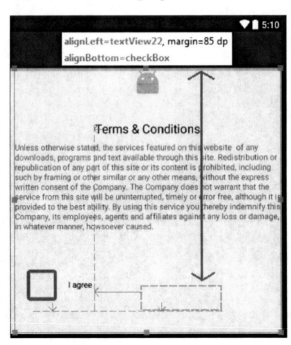

29. Change the **text** property to `Can't wait! Sign me up!`.

30. Next, you will notice that the base of the button is in line with the check box base but the top isn't. In the **Properties** window find the **layout:alignComponent** property and in the **top:top** sub-property select the **checkBox** widget.

31. Now go to the root `LinearLayout` and find the **padding** property and set its sub-property **all** to `20dp`.

32. Change the call to `setContentView` in `MainActivity.java` to the same as the next line of code:

```
setContentView(R.layout.form_layout);
```

33. The code will now set our new layout as the layout for our app. Run the app on the Nexus 7 emulator.

You should have a nearly-identical layout to the image we saw before the start of the tutorial. We achieved these tidy results by inserting two `RelativeLayouts` in a parent horizontal `LinearLayout`. Actually we could have achieved an initially neat looking layout in just one `RelativeLayout`. The problem is that if we had done this, the second column of widgets would have been positioned using a margin from the left-hand column. The `dp` units are perfect for creating small margins and padding, but when we use them across a significant amount of screen real estate then we get very inconsistent results on different devices.

By first dividing the screen into two halves, based on the `weight` property, we get a consistently neat layout. If the form was more complicated we would probably want to further sub-divide the screen to be even more sure that when we lay out the individual widgets relatively, they are always consistent.

As an experiment, try rotating the screen to portrait orientation. You can do so on an emulator with the *Ctrl + F11* keyboard combination.

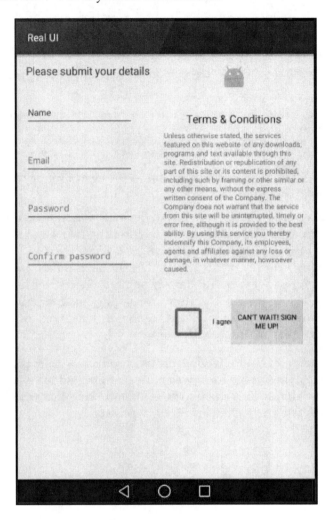

Not too bad but certainly imperfect. There are a few possible solutions to this problem:

1. Provide an additional layout in a file with the same name and put it in a folder named `layout-portrait` in the `res` folder.

2. Lock the layout to landscape and prevent the user from rotating the layout. We can do this in either XML or Java code.

3. Come up with an entirely more elegant but slightly more complex solution using **Fragments**.

We will use the second solution when we build our first full app from *Chapter 12, Having a Dialogue with the User* to *Chapter 17, Sound FX and Supporting Different Versions of Android*. We will see the third solution when we build more advanced apps starting from *Chapter 18, Design Patterns, Fragments, and the Real World*. There are pros and cons to all of the solutions, and which one you use depends upon the experience you want your user to have. They are all as valid as each other.

Summary

The main thing to learn from this chapter is that experience and practice are a lot more valuable than vast volumes of knowledge. If you have a neat idea for a cool new UI, but this chapter hasn't shown you how to do it, then chances are somebody else has already shared that knowledge, and a quick web search will usually provide a tutorial or discussion that provides your solutions. Now you know your way around the UI designer, tutorials on the web should be easily understandable.

As we progress through the book we will look at much more advanced UIs than we have so far. Hopefully this chapter will have been a good all-round introduction to building more real-world UIs in the Android Studio visual designer.

Despite significant progress, there is a very big elephant in the room. Of course, our UI doesn't actually do anything! Our neat looking form will not collect a single scrap of data and our smart scrolling list doesn't show any details when we click on one of the items.

To solve these problems we first need to get really familiar with Java. That is what we will start to do in the next chapter.

6

The Life and Times of an Android App

In this short chapter, we will look at the lifecycle of an Android app. At first, it might sound a bit strange that a computer program has a lifecycle, but it will soon make sense. We will see the phases an app goes through, from creation to destruction, and how this helps us know *where* to put our Java code, depending on what we are trying to achieve.

In brief, we will look at:

- An introduction to the Android lifecycle
- What method overriding @Override is
- The phases of the Android lifecycle
- What exactly we need to know and do to code our apps
- A lifecycle demonstration mini app
- A quick look at code structure, ready to get Java coding in the next chapter

Let's start learning about the Android lifecycle.

Introduction to the Android lifecycle

We have talked a bit about the structure of our code; that we write classes, and within those classes we have methods that contain our code. We also know that when we want the code within a method to run (be **executed**), we **call** that method by using its name.

Also, in *Chapter 2, Java - First Contact*, we learned that Android itself calls the onCreate method just before the app is ready to start. We saw this when we outputted to the logcat and used the Toast class to send a pop-up message to the user.

What we will look at now is what happens throughout the lifecycle of every app we write: when it starts and ends, as well as a few stages in between. And what we will see is that Android actually interacts with our app on numerous occasions, each and every time it is run.

It does so by calling methods that are contained within the Activity class. Even if the method is not visible within our Java code, it is still being called by Android at the appropriate time. If this doesn't seem to make any sense, then read on.

Did you ever wonder why the onCreate method had the strange-looking line of code just before it?

```
@Override
```

What is going on here is that, when you call onCreate, we are asking Android to please use our overridden version, because we have some things to do at that time.

Furthermore, you might remember the odd-looking first line of code in the onCreate method:

```
super.onCreate(savedInstanceState)
```

This is telling Android to call the original/official version of onCreate before proceeding with our overridden version. This is not just a quirk of Android, **method overriding** is built into Java.

There are also quite a lot of other methods that we can optionally override, and they allow us to add our code at appropriate times within the lifecycle of our Android app.

The reason we need to care about the methods of *our* app that Android calls whenever it wants, is because they control the very life and death of our code. For instance, what if our app allows the user to type a moment of inspiration, perhaps a poem or vital reminder, into our hypothetical note-taking app, when halfway through the phone rings, our app disappears and the data (the note) is gone?

It is vital, and thankfully quite straightforward, that we learn when, why, and which methods Android will call as part of the lifecycle of our app. We can then know where we need to override methods to add our own code and where to add the real functionality (code) that defines our app. Let's examine the Android lifecycle, then we can move on to the ins and outs of Java, and we will know exactly where to put the code that we write.

A simplified explanation of the Android lifecycle

If you have ever used an Android device, you have probably noticed it works quite differently than many other operating systems. For example, you can be using an app, say you're checking what people are doing on Facebook. Then you get an e-mail notification and you tap the e-mail icon to read it. Mid-way through reading the e-mail you might get a Twitter notification, and because you're waiting on important news from someone you follow, you interrupt your e-mail reading and change apps to Twitter, with one touch.

After reading the tweet, you fancy a game of Angry Birds, but mid-way through the first daring fling you suddenly remember that Facebook post. So you quit Angry Birds and tap the Facebook icon.

Then you resume Facebook, probably at the same point you left it. You could have resumed reading the e-mail, decided to reply to the tweet, or started an entirely new app.

All this backwards and forwards takes quite a lot of management on the part of the operating system, apparently independent from the individual apps themselves.

The difference between, say, a Windows PC and Android in the context we have just discussed is this: with Android, although the user decides which app they are using, the OS decides if and when to actually close down (destroy) an application, and **our user's data** (like the hypothetical note) along with it. We just need to consider this when coding our apps.

Lifecycle phases – what we need to know

The Android system has multiple different *phases* that any given app can be in. Depending upon the phase, the Android system determines how the app is viewed by the user or whether it is viewed at all. Android has these phases, so it can decide which app is in current use and then allocate the right amount of resources, such as memory and processing power. But it also allows us as app developers to interact with these phases.

We have already raised the issue of what will happen if the user quits our app to answer a phone call, will they lose their progress/data/important note?

Android has a fairly complex system that, when simplified a little for the purposes of explanation, means that every app on an Android device is in one of the following phases:

- Being created
- Starting
- Resuming
- Running
- Pausing
- Stopping
- Being destroyed

The list of phases will hopefully appear fairly logical. As an example, the user presses the Facebook app icon and the app is **created**. Then it is **started**. All fairly straightforward so far, but next in the list is **resuming**. It is not as illogical as it might first appear. If, for a moment, we can just accept that the app resumes after it starts, then all will become clear as we proceed.

After **resuming**, the app is **running**. This is when the Facebook app has control of the screen and probably the greater share of system memory and processing power. Now, what about our example when we switched from the Facebook app to the e-mail app?

As we tap to go to read our e-mail, the Facebook app will probably have entered the **paused** phase, followed by stopping, and the e-mail app will enter the being **created** phase, followed by **resuming**, then **running**. If we decide to revisit Facebook, as in the scenario earlier, the Facebook app will probably skip being created, then it will **restart**, **resume**, and be **running** again, most likely exactly on the post we left it on.

Note that, at any time, Android can decide to **stop**, then **destroy** an app. In which case, when we run the app again, it will need to be **created** at the first phase all over again. So, had the Facebook app been inactive long enough, or had Angry Birds required so many system resources that Android had **destroyed** the Facebook app, then our experience of finding the exact post we were previously reading might have been different.

If all this phase stuff is starting to get confusing then you will be pleased to know that the only reason to mention it is so that:

- You know it exists
- We occasionally need to interact with it
- We will take things step by step when we do

Lifecycle phases – what we need to do

When we are programming an app, how do we possibly interact with this complexity? The good news is that the Android code that was auto-generated when we created our first project does most of it for us. As we have discussed, we just don't see the methods that handle this, but we do have the opportunity to **override** them and add our own code to that phase.

This means we can get on with learning Java and making Android apps until we come to one of the few instances for which we need to do something, specifically in one of the phases.

> **Each Activity has its own lifecycle**
>
> Actually, this discussion is relevant to just an Activity. So, if our app has more than one Activity, they will each have their own lifecycle. This doesn't have to complicate things, and in the long run it will make things easier for us.

Here is a quick explanation of the methods provided by Android, for our convenience, to manage the lifecycle phases. To clarify our discussion of lifecycle methods, they are listed next to their corresponding phases, which we have been discussing. However, as you will see, the method names make it fairly clear on their own where they fit in.

There is also a brief explanation or suggestion about when we might use a given method, and thereby interact during a specific phase. We will meet most of these methods as we progress through the book. We have of course already seen onCreate:

- onCreate: This method is executed when the Activity is being created. Here we get everything ready for the app including UI (such as calling setContentView), graphics, and sound.

- onStart: This method is executed when the app is in the starting phase.

- onResume: This method runs after onStart but can also be entered, perhaps most logically, if our Activity is resumed after being previously paused. We might reload previously saved user data (such as an important note) from when the app had been interrupted, perhaps by a phone call or the user running another app.

- onPause: You are probably getting the hang of these methods. This occurs when our app is pausing. Here we might save unsaved data (such as the note) that could be reloaded in onResume. Activities always transition into a paused state when another UI element is displayed on top of the current activity (for example, a pop-up dialog), or when the activity is about to be stopped (for example, when the user navigates to a different activity).

- onStop: This relates to the stopping phase. This is where we might undo everything we did in onCreate, such as releasing system resources or writing information to a database. If we reach here, we are probably going to get destroyed sometime soon.

- onDestroy: This is when our activity is finally being destroyed. There is no turning back at this phase. This is our last chance to dismantle our app in an orderly manner. If we reach here, we will definitely be going through the lifecycle phases from the beginning next time.

All the method descriptions and their related phases should appear straightforward. Perhaps the only real question is: what about the running phase? As we will see when we write our code in the other methods/phases, the onCreate, onStart, and onResume methods will prepare the app, which then persists, forming the running phase. Then the onPause, onStop, and onDestroy methods will occur afterwards. Now, we can actually take a look at these lifecycle methods in action. We will do so by overriding them all and adding a Log message and a Toast message to each.

The lifecycle demonstration app

This quick experiment will help familiarize ourselves with the lifecycle methods our app uses, as well as give us a chance to play around with a bit more Java code:

1. Start a new project and call it Lifecycle Demonstration. Of course, the code is in the download bundle in the Chapter 6/Lifecycle Demonstration folder should you wish to refer to it or copy and paste it.

2. Accept the default target devices.

3. Choose **Blank Activity** and don't worry about customizing the activity options at all.

4. Open the MainActivity.java file in the code editor, if it is not opened for you by default, by left-clicking on the **MainActivity** tab above the editor.

 If the previous steps were not detailed enough, check back to any of the previous occasions when we created a new project for further details.

You have created a new project with all the settings on default. We will only need the MainActivity.java file for this demonstration and we will not be building a UI.

In the `MainActivity.java` file, find the `onCreate` method and add these two lines of code just before the closing curly brace }, which marks the end of the `onCreate` method:

```
Toast.makeText(this, "In onCreate", Toast.LENGTH_SHORT).show();
Log.i("info", "In onCreate");
```

The entire `onCreate` method should now look exactly like this, where the highlighted code is the two lines we just added:

```
@Override
protected void onCreate(Bundle savedInstanceState) {
    super.onCreate(savedInstanceState);
    setContentView(R.layout.activity_main);

    Toast.makeText(this, "In onCreate", Toast.LENGTH_SHORT).show();
    Log.i("info", "In onCreate");
}
```

After the closing curly brace } of the `onCreate` method, leave one clear line and add the following five lifecycle methods and their contained code. Remember, you will need to use the *Alt + Enter* keyboard combination twice to import the classes needed for `Toast` and `Log`. Also note that it doesn't matter what order we add our overridden methods. Android will call them in the correct order regardless of the order we type them:

```
@Override
public void onStart() {
    // First call the "official" version of this method
    super.onStart();

    Toast.makeText(this, "In onStart", Toast.LENGTH_SHORT).show();
    Log.i("info", "In onStart");
}

@Override
public void onResume() {
    // First call the "official" version of this method
    super.onResume();

    Toast.makeText(this, "In onResume", Toast.LENGTH_SHORT).show();
    Log.i("info", "In onResume");
}

@Override
```

```
public void onPause() {
  // First call the "official" version of this method
  super.onPause();

  Toast.makeText(this, "In onPause", Toast.LENGTH_SHORT).show();
  Log.i("info", "In onPause");
}

@Override
public void onStop() {
  // First call the "official" version of this method
  super.onStop();

  Toast.makeText(this, "In onStop", Toast.LENGTH_SHORT).show();
  Log.i("info", "In onStop");
}

@Override
public void onDestroy() {
  // First call the "official" version of this method
  super.onDestroy();

  Toast.makeText(this, "In onDestroy", Toast.LENGTH_SHORT).show();
  Log.i("info", "In onDestroy");
}
```

First of all, let's talk about the code itself. Notice that the method names all correspond to the lifecycle methods and phases we have just discussed. Notice that all of the method declarations are preceded by the @Override line of code. Also see that the first line of code inside each method is super.on....

What it is that is going on here is this:

- Android calls our methods at the various times we have already discussed.

- The @Override keyword indicates that these methods replace/override the original version of the method that is provided as part of the Android API. Note we don't see these overridden methods but they are there, and if we didn't override them, these original versions would be called by Android instead of ours.

- The super.on... syntax, which is the first line of code within each of the overridden methods, then calls these original versions.

So, we don't simply override these original methods in order to add our own code, we also call them and their code is executed too.

> For the curious, the keyword super is for super-class. We will explore method overriding and super classes in several chapters as we progress.

Finally, the code that you added will make each of the methods output one Toast message and one Log message. However, the messages that are output vary, as can be seen by the text in between the double quote marks "". The messages that are output will make it plain which method produced them.

Now that we have looked at the code, we can play with our app and learn about the lifecycle from what happens:

1. Run the app on either a device or an emulator.

2. Watch the screen of the emulator and you will see the following appear, one after the other, as Toast messages on the screen: **In onCreate**, **In onStart**, and **In onResume**.

3. Notice the following messages in the logcat window. If there are too many messages, remember you can filter them by setting the **Log level** drop-down to **Info**:

    ```
    info:in onCreate
    info:in onStart
    info:in onResume
    ```

4. Now tap the back button on the emulator or the device. Notice you get the following three Toast messages in exactly this order. **In onPause**, **In onStop**, **In onDestroy**. Verify that we have matching output in the logcat window.

5. Next, run a different app. Perhaps the Hello Android app from *Chapter 1, The First App* by tapping its icon on the emulator screen.

6. Now try this: tap the task manager button. This is a square (as shown next) on the emulator but does vary a little on different devices:

7. You should now see all the recently run apps on the device. Here is what my Nexus 5 emulator looks like at this point:

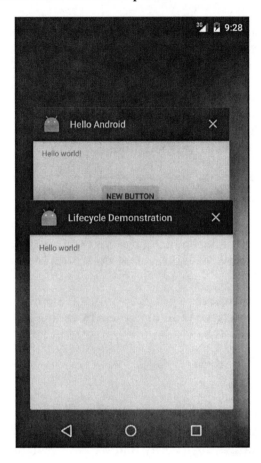

8. Tap the **Lifecycle Demonstration** app and notice that the usual three starting messages are shown. This is because our app was previously destroyed.

9. However, now tap the task manager button again and switch to the **Hello Android** app. Notice that this time, only the **In onPause** and **In onStop** messages are shown. Verify that we have matching output in the logcat. The app has **not** been destroyed.

10. Now, again using the task manager button, switch to the **Lifecycle Demonstration** app. You will see that only the **In onStart** and **In onResume** messages were shown, indicating that onCreate was not required to get the app running again. This is as expected because the app was not previously destroyed, merely stopped.

Next let's talk about what we saw when we ran the app. When we started the *Lifecycle Demonstration* app for the first time, we saw that the onCreate, onStart, and onResume methods were called. Then, when we closed the app using the back button, the onPause, onStop, and onDestroy methods were called. Furthermore, we know from our code that the original versions of all these methods are also called because we are calling them ourselves with the super.on... code, which is the first thing we do in each of our overridden methods.

The quirk in our apps' behavior came when we used the task manager to switch between apps, and also, when switching away from Lifecycle Demonstration, it was not destroyed; subsequently, when switching back, it was not necessary to run onCreate.

Where's my Toast?

Actually, the opening three and closing three Toast messages are queued and the methods have already completed by the time they are shown. You can verify this by running the experiments again and seeing that all three starting/closing log messages are output before even the second Toast message is shown. However, the Toast messages do reinforce our knowledge about the order, if not the timing.

It is entirely possible (but not that likely) that you got slightly different results when you followed the previous steps. What is for sure is that when our apps are run on thousands of different devices by millions of different users who have different preferences for interacting with their devices, Android will be calling the lifecycle methods at times we cannot really predict.

For example, what happens when the user exits the app by pressing the home button? When we open two apps, one after the other, and then use the back button to switch to the previous app: will that destroy or just stop the app? What happens when the user has a dozen apps in his task manager and the operating system needs to destroy some apps that were previously only stopped: will our app be one of the "victims"?

You can of course test out all of these scenarios on the emulator, but the results will only be true for the one time you test it. It is not guaranteed that the same behavior will be exhibited every time, and certainly not on every different Android device.

At last some good news! The solution to all this complexity is to follow a few simple rules:

- Set up your app ready to run in the onCreate method
- Load your user's data in the onResume method
- Save your user's data in the onPause method

- Tidy up your app and make it a good Android citizen in the `onDestroy` method
- Watch out throughout the book for a couple of occasions when we might like to use `onStart` and `onStop`

If we do these things, and we will see how to over the course of the book, we can just stop worrying about all this lifecycle stuff and let Android handle it!

There are a few more methods we can override as well. So let's take a look at them.

Some other overridden methods

Almost certainly you have noticed that there are two other auto-generated methods in the code of all our projects so far. They are `onCreateOptionsMenu` and `onOptionsItemSelected`. Most Android apps have a pop-up menu, so Android Studio generates one by default; including the basic code to make it work.

You can see the XML that describes the menu in `menu/menu_main.xml` from the project explorer. The key line of XML code is this:

```
<item android:id="@+id/action_settings"
    android:title="@string/action_settings"
    android:orderInCategory="100" app:showAsAction="never" />
```

This describes a **menu item** with the text, **Settings**. If you run any of the apps we have created so far you can see the button, as shown next:

If you tap the button you can see it in action, as shown next:

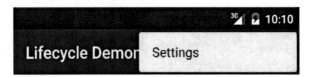

So, how do the `onCreateOptionsMenu` and `onOptionsItemSelected` methods produce these results?

The `onCreateOptionsMenu` method loads the menu from the `menu_main.xml` file with this line of code:

```
getMenuInflater().inflate(R.menu.menu_main, menu);
```

It is called by the default version of the `onCreate` method, which is why we don't see it happen.

 Some very old versions of Android do this slightly differently but we will not need to concern ourselves with this in the context of this book.

The `onOptionsItemSelected` method is called when the user taps the menu button. This method handles what will happen when a particular item is selected. At the moment nothing happens, it just returns `true`.

Feel free to add `Toast` and `Log` messages to these methods to test out the order and timing I have just described.

We will be using menus in our first major app project. I just thought it a good time to quickly introduce these two methods because they have been lurking around in our code without an introduction and I didn't want them to feel left out.

Now that we have seen how the Android lifecycle works and have been introduced to a whole bunch of methods we can override to interact with the lifecycle, we had better learn the fundamentals of Java so that we can write some code to go in these methods, as well as our own methods.

The structure of Java code – revisited

We have already seen that each time we create a new Android project we also create a new Java **package**, as a kind of container for the code we will write.

We have also learned about and played around with **classes**. We have imported and taken direct advantage of classes from the Android API such as `Log` and `Toast`. We have also used the `AppCompatActivity` class, but in a different manner to that of `Log` and `Toast`. You might remember the first line of code in all our projects so far, after the `import` statements, used the `extends` keyword:

```
public class MyActivity extends AppCompatActivity {
```

When we extend a class as opposed to just importing it, we are kind of making it our own. In fact, if you take another look at the line of code you can see that we are making a new class, with a new name, `MyActivity`, but basing it on the `AppCompatActivity` class from the Android API.

AppCompatActivity is a slightly modified version of Activity. It basically provides extra features for older versions of Android that would otherwise not be present. Everything we have discussed about Activity is equally true for AppCompatActivity. We will see some more variations on the Activity class as we progress. It is entirely possible that you have a different class in place of AppCompatActivity, dependent upon changes that have taken place since this was written. Updates of Android Studio will often change the default Activity class that it uses when it creates a new project. As long as the name ends in ...Activity it doesn't matter because everything we have discussed and will discuss is equally true. I will usually just refer to this class simply as Activity.

In summary, we can import classes to use them, we can extend classes to use them and, very importantly, we will eventually make our own classes.

The important point

Classes, in their various forms, are the foundation of every single line of code in Java. Everything in Java is, or is part of, a class.

Our own classes and those written by others are the building blocks of our code, and the methods within the classes wrap the functional code, the code that actually does the work.

We can write methods within the classes that we extend, as we did with topClick and bottomClick in *Chapter 2, Java – First Contact*. Furthermore, we overrode methods that are already part of classes written by others, such as onCreate, onPause, and so on.

However, the only code that we put in these methods was a few calls using Toast and Log. We aren't going to code the next killer app with just that.

Summary

In this chapter we have seen that it is not only us who can call our code. The operating system can also call the code contained within the methods we have overridden. By adding the appropriate code into the appropriate overridden lifecycle methods, we can be sure that the right code will be executed at the right time.

What we need to do now is learn how to write some more Java code.

7

Coding in Java
Part 1 – Variables,
Decisions, and Loops

In this chapter, we are going to learn and practice the core fundamentals of Java, that is, the code that goes into the classes, and the methods that we create, along with the data that the code acts upon.

We will also quickly recap on what we learned in the previous chapters about Java and then immediately dive into learning how to write our very own Java code. The principles we are about to learn are not limited to Java but are also applicable to other programming languages as well. By the end of the chapter, you will be comfortable writing Java code that actually creates and uses data within Android.

This chapter takes you through:

- Java syntax and jargon
- Variables, operators, and expressions
- Decisions and branching
- Loops

Java is everywhere

The core Java fundamentals that we are about to learn apply to classes that we inherit from (such as `Activity`), as well as classes that we write ourselves (as we will start to do in *Chapter 9, Object-Oriented Programming*). As it is more logical to learn the basics before we write our own classes, we will be using the extended `Activity` class in a whole bunch of mini-projects in this chapter to learn and practice Java, and we will use `Log` and `Toast` again to observe the results of our coding. In addition, we will use more methods that we will write ourselves (called from buttons), as well as the overridden methods of the `Activity` class to trigger the execution of our code.

However, when we move onto *Chapter 9, Object-Oriented Programming* and start to write our own classes, as well as understand more about how classes written by others work, everything we have learned here will apply then too. In fact, all the Java that you learn in this chapter will work in the following Java environments if you strip it out of the `Activity` class and paste it into these environments:

- Any of the major desktop operating systems
- Many modern televisions
- Sat nav
- Smart fridges and more...

Calling all Java gurus

If you have already done some Java programming and understand the following words: `if`, `else`, `while`, `do while`, `switch`, and `for`, you can probably skip to the next chapter. Or you might like to skim over this information as a refresher.

Let's get on with learning how to code in Java.

Syntax and jargon

Throughout this book we will use plain English to discuss some fairly technical things. You will never be asked to read a technical explanation of a Java or Android concept that has not been previously explained in non-technical language.

So far, on a few occasions, I have asked that you accept a simplified explanation in order to offer a fuller explanation at a more appropriate time, like with classes and methods.

Having said that, the Java and Android communities are full of people who speak in technical terms, and to join in and learn from these communities you need to understand the terms they use. So, the approach this book takes is to learn a concept or appreciate an idea using entirely plain-speaking language, but, at the same time, introduce the jargon/technical term as part of the learning.

Java syntax is the way we put together the language elements of Java in order to produce code that works in the Dalvik virtual machine. The Java syntax is a combination of the words we use and the formation of those words into the sentence-like structures that are our code.

These Java "words" are many in number, but taken in small chunks are almost certainly easier to learn than any human spoken language. We call these words **keywords**.

I am confident that if you can read then you can learn Java because learning Java is much easier. What then separates someone who has finished an elementary Java course and an expert programmer? The exact same thing that separates a student of language and a master poet. Expertise in Java comes not in the number of Java keywords we know how to use but rather in the way we use them. Mastery of the language comes through practice, further study, and using the keywords more skillfully. Many consider programming an art as much as a science and there is probably some truth to this.

More code comments

As you become more advanced at writing Java programs, the solutions you use to create your programs will become longer and more complicated. Furthermore, as we will see in later chapters, Java was designed to manage complexity by having us divide up our code into separate classes, very often across multiple files.

Code comments are a part of the Java program that do not have any function in the program itself. The compiler ignores them. They serve to help the programmer document, explain, and clarify their code to make it more understandable to themselves at a later date, or to other programmers who might need to use or modify it.

We have already seen a single-line comment:

```
// this is a comment explaining what is going on
```

The previous comment begins with the two forward slash characters //. The comment ends at the end of the line. So, anything on that line is for humans only, whereas anything on the next line (unless it's another comment) needs to be syntactically correct Java code:

```
// I can write anything I like here
but this line will cause an error
```

We can use multiple single-line comments:

```
// Below is an important note
// I am an important note
// We can have as many single line comments like this as we like
```

Single-line comments are also useful if we want to temporarily disable a line of code. We can put // in front of the code and it will not be included in the program. Remember this code, which tells Android to load our layout?

```
// setContentView(R.layout.activity_main);
```

In the previous situation, the layout will not be loaded and the app will have a blank screen when run, as the entire line of code is ignored by the compiler.

There is another type of comment in Java known as the **multi-line comment**. The multi-line comment is useful for longer comments that span across multiple lines, and also for adding things such as copyright information at the top of a code file. Similar to the single-line comment, a multi-line comment can be used to temporarily disable code, in this case across multiple lines.

Everything in between the leading /* and the ending */ is ignored by the compiler. Here are some examples:

```
/*
    You can tell I am good at this because my
    code has so many helpful comments in it.
*/
```

There is no limit to the number of lines in a multi-line comment. Which type of comment is best to use will depend upon the situation. In this book, I will always explain every line of code explicitly in the text but you will often find liberally sprinkled comments within the code itself that add further explanation, insight, or context. So, it's always a good idea to read all the code thoroughly too:

```
/*
    The winning lottery numbers for next Saturday are
    9,7,12,34,29,22
    But you still want to make Android apps?
*/
```

All the best Java programmers liberally sprinkle their code with comments!

Storing and using data with variables

We can think of a **variable** as a named storage box. We choose a name, perhaps variableA. These names are kind of like our programmer's window into the memory of the user's Android device.

Variables are values in memory ready to be used or altered when necessary by using the appropriate name.

Computer memory has a highly complex system of addressing, which fortunately we do not need to interact with. Java variables allow us to devise our own convenient names for all the data we need our program to work with. The DVM will handle all the technicalities of interacting with the operating system, and the operating system will, in turn, interact with the physical memory.

So, we can think of our Android device's memory as a huge warehouse just waiting for us to add our variables. When we assign names to our variables, they are stored in the warehouse, ready for when we need them. When we use our variable's name, the device knows exactly what we are referring to. We can then tell it to do things such as: get variableA and add it to variableC, delete variableB, and so on.

In a typical app, we might have a variable named unreadMessages, perhaps to hold the number of unread messages the user has. We could add to it when a new message arrives, take away from it when the user reads a message, and show it to the user somewhere in the app layout, so they know how many unread messages they have.

Some situations that might arise are:

- User gets three new messages so add three to the value of unreadMessages.
- User logs into app so use Toast to display a message along with the value stored in unreadMessages.
- User sees that a bunch of the messages are from someone she doesn't like and deletes six messages. We could then subtract six from unreadMessages.

These are fairly arbitrary examples of names for variables and as long as you don't use any of the characters or keywords that Java restricts, you can actually call your variables whatever you like.

In practice, however, it is best to adopt a **naming convention** so that your variable names will be consistent. In this book, we will use a loose convention of variable names starting with a lowercase letter. When there is more than one word in the variable's name, the second word will begin with an uppercase letter. This is called **camel casing**.

Something like:

- `unreadMessages`
- `contactName`
- `isFriend`

Before we look at some real Java code with some variables, we need to first look at the **types** of variables we can create and use.

Types of variables

It is not hard to imagine that even a simple app will probably have quite a few variables. In the previous section, we introduced the `unreadMessages` variable as a hypothetical example. What if the app has a list of contacts and needs to remember each of their names? We might then need variables for each contact.

And what about when an app needs to know whether a contact is also a friend, or just a regular contact? We might need code that tests for friend status and then adds messages from that contact into an appropriate folder so the user knows whether they were messages from a friend or not.

Another common requirement in a computer program, including Android apps, is the right or wrong calculation. Computer programs represent right or wrong calculations using true or false.

To cover these and many other types of data you might want to store or manipulate, Java has **types**.

Primitive types

There are many types of variables and we can even invent our own types as well. But for now, we will look at the most used built-in Java types. And to be fair, they cover just about every situation we are likely to run into for a while. These examples are the best way to explain *types*.

We have already discussed the hypothetical `unreadMessages` variable. This variable is of course a number, so we have to tell the Java compiler this by giving it an appropriate type. The hypothetical `contactName` will of course hold the characters that make up the contact name. Jumping ahead a couple of paragraphs, the type that holds a regular number is called `int` and the type that holds name-like data is called `String`. And if we try to store a contact name, perhaps "Ada Lovelace" in an `int` like `unreadMessages`, meant for numbers, we will certainly run into trouble, as we can see from the next screenshot:

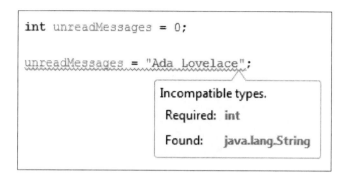

As we can see, Java was designed to make it impossible for such errors to make it into a running program. With the compiler protecting us from ourselves, what could possibly go wrong?

Here are the main types in Java, then we will see how to start using them:

- `int`: The `int` type is for storing integers, whole numbers. This type uses 32 pieces (**bits**) of memory and can therefore store values with a magnitude a little in excess of two billion, including negative values too.

- `long`: As the name hints at, `long` data types can be used when even larger numbers are required. A `long` type uses 64 bits of memory and 2 to the power of 63 is what we can store in this. If you want to see what that looks like, here it is: 9,223,372,036,854,775,807. Perhaps, surprisingly, there are uses for `long` variables but the point is, if a smaller variable will do, we should use it because our program will use less memory.

You might be wondering when you might use numbers of this magnitude. The obvious examples would be math or science applications that do complex calculations, but another use might be for timing. When you time how long something takes, the Java `Date` class uses the number of milliseconds since January 1, 1970. A millisecond is one thousandth of a second, so there have been quite a few of them since 1970.

- `float`: This is for floating point numbers. That is, numbers where there is precision beyond the decimal point. As the fractional part of a number takes memory space just as the whole number portion, the range of a number possible in a `float` is therefore decreased compared to non-floating point numbers. So, unless our variable will definitely use the extra precision, `float` would not be our data type of choice.

- `double`: When the precision in `float` is not enough we have `double`.

- `boolean`: We will be using plenty of Booleans throughout the book. The `boolean` variable type can be either `true` or `false`; nothing else. Perhaps Booleans answer questions such as:
    - Is the contact a friend?
    - Are there any new messages?
    - Are two examples for Boolean enough?

- `char`: A single alphanumeric character is stored in `char`. It's not going to change the world on its own but could be useful if we put lots of them together.

> I have kept this discussion of data types to a practical level that is useful in the context of this book. If you are interested in how a data type's value is stored and why the limits are what they are, then have a look on the Oracle Java tutorials site here: `http://docs.oracle.com/javase/tutorial/java/nutsandbolts/datatypes.html`. Note that you do not need any more information than we have already discussed to continue with this book.

As we just learned, each type of data that we might want to store will require a specific amount of memory; so we must let the Java compiler know the type of the variable before we begin to use it.

The previous variables are known as the **primitive** types. They use predefined amounts of memory and so, using our warehouse storage analogy, fit into predefined sizes of storage box.

As the "primitive" label suggests, they are not as sophisticated as **reference** types.

Reference types

You might have noticed that we didn't cover the `String` variable type that we previously used to introduce the concept of variables that hold alphanumeric data such as a contact's name.

Strings are one of a special type of variable known as a **reference** type. They quite simply refer to a place in memory where storage of the variable begins but the reference type itself does not define a specific amount of memory. The reason for this is fairly straightforward.

It's because we don't always know how much data will need to be stored in it until the program is actually run.

We can think of Strings and other reference types as continually expanding and contracting storage boxes. So won't one of these `String` reference types bump into another variable eventually?

As we are thinking about the device's memory as a huge warehouse full of racks of labeled storage boxes, then you can think of the DVM as a super-efficient forklift truck driver that puts the different types of storage boxes in the most appropriate place.

And if it becomes necessary, the DVM will quickly move stuff around in a fraction of a second to avoid collisions. Also, when appropriate, Dalvik, the forklift driver, will even incinerate unwanted storage boxes. This happens at the same time as constantly unloading new storage boxes of all types and placing them in the best place, for that type of variable. Dalvik keeps reference variables in a different part of the warehouse to the primitive variables. And we will learn more details about this in *Chapter 9, Object-Oriented Programming*.

So, Strings can be used to store any keyboard character. Kind of like `char` but of almost any length. Anything from a contact's name to an entire book can be stored in a single `String`. We will be using Strings regularly, including in this chapter.

There are a couple more reference types we will explore as well. **Arrays** are a way to store lots of variables of the same type, ready for quick and efficient access. We will look at arrays in *Chapter 13, Handling and Displaying Arrays of Data*.

Think of an array as an aisle in our warehouse with all the variables of a certain type lined up in a precise order. Arrays are reference types, so Dalvik keeps these in the same part of the warehouse as Strings. We might, for example, use an array to store dozens of contacts in.

The other reference type is the class that we have already discussed but not explained properly. We will be getting familiar with classes in *Chapter 9, Object-Oriented Programming*.

Now we know that each type of data that we might want to store will require an amount of memory. Hence, we must let the Java compiler know the type of the variable before we begin to use it. We do this with a variable **declaration**.

Variable declaration

That's enough theory. Let's see how we would actually use our variables and types. Remember that each primitive type requires a specific amount of real device memory. This is one of the reasons that the compiler needs to know what type a variable will be. So, we must first declare a variable and its type before we attempt to do anything with it.

To declare a variable of type `int` with the name `unreadMessages`, we would type:

```
int unreadMessages;
```

That's it, simply state the type, in this case `int`, then leave a space and type the name you want to use for this variable. Note also the semicolon `;` on the end of the line will tell the compiler that we are done with this line and what follows, if anything, is not part of the declaration.

Similarly, for almost all the other variable types, declaration would occur in the same way. Here are some examples. The variable names in the examples are arbitrary. This is like reserving a labeled storage box in the warehouse:

```
long millisecondsElapsed;
float accountBalance;
boolean isFriend;
char contactFirstInitial;
String messageText;
```

Variable initialization

Initialization is the next step. Here, for each type, we initialize a value to the variable. Think about placing a value inside the storage box:

```
unreadMessages = 10;
millisecondsElapsed = 14381651168411;// 29th July 2016 11:19am
accountBalance = 129.52f;
isFriend = true;
contactFirstInitial = 'C';
messageText = "Hi reader, Just thought I would let you know that
Charles Babbage was an early computing pioneer and he invented the
difference engine. If you want to know more about him you can click
this link www.charlesbabbage.net. Thanks, John";
```

Notice that the char variable uses single quotes ' around the initialized value while the String uses double quotes ".

We can also combine the declaration and initialization steps. In the following we declare and initialize the same variables as we have previously, but in one step:

```
int unreadMessages = 10;
long millisecondsElapsed = 1438165116841l;//29th July 2016 11:19am
float accountBalance = 129.52f;
boolean isFriend = true;
char contactFirstInitial = 'C';
String messageText = "Hi reader, Just thought I would let you know
that Charles Babbage was an early computing pioneer and he invented
the difference engine. If you want to know more about him you can
click this link http://www.charlesbabbage.net/. Thanks, John";
```

Whether we declare and initialize separately or together is probably dependent upon the specific situation. The important thing is that we must do both:

```
int a;
// That's me declared and ready to go?
// The line below attempts to output a to the console
Log.i("info", "int a = " + a);
// Oh no I forgot to initialize a!!
```

This would cause the following:

Compiler Error: Variable a might not have been initialized

There is a significant exception to this rule. Under certain circumstances variables can have **default values**. We will see this in *Chapter 9, Object-Oriented Programming*; however, it is good practice to both declare and initialize variables.

Changing values in variables with operators

Of course, in almost any program, we are going to need to do things with these values. We manipulate (change) variables with **operators**. Here is a list of perhaps the most common Java operators that allow us to manipulate variables. You do not need to memorize them as we will look at every line of code as and when we use them for the first time. We have already seen the first operator when we initialized our variables but we will see it again being a bit more adventurous:

- The **assignment** operator (=): This makes the variable to the left of the operator the same as the value to the right. For example, unreadMessages = newMessages;.

- The **addition** operator (**+**): This adds together values on either side of the operator. It is usually used in conjunction with the assignment operator, or slightly differently; add together two variables that contain numeric values. Perhaps like this `unreadMessages = newMessages + unreadMessages;` or `accountBalance = yesterdaysBalance + todaysDeposits;`. Notice it is perfectly acceptable to use the same variable, simultaneously on both sides of an operator.

- The **subtraction** operator (**-**): This subtracts the value on the right side of the operator from the value on the left. Usually used in conjunction with the assignment operator. Perhaps, `unreadMessages = unreadMessages - 1;` or `accountBalance = accountBalance - withdrawals;`.

- The **division** operator (**/**): This divides the number on the left by the number on the right. Again, usually used in conjunction with the assignment operator. For example, `fairShare = numSweets / numChildren;`.

- The **multiplication** operator (*****): This multiplies variables and numbers together. For example, `answer = 10 * 10;` or `biggerAnswer = 10 * 10 * 10;`.

- The **increment** operator (**++**): This is a really neat way to add 1 to something. `myVariable = myVariable + 1;` is the same as `myVariable ++;`.

- The **decrement** operator (**--**): You guessed it. This is a really neat way to subtract 1 from something. `myVariable = myVariable -1;` is the same as `myVariable --;`.

>
> The formal names for these operators are slightly different to that previously explained. For example, the division operator is actually one of the multiplicative operators, but the names given previously are far more useful for the purpose of learning Java, and if you used the term division operator while conversing with someone from the Java community, they would know exactly what you mean.

There are actually many more operators than this in Java. We will meet a whole bunch more later in this chapter when we learn about decisions in Java.

>
> If you are curious about operators, there is a complete list of them on the Java website here: `http://docs.oracle.com/javase/tutorial/java/nutsandbolts/operators.html`. All the operators required to complete the projects will be fully explained in this book. The link is provided for the curious among us.

Expressing yourself demo app

Let's try using some declarations, assignments, and operators. When we bundle these elements together into some meaningful syntax, we call it an **expression**. So let's write a quick app to try some out. We will then use Toast and Log to check our results.

Create a new project called Expressing Yourself, use a **Blank Activity**, and leave all the other settings at their defaults. The completed code that we will write in this project can be found in the Chapter 7/Expressing Yourself folder of the download bundle.

Switch to the **MainActivity** tab in the editor and we will write some code. In the onCreate method, just before the closing curly brace }, add this code:

```
int numMessages;
```

Directly below the previous line of code we will assign a value to numMessages. But as you begin to type nu notice we get a little pop-up message like this:

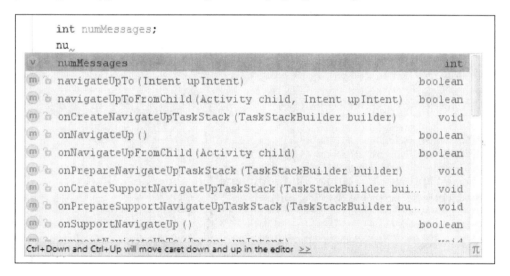

If you look at the first option in the pop-up message it is in fact numMessages. Android Studio is offering to complete our typing for us. We can either left-click numMessages to have the variable name auto-completed or simply select it because it is already highlighted by pressing *Enter* on the keyboard. Whenever Android Studio thinks it might know what we want to type, it will pop up some options. It is a great time-saving habit to get into.

Add this line of code using auto-complete:

```
numMessages = 10;
```

Now that we have introduced the really handy code completion feature we will add a larger chunk of code. Immediately after the previous line of code and before the closing } of onCreate, add the following code:

```
// Output the value of numMessages
Log.i("numMessages = ", "" + numMessages);

numMessages++;
numMessages = numMessages + 1;
Log.i("numMessages = ", "" + numMessages);

// Now a boolean (just true or false)
boolean isFriend = true;
Log.i("isFriend = ", "" + isFriend);

// A contact and an important message
String contact = "James Gosling";
String message = "Dear reader, I invented Java.";

// Now let's play with those String variables
Toast.makeText(this, "Message from" + contact,
  Toast.LENGTH_SHORT).show();

Toast.makeText(this, "Message is:" + message,
  Toast.LENGTH_SHORT).show();
```

Run the app and we can examine the output and then the code. In the logcat window, you will see the following output:

```
numMessages =: 10
numMessages =: 12
isFriend =: true
```

On the screen, you will see two pop-up `Toast` messages. The first says **Message from James Gosling**. The second says **Message is: Dear Reader, I invented Java.** and is shown in the next screenshot:

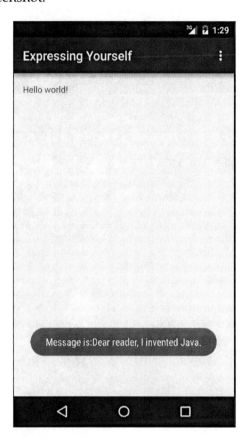

Let's step through the code and make sure that each line is clear before moving on.

First, we declared and initialized an `int` type variable called `numMessages`. We could have done it on one line but we did it like this:

```
int numMessages;
numMessages = 10;
```

Next we used `Log` to output a message. Instead of simply typing the message between the double quote marks `""`, this time we used the `+` operator to add `numMessages` onto the output. And as we saw in the console, the actual value of `numMessages` was output:

```
// Output the value of numMessages
Log.i("numMessages = ", "" + numMessages);
```

Just to further prove that our `numMessages` variable is as versatile as it should be, we use the `++` operator, which should increase its value by one and then add `numMessages` to itself `+1`. We then output the new value of `numMessages` and indeed found its value was increased to `12` from `10`:

```
numMessages ++;
numMessages = numMessages + 1;
Log.i("numMessages = ", "" + numMessages);
```

Next, we created a `boolean` type variable called `isFriend` and output that to the console. We saw from the output that `true` was displayed. This variable type will fully demonstrate its usefulness when we look at decision-making in the next section:

```
// Now a boolean (just true or false)
boolean isFriend = true;
Log.i("isFriend = ", "" + isFriend);
```

After this, we declared and initialized two `String` type variables:

```
// A contact and an important message
String contact = "James Gosling";
String message = "Dear reader, I invented Java.";
```

Finally, we output the `String` variables using `Toast`. We used a hard-coded part of the message `"Message from "` and added the variable part of the message with `+ contact`. We used the same technique to form the second `Toast` message as well. When we add two Strings together to make a longer String, it is called **concatenation**:

```
// Now let's play with those String variables
Toast.makeText(this, "Message from " + contact,
   Toast.LENGTH_SHORT).show();

Toast.makeText(this, "Message is:" + message,
   Toast.LENGTH_SHORT).show();
```

Now we can declare variables, initialize them to a value, change them around a bit, and output them using `Toast` or `Log`. Now let's look at how we can make decisions based on the value of these variables and how this is useful to us.

Decisions

Our Java code will constantly be making decisions. For example, we might need to know whether the user has new messages or whether they have a certain number of friends. We need to be able to test our variables to see whether they meet certain conditions and then execute a certain section of code depending upon whether it did or not.

In this section, as our code gets more in-depth, it helps to present it in a way that makes it more readable. Let's take a look at code indenting to make our discussion about decisions easier.

Indenting our code

You have probably noticed that the Java code in our projects is indented. For example, the first line of code inside the `MainActivity` class is indented by one tab. And the first line of code is indented inside each method. Here is an annotated image as another quick example to make this clear:

Notice also that when the indented block has ended, often with a closing curly brace }, that } is indented to the same extent as the line of code that began the block.

We do this to make the code more readable. It is not part of the Java syntax however, and the code will still compile if we don't bother to do this.

As our code gets more complicated, indenting along with comments helps to keep the meaning and structure of our code clear. I mention this now because when we start to learn the syntax for making decisions in Java, indenting becomes especially useful, and it is recommended that you indent your code the same way.

Much of this indenting is done for us by Android Studio, but not all of it.

Now that we know how to present our code more clearly, let's learn some more operators and then we can really get to work taking decisions with Java.

More operators

We can already add (+), take away (-), multiply (*), divide (/), assign (=), increment (++), and decrement (--) with operators. Let's introduce some more super-useful operators, and then we will go straight on to actually understanding how to use them in Java.

 Don't worry about memorizing each of the following operators. Glance over them and their explanations, and then move quickly on to the next section. There we will put some operators to use and they will become much clearer as we see a few examples of what they allow us to do. They are presented here in a list just to make the variety and scope of operators plain from the start. The list will also be more convenient to refer back to when not intermingled with the discussion about implementation that follows it.

We use operators to create an expression that is either `true` or `false`. We wrap that expression in parentheses like this, (expression goes here):

- **==**: This **comparison** operator tests for equality and is either true or false. An expression such as `(10 == 9)`, for example, is `false`. 10 is obviously not equal to 9.

- **!**: This is the logical **NOT** operator. The expression `(! (2+2 == 5))` is `true` because 2+2 is not 5.

- **!=**: Another comparison operator. This tests whether something is **not equal**. For example, the expression `(10 != 9)` is `true`. 10 is not equal to 9.

- **>**: Another comparison operator; actually, there are a few more as well. This tests whether something is **greater than** something else. The expression `(10 > 9)` is `true`.

- **<**: You guessed it. This tests for values **less than**. The expression `(10 < 9)` is `false`.

- **>=**: This operator tests for whether one value is **greater than or equal** to the other and if either is `true`, the result is `true`. For example, the expression `(10 >= 9)` is `true`. The expression `(10 >= 10)` is also `true`.

- **<=**: Like the previous operator, this one tests for two conditions but this time **less than or equal** to. The expression `(10 <= 9)` is `false`. The expression `(10 <= 10)` is `true`.

- **&&**: This operator is known as logical **AND**. It tests two or more separate parts of an expression and **all parts** must be `true` in order for the result to be `true`. Logical AND is usually used in conjunction with the other operators to build more complex tests. The expression `((10 > 9) && (10 < 11))` is `true` because both parts are `true` so the expression is `true`. The expression `((10 > 9) && (10 < 9))` is `false` because only one part of the expression is `true` and the other is `false`.

- **||**: This operator is called logical **OR** and it is just like logical AND except that **only one** of two or more parts of an expression need to be `true` for the expression to be `true`. Let's look at the last example we used but switch the `&&` for `||`. The expression `((10 > 9) || (10 < 9))` is now `true` because one part of the expression is `true`.

All these operators are virtually useless without a way of properly using them to make real decisions that affect real variables and code.

Now we have all the information we need, we can look at a hypothetical situation then actually see some code for decision-making.

If they come over the bridge, shoot them

As we saw, operators serve very little purpose on their own but it was probably useful to see just part of the wide and varied range available to us. Now, when we look at putting the most common operator `==` to use, we can start to see the powerful yet fine control that they offer us.

Let's make the previous examples less abstract. Meet the Java `if` keyword. We will use `if` and a few conditional operators along with a small story to demonstrate their use. Next follows a made up military situation that will hopefully be less abstract than the previous examples.

The captain is dying and knowing that his remaining subordinates are not very experienced, he decides to write a Java program to convey his last orders after he has died. The troops must hold one side of a bridge while awaiting reinforcements.

The first command the captain wants to make sure his troops understand is this:

If they come over the bridge, shoot them.

So, how do we simulate this situation in Java? We need a Boolean variable `isComingOverBridge`. The next bit of code assumes that the `isComingOverBridge` variable has been declared and initialized to either `true` or `false`.

We can then use `if` like this:

```
if(isComingOverBridge){

    // Shoot them

}
```

If the `isComingOverBridge` Boolean is `true`, the code inside the opening and closing curly braces will run. If not, the program continues after the `if` block and without running the code within it.

Else do this instead

The captain also wants to tell his troops what to do (stay put) if the enemy is not coming over the bridge.

Now we introduce another Java keyword, `else`. When we want to explicitly do something when the `if` does not evaluate to `true`, we can use `else`.

For example, to tell the troops to stay put if the enemy is not coming over the bridge, we could write this code:

```
if(isComingOverBridge){

    // Shoot them

}else{

    // Hold position

}
```

The captain then realized that the problem wasn't as simple as he first thought. What if the enemy comes over the bridge, but has too many troops? His squad would be overrun. So, he came up with this code (we'll use some variables as well this time):

```
boolean isComingOverBridge;
int enemyTroops;
int friendlyTroops;
// Code that initializes the above variables one way or another

// Now the if
if(isComingOverBridge && friendlyTroops > enemyTroops){

    // shoot them
```

```
}else if(isComingOveBridge && friendlyTroops < enemyTroops) {

    // blow the bridge

}else{

    // Hold position

}
```

The previous code has three possible paths of execution. First, if the enemy is coming over the bridge and the friendly troops are greater in number:

```
if(isComingOverBridge && friendlyTroops > enemyTroops)
```

Second, if the enemy troops are coming over the bridge but outnumber the friendly troops:

```
else if(isComingOveBridge && friendlyTroops < enemyTroops)
```

Then the third and final possible outcome, which will execute if neither of the others is true, is captured by the final `else` without an `if` condition.

Readers challenge

Can you spot a flaw with the previous code? One that might leave a bunch of inexperienced troops in complete disarray? The possibility of the enemy troops and friendly troops being exactly equal in number has not been handled explicitly and would therefore be handled by the final `else`, which is meant for when there is no enemy troops. I guess any self-respecting captain would expect his troops to fight in this situation, and he could have changed the first `if` statement to accommodate this possibility:

```
if(isComingOverBridge && friendlyTroops >=
enemyTroops)
```

And finally, the captain's last concern was that if the enemy came over the bridge waving the white flag of surrender and were promptly slaughtered, then his men would end up as war criminals. The Java code that was needed was obvious. Using the `wavingWhiteFlag` Boolean variable, he wrote this test:

```
if (wavingWhiteFlag){

    // Take prisoners

}
```

But where to put this code was less clear. In the end, the captain opted for the following nested solution and for changing the test for `wavingWhiteFlag` to logical NOT, like this:

```
if (!wavingWhiteFlag){

   // not surrendering so check everything else

   if(isComingOverTheBridge && friendlyTroops >= enemyTroops){

     // shoot them

   }else if(isComingOverTheBridge && friendlyTroops
     < enemyTroops) {

     // blow the bridge

   }

}else{

   // this is the else for our first if
   // Take prisoners

}

// Holding position
```

This demonstrates that we can nest `if` and `else` statements inside of one another to create quite deep and detailed decisions.

We could go on making more and more complicated decisions with `if` and `else` but what we have seen is more than sufficient as an introduction. It is probably worth pointing out that very often there is more than one way to arrive at a solution to a problem. The *right* way will usually be the way that solves the problem in the clearest and simplest manner.

Let's look at some other ways to make decisions in Java and then we can put them all together in an app.

Switching to make decisions

We have seen the vast and virtually limitless possibilities of combining the Java operators with `if` and `else` statements. But sometimes a decision in Java can be better made in other ways.

When we have to make a decision based on a clear list of possibilities that doesn't involve complex combinations, then `switch` is usually the way to go.

We start a `switch` decision like this:

```
switch(argument){


}
```

In the previous example, an **argument** could be an expression or a variable. Within the curly braces { } we can make decisions based on the argument with `case` and `break` elements:

```
case x:
  // code to for case x
  break;

case y:
  // code for case y
  break;
```

You can see in the previous example each `case` states a possible result and each `break` denotes the end of that `case`, and also the point at which no further `case` statements should be evaluated.

The first break encountered breaks out of the `switch` block to proceed with the next line of code after the closing brace } of the entire `switch` block.

We can also use `default` without a value to run some code in case none of the case statements evaluate to true. Like this:

```
default:// Look no value
  // Do something here if no other case statements are true
  break;
```

Let's write a quick demo app that uses `switch`.

The Switch Demo app

To get started, create a new Android project called `Switch Demo`, use a **Blank Activity**, and leave all the other settings at their default. Switch to the `MainActivity.java` file by left-clicking the **MainActivity.java** tab above the editor and we can start coding.

Let's pretend we are writing an old-fashioned text adventure game, the kind of game where the player types commands such as "Go East", "Go West", "Take Sword", and so on. In this case, `switch` could handle that situation with this code and we could use `default` to handle the player typing a command that is not specifically handled.

Enter the following code in the `onCreate` method just before the closing curly brace `}`:

```java
// get input from user in a String variable called command
String command = "go east";

switch(command){

  case "go east":
    Log.i("Player: ", "Moves to the east" );
    break;

  case "go west":
    Log.i("Player: ", "Moves to the West" );
    break;

  case "go north":
    Log.i("Player: ", "Moves to the North" );
    break;

  case "go south":
    Log.i("Player: ", "Moves to the South" );
    break;

  case "take sword":
    Log.i("Player: ", "Takes the silver sword" );
    break;

  // more possible cases

  default:
    Log.i("Message: ", "Sorry I don't speak Elfish" );
    break;

}
```

Run the app a few times. Each time, change the initialization of `command` to something new. Notice that when you initialize `command` to something that is explicitly handled by a `case` statement, we get the expected output. Otherwise we get the default **Sorry I don't speak Elfish**.

If we had a lot of code to execute for a particular case, we could contain it all in a method, perhaps, like this next piece of code. I have highlighted the new line:

```
default:
    goWest();
    break;
```

Of course, we would then need to write the new goWest method. Then, when command was initialized to "go west", the goWest method would be executed and execution would return to the break statement, which would cause the code to continue after the switch block.

Of course, one of the things this code seriously lacks is interaction with a UI. We have seen how we can call methods from button clicks but even that isn't enough to make this code worthwhile in a real app. We will see how we solve this problem in *Chapter 10, Everything's a Class.*

The other problem we have is that after the code has been executed, that's it. We need it to continually ask the player for instructions, not just once but over and over. We will look at a solution to this problem next.

Repeating code with loops

Here we will learn how to repeatedly execute portions of our code in a controlled and precise way by looking at different types of loops in Java. These include while loops, do while loops, and for loops. We will also learn the most appropriate situations to use the different types of loops.

It would be completely reasonable to ask what loops have to do with programming, but they are exactly what the name implies. They are a way of repeating the same part of the code more than once, or looping over the same part of code although potentially for a different outcome each time.

This can simply mean doing the same thing until the code being looped over (**iterated**) prompts the loop to end. It could be a predetermined number of iterations as specified by the loop code itself. It might be until a predetermined situation or **condition** is met. Or it could be a combination of more than one of these things. Along with if, else, and switch, loops are part of the Java **control flow statements**.

We will look at all the major types of loops that Java offers us to control our code and we will use some of them to implement a working mini-app to make sure we understand them completely. Let's look at the first and simplest loop type in Java called the while loop.

While loops

Java `while` loops have the simplest syntax. Think back to the `if` statements for a moment. We could put virtually any combination of operators and variables in the conditional expression of the `if` statement. If the expression evaluated to `true` then the code in the body of the `if` block is executed. With the `while` loop we also put an expression that can evaluate to `true` or `false`. Take a look at this code:

```
int x = 10;

while(x > 0){
   x--;
   // x decreases by one each pass through the loop
}
```

What happens here is this: outside of the `while` loop an `int` named `x` is declared and initialized to `10`. Then, the `while` loop begins. Its condition is `x > 0`. So, the `while` loop will continue looping through the code in its body until the condition evaluates to `false`. So the previous code will execute 10 times.

On the first pass `x = 10` then `9` then `8`, and so on. But once `x` is equal to `0`, it is of course no longer greater than `0`, the program will exit the loop and continue with the first line of code after the `while` loop.

Just like an `if` statement, it is possible that the `while` loop will not execute even once. Take a look at this:

```
int x = 10;

while(x > 10){
   // more code here.
   // but it will never run unless x is greater than 10.
}
```

Moreover, there is no limit to the complexity of the conditional expression or the amount of code that can go into the loop body:

```
int newMessages = 3;
int unreadMessages = 0;

while(newMessages > 0 || unreadMessages > 0){
   // Display next message
   // etc.
}

// continue here when newMessages and unreadMessages equal 0
```

The previous `while` loop would continue to execute until both `newMessages` and `unreadMessages` were equal to or less than zero. As the condition uses logical OR operator `||` either one of those conditions being `true` will cause the `while` loop to continue executing.

It is worth noting that once the body of the loop has been entered, it will always complete, even if the expression evaluates to `false` part way through, as it is not tested again until the code tries to start another pass. For example:

```
int x = 1;

while(x > 0){
  x--;
  // x is now 0 so the condition is false
  // But this line still runs
  // and this one
  // and me!

}
```

The previous loop body will execute exactly once. We can also set a `while` loop that will run forever; unsurprisingly called an **infinite loop**. Here is one:

```
int x = 0;

while(true){
  x++; // I am going to get mighty big!
}
```

Breaking out of a loop

We might use an infinite loop like this so that we can decide when to exit the loop from within its body. We would do this by using the `break` keyword when we are ready to leave the loop body. Like this:

```
int x = 0;

while(true){
  x++; //I am going to get mighty big!
  break; // No you're not haha.
  // code doesn't reach here
}
```

And you might have been able to guess that we can combine any of the decision-making tools like `if`, `else`, and `switch` within our `while` loops and all the rest of the loops we will look at in a minute. For example:

```
int x = 0;
int tooBig = 10;

while(true){
  x++; // I am going to get mighty big!
  if(x == tooBig){
    break;
  } // No you're not haha.

  // code reaches here only until x = 10
}
```

It would be simple to go on for many more pages demonstrating the versatility of `while` loops, but at some point we want to get back to doing some real programming. So, here is one last concept combined with `while` loops.

Continue

The `continue` keyword acts in a similar way to `break`, up to a point. The `continue` keyword will break out of the loop body but will also check the condition expression afterwards so the loop *could* run again. An example will help:

```
int x = 0;
int tooBig = 10;
int tooBigToPrint = 5;

while(true){
  x++; // I am going to get mighty big!
  if(x == tooBig){
    break;
  } // No you're not haha.

  // code reaches here only until x = 10

  if(x >= tooBigToPrint){
    // No more printing but keep looping
    continue;
  }
  // code reaches here only until x = 5

  // Print out x

}
```

Do while loops

A do while loop is very much the same as a while loop with the exception that a do while loop evaluates its expression *after* the body. This means that a do while loop will always execute at least once before checking the loop condition:

```
int x= 0
do{
  x++;
}while(x < 10);
// x now = 10
```

 Note that break and continue can also be used in do while loops.

For loops

A for loop has a slightly more complicated syntax than while or do while loops as it takes three parts to initialize. Have a look at the code first then we will break it apart:

```
for(int i = 0; i < 10;  i++){

   //Something that needs to happen 10 times goes here

}
```

The apparently obscure form of the for loop is clearer when put like this:

```
for(declaration and initialization; condition;
   change after each pass through loop)
```

To clarify further we have:

- **Declaration and initialization**: We create a new int variable i and initialize it to zero.

- **Condition**: Just like the other loops, it refers to the condition that must evaluate to true for the loop to continue.

- **Change after each pass through loop**: In the example, i++ means that 1 is added/incremented to i on each pass. We could also use i-- to reduce/decrement i each pass. Consider the following code:
  ```
  for(int i = 10; i > 0;  i--){
    // countdown
  }
  // blast off i = 0
  ```

Note that break and continue can also be used in for loops.

The for loop essentially takes control of initialization, condition evaluation, and the control variable itself.

Loops demo app

To get started, create a new Android project called Loops, use a **Blank Activity**, and leave all the other settings at their default.

Let's add a few buttons to our UI to make this more fun:

1. Drag a button onto the UI and center it horizontally near the top.

2. In the **Properties** window change the text property to countUp.

3. In the properties window change the onClick property to countUp.

4. Place a new button just below the previous one and repeat steps 2 and 3, but this time use countDown for the text property and the onClick property.

5. Place a new button just below the previous one and repeat steps 2 and 3, but this time use nested for the text property and the onClick property.

Looks are not important for this demo but the layout should look something like this next screenshot:

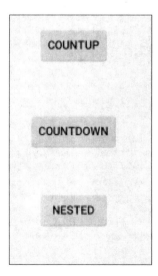

What is important is that we have three buttons labeled **COUNTUP**, **COUNTDOWN**, and **NESTED**, which call methods named countUp, countDown, and nested.

Switch to the MainActivity.java file by left-clicking the **MainActivity.java** tab above the editor and we can start coding our methods.

After the closing curly brace of the onCreate method, add the countUp method as shown next:

```java
public void countUp(View v){
   Log.i("message:","In countUp method");

   int x = 0;

   // Now an apparently infinite while loop
   while(true){

      // Add 1 to x each time
      x++;
      Log.i("x =", "" + x);

      if(x == 3){
        // Get me out of here
        break;
      }
   }
}
```

We will be able to call this method we have just written, from the appropriately labeled button.

After the closing curly brace of the countUp method, add the countDown method:

```java
public void countDown(View v){
   Log.i("message:","In countDown method");
   int x = 4;
   // Now an apparently infinite while loop
   while(true){
     // Add 1 to x each time
     x--;
     Log.i("x =", "" + x);
     if(x == 1){
       // Get me out of here
       break;
     }
   }
}
```

We will be able to call this method we have just written, from the appropriately labeled button.

After the closing curly brace of the `countDown` method, add the `nested` method:

```java
public void nested(View v){
  Log.i("message:","In nested method");

  // a nested for loop
  for(int i = 0; i < 3; i ++){

    for(int j = 3; j > 0; j --){

      // Output the values of i and j
      Log.i("i =" + i,"j=" + j);
    }
  }
}
```

We will be able to call this method we have just written, from the appropriately labeled button.

Now, let's run the app and start tapping buttons. If you tap each of the buttons once from top to bottom, this is the console output you will see:

```
message:: In countUp method
x =: 1
x =: 2
x =: 3
message:: In countDown method
x =: 3
x =: 2
x =: 1
message:: In nested method
i =0: j=3
i =0: j=2
i =0: j=1
i =1: j=3
```

```
i =1: j=2
i =1: j=1
i =2: j=3
i =2: j=2
i =2: j=1
```

We can see that the countUp method does exactly that. The int x variable is initialized to zero, an infinite while loop is entered, and x is incremented with the increment ++ operator. Fortunately, on each iteration of the loop, we test for x being equal to 3 with if (x == 3) and break when this is true.

Next, in the countDown method, we do the same in reverse. The int x variable is initialized to 4, an infinite while loop is entered, and x is decremented with the decrement -- operator. This time, on each iteration of the loop, we test for x being equal to 1 with if (x == 1) and break when this is true.

Finally, we nest two for loops within each other. We can see from the output that for each time i (which is controlled by the outer loop) is incremented, j (which is controlled by the inner loop) is decremented from 3 to 1. Look carefully at this image that shows where the start and end of each for loop is, to help fully understand this:

```
// a nested for loop
for(int i = 0; i < 3; i ++){

    for(int j = 3; j > 0; j --){

        // Output the values of i and j
        Log.i("i =" + i,"j=" + j);
    }
}
```

You can of course keep tapping to observe each button's output for as long as you like. As an experiment, try making the loops longer, perhaps 1,000.

Summary

At last we have used some serious Java. We learned about variables, declaration, and initialization. We saw how to use operators to change the value of variables, we used `if`, `else`, and `switch` to make decisions with expressions and branch our code. We saw and practiced `while`, `for`, and `do while` to repeat parts of our code.

It doesn't matter if you don't remember everything straight away as we will constantly be using these techniques and keywords throughout the book.

Next, we will take a much closer look at Java methods, which is where all our code will go.

8
Coding in Java
Part 2 – Methods

As we are starting to get comfortable with Java programming, in this chapter, we will take a closer look at methods because although we know that you can **call** them to make them execute their code, it is plain that there is more to them than has been discussed so far.

In this chapter, we will look at the following topics:

- The method structure
- Method overloading versus overriding
- A method's demo mini app
- How methods affect our variables

First, let's go through a quick method recap.

Methods revisited

This figure probably roughly sums up where our understanding of methods is at the moment:

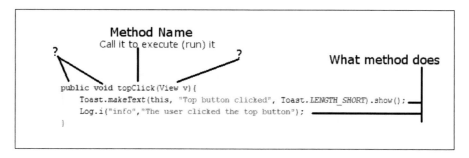

As we can see in the previous figure, there are still a couple of question marks around methods. We will completely take the lid off of methods and see how they work, and what exactly the other parts of the method are doing for us later in the chapter. In *Chapter 9, Object-Oriented Programming*, we will clear up the last few parts of the mystery of methods.

So, what exactly are Java methods? A method is a collection of variables, expressions, and control flow statements bundled together inside an opening curly brace and closing curly brace preceded by a name. We have already been using lots of methods, but we just haven't looked very closely at them yet.

Let's start with the method structure.

The method structure

The first part of a method that we write is called the **signature**. Here is a hypothetical method signature:

```
public boolean addContact(boolean isFriend, String name)
```

If we add an opening and closing pair of curly braces, {}, with some code that the method performs, then we have a complete method—a **definition**. Here is another made up, yet syntactically correct, method:

```
private void setCoordinates(int x, int y){
  // code to set coordinates goes here
}
```

As we have seen, we could then use our new method from another part of our code like this:

```
// I like it here

setCoordinates(4,6);
// now I am going off to setCoordinates method

// Phew, I'm back again - code continues here
```

At the point where we call `setCoordinates`, our program's execution would branch out to the code that is contained within that method. The method would execute all the statements inside it step by step until it reaches the end and returns the control to the code that called it, or sooner if it hits a `return` statement. Then, the code would continue running from the first line after the method call.

Here is another example of a method complete with the code to make the method return to the code that called it:

```
int addAToB(int a, int b){
   int answer = a + b;
   return answer;
}
```

The call to use the preceding method could look like this:

```
int myAnswer = addAToB(2, 4);
```

Clearly, we don't need to write methods to add two `int` variables together but, the example helps us see a little more into the workings of methods. First, we pass in the values 2 and 4. In the signature, the value 2 is assigned to `int` a and the value 4 is assigned to `int` b.

Within the method body, the variables a and b are added together and used to initialize the new `int` answer variable. The `return answer` line returns the value stored in `answer` to the calling code, causing `myAnswer` to be initialized with the value 6.

Note that each of the method signatures in the preceding examples varies a little. The reason for this is that the Java method signature is quite flexible and allows us to build exactly the methods we require.

Exactly how the method signature defines how the method must be called and how the method must return a value deserves further discussion. Let's give each part of the signature a name, so we can break it into chunks and learn about the parts.

Here is a signature of a method with its parts labeled up and ready for discussion. Also, have a look at the table to further identify which part of the signature is which. This will make the rest of our discussions on methods straightforward:

```
modifier | return type | name of method (parameters)
```

And here are a few examples that we have used so far so you can clearly identify the part of the signature under discussion:

Part of signature	Examples
Modifier	public, private, and package-private (without modifier specified)
Return type	int, you can also use any of the Java primitive types (such as boolean, float, double, char, int and long) or any predefined reference types (such as String) and user-defined types (such as Employee, Person)

Part of signature	Examples
Name of method	addContact, setCoordinates, and addAToB
Parameters	(boolean isFriend, String name), (int x, int y), and (int a, int b)

Modifiers

In our previous examples, we only used a modifier in a couple of examples, partly because the method doesn't have to use the modifier. The modifier is a way of specifying which code can use (call) your method using modifiers such as `public` and `private`. Actually, regular variables can have modifiers too, for example:

```
// Most code can see me
public int a;

// Code in other classes can't see me
private String secret = "Shhh, I am private";
```

Modifiers (for methods and variables) are an essential Java topic, but they are best dealt with when we are discussing the other vital Java topic that we have skirted around so many times already—classes. We will discuss them in the next chapter.

 As we can see from our example methods and the fact that all the code we have written so far works just fine, modifiers are not necessary to facilitate our learning so far, although they will be a big part of our future learning from *Chapter 9, Object-Oriented Programming* onwards.

Return types

Next up is the return type. Like a modifier, a return type is optional. So, let's look a bit closer at it. We have seen that our methods do stuff. But what if we need the results from what they have done? The simplest example of a return type we have seen so far is:

```
int addAToB(int a, int b){
   int answer = a + b;
   return answer;
}
```

Here, the return type in the signature is highlighted, so the return type is `int`. The addAToB method sends back (returns) to the code that called it a value that will fit in an `int` variable.

The return type can be of any Java type that we have seen so far. The method does not have to return a value at all, however. In this case, the signature must use the void keyword as the return type. When the void keyword is used, the method body must not attempt to return a value, as this will cause a compiler error. It can, however, use the return keyword without a value. Here are some combinations of the return type and the use of the return keyword that are valid:

```java
void doSomething(){
  // our code

  // I'm done going back to calling code here
  // no return is necessary
}
```

Another combination of them is as follows:

```java
void doSomethingElse(){
  // our code

  // I can do this as long as I don't try and add a value
  return;
}
```

The following code is yet another combination:

```java
void doYetAnotherThing(){
  // some code
  if(someCondition){

    // if someCondition is true returning to calling code
    // before the end of the method body
    return;
  }

  // More code that might or might not get executed

  return;
  /*
    As I'm at the bottom of the method body
    and the return type is void, I'm
    really not necessary but I suppose I make it
    clear that the method is over.
  */
}
```

And in this final example we return a String:

```
String joinTogether(String firstName, String lastName){
  return firstName + lastName;
}
```

We could call each of the preceding methods, in turn, like this:

```
// OK time to call some methods

doSomething();
doSomethingElse();
doYetAnotherThing();
String fullName = joinTogether("Alan ","Turing")

// fullName now = Alan Turing
// continue with code from here
```

The preceding code would execute all the code in each method in turn.

The name of a method

The method name when we design our own methods is arbitrary. But it is a convention to use verbs that clearly explain what the method will do. Also, use the convention of the first letter of the first word of the name being lower case and the first letter of subsequent words being upper case. This is called camel case as we learned while learning about variable names, for example:

```
XGHHY78802c(){
  // code here
}
```

The preceding method is perfectly legal and will work; however, let's take a look at a much clearer example that uses the conventions:

```
doSomeVerySpecificTask(){
  // code here
}

getMyFriendsList(){
  // code here
}

startNewMessage(){
  // code here
}
```

Now that this is much clearer, let's have a look at the parameters in methods.

Parameters

We know that a method can return a result to the calling code. But what if we need to share some data values *from* the calling code *with* the method? **Parameters** allow us to share values with the method. We have actually already seen an example with parameters when we looked at return types. We will look at the same example but a little more closely at the parameters:

```
int addAToB(int a, int b){
   int answer = a + b;
   return answer;
}
```

In the preceding code, the parameters are highlighted. Parameters are contained in the parentheses (parameters go here) immediately after the method name. Note that in the first line of the method body, we use a + b as if they are already declared and initialized variables. This is because they are. The parameters of the method signature is their declaration, and the code that calls the method, initializes them as highlighted in the next line of code:

```
int returnedAnswer = addAToB(10,5);
```

Also, as we have partly seen in the previous examples, we don't have to use just int in our parameters, we can use any Java type, including types that we design ourselves. What's more is that we can mix and match types as well. We can also use as many parameters as necessary to solve our problem. This example might help:

```
void addToAddressBook
   (char firstInitial, String lastName, String city, int age){

   /*
      all the parameters are now living breathing,
      declared and initialized variables.

      The code to add details to address book goes here.
   */
}
```

Now, it's time to get serious about our bodies (method bodies, obviously).

Working in the method body

The body is the part that we have been kind of avoiding with comments such as:

```
// code here
```

Or comments like:

```
// some code
```

But actually, we know exactly what to do in the body already. Any Java syntax that we have learned so far will work in the body of a method. In fact, if we think back, all the code we have written so far *has* been in a method.

The best thing we can do next is write a few methods that actually do something in the body.

Using methods – demo apps

Here, we will quickly build two apps to explore methods a bit further. First, we will look into the fundamentals with the `Real World Methods` app and then we will glimpse at a new topic, **method overloading**, in action with the `Exploring Method Overloading` app.

As usual, you can open the ready-typed code files in the usual way. The next two examples on methods can be found in the download bundle in the `chapter 8` folder and the `Real World Methods` and `Exploring Method Overloading` subfolders.

Real-world methods

First, let's make ourselves some simple working methods complete with the return types parameters and fully functioning bodies.

To get started, create a new Android project called `Real World Methods`, use a **Blank Activity** template, and leave all the other settings at their default. Switch to the `MainActivity.java` file by clicking on the **MainActivity.java** tab above the editor, and then we can start coding.

First, add these three methods to `MainActivity`. Add them just after the closing curly brace, }, of the `onCreate` method:

```
String  joinThese(String a, String b, String c){
  return a + b + c;
}

float getAreaCircle(float radius){
  return 3.141f * radius * radius;
}

void changeA(int a){
  a++;
}
```

The first method that we added is called `joinThese`. It will return a `String` variable and requires three `String` variables passed into it. In the method body, there is only one line of code. The `return a + b + c` code will concatenate the three Strings that are passed into it and return the joined Strings as the result.

The next method `getAreaCircle` takes a `float` variable as an argument and then returns a `float` variable too. The body of the method simply uses the formula for the area of a circle to incorporate the passed-in radius and then returns the answer to the calling code. The odd-looking `f` at the end of `3.141` is to let the compiler know that the number is of the type `float`. Any floating point number is assumed to be of the type `double` unless it has the trailing `f`.

The third and final method is the simplest of all the methods. Note that it doesn't return anything; it has a `void` return type. We have included this method to make clear an important point that we want to remember about methods. But, let's see it in action before we talk about it.

Now in `onCreate`, after the call to `setContentView`, add this code that calls our methods:

```
String joinedString =
    joinThese("Methods ", "are ", "cool ");
Log.i("joinedString = ","" + joinedString);

float area  = getAreaCircle(5f);
Log.i("area = ","" + area);

int a = 0;
changeA(a);
Log.i("a = ","" + a);
```

Run the app and observe the output in the logcat window, which is shown next for your convenience:

joinedString =: Methods are cool

area =: 78.525

a =: 0

In the logcat output, the first thing we can see is the value of the String: `joinedString`. As expected, it is the concatenation of the three words we passed into the `joinThese` method.

Next, we can see that `getAreaCircle` has indeed calculated and returned the area of a circle based on the length of the radius passed in.

The final line of output is perhaps the most interesting: `a=: 0`. In the `onCreate` method, we declared and initialized `int` a to 0 and then we called `changeA`. In the body of `changeA`, we incremented a with the `a++` code. Yet back in `onCreate`, we see that when we use `Log` to print the value of a on the logcat window, it is still `0`.

So, when we passed in a to the `changeA` method, we were actually passing the *value stored in* a and not the actual variable a. This is referred to as passing by value in Java.

When we declare a variable in a method, it can only be *seen* in that method. When we declare a variable in another method, even if it has the exact same name, it is *not* the same variable. A variable only has **scope** within the method that it was declared in.

With all primitive variables, this is how passing them to methods works. With reference variables, it works slightly different, and we will see how it works in the next chapter.

I have talked about this scope concept with a number of people who are new to Java. To some, it seems blindingly obvious, even natural. To others, however, it is a cause of constant confusion. Should you fall into the latter category, don't worry because we will talk a bit more about this later in the chapter, and in subsequent chapters, we will go into great detail exploring scope and make sure that it is no longer an issue.

Let's look at another practical example of methods and learn something new at the same time.

Exploring method overloading

As you can see, methods are really quite diverse and deep as a topic. But hopefully, by taking them a step at a time, we will see that they are not daunting in any way. We will also be returning to methods in the next chapter. For now, let's create a new project to explore **method overloading**.

Create a new blank project called `Exploring Method Overloading`, and then we will get on with writing three methods, but with a slight twist.

As we will now see, we can create more than one method with the same name provided that the parameters are different. The code in this project is very simple. It is how it works that might appear slightly curious until we analyze it after.

In the first method, we will simply call it `printStuff` and pass in an `int` variable via a parameter that is to be printed. Insert this method after the closing brace, }, of `onCreate` but before the closing brace, }, of `MainActivity`. Remember to import the `Log` class in the usual way:

```
void printStuff(int myInt){
   Log.i("info", "This is the int only version");
   Log.i("info", "myInt = "+ myInt);
}
```

In this second method, we will also call it `printStuff` but pass in a `String` variable that is to be printed. Insert this method after the closing brace, }, of `onCreate` but before the closing brace, }, of `MainActivity`:

```
void printStuff(String myString){
   Log.i("info", "This is the String only version");
   Log.i("info", "myString = "+ myString);
}
```

In this third method, we will call it `printStuff` but pass in a `String` variable and `int` that is to be printed. Insert this method after the closing brace, }, of `onCreate` but before the closing brace, }, of `MainActivity`:

```
void printStuff(int myInt, String myString){
   Log.i("info", "This is the combined int and String version");
   Log.i("info", "myInt = "+ myInt);
   Log.i("info", "myString = "+ myString);
}
```

Now, insert this code just before the closing brace, }, of the `onCreate` method to call the methods and print some values on the Android console:

```
// Declare and initialize a String and an int
int anInt = 10;
String aString = "I am a string";

// Now call the different versions of printStuff
// The name stays the same, only the parameters vary
printStuff(anInt);
printStuff(aString);
printStuff(anInt, aString);
```

Now, we can run the app on the emulator or a real device. Here is the console output:

```
info: This is the int only version
info: myInt = 10
```

```
info: This is the String only version
info: myString = I am a string
info: This is the combined int and String version
info: myInt = 10
info: myString = I am a string
```

As you can see, Java has treated three methods with the same name as totally different methods. This, as we have just demonstrated, can be really useful. It is called **method overloading**.

Method overloading and overriding confusion

Overloading is when we have more than one method with the same name but different parameters.

Overriding is when we essentially replace a method with the same name and the same parameter list.

We know enough about overloading and overriding to complete this book, but if you are brave and your mind is wandering, yes you can override an overloaded method; however, that is something that we've kept for another time.

This is how it all works. In each of the steps in which we wrote code, we created a method called printStuff. But each printStuff method has different parameters, so each is actually a different method that can be called individually:

```java
void printStuff(int myInt){
    . . .
}

void printStuff(String myString){
    . . .
}

void printStuff(int myInt, String myString){
    . . .
}
```

The body of each of the methods is simple and just prints out the passed-in parameters and confirms which version of the method is being called currently.

The next important part of our code is when we make it plain, which we mean to call by using the appropriate arguments that match the parameters in the signature. Then, we call each method in turn, using the appropriate parameters so that the compiler knows the exact method required:

```
printStuff(anInt);
printStuff(aString);
printStuff(anInt, aString);
```

We now know all we need to about methods, so let's take a quick second look at the relationship between methods and variables. Then, we'll get our heads around this scope phenomenon a bit more.

Scope and variables revisited

You might remember that in the `Real World Methods` project, the slightly disturbing anomaly was that variables in one method were not apparently the same as those from another, even if they did have the same name. If you declare a variable in a method, whether that is one of the lifecycle methods or one of our own methods, it can only be used within that method.

It is no use doing this in `onCreate`:

```
int a = 0;
```

And then, trying to do this in `onPause` or some other method:

```
a++;
```

We will get an error because `a` is only visible within the method it was declared in. At first, this might seem like a problem, but perhaps surprisingly, it is actually a very useful feature of Java.

The term used to describe this is "**scope**". A variable is said to be in a scope when it is usable and out of the scope when it is not. The topic of scope is best discussed along with classes, and we will in the next chapter, but as a sneak look at what lies ahead you might like to know that a class can have its very own variables, and when it does, they have a scope for the whole class. That is, all its methods can see and use them. We call them **member** variables or **fields**.

To declare a member variable, you can simply use the usual syntax after the start of the class, outside of any method declared in the class. If our app started like this:

```
public class MainActivity extends AppCompatActivity {

    int mSomeVariable = 0;
```

```
// Rest of code and methods follow as usual
// ...
```

We could use `mSomeVariable` anywhere, inside any method in this class. Our new variable, `mSomeVariable`, has class scope. We append `m` to the variable name simply to remind us when we see it that it is a member variable. This is not required, but it is a useful convention.

Here are a couple of hypothetical method questions to try and make some of what we have learned stick a little more. Try and answer them yourself.

FAQ

1. What is wrong with this method definition?

```
doSomething(){
   // Do something here
}
```

No return type is declared. You do not have to return a value from a method, but its return type must be void in this case. This is how the method should look:

```
void doSomething(){
   // Do something here
}
```

2. What is wrong with this method definition?

```
float getBalance(){
   String customerName = "Linus Torvalds";
   float balance = 429.66f;
   return customerName;
}
```

The method returns a String (`userName`) variable, but the signature states that it must return a float. With a method name like `getBalance`, this code is probably what was intended:

```
float getBalance(){
   String customerName = "Linus Torvalds";
   float balance = 429.66f;
   return balance;
}
```

3. When do we call the `onCreate` method? !Trick question alert!

    We don't. Android decides when to call `onCreate` as well as all the other methods that make up the lifecycle of an Activity. We just override the ones that are useful to us. We do, however, call `super.onCreate` so that our overridden version and the original version both get executed.

 For the sake of technical accuracy, it is possible to call the lifecycle methods from our code, but we will never need to do this in the context of this book. It is best to leave these things to Android.

Further reading

You have learned enough Java to proceed with this book. It is always beneficial, however, to see more examples of Java in action and to go beyond the minimum necessary to proceed. If you want a good source to learn Java in greater depth, then the official Oracle website is good. Note that you do not need to study this website to continue with this book. Also note that the tutorials are not set in an Android context. The site is a useful resource to bookmark and browse all the same. The official Java tutorials can be found at `https://docs.oracle.com/javase/tutorial/`.

Summary

In previous chapters, we got quite proficient with a whole array of widgets and other UI elements and we built a fairly good selection of UI layouts. In this chapter and the previous two, we explored Java and the Android Activity lifecycle in quite significant depth, especially considering how quickly we have done it.

What we really need to do now is bring these things together so that we can begin to display and manipulate our data using the Android UI. To achieve this, we need to understand a bit more about classes. They have been lurking in our code since *Chapter 1, The First App*, and we have even used them a bit. Up until now, however, we haven't tackled them properly other than constantly referring to *Chapter 9, Object-Oriented Programming*. In the next chapter, we will quickly get to grips with classes and then we can finally start to build apps in which the UI designs and our Java code work in perfect harmony.

9
Object-Oriented Programming

In this chapter we will discover that in Java, classes are fundamental to just about everything. We will begin to understand why the software engineers at Sun Microsystems back in the early 1990's made Java the way they did.

We have already talked about reusing other people's code, specifically the Android API, but in this chapter, we will really get to grips with how this works and learn about **object-oriented programming** (OOP) and how to use it.

In short, we will cover the following topics:

- What OOP is including encapsulation, inheritance, and polymorphism
- Writing and using our first, very own class
- Encapsulation in depth and how it helps us
- Inheritance in depth and how to take full advantage of it
- Polymorphism explained in greater detail
- Static classes and how we have been using them already
- Abstract classes and interfaces

Important memory management warning

Before we get into exactly what OOP is, a quick warning.

I'm referring to our memories for a change. If you try to memorize this chapter, you will have to make a lot of room in your brain and you will probably forget something really important in its place, like going to work or thanking the author for telling you not to try and memorize this stuff.

A good goal would be to try and *just about get it*. This way, your understanding will become more rounded. You can then refer back to this chapter for a refresher when needed.

> It doesn't matter if you don't completely understand everything in this chapter straight away! Keep on reading and make sure to complete all the apps and mini apps.

Introducing OOP

In *Chapter 1, The First App,* we mentioned that Java was an object-oriented language. An object-oriented language requires us to use object-oriented programming.

> My ten-year-old son has been especially helpful in devising a unique way of remembering OOP. He suggests simply reversing its letters. I will let the reader decide whether to use this particular memory jogger or one of his or her own.

Let's find out a little bit more.

What is OOP exactly?

OOP is a way of programming that involves breaking our requirements down into chunks that are more manageable than the whole.

Each chunk is self-contained yet potentially reusable by other programs, while working together as a whole with the other chunks.

These chunks are what we have been referring to as objects. When we plan/code an object, we do so with a class. A class can be thought of as the blueprint of an object.

We implement an object *of* a class. This is called an **instance** of a class. Think about a house blueprint. You can't live in it, but you can build a house from it; you build an instance of it. Often, when we design classes for our apps, we write them to represent real world *things*.

However, OOP is more than this. It is also a *way* of doing things, a methodology that defines best practices.

The three core principles of OOP are **encapsulation**, **polymorphism**, and **inheritance**. This might sound complex but actually, when taken a step at a time, is reasonably straightforward.

Encapsulation

Encapsulation means keeping the internal workings of your code safe from interference from the code that uses it, by allowing only the variables and methods you choose to be accessed. This means your code can always be updated, extended, or improved without affecting the programs that use it, as long as the exposed parts are still accessed in the same way.

Remember this line of code from *Chapter 1, The First App*?

```
locationManager.getLastKnownLocation
  (LocationManager.GPS_PROVIDER);
```

With proper encapsulation, it doesn't matter if the satellite company or the Android API team need to update the way their code works. As long as the getLastKnownLocation method signature remains the same, we don't have to worry about what goes on inside. Our code written before the update will still work after the update. If the manufacturers of a car get rid of the wheels and make it an electrically powered hover car, as long as it still has a steering wheel, accelerator, and brake pedal, driving it should not be a challenge.

When we use the classes of the Android API, we are doing so in the way the Android developers designed their classes to allow us to.

Polymorphism

Polymorphism allows us to write code that is less dependent on the *types* we are trying to manipulate, making our code clearer and more efficient. Polymorphism means *different forms*. If the objects that we code can be more than one type of thing, then we can take advantage of this. Some examples later in the chapter will make this clear.

Inheritance

Just like it sounds, inheritance means we can harness all the features and benefits of other people's classes, including encapsulation and polymorphism, while further refining their code specifically to our situation. Actually, we have done this already, every time we used the extends keyword:

```
public class MyActivity extends AppCompatActivity {
```

The AppCompatActivity class itself inherits from Activity. So, we inherited from Activity every time we created a new Android project. We can go further than this, and we will see how it is useful.

Why do it like this?

When written properly, all this OOP allows you to add new features without worrying as much about how they interact with existing features. When you do have to change a class, its self-contained (encapsulated) nature means less or perhaps even zero consequences for other parts of the program. This is the encapsulation part.

You can use other people's code (like the Android API) without knowing or perhaps even caring how it works. Think about the Android lifecycle, Toast, Log, all the UI widgets, listening to satellites, and so on. For example, the Button class has nearly 50 methods—do we really want to write all that ourselves, just for a button? Much better to use someone else's Button class.

OOP allows you to write apps for highly complex situations without breaking a sweat.

You can create multiple, similar, and yet different versions of a class without starting the class from scratch by using inheritance; and you can still use the methods intended for the original type of object with your new object because of polymorphism.

It makes sense, really. And Java was designed from the start with all of this in mind, so we are forced into using all this OOP; however, this is a definitely a good thing. Let's have a quick class recap.

A class recap

A class is a bunch of code that can contain methods, variables, loops, and all the other Java syntax we have learned. A class is part of a Java package, and most packages will normally have multiple classes. Usually, although not always, each new class will be defined in its own .java code file with the same name as the class, as with all our Activity classes so far.

Once we have written a class, we can use it to make as many objects from it as we want. Remember, the class is the blueprint, and we make objects based on the blueprint. The house isn't the blueprint, just as the object isn't the class; it is an object made from the class. An object is a reference variable, just like a String, and later we will discover exactly what being a reference variable means. For now, let's take a look at some actual code.

Taking a look at the code for a class

Let's say we are making an app for the military. It is designed for use by senior officers to micromanage their troops in the battle. Among others, we would probably need a class to represent a soldier.

The class implementation

Here is real code for our hypothetical class. We call it a class **implementation**. Because the class is called `Soldier`, if we implement this for real, we would do so in a file called `Soldier.java`:

```java
public class Soldier {

  // Member variables
  int health;
  String soldierType;

  // Method of the class
  void shootEnemy(){
    // bang bang
  }

}
```

The code snippet in the preceding example is the implementation for a class called `Soldier`. There are two **member variables** or **fields**, an `int` variable called `health` and a `String` variable called `soldierType`.

There is also a method called `shootEnemy`. The method has no parameters and a `void` return type, but class methods can be of any shape or size as we discussed in *Chapter 8, Coding in Java Part 2 – Methods*.

To be precise about member variables and fields, when the class is instantiated into a real object, the fields become variables of the object itself, and we call them **instance** or **member** variables.

They are just variables of the class, whichever fancy name they are referred to by. However, the difference between fields and variables declared in methods (called **local** variables) does become more important as we progress. We briefly discussed variable scope at the end of *Chapter 8, Coding in Java Part 2 – Methods*. We will look at all types of variables again later in this chapter.

Declaring, initializing, and using an object of the class

Remember that `Soldier` is just a class, not an actual usable object. It is a blueprint for a soldier and not an actual soldier object, just as `int`, `String`, and `boolean` are not variables; they are just types we can make variables of. This is how we make an object of the type `Soldier` from our `Soldier` class:

```
Soldier mySoldier = new Soldier();
```

In the first part of the code, `Soldier mySoldier` declares a new variable of the type `Soldier` called `mySoldier`. The last part of the code, `new Soldier()`, calls a special method called a **constructor** that is automatically made for all classes by the compiler that creates an actual `Soldier` object. As you can see, the constructor method has the same name as the class. We will look at constructors in more depth later in the chapter.

And, of course, the assignment operator `=` in the middle of the two parts assigns the result of the second part to that of the first. The next image summarizes all this information:

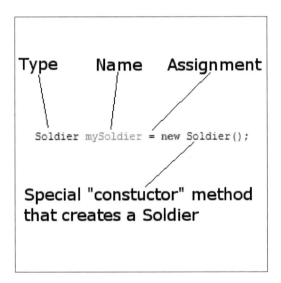

This is not far off how we deal with a regular variable, apart from the odd-looking parentheses `()` on the end of the line of code. These parentheses will be explained shortly.

Hmm, looks a bit like a method call, right?

Just like regular variables, we could also have done it in two parts, like this:

```
Soldier mySoldier;
mySoldier = new Soldier();
```

This is how we would assign and use the variables of our hypothetical class:

```
mySoldier.health = 100;
mySoldier.soldierType = "sniper";

// Notice that we use the object name mySoldier.
// Not the class name Soldier.
// We didn't do this:
// Soldier.health = 100;
// ERROR!
```

In the preceding code, the dot operator . is used to access the variables of the class; and this is how we would call the method, again, by using the object name and not the class name and followed by the dot operator:

```
mySoldier.shootEnemy();
```

We can summarize the use of the dot operator with a diagram:

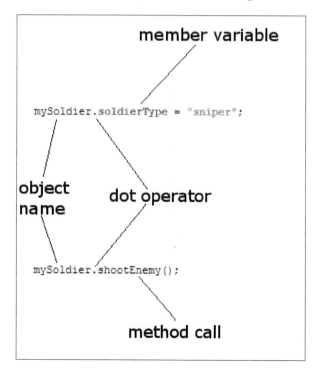

We can think of a class's methods in terms of what it can *do* and its instance/member variables as what it *knows* about itself.

We can also go ahead and make another `Soldier` object and access its methods and variables:

```
Soldier mySoldier2 = new Soldier();
mySoldier2.health = 150;
mySoldier2.soldierType = "special forces";
mySoldier2.shootEnemy();
```

It is important to realize that `mySoldier2` is a totally separate object with completely separate instance variables to `mySoldier`:

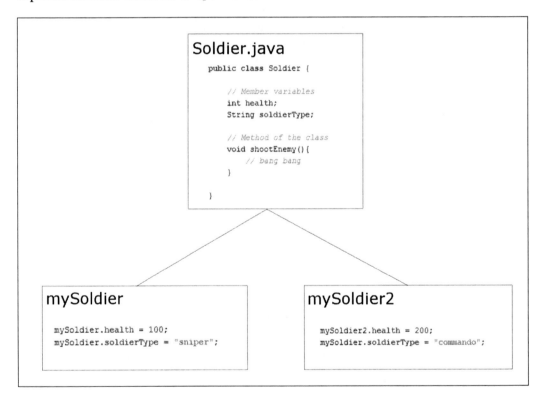

What is also key here is that this previous code would not be written within the class itself. For example, we could create the `Soldier` class in an external file called `Soldier.java` and then use the code that we have just seen, perhaps in our `MainActivity` class.

This will become clearer when we write our first class in an actual project shortly.

Also, notice that everything is done *on* the object itself. We must create objects of classes in order to make them useful.

 As always, there are exceptions to this rule. But they are in the minority, and we will look at the exception later in the chapter. In fact, we have already seen two exceptions in the book so far: the Toast and Log classes. Exactly what is going on with them will be explained soon.

Let's explore basic classes a little more deeply by writing one for real.

The basic classes mini app

The generals who will be using our app will need more than one Soldier object. In our app that we are about to build, we will instantiate and use multiple objects. We will also demonstrate using the dot operator on variables and methods to show that different objects have their very own instance variables.

You can get the completed code for this example in the code download. It is in the chapter 9/Basic Classes folder. Alternatively, read on to create your own working example.

Create a project with a blank activity. Call the application BasicClasses. Now, we create a new class called Soldier:

1. Right-click the com.gamecodeschool.basicclasses (or whatever your package name is) folder in the project explorer window.
2. Select **New | Java Class**.
3. In the **Name** field, type Soldier and left-click on **OK**.

The new class is created for us with a code template ready to put our implementation within it, just like the next image shows:

```
package com.gamecodeschool.basicclasses;

/**
 * Created by John on 27/02/2016
 */
public class Soldier {
}
```

Notice that Android Studio has put the class in the same package as the rest of our app. And now, we can write its implementation.

Write the following class implementation code within the opening and closing curly braces of the Soldier class as shown. The new code to type is highlighted:

```
public class Soldier {
    int health;
    String soldierType;

    void shootEnemy(){
        //let's print which type of soldier is shooting
        Log.i(soldierType, " is shooting");
    }
}
```

Now that we have a class, a blueprint for our future objects of the type Soldier, we can start to build our army. In the editor window, left-click on the tab **MainActivity.java**. We will write this code within the onCreate method just after the call to setContentView. Type this code:

```
// first we make an object of type soldier
Soldier rambo = new Soldier();
rambo.soldierType = "Green Beret";
rambo.health = 150;
// It takes allot to kill Rambo

// Now we make another Soldier object
Soldier vassily = new Soldier();
vassily.soldierType = "Sniper";
vassily.health = 50;
// Snipers have less health

// And one more Soldier object
Soldier wellington = new Soldier();
wellington.soldierType = "Sailor";
wellington.health = 100;
// He's tough but no green beret
```

 If you aren't doing so already, this is a really good time to start taking advantage of the auto-complete feature in Android Studio. Notice after you have declared and created a new object, all you have to do is begin typing the object's name and all the auto-complete options present themselves.

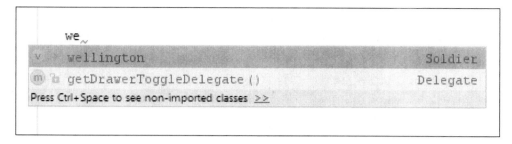

Now that we have our extremely varied and somewhat unlikely army, we can use it and also verify the identity of each object. Type the following code below the code in the previous step:

```
Log.i("Rambo's health = ", "" + rambo.health);
Log.i("Vassily's health = ", "" + vassily.health);
Log.i("Wellington's health = ", "" + wellington.health);

rambo.shootEnemy();
vassily.shootEnemy();
wellington.shootEnemy();
```

Now, we can run our app. All the output will be in the logcat console window.

This is how it works. First, we created a template for our new `Soldier` class. Then, we implemented our class including the declaring of two fields (member variables), an `int` and a `String` called `health` and `soldierType`.

We also have a method in our class called `shootEnemy`. Let's look at it again and examine what is going on:

```
void shootEnemy(){
  //lets print which type of soldier is shooting
  Log.i(soldierType, " is shooting");
}
```

In the body of the method, we print to the console, first the string `soldierType` and then the arbitrary `" is shooting"`. What's neat here is that the string `soldierType` will be different depending upon which object we call the `shootEnemy` method on.

Next, we declared and created three new objects of the type `Soldier`. They were `rambo`, `vassily`, and `wellington`. Finally, we initialized each with a different value for `health` as well as `soldierType`.

Here is the output:

```
Rambo's health =: 150
Vassily>s health =: 50
Wellington>s health =: 100
Green Beret: is shooting
Sniper: is shooting
Sailor: is shooting
```

Notice that each time we access the `health` variable of each `Soldier` object, it prints the value we assigned it, demonstrating that although the three objects are of the same type, they are completely separate, individual instances/objects.

Perhaps more interesting is the three calls to `shootEnemy`. One by one, each of our `Soldier` object's `shootEnemy` methods is called and we print the `soldierType` variable to the console. The method has the appropriate value for each individual object, further demonstrating that we have three distinct objects (instances of the class), albeit created from the same `Soldier` class.

We saw how each object is completely independent of the other objects. However, if we imagine whole armies of `Soldier` objects in our app, then we realize we are going to need to learn new ways of handling large numbers of objects (and regular variables, too).

Think about managing just 100 separate `Soldier` objects. What about when we have thousands of objects? In addition, this isn't very dynamic. The way we are writing the code at the moment relies on us (the developers) knowing the exact details of the soldiers that the generals (the user) will be commanding. We will see the solution for this in *Chapter 13, Handling and Displaying Arrays of Data*.

More things we can do with our first class

We can treat a class much like we can other variables. We can use a class as a parameter in a method signature:

```
public void healSoldier(Soldier soldierToBeHealed){
```

And when we actually call the method, we must, of course, pass an object of that type. Here is a hypothetical call to a `healSoldier` method:

```
// Perhaps healSoldier could add to the health instance variable
healSoldier(rambo);
```

Of course, the preceding example might raise questions like, should the `healSoldier` method be a method of a class?

```
fieldhospital.healSoldier(rambo);
```

It could be or not. It would depend upon what the best solution is for the situation. We will look at more OOP, and then the best solution for lots of similar conundrums should present themselves more easily.

And, as you might guess, we can also use an object as the return value of a method. Here is what the updated hypothetical `healSoldier` signature and implementation might look like now:

```
Soldier healSoldier(Soldier soldierToBeHealed){
   soldierToBeHealed.health++;

   return soldierToBeHealed;
}
```

In fact, we have already seen classes being used as parameters. For example, here is our `topClick` method from *Chapter 2, Java – First Contact*. It receives an object called v of the type `View`:

```
public void topClick(View v){
```

Although, in the case of `topClick`, we didn't do anything with the passed in object of the type `View`, partly because we didn't need to and partly because we don't know what we can do with an object of the type `View` yet.

All this information will likely raise a few questions. OOP is like that. So, let's try and consolidate all this class stuff with what we already know by taking another look at variables and encapsulation.

Remember that encapsulation thing?

So far, what we have really seen is what amounts to a kind of code-organizing convention; although, we did discuss the wider goals of all this OOP stuff. So, now we will take things further and begin to see how we actually manage to achieve encapsulation with OOP.

Definition of encapsulation

Encapsulation involves keeping the internal workings of your code safe from interference from the programs that use it, allowing only the variables and methods you choose, to be accessed. This means your code can always be updated, extended, or improved without affecting the programs that use it, as long as the exposed parts are still made available in the same way. It also allows the code that uses your encapsulated code to be much simpler and easier to maintain because much of the complexity of the task is encapsulated in your code.

But didn't you say we don't have to know what is going on inside? So, you might question what we have seen so far, for example, if we are constantly setting the instance variables like this: `rambo.health = 100;`, isn't it possible that eventually things could start to go wrong, perhaps like this?

```
rambo.soldierType = "fluffy bunny";
```

Encapsulation protects your class/objects of your class/code from being used in a way that it wasn't meant to be. By strictly controlling the way your code is used, it can only ever do what you want it to do and with value ranges that you can control.

It can't be forced into errors or crashes. Also, you are then free to make changes to the way your code works internally, without breaking the rest of your program or any other programs that are using an older version of the code:

```
weightlifter.legstrength = 100;
weightlifter.armstrength = -100;
weightlifter.liftHeavyWeight();

// one typo and weightlifter rips own arms off
```

We can encapsulate our classes to avoid this and here is how.

Controlling class use with access modifiers

The designer of the class controls what can be seen and manipulated by any program that uses their class. We can add an **access modifier** before the class keyword, like this:

```
public class Soldier{
  //Implementation goes here
}
```

There are two main access modifiers for classes in the context we have discussed so far. Let's briefly look at each in turn:

- `public`: This is straightforward. A class declared as public can be seen by all other classes.

- `default`: A class has default access when no access modifier is specified. This will make it public, but only to classes in the same package, and inaccessible to all others.

So, now we can make a start at this encapsulation thing. But even at a glance, the access modifiers described are not very fine-grained. We seem to be limited to complete lock down to anything outside the package or a complete free-for-all.

Actually, the benefits here are easily taken advantage of. The idea would be to design a package that fulfills a set of tasks. Then, all the complex inner workings of the package, the stuff that shouldn't be messed with by anybody but our package, should be given default access (only accessible to classes within the package). We can then make available a careful selection of public classes that can be used by others (or other distinct parts of our program).

 For the size and complexity of the apps in this book, creating multiple packages is probably overkill. We will, of course, be using other people's packages and classes, so this stuff is worth knowing.

Class access in a nutshell

A well-designed app will probably consist of one or more packages, each containing only default or default and public classes.

In addition to class level privacy controls, Java gives us programmers very fine-grained controls, but to use these controls, we have to look into variables with a little more detail.

Controlling variable use with access modifiers

To build on the class visibility controls, we have variable access modifiers. Here is a variable with the `private` access modifier being declared:

```
private int myInt;
```

Note also that all our discussion of variable access modifiers applies to object variables, too. For example, here is an instance of our `Soldier` class being declared, created, and assigned. As you can see, the access specified in this case is public:

```
public Soldier mySoldier  = new Soldier();
```

Before you apply a modifier to a variable, you must first consider the class visibility. If class *a* is not visible to class *b*, say because class *a* has default access and class *b* is in another package, then it doesn't make any difference what access modifiers you use on the variables in class *a*; class *b* can't see any of them.

So, it makes sense to show a class to another class when necessary but only to expose the variables that are needed, not everything.

Here is an explanation of the different variable access modifiers. They are more numerous and finely-grained than the class access modifiers. The depth and complexity of access modification is not so much in the range of modifiers but rather in the smart ways we can combine them to achieve the worthy goals of encapsulation. Here are the variable access modifiers:

- `public`: You guessed it, any class or method from any package can see this variable. Use `public` only when you are sure this is what you want.

- `protected`: This is the next least restrictive after public. Protected variables can be seen by any class and any method as long as they are in the same package.

- `default`: Default doesn't sound as restrictive as protected, but it is more so. A variable has default access when no access is specified. The fact that default is restrictive perhaps implies we should be thinking on the side of hiding our variables more than we should be exposing them. At this point, we need to introduce a new concept. Do you remember we briefly discussed inheritance and how we can quickly take on the attributes of a class and yet refine it by using the `extends` keyword? Just for the record, default access variables are not visible to sub classes; that is, when we `extend` a class like we did with `Activity`, we cannot see it's default variables. We will look at inheritance in more detail later in the chapter.

- `private`: Private variables can only be seen within the class they are declared. Including default access, they cannot be seen by subclasses (classes that inherit from the class in question).

Variable access summary

A well-designed app will probably consist of one or more packages, each containing only `default` or `default` and `public` classes. Within these classes, variables will have carefully chosen and most likely varied access modifiers, chosen with a view to achieving our goal of encapsulation.

One more twist in all this access modification stuff before we get practical with it.

Methods have access modifiers too

We already briefly mentioned in the previous chapter that methods have access modifiers. It makes sense as methods are the things that our classes can *do*. We will want to control what users of our class can and can't do.

The general idea here is that some methods will do things internally only and are therefore not needed by users of the class, and some methods will be fundamental to how users of the class use your class.

The access modifiers for methods are the same as for the class variables. This makes things easy to remember but suggests, again, that successful encapsulation is a matter of design rather than of following any specific set of rules.

As an example, this method, provided it is in a `public` class, could be used by any other class:

```
public useMeEverybody(){
  //do something everyone needs to do here
}
```

Whereas this method could only be used internally by the class that created it:

```
private secretInternalTask(){
  /*
    do something that helps the class function internally
    Perhaps, if it is part of the same class,
    useMeEverybody could use this method...
    On behalf of the classes outside of this class.
    Neat!
  */
}
```

And this next method with no access specified has `default` visibility. It can be used only by other classes in the same package. If we extend the class containing this default access method, the class will not have access to this method:

```
fairlySecretTask(){
  // allow just the classes in the package
  // Not for external use
}
```

As a last example before we move on, here is a protected method, only visible to the package but usable by our classes that extend it, just like `onCreate`:

```
protected packageTask(){
  // Allow just the classes in the package
  // And you can use me if you extend me too
}
```

A method access summary

Method access should be chosen to best enforce the principles we have already discussed. It should provide the users of your class with just the access they need and preferably nothing more, Thereby, we achieve our encapsulation goals, like keeping the internal workings of our code safe from interference from the programs that use it, for all the reasons we have discussed.

Accessing private variables with getters and setters

Now, we need to consider, if it is best practice to hide our variables away as private; how do we allow access to them without spoiling our encapsulation? What if an object of the class `Hospital` wanted access to the `health` member variable from an object of the type `Soldier`, so it could increase it? The `health` variable should be private because we don't want just any piece of code changing it.

In order to be able to make as many member variables as possible private and yet still allow some kind of limited access to some of them, we use **getters** and **setters**. Getters and setters are just methods that get and set variable values.

This is not some special new Java thing we have to learn. It is just a convention for using what we already know. Let's have a look at getters and setters using our `Soldier` and `Hospital` class example.

In this example, each of our two classes are created in their own file but the same package. First of all, here is our hypothetical `Hospital` class:

```
class Hospital{
  public void healSoldier(Soldier soldierToHeal){
    int health = soldierToHeal.getHealth();
    health = health + 10;
    soldierToHeal.setHealth(health);
  }
}
```

Our implementation of the `Hospital` class has just one method, `healSoldier`. It receives a reference to a `Soldier` object as a parameter. So, this method will work on whichever `Soldier` object is passed in: `vassily`, `wellington`, `Rambo`, or whoever.

It also has a local `health` variable that it uses to temporarily hold and increase the soldier's health. In the same line, it initializes the `health` variable to the `Soldier` object's current health. The `Soldier` object's health is private, so the public getter method `getHealth` is used instead.

Then, `health` is increased by `10` and the `setHealth` setter method loads up the new revived health value back to the `Soldier` object.

The key here is that although a `Hospital` object can change a `Soldier` object's health, it only does so within the bounds of the getter and setter methods. The getter and setter methods can be written to control and check for potentially erroneous or harmful values.

Next, look at our hypothetical `Soldier` class with the simplest implementation possible of its getter and setter methods:

```
public class Soldier{

  private int health;

  public int getHealth(){
    return health;
  }

  public void setHealth(int newHealth){

    // Check for stupid values of newHealth
    health = newHealth;
  }
}
```

We have one instance variable called `health`, and it is private. Private means it can only be changed by methods of the `Soldier` class. We then have a public `getHealth` method that unsurprisingly returns the value held in the private `health` `int` variable. As this method is public, any code with access to an object of the type `Soldier` can use it.

Next, the `setHealth` method is implemented. Again, it is public, but this time it takes an `int` data type as a parameter and assigns whatever is passed in to the private `health` variable. In a more lifelike example, we would write some more code here to make sure the value passed in is within the bounds we expect.

Now, we declare, create, and assign to make an object of each of our two new classes and see how our getters and setters work:

```
Soldier mySoldier = new Soldier();
// mySoldier.health = 100;//Doesn't work, private

// we can use the public setter setHealth()
mySoldier.setHealth(100);//That's better

Hospital militaryHospital = new Hospital();

// Oh no mySoldier has been wounded
mySoldier.setHealth(10);

/*
  Take him to the hospital
  But my health variable is private
  And Hospital won't be able to access it
  I'm doomed - tell Laura I love her

  No wait- what about my public getters and setters?
  We can use the public getters and setters from another class
*/

militaryHospital.healSoldier(mySoldier);

// mySoldiers private variable health has been increased by 10
// I'm feeling much better thanks!
```

We see that we can call our public `setHealth` and `getHealth` methods directly on our object of the type `Soldier`. Not only that, we can call the `healSoldier` method of the `Hospital` object, passing in a reference to the `Soldier` object, which can also use the public getters and setters to manipulate the private `health` variable.

We see that the private `health` variable is simply accessible, yet totally within the control of the designer of the `Soldier` class.

If you want to play around with this example, there is code for a working app in the code bundle in the `Chapter 9` folder called `GettersAndSetters`. I have added a few lines of code to print to the console. We deliberately covered this the way we did to keep the key parts of the code as clear as possible.

> Getters and setters are sometimes referred to by their more correct names, **accessors** and **mutators**. We will stick to getters and setters. I just thought you might like to know the jargon.

Yet again, our example and the explanation is probably raising more questions. That's good.

By using encapsulation features (like access control), it is kind of like signing a really important deal about how to use and access a class and its methods and variables. The contract is not just an agreement about now, but an implied guarantee for the future. We will see that as we proceed through this chapter, there are more ways that we refine and strengthen this contract.

> Use encapsulation where it is needed or, of course, if you are being paid to use it by an employer. Often, encapsulation is overkill on small learning projects, like some of the examples in this book, except, of course, when the topic you are learning is encapsulation itself.
>
> We are learning this Java OOP stuff under the assumption that you will one day want to write much more complex apps, whether on Android or some other platform that uses OOP. In addition, we will be using classes from the Android API that uses it extensively, and it will help us understand what is happening then, as well. Typically, throughout this book, we will use encapsulation when implementing full projects and often overlook it when showing small code samples to demonstrate a single idea or topic.

Setting up our objects with constructors

With all these private variables and their getters and setters, does it mean that we need a getter and a setter for every private variable? What about a class with lots of variables that need initializing at the start? Think about:

```
mySoldier.name
mysoldier.type
mySoldier.weapon
mySoldier.regiment
...
```

Some of these variables might need getters and setters, but what if we just want to set things up when the object is first created, to make the object function correctly?

Surely, we don't need two methods (a getter and a setter) for each?

Fortunately, this is unnecessary. For solving this potential problem, there is a special method called a **constructor**. We briefly mentioned the existence of a constructor when we discussed instantiating an object from a class. Let's take a look again. Here, we create an object of the type `Soldier` and assign it to an object called `mySoldier`:

```
Soldier mySoldier = new Soldier();
```

Nothing new here, but look at the last part of that line of code:

```
...Soldier();
```

This looks suspiciously like a method.

All along, we have been calling a special method known as a constructor that has been created behind the scenes automatically by the compiler.

However, and this is getting to the point now, like a method, we can override it, which means we can do really useful things to set up our new object *before* it is used. This next code shows how we could do this:

```
public Soldier(){
   // Someone is creating a new Soldier object

   health = 200;
   // more setup here
}
```

The constructor has a lot of syntactical similarities to a method. It can, however, only be called with the use of the `new` keyword, and it is created for us automatically by the compiler, unless we create our own like in the previous code.

Constructors have the following attributes:

- They have no return type

- They have the exact same name as the class

- They can have parameters

- They can be overloaded

One more piece of Java syntax that is useful to introduce at this point is the Java `this` keyword.

The `this` keyword is used when we want to be explicit about exactly which variables we are referring to. Look at this example constructor, again for a hypothetical variation of the `Soldier` class:

```java
public class Soldier{

    String name;
    String type;
    int health;


    public Soldier(String name, String type, int health){

        // Someone is creating a new Soldier object

        this.name = name;
        this.type = type;
        this.health = health;

        // more setup here
    }
}
```

This time, the constructor has a parameter for each of the variables we want to initialize. By using the `this` keyword, it is clear when we mean the member variable or the parameter.

There are more twists and turns to be learned with regard to variables and `this`, and they make much more sense when applied to a practical project. In the next mini app, we will explore all we have learned so far in this chapter and some more new ideas, too.

But first, a bit more OOP.

Static methods

We know quite a lot about classes—how to turn them into objects and use their methods and variables. But something isn't quite right. Since the very start of the book, we have been using two classes more than any other. We have repeatedly used `Log` and `Toast` to output to the logcat or the user's screen, but have not instantiated them once! How can this be?

The `static` methods of classes can be used *without* first instantiating an object of the class. We can think of this as a static method belonging to the class and all other methods belonging to an object of a class.

And as you have probably realized by now, `Log` and `Toast` both contain static methods. To be clear: `Log` and `Toast` *contain* static methods; they themselves are still classes.

Classes can have both static and regular methods, as well, but the regular methods would need to be used in the regular way, via an instance of the class.

Take another look at `Log.i` in action:

```
Log.i("info","our message here");
```

Here, `i` is the method being statically accessed, and the method takes two parameters, both of the type `String`.

Next, we see the static method `makeText` of the `Toast` class in use:

```
Toast.makeText(this, "our message", Toast.LENGTH_SHORT).show();
```

The `makeText` method of the `Toast` class takes three arguments.

The first argument is `this`, which takes some explaining. We saw when talking about constructors that to explicitly refer to the member variables of the current instance of an object, we can use `this.health`, `this.regiment`, and so on.

When we use `this` as we do in the previous line of code, we are referring to the instance of the class itself. It is not the `Toast` class but the `this` keyword in the previous line of code is a reference to the class the method is being used *from*. In our case, we have used it from `MainActivity`. Many things in Android require a reference to an instance of `Activity` to do their job. We will fairly regularly, throughout this book, pass in `this` (a reference to `Activity`) in order to help a class/object from the Android API do its work. We will also write classes that need `this` as an argument in one or more of its methods. So, we will see how to handle `this` when it is passed in, as well.

The second argument is, of course, a `String`.

The third argument is accessing a `final` variable, `LENGTH_SHORT`, again via the class name, not an instance of the class. If we declare a variable like this next line of code:

```
public static final int LENGTH_SHORT = 1;
```

Assuming that the variable was declared in a class called `MyClass`, we could access the variable like this: `MyClass.LENGTH_SHORT` and use it like any other variable, but the `final` keyword makes sure that the value of the variable can never be changed. This type of variable is called a **constant**.

The `static` keyword also has another consequence for a variable, especially when it is not a constant (can be changed), and we will see this in action in our next mini app.

Now, if you look carefully at the very end of the line of code that shows a `Toast` message to the user, you will see something else new: `.show()`.

This is called **chaining**, and all we are doing is calling a second method of the `Toast` class but using just one line of code. It is the `show` method that actually triggers the message.

We will see some more chaining as we proceed through the book, like in *Chapter 12, Having a Dialogue with the User*, when we make pop-up dialog windows, and in *Chapter 17, Sound FX and Supporting Different Versions of Android*, when we start to use sound in our apps.

> If you want to read about the `Toast` class and some of its other methods in detail, you can do so here: `http://developer.android.com/reference/android/widget/Toast.html`.

Static methods are often provided in classes with uses that are so generic, it doesn't make sense to have to create an object of the class. Another really useful class with static methods is `Math`. This class is actually a part of the Java API, not the Android API.

> Want to write a calculator app? It's easier than you think with the static methods of the `Math` class. You can take a look at them here: `http://docs.oracle.com/javase/7/docs/api/java/lang/Math.html`.

If you try this out, you will need to import the `Math` class the same way you imported all the other classes we have used.

Encapsulation and static methods mini app

We have looked at the intricate way that access to variables and their scope is controlled, and it would probably serve us well to look at an example of them in action. These will not so much be practical real-world examples of variable use, but more a demonstration to help understand access modifiers for classes, methods, and variables. This is alongside the different types of variable-like references or primitive and local instances, along with the new concepts of static and final variables and the `this` keyword. The completed code is in the `chapter 9` folder of the download bundle. It is called `Access Scope This And Static`.

Create a new blank activity project and call it `Access Scope This And Static`.

Create a new class by right-clicking on the existing `MainActivity` class in the project explorer and clicking **New | Class**. Name the new class `AlienShip`.

Now, we declare our new class and some member variables. Note that `numShips` is `private` and `static`. We will see how this variable is the same across all instances of the class soon. The `shieldStrength` variable is `private`. `shipName` is public:

```
public class AlienShip {

    private static int numShips;
    private int shieldStrength;
    public String shipName;
```

Next is the constructor. We can see that the constructor is public, has no return type, and has the same name as the class—as per the rules. In it, we increment the private static `numShips` variable. Remember, this will happen each time we create a new object of the type `AlienShip`. Also, the constructor sets a value for the private variable `shieldStrength` using the private `setShieldStrength` method:

```
public AlienShip(){
    numShips++;

    /*
        Can call private methods from here because I am part
        of the class.
        If didn't have "this" then this call
        might be less   clear
        But this "this" isn't strictly necessary
```

```
        Because of "this" I am sure I am setting
        the correct shieldStrength
    */

    this.setShieldStrength(100);

}
```

Here is the `public static` getter method so classes outside of `AlienShip` can find out how many `AlienShip` objects there are. We will also explore the way in which we use static methods:

```
public static int getNumShips(){
    return numShips;

}
```

And this is our private `setShieldStrength` method. We could have just set `shieldStrength` directly from within the class, but the following code shows how we distinguish between the `shieldStrength` local variable/parameter and the `shieldStrength` member variable by using the `this` keyword:

```
private void setShieldStrength(int shieldStrength){

    // "this" distinguishes between the
    // member variable shieldStrength
    // And the local variable/paramater of the same name
    this.shieldStrength = shieldStrength;

}
```

This next method is the getter, so other classes can read but not alter the shield strength of each `AlienShip` object:

```
public int getShieldStrength(){
    return this.shieldStrength;
}
```

Now, we have a `public` method that can be called every time an `AlienShip` object is hit. It just prints to the console and then detects if that particular object's `shieldStrength` is zero. If it is, it calls the `destroyShip` method that we'll look at next:

```
public void hitDetected(){

    shieldStrength -=25;
```

```
    Log.i("Incomiming: ","Bam!!");
    if (shieldStrength == 0){
      destroyShip();
    }

  }
```

And lastly, for our `AlienShip` class, we have the `destroyShip` method. We print a message that indicates which ship has been destroyed based on its `shipName`, as well as decrement the `numShips` static variable so we can keep track of how many objects of the type `AlienShip` we have:

```
private void destroyShip(){
  numShips--;
  Log.i("Explosion: ", ""+this.shipName + " destroyed");
} // End of the class
```

Now, we switch over to our `MainActivity` class and write some code that uses our new `AlienShip` class. All the code goes in the `onCreate` method after the call to `setContentView`. First, we create two new `AlienShip` objects called `girlShip` and `boyShip`:

```
// every time we do this the constructor runs
AlienShip girlShip = new AlienShip();
AlienShip boyShip = new AlienShip();
```

Look how we get the value in `numShips`. We use the `getNumShips` method as we might expect. However, look closely at the syntax. We are using the class name and not an object. We can also access static variables with methods that are not static. We did it this way to see a static method in action:

```
// Look no objects but using the static method
Log.i("numShips: ", "" + AlienShip.getNumShips());
```

Now, we assign names to our public `shipName` String variables:

```
// This works because shipName is public
girlShip.shipName = "Corrine Yu";
boyShip.shipName = "Andre LaMothe";
```

If we attempt to assign a value directly to a private variable, it won't work. So, we use the public getter method `getShieldStrength` to print out the `shieldStrength` that was assigned in the constructor:

```
// This won't work because shieldStrength is private
// girlship.shieldStrength = 999;

// But we have a public getter
```

```
Log.i("girlShip shieldStrngth: ", "" +
  girlShip.getShieldStrength());

Log.i("boyShip shieldStrngth: ", "" +
  boyShip.getShieldStrength());

// And we can't do this because it's private
// boyship.setShieldStrength(1000000);
```

Finally, we get to blow some stuff up by playing with the hitDetected method and occasionally checking the shieldStrength of our two objects:

```
// lets shoot some ships
girlShip.hitDetected();
Log.i("girlShip shieldStrngth: ", "" +
  girlShip.getShieldStrength());

Log.i("boyShip shieldStrngth: ", "" +
  boyShip.getShieldStrength());

boyShip.hitDetected();
boyShip.hitDetected();
boyShip.hitDetected();

Log.i("girlShip shieldStrngth: ", "" +
  girlShip.getShieldStrength());

Log.i("boyShip shieldStrngth: ", "" +
  boyShip.getShieldStrength());

boyShip.hitDetected(); //ahhh

Log.i("girlShip shieldStrngth: ", "" +
  girlShip.getShieldStrength());

Log.i("boyShip shieldStrngth: ", "" +
  boyShip.getShieldStrength());
```

When we think we have destroyed a ship, we again use our static getNumShips method to see if our static variable numShips was changed by the destroyShip method:

```
Log.i("numShips: ", "" + AlienShip.getNumShips());
```

Run the demo and look at the console output:

```
numShips: 2
girlShip shieldStrngth: 100
boyShip shieldStrngth: 100
Incomiming: Bam!!
girlShip shieldStrngth:: 75
boyShip shieldStrngth:: 100
Incomiming: Bam!!
Incomiming: Bam!!
Incomiming: Bam!!
girlShip shieldStrngth:: 75
boyShip shieldStrngth:: 25
Incomiming: Bam!!
Explosion: Andre LaMothe destroyed
girlShip shieldStrngth: 75
boyShip shieldStrngth: 0
numShips: 1
boyShip shieldStrngth: 0
numShips: 1
```

In the previous example, we saw that we can distinguish between local and member variables of the same name by using the this keyword. We can also use the this keyword to write code that refers to whatever the current object being acted upon is.

We saw that a static variable, in this case numShips, is consistent across all instances; moreover, by incrementing it in the constructor and decrementing it in our destroyShip method, we can keep track of the number of AlienShip objects we created.

We also saw that we can use static methods by using the class name with the dot operator instead of an actual object. Yes, I know it is kind of like living in the blueprint of a house, but it's quite useful.

Finally, we demonstrated how we could hide and expose certain methods and variables using an access specifier.

OOP and inheritance

We have seen how we can use other people's hard work by instantiating/creating objects from the classes of an API like Android. But this whole OOP thing goes even further than that.

What if there is a class that has loads of useful functionality in it but is not quite what we want? We can inherit from the class and then further refine or add to how it works and what it does.

You might be surprised to hear that we have done this already. In fact, we have done this with every single app we have created. When we use the extends keyword, we are inheriting. Remember this?

```
public class MainActivity extends AppCompatActivity ...
```

Here, we are inheriting the AppCompatActivity class along with all its functionality—or more specifically, all the functionality that the class designers want us to have access to. Now, we will discuss some of the things we can do to classes we have extended.

We can even override a method *and* still rely in part on the overridden method in the class we inherit from. For example, we overrode the onCreate method every time we extended the AppCompatActivity class. But we also called on the default implementation provided by the class designers when we did this:

```
super.onCreate(...
```

And in *Chapter 6, The Life and Times of an Android App*, we overrode just about all of the Activity class's lifecycle methods.

We discuss inheritance mainly so that we understand what is going on around us and as the first step toward being able to eventually design useful classes that we or others can extend.

With this in mind, let's look at some example classes and see how we can extend them, just to see the syntax and as a first step, and also to be able to say we have done it.

When we look at the final major topic of this chapter, polymorphism, we will also dig a little deeper into inheritance at the same time. Here is some code using inheritance:

This code would go in a file named `Animal.java`:

```java
public class Animal{

  // Some member variables
  public int age;
  public int weight;
  public String type;
  public int hungerLevel;

  public void eat(){
    hungerLevel--;
  }

  public void walk(){
    hungerLevel++;
  }


}
```

Then, in a separate file named `Elephant.java`, we could do this:

```java
public class Elelphant extends Animal{

  public Elephant(int age, int weight){
    this.age = 57;
    this.weight = 1000;
    this.type = "Elephant";
    int hungerLevel = 0;
  }

}
```

We can see in the previous code that we have implemented a class called `Animal`, and it has four member variables: age, weight, type, and hungerLevel. It also has two methods, eat and walk.

We then extended `Animal` with `Elephant`. Elephant can now do anything `Animal` can, and it also has all its variables. We initialized the variables from `Animal`, which `Elephant` has in the `Elephant` constructor. Two variables (age and weight) are passed into the constructor when an `Elephant` object is created, and two variables (type and hungerLevel) are assigned the same for all `Elephant` objects.

We could go ahead and write a bunch of other classes that are an extension of the Animal class, perhaps Lion, Tiger, and ThreeToedSloth. Each would have an age, weight, type, hungerLevel, and each would be able to walk and eat.

As if OOP were not useful enough already, we can now model real-world objects. We have also seen we can make OOP even more useful by subclassing/extending/inheriting from other classes. The terminology we might like to learn here is that the class that is extended from is the **super class**, and the class that inherits from the super class is the **subclass**. We can also say parent and child class.

 As usual, we might find ourselves asking this question about inheritance. Why? The reason is something like this: we can write common code once; in the parent class, we can update that common code and all classes that inherit from it are also updated. Furthermore, a subclass only gets to use public/protected instance variables and methods. So, designed properly, this also further enhances the goals of encapsulation.

Let's take a closer look at the final major OOP concept. Then, we will be able to do some more really practical things with the Android API.

The inheritance mini app

We have looked at the way we can create hierarchies of classes to model the system that fits our app. So, let's try out some simple code that uses inheritance. The completed code is in the Chapter 9 folder of the code download. It is called Inheritance Example.

Create three new classes in the usual way. Name one AlienShip, another Fighter, and the last one Bomber.

The following is the code for the AlienShip class. It is very similar to our previous class demo, AlienShip. The differences are that the constructor now takes an int parameter, which it uses to set the shield strength.

The constructor also outputs a message to the console, so we can see when it is being used. Additionally, the AlienShip class has a new method, fireWeapon, that is declared abstract. This guarantees that any class that subclasses AlienShip must implement its own version of fireWeapon. Notice the class has the abstract keyword as part of its declaration. We have to do this because one of its methods also uses the keyword abstract. We will explain the abstract method when discussing this demo and the abstract class when we talk about polymorphism. Create a class called AlienShip and type this code:

```
public abstract class AlienShip {
  private static int numShips;
  private int shieldStrength;
  public String shipName;

  public AlienShip(int shieldStrength){
    Log.i("Location: ", "AlienShip constructor");
    numShips++;
    setShieldStrength(shieldStrength);
  }

  public abstract void fireWeapon();
  // Ahh my body where is it?

  public static int getNumShips(){
    return numShips;
  }

  private void setShieldStrength(int shieldStrength){
    this.shieldStrength = shieldStrength;
  }

  public int getShieldStrength(){
    return this.shieldStrength;
  }

  public void hitDetected(){
    shieldStrength -=25;
    Log.i("Incoming: ", "Bam!!");
    if (shieldStrength == 0){
      destroyShip();
    }

  }

  private void destroyShip(){
```

```
      numShips--;
      Log.i("Explosion: ", "" + this.shipName + " destroyed");
   }


}
```

Now, we will implement the `Bomber` class. Notice the call to `super(100)`. This calls the constructor of the super class with the value for `shieldStrength`. We could do further specific `Bomber` initialization in this constructor, but for now, we just print out the location so we can see when the `Bomber` constructor is being executed. Because we must, we also implement a `Bomber` specific version of the abstract `fireWeapon` method. Create a class called `Bomber` and type this code:

```
   public class Bomber extends AlienShip {

      public Bomber(){
        super(100);
        // Weak shields for a bomber
        Log.i("Location: ", "Bomber constructor");
      }

      public void fireWeapon(){
        Log.i("Firing weapon: ", "bombs away");
      }
   }
```

Now, we will implement the `Fighter` class. Notice the call to `super(400)`. This calls the constructor of the super class with the value for `shieldStrength`. We could do further specific `Fighter` initialization in this constructor, but for now, we just print out the location so we can see when the `Fighter` constructor is being executed. Because we must, we also implement `Fighter` specific version of the abstract `fireWeapon` method. Create a class called `Fighter` and type this code:

```
   public class Fighter extends AlienShip{

      public Fighter(){
        super(400);
        // Strong shields for a fighter
        Log.i("Location: ", "Fighter constructor");
      }

      public void fireWeapon(){
        Log.i("Firing weapon: ", "lasers firing");
      }

   }
```

And here is our code in the `onCreate` method of `MainActivity`. As usual, enter this code after the call to `setContentView`. This is the code that uses our three new classes. The code looks quite ordinary and is nothing new; it is the output that is interesting:

```
Fighter aFighter = new Fighter();
Bomber aBomber = new Bomber();

// Can't do this AlienShip is abstract -
// Literally speaking as well as in code
// AlienShip alienShip = new AlienShip(500);

// But our objects of the subclasses can still do
// everything the AlienShip is meant to do

aBomber.shipName = "Newell Bomber";
aFighter.shipName = "Meier Fighter";

// And because of the overridden constructor
// That still calls the super constructor
// They have unique properties
Log.i("aFighter Shield:", ""+ aFighter.getShieldStrength());
Log.i("aBomber Shield:", ""+ aBomber.getShieldStrength());

// As well as certain things in certain ways
// That are unique to the subclass
aBomber.fireWeapon();
aFighter.fireWeapon();

// Take down those alien ships
// Focus on the bomber it has a weaker shield
aBomber.hitDetected();
aBomber.hitDetected();
aBomber.hitDetected();
aBomber.hitDetected();
```

Run the app and you will get the following output in the logcat window:

```
Location:: AlienShip constructor
Location:: Fighter constructor
Location:: AlienShip constructor
Location:: Bomber constructor
aFighter Shield:: 400
aBomber Shield:: 100
```

```
Firing weapon:: bombs away
Firing weapon:: lasers firing
Incomiming:: Bam!!
Incomiming:: Bam!!
Incomiming:: Bam!!
Incomiming:: Bam!!
Explosion:: Newell Bomber destroyed
```

We can see how the constructor of the subclass can call the constructor of the super class. We can also clearly see that the individual implementations of the `fireWeapon` method work exactly as expected.

Polymorphism

We already know that polymorphism means *different forms*. But what does it mean to us?

Boiled down to its simplest definition, polymorphism is: any subclass can be used as part of the code that uses the super class.

This means we can write code that is simpler and easier to understand and also easier to modify or change.

Also, we can write code for the super class and rely on the fact that no matter how many times it is subclassed, within certain parameters, the code will still work.

Let's discuss an example.

Suppose we want to use polymorphism to help write a zoo management app. We will probably want to have a method like `feed`. We will also probably want to pass a reference to the animal to be fed into the `feed` method. This might seem like we need to write a `feed` method for each and every type of `Animal`.

However, we can write polymorphic methods with polymorphic return types and arguments:

```
Animal feed(Animal animalToFeed){
   // Feed any animal here
   return animalToFeed;
}
```

The preceding method has `Animal` as a parameter, meaning that *any* object that is built from a class that extends `Animal` can be passed into it. And as you can see in the preceding code, the method also returns `Animal`, which has exactly the same benefits.

There is a small gotcha with polymorphic return types, and that is why we need to be aware of what is being returned and make it explicit in the code that calls the method.

For example, we could handle `Elephant` being passed into the `feed` method like this:

```
someElephant = (Elephant) feed(someElephant);
```

Notice the highlighted `(Elephant)` in the previous code. This makes it clear that we want `Elephant` from the returned `Animal`. This is called **casting**. We will use casting with methods from the Android API in the next chapter and throughout the rest of the book, when we look at how to interact with our UI from our Java code.

So, you can even write code *today* and make another subclass in a week, month, or year, and the very same methods and data structures will still work.

Also, we can enforce upon our subclasses a set of rules as to what they can and cannot do, as well as how they do it. So, good design in one stage can influence it at other stages.

But will we ever really want to instantiate an actual `Animal`?

Abstract classes

An abstract class is a class that cannot be instantiated and therefore cannot be made into an object. So, it's a blueprint that will never be used, then? But that's like paying an architect to design your home and then never building it! You might be saying to yourself, "I kind of got the idea of an abstract method, but abstract classes are just silly."

If we, or the designer of a class, wants to force us to inherit *before* we use their class, they can declare a class **abstract.** Then, we cannot make an object from it; therefore, we must extend it first and make an object from the subclass.

We can also declare a method `abstract` and then that method must be overridden in any class that extends the class with the `abstract` method.

Let's look at an example; it will help. We make a class abstract by declaring it with the abstract keyword, like this:

```
abstract class someClass{
  /*
    All methods and variables here.
    As usual!
    Just don't try and make
    an object out of me!
  */
}
```

Yes, but why?

Sometimes, we want a class that can be used as a polymorphic type, but we need to guarantee it can never be used as an object. For example, Animal doesn't really make sense on its own.

We don't talk about animals; we talk about types of animals. We don't say, "ooh, look at that lovely, fluffy, white animal!" Or, "yesterday we went to the pet shop and got an animal and an animal bed." It's just too, well, *abstract*.

So, an abstract class is kind of like a template to be used by any class that extends it (inherits from it).

We might want a Worker class, for example, and extend it to make, Miner, Steelworker, OfficeWorker, and, of course, Programmer. But what exactly does a plain Worker do? Why would we ever want to instantiate one?

The answer is we wouldn't want to instantiate one, but we might want to use it as a polymorphic type so we can pass multiple worker subclasses between methods and have data structures that can hold all types of Workers.

We call this type of class an abstract class, and when a class has even one abstract method, it must be declared abstract itself. And all abstract methods must be overridden by any class that extends it. This means that the abstract class can provide some of the common functionality that would be available in all its subclasses. For example, the Worker class might have the height, weight, and age member variables.

It might have the getPayCheck method, which is not abstract and is the same in all the subclasses, but a doWork method instead, which is abstract and must be overridden, because all the different types of worker doWork very differently.

This leads us neatly to another area of polymorphism that is going to make life easier for us throughout this book.

Interfaces

An interface is like a class. Phew! Nothing complicated here, then. But it's like a class that is always abstract and with only abstract methods.

We can think of an interface as an entirely abstract class with all its methods abstract and no member variables either. OK, so you can just about wrap your head around an abstract class because at least it can pass on some functionality in its methods that are not abstract and serve as a polymorphic type.

But seriously, this interface seems a bit pointless. Let's look at the simplest possible generic example of an interface, and then we can discuss it further.

To define an interface, we type:

```
public interface myInterface{
   void someAbstractMethod();
   // omg I've got no body

   int anotherAbstractMethod();
   // Ahh! Me too

   // Interface methods are always abstract and public implicitly
   // but we could make it explicit if we prefer

   public abstract explicitlyAbstractAndPublicMethod();
   // still no body though


}
```

The methods of an interface have no body because they are abstract, but they can still have return types and parameters, or not.

To use an interface, we use the `implements` keyword after the class declaration:

```
public class someClass implements someInterface{

   // class stuff here

   /*
      Better implement the methods of the interface
      or we will have errors.
```

```
    And nothing will work
*/

public void someAbstractMethod(){
  // code here if you like
  // but just an empty implementation will do
}

public int anotherAbstractMethod(){
  // code here if you like
  // but just an empty implementation will do

  // Must have a return type though
  // as that is part of the contract
  return 1;
}
}
```

This enables us to use polymorphism with multiple different objects that are from completely unrelated inheritance hierarchies. As long as a class implements an interface, the whole thing can be passed along or used as if it is that thing, because it is that thing. It is polymorphic (many things).

We can even have a class implement multiple different interfaces at the same time. Just add a comma between each interface and list them after the `implements` keyword. Just be sure to implement all the necessary methods.

In this book, we will use the interfaces of the Android API a lot more frequently than we write our own. In the next chapter, one such interface we will use in the Java Meet UI mini app is the `OnClickListener` interface.

Anything might like to know when it is being clicked, perhaps a **Button** or a **TextView** widget and so on. So, using an interface, we don't need different methods for every type of UI element we might like to click.

FAQ

1. What is wrong with this class declaration?

```
private class someClass{
  // class implementation goes here
}
```

There are no private classes. Classes can be public or default. Public is public; default is like being private within its own package.

2. What is encapsulation?

    Encapsulation is how we contain our variables, code, and methods in a manner that exposes just the parts and functionality we want for the code that uses it.

Summary

In this chapter, we covered more theory than in any other chapter. If you haven't memorized everything or some of the code seemed a bit too in-depth, then you have still succeeded completely. If you just understand that OOP is about writing reusable, extendable, and efficient code through encapsulation, inheritance, and polymorphism, then you have the potential to be a Java master. Simply put, OOP enables us to use other people's code even when those other people were not aware of exactly what we would be doing at the time they did the work. All you have to do is keep practicing.

We will constantly be using these same concepts over and over again throughout the book, so you *do not* need to have even begun to master them at this point.

In the next chapter, we will be revisiting some concepts from this one as well as looking at some new aspects of OOP and how that enables our Java to interact with our XML layouts.

But first, there is an important incoming news flash!

10
Everything's a Class

In this chapter, we will indeed see that everything's a class. By the end of this chapter, the missing link between Java and our XML layouts will be fully revealed, leaving us with the power to add all kinds of widgets to our apps.

Here, you will learn about the following topics:

- Android UI elements as classes
- Garbage collection
- Our UI on the heap
- Special types of a class that includes inner and anonymous

So, what do I mean by everything's a class?

All Android UI elements are classes too

When our app is run and the setContentView method is called from onCreate, the layout is **inflated** from XML UI classes and loaded into memory as usable objects. They are stored in a part of the DVM memory called the **heap**.

Reintroducing references

However, where are all these UI objects/classes? We certainly can't see them in our code. And how on earth do we get our hands on them?

The DVM inside every Android device takes care of memory allocation to our apps. In addition, it stores different types of variables in different places.

Variables that we declare and initialize in methods are stored in the area of memory that is known as the **stack**. We can stick to our existing warehouse analogy when talking about the stack—almost. We already know how we can manipulate variables on the stack. So, let's talk about the heap and what is stored there.

 Important fact: **All objects of classes are reference type variables and are just references to the actual objects that are stored on the heap**; they are not actual objects.

Think of the heap as a separate area of the same warehouse. The heap has lots of floor space for odd-shaped objects, racks for smaller objects, lots of long rows with small-sized cubby holes, and so on. This is where objects are stored. The problem is we have no direct access to the heap. Let's look at what exactly a reference variable is.

It is a variable that we refer to and use via a reference. A reference can be loosely, but usefully, defined as an address or a location. The reference (address or location) of the object is on the stack. So, when we use the dot operator, we are asking Dalvik to perform a task *at* a specific location, a location that is stored in the reference.

 Reference variables are just that—a reference. A way to access and manipulate the object (variables and methods), but they are not the actual variable itself.

Why, oh why would we ever want a system like this? Just give me my objects on the Stack already. Here is why.

A quick break to throw out the trash

This is what the whole stack and heap thing does for us. As we know, the DVM keeps track of all our objects for us and stores them in a special area of our warehouse called the heap. Regularly, while our app is running, the DVM will scan the stack, the regular racks of our warehouse, and match up references to objects that are on the heap. And it destroys any objects that it finds without a matching reference. Or in Java terminology, it collects garbage.

Think of a very discriminating refuse vehicle driving through the middle of our heap, scanning objects to match up references (on the stack). No reference, you're garbage now. After all, if an object has no reference variable, we can't possibly do anything with it anyway because we have no way to access it. This system of garbage collection helps our apps run more efficiently by freeing up unused memory.

If this task was left to us, our apps would be much more complicated to code.

So, the variables declared in a method are local, on the stack, and only visible within the method they were declared in. A member variable (in an object) is on the heap and can be referenced from anywhere there is a reference to it and from anywhere that the access specification (encapsulation) allows.

Stack and heap – a quick summary

Let's take a quick look at what you learned about a stack and heap:

- You don't delete objects, but the VM sends the garbage collector when it thinks it's appropriate. This is usually when there is no active reference to the object.

- Local variables and methods are on the stack, and the local variables are local to the specific method within which they were declared.

- Instance/class variables are on the heap (with their objects), but the reference *to* the object, the address, is a local variable on the stack.

- We control what goes onto the stack. We can use the objects on the heap, but only by referencing them.

- The heap is maintained by the garbage collector.

- An object is garbage collected when there is no longer a valid reference to it. So, when a reference variable, either local or instance, is removed from the stack, then its related object becomes viable for garbage collection. And when the DVM decides the time is right (usually very promptly), it will free up the RAM memory to avoid running out of memory.

- If we try to reference an object that doesn't exist, we will get a `NullPointerException` error and the app will crash.

So, how does this heap thing help me?

Any UI element that has its `id` property set can have its reference retrieved from the heap using the `findViewById` method, which is part of the Activity, the `AppCompatActivity` class. As it is part of the class that we extend, we have access to it:

```
myButton = (Button) findViewById(R.id.myButton);
```

The preceding code assumes that `myButton` has been declared previously to an appropriate type; in this case, `Button`. Also, the preceding code assumes that within the XML layout, there is a button with an ID property set to `myButton`.

Note that `findViewById` is also polymorphic. We know this because we use a cast, `(Button)`, to be explicit about making the returned object `Button` from its `View` parent type, just like we did with our object of the type `Elephant` with the `feed` method in the last chapter.

This is quite exciting because it implies that we can grab a reference to a whole bunch of stuff from our layout. We can then start using all the methods that these objects have. Here are some examples of the methods we can use for `Button` objects:

```
myButton.setText
myButton.setHeight
myButton.setOnCLickListener
myButton.setVisibility
```

Remember that `Button` alone has around 50 methods! If you think that after nearly 10 chapters we are finally going to start doing some really neat stuff with Android, you would be right!

Using Button and TextView widgets from our layout

To follow along with this mini project, create a new Android Studio project, call it `Java Meet UI`, and leave all the other options at their default values. As usual, you can find the Java code and the XML layout code in the `Chapter 10/Java Meet UI` folder.

First, let's build a simple UI:

1. Delete the autogenerated **TextView** widget, the one that reads "Hello world!".
2. Add a **Large Text** widget on the top and at the center of the layout.
3. Set its **text** property to `0` and its **id** property to `txtValue`. Pay careful attention to the case of the ID. It has an uppercase `V`.

4. Now, drag-and-drop six buttons on the layout so that it looks fairly similar to this next screenshot. The exact layout isn't important:

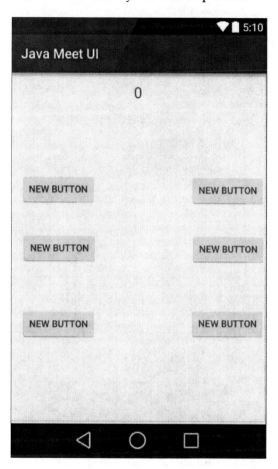

5. Double-click on each button in turn (left to right and then top to bottom) and set the `text` and `id` properties as shown in the next table. When you see the pop-up message as shown in the next figure, choose **Yes** each time:

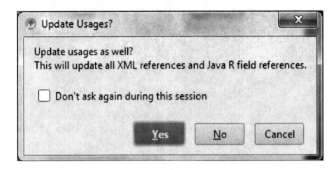

The text property	The id property
add	btnAdd
take	btnTake
grow	btnGrow
shrink	btnShrink
Hide	btnHide
Reset	btnReset

When you're done, your layout should look as shown in the next screenshot:

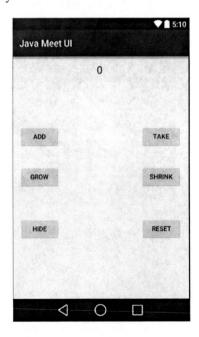

The precise position and text on the buttons is not very important, but the values given to the id properties must be exactly the same. The reason for this is we will be using these IDs to get a reference to the buttons and TextView in this layout from our Java code.

Switch to the **MainActivity.java** tab in the editor and find the following code:

```
public class MainActivity extends AppCompatActivity{
```

Amend the preceding line to:

```
public class MainActivity extends
    AppCompatActivity implements View.OnClickListener{
```

Note that the entire line we just amended is underlined in red, indicating an error. Now, because we have made MainActivity into OnClickListener by adding it as an interface, we must implement the abstract method of OnClickListener. The method is called onClick. When we add the method, the error will be gone.

We can get Android Studio to add it for us by clicking anywhere on the line with an error and then using the keyboard combination *Alt + Enter*. After this, click on the **Implement methods** option, as shown in the next figure:

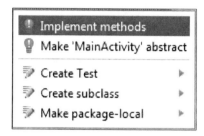

Now, click on **OK** to confirm that we want Android Studio to add the onClick method. The error goes away and we can carry on with adding code. We also have an onClick method, and we will soon see what we will do with that.

Now, we will declare a int variable called value and initialize it to 0. We will also declare six Button objects and a TextView object. We will give them the same names that we gave the id property values in our UI layout. This name association is not required, but it is useful to keep track of which Button in our Java code will be holding a reference to which Button from our UI.

Furthermore, we are declaring them all with the private access specification because we know that they will not be needed outside of this class.

Before you go ahead and type the code, note that all these variables are members of the `MainActivity` class. This means that we enter all the code that is shown next immediately after the class declaration that we amended in the previous step.

Making all these variables into members/fields means that they have a class scope, and we can access them from anywhere within the `MainActivity` class. This will be essential for this project because we will need to use them all in `onCreate` and in our new `onClick` method.

Enter this next code that we just discussed after the opening curly brace, {, of the `MainActivity` class and before the `onCreate` method:

```java
// An int variable to hold a value
private int value = 0;

// A bunch of Buttons and a TextView
private Button btnAdd;
private Button btnTake;
private TextView txtValue;
private Button btnGrow;
private Button btnShrink;
private Button btnReset;
private Button btnHide;
```

 Remember to use the *Alt + Enter* keyboard combination to import new classes.

Next, we want to prepare all our variables ready for action. The best place for this to happen is in the `onCreate` method because we know that will be called by Android just before the app is shown to the user. This code uses the `findViewById` method to associate each of our Java objects with a widget from our UI.

It does so by returning a reference to the object that is associated with the UI widget on the heap. It *knows* which one we are after because we use the appropriate `id` as an argument. For example, `... (R.id.btnAdd)` will return `Button` with the `ADD` text that we created in our layout.

As a reminder, we use the odd-looking `= (Button)` syntax because the method is polymorphic and could potentially return any object type that is a subclass of the `View` class. This is called **casting**.

Enter the following code just after the call to `setContentView` in the `onCreate` method:

```
// Get a reference to all the buttons in our UI
// Match them up to all our Button objects we declared earlier
btnAdd = (Button) findViewById(R.id.btnAdd);
btnTake = (Button) findViewById(R.id.btnTake);
txtValue = (TextView) findViewById(R.id.txtValue);
btnGrow = (Button) findViewById(R.id.btnGrow);
btnShrink = (Button) findViewById(R.id.btnShrink);
btnReset = (Button) findViewById(R.id.btnReset);
btnHide = (Button) findViewById(R.id.btnHide);
```

Now that we have a reference to all of our `Button` objects and `TextView`, we can start using their methods. In the code that follows, we use the `setOnClickListener` method on each of the `Button` references to make Android pass any clicks from the user onto our `onClick` method.

This works because when we implemented the `View.OnClickListener` interface, our `MainActivity` class effectively *became* an `OnClickListener`.

So, all we have to do is call `setOnClickListener` on each button in turn. As a reminder, the `this` argument is a reference to `MainActivity`. So, the method call says, "hey Android, I want an `OnClickListener` and I want it to be the `MainActivity` class". Android now knows which class to call `onClick` on. This next code wouldn't work if we hadn't implemented the interface first. Also, we must set up these listeners before the Activity starts, which is why we do it in `onCreate`.

We will add code to `onClick` to actually handle what happens soon.

Add this code after the previous code inside the `onCreate` method:

```
// Listen for all the button clicks
btnAdd.setOnClickListener(this);
btnTake.setOnClickListener(this);
txtValue.setOnClickListener(this);
btnGrow.setOnClickListener(this);
btnShrink.setOnClickListener(this);
btnReset.setOnClickListener(this);
btnHide.setOnClickListener(this);
```

Now, scroll down to the `onClick` method that Android Studio added for us after we implemented the `OnClickListener` interface. Add the `float size;` variable declaration and an empty switch block inside it so that it looks like this next code. The new code to be added is highlighted here:

```
public void onClick(View v)

    // A local variable to use later
    float size;

    switch(v.getId()){


    }
}
```

Remember that `switch` will check for `case` to match the condition inside the `switch` statement.

In the previous code, the `switch` condition is `v.getId()`. Let's step through and understand this. The `v` variable is a reference to an object of the type `View`, which was passed into the `onClick` method by Android:

```
public void onClick(View v)
```

`View` is the parent class for `Button`, `TextView`, and more. So, perhaps, as we might expect, calling `v.getId()` will return the ID property of the UI widget that has been clicked, the widget that triggered the call to `onClick` in the first place.

All we need to do then is provide a `case` statement (and appropriate action) for each of the `Button` references we want to respond to.

We will see that this next code has the first three `case` statements. They handle `R.id.btnAdd`, `R.id.btnTake`, and `R.id.btnReset`.

The code in the `R.id.btnAdd` case simply increments the `value` variable, and then it does something new. It calls the `setText` method on the `txtValue` object. Here is the argument `(""+ value)`. This argument uses an empty string and adds (concatenates) whatever value is stored in `value` to it. This has the effect of causing our `TextView` `txtValue` widget to display whatever value is stored in `value`.

The **TAKE** button (`R.id.btnTake`) does exactly the same, but subtracts `1` from `value` instead of adding `1`.

The third case statement handles the **RESET** button, sets `value` to `0`, and again updates the `text` property of `txtValue`.

Then, at the end of each `case`, there is a `break` statement. At this point, the `switch` block exits, the `onClick` method returns, and life returns to normal—until the user's next click.

Enter this code that we just discussed inside the `switch` block after the opening curly brace, {:

```
case R.id.btnAdd:
  value ++;
  txtValue.setText(""+ value);

  break;

case R.id.btnTake:
  value--;
  txtValue.setText(""+ value);

  break;

case R.id.btnReset:
  value = 0;
  txtValue.setText(""+ value);

  break;
```

The next two case statements handle the **SHRINK** and **GROW** buttons from our UI. We can confirm this from the `R.id.btnGrow` and `R.id.btnShrink` IDs. What is new and more interesting are the two new methods that are used.

The `getTextScaleX` method returns the horizontal scale of the text within the object it is used on. We can see that the object it is used on is our `TextView txtValue`. The `size =` at the start of the line of code assigns the returned value to our `float` variable, `size`.

The next line of code in each `case` statement changes the horizontal scale of the text using `setTextScaleX`. When the **GROW** button is pressed, the scale is set to `size + 1`, and when the **SHRINK** button is pressed, the scale is set to `size - 1`.

The overall effect is to allow these two buttons to grow and shrink the text in `txtValue` by a scale of `1` on each click.

Enter the next two `case` statements that we just discussed below the previous code:

```
case R.id.btnGrow:
  size = txtValue.getTextScaleX();
  txtValue.setTextScaleX(size + 1);

  break;

case R.id.btnShrink:
  size = txtValue.getTextScaleX();
  txtValue.setTextScaleX(size - 1);

  break;
```

In our last `case` statement, which we will code next, we have an `if-else` block. The condition takes a little bit of explaining. Here it goes.

The condition to be evaluated is `txtValue.getVisibility() == View.VISIBLE`. The first part of this condition before the `==` operator returns the `visibility` property of `txtValue TextView`. The return value will be one of the three possible constant values defined in the `View` class. They are `View.VISIBLE`, `View.INVISIBLE`, and `View.GONE`.

If `TextView` is visible to the user on the UI, the method returns `View.VISIBLE`, the condition is evaluated as `true`, and the `if` block is executed.

Inside the `if` block, we use the `setVisibility` method on `txtValue` and make it invisible to the user with the `View.INVISIBLE` argument.

In addition to this, we change the text on `btnHide` to `SHOW` using the `setText` method.

After the `if` block is executed, `txtValue` becomes invisible, and we have a button on our UI that says **SHOW**. When the user clicks on it in this state, the `if` statement will be `false` and the `else` block will be executed. In the `else` block, we reverse the situation. We set `txtValue` back to `View.VISIBLE` and the `text` property on `btnHide` back to `HIDE`.

If this is in anyway unclear, just enter the code, run the app, and revisit this last code and explanation once you have seen it in action:

```
case R.id.btnHide:
  if(txtValue.getVisibility() == View.VISIBLE)
  {
    // Currently visible so hide it
```

```
    txtValue.setVisibility(View.INVISIBLE);

    // Change text on the button
    btnHide.setText("SHOW");

}else{
    // Currently hidden so show it
    txtValue.setVisibility(View.VISIBLE);

    // Change text on the button
    btnHide.setText("HIDE");
}


    break;
```

We have the UI and the code in place, so it is time to run the app. Try out all the buttons. Note that the **ADD** and **TAKE** buttons change the value of `value` by 1 in either direction and then display the result in `TextView`. Also note that the **SHRINK** and **GROW** buttons decrease and increase the width of the text and **RESET** sets the `value` variable to `0` and displays it on `TextView`. Finally, the **HIDE** button not only hides `TextView`, but also changes its own text to **SHOW**, and it will indeed reshow `TextView` if it is tapped again.

Note that there was no need for `Log` or `Toast` in this app, as we are finally manipulating the UI using our Java code.

Inner and anonymous classes

Before we proceed to the next chapter and build apps with loads of different widgets, which will put into practice and reinforce everything you have learned in this chapter, we will have a very brief introduction to anonymous and inner classes.

When we implemented our Basic Classes demo app in the last chapter, we declared and implemented the class in a separate file to our `MainActivity` class. That file had to have the same name as the class.

We can also declare and implement classes within a class. The only question remaining, of course, is why would we do this? When we implement an inner class, the inner class can access the member variables of the enclosing class, and the enclosing class can access the members of the inner class. This often makes the structure of our code more straightforward. So, inner classes are sometimes the way to go.

In addition, we can also declare and implement an entire class within a method of one of our classes. When we do so, we use a slightly different syntax and do not use a name with the class. This is an **anonymous** class.

We will see both inner and anonymous classes in action throughout the rest of the book, and we will thoroughly discuss them when we use them.

FAQ

1. I don't get it all, and actually, I have more questions now than I had at the start of the chapter. What should I do?

    You know enough about OOP to make significant progress with Android and any other type of Java programming. If you are desperate to know more about OOP right now, there are plenty of highly rated books that discuss nothing but OOP. However, practice and familiarity with the syntax will go a long way to achieve the same thing and will probably be more fun. This is exactly what we will do for the rest of the book.

Summary

In this chapter, we finally had some real interaction between our code and our UI. It turns out that every time we add a widget to our UI, we are actually adding a Java object of a class that we can access with an appropriate reference in our Java code. All these objects are stored in a separate area of memory called the heap.

You are now in a position where you can learn about and do cool things with some of the more interesting widgets. We will look at loads of them in the next chapter, and then, we will keep introducing further new widgets throughout the rest of the book as well.

11
Widget Mania

Now that we have a really good overview of the layout and coding of an Android app, our newly acquired insight into object-oriented programming, and how we can manipulate a UI from our Java code, we are ready to experiment with more widgets from the palette.

OOP is tricky at times, but by gradually learning new concepts, practicing, and becoming familiar with them, over time, it will actually become our friend.

In this chapter, we will diversify a lot by going back to the Android Studio palette and looking around at half a dozen widgets that we have either not seen at all or have not used fully yet.

Once we have done so, we will put them all into a layout and practice manipulating them with Java code. In this chapter, we will:

- Refresh our memories on how to declare and initialize layout widgets
- Quickly see how to create widgets with just Java code
- Take a look at the `EditText`, `ImageView`, `RadioButton` (and `RadioGroup`), `Switch`, `CheckBox`, `WebView`, and `TextClock` widgets
- Learn how to use an anonymous class
- Make a widget demo mini app using all of the preceding widgets

Let's start with a quick recap.

Exploring Android UI objects

Let's power up Android Studio and get ready to dig a little deeper into the palette. While we are waiting for it to boot up, let's have a quick object recap, especially using objects from our UI layout.

Declaring and initializing objects

We know that when we call setContentView in the onCreate method, Android inflates all the widgets and layouts and turns them into *real* Java objects on the heap.

We know that to use a widget from the heap, we must first declare an object of the correct type and then use it to get a reference to the UI widget object on the heap using its unique id property. For example, we get a reference to TextView with an id property of txtTitle and assign it to a new object called myTextView like this:

```
// Grab a reference to an object on the heap
TextView myTextView = (TextView) findViewById(R.id.txtTitle);
```

Now, using our myTextView instance variable, we can do anything that the TextView class was designed to do. For example, we can set the text so that it is displayed like this:

```
myTextView.setText("Hi there");
```

We can make it disappear like this:

```
// Bye bye
myTextView.setVisibility(View.GONE)
```

We can change its text again and make it reappear:

```
myTextView.setText("BOO!");

// Surprise
myTextView.setVisibility(View.VISIBLE)
```

It is worth mentioning that we can manipulate any property in Java that we set using XML in the previous chapters. Furthermore, we have hinted at, but not actually seen, that we can create widgets from nothing using just Java code.

Widget news flash

We can also create widgets from Java objects that are not a reference to an object in our layout. We can declare, instantiate, and set a widget's properties, all in code, like this:

```
Button myButton = new Button();
```

The preceding code creates a new button using new(). The only caveat is that Button has to be part of a layout before it can be shown. So, we could either get a reference to a layout element from our XML layout or create a new one in code.

If we assume that we have `LinearLayout` in our XML layout with an `id` property equal to `linearLayout1`, we could put our button from the previous line of code into it, like this:

```
// Get a reference to the LinearLayout
LinearLayout linearLayout = (LinearLayout) findViewById
  (R.id.linearLayout1);

// Add our Button to it
linearLayout.addView(myButton)
```

We could even create an entire layout in pure Java code by first creating a new layout, then all the widgets that we want to add, and finally by calling `setContentView` on the layout that contains our widgets. In this next code, we create a layout just in Java, albeit a very simple one with a single `Button` widget inside `LinearLayout`:

```
// Create a new LinearLayout
LinearLayout linearLayout = new LinearLayout();

// Create a new Button
Button myButton = new Button();

// Add myButton to the LinearLayout
linearLayout.addView(myButton);

// Make the LinearLayout the main view
setContentView(linearLayout);
```

It is probably obvious, but well worth pointing out as well, that designing a detailed and nuanced layout in Java only is significantly more awkward, harder to visualize, and not the way it is most commonly done. There are times, however, when we will find it useful to do things in this way.

We are getting quite advanced now with layouts and widgets. It is plain to see, however, that there is a whole bunch of other widgets (and UI elements) from the palette that we have not explored yet. So, let's do that.

Exploring the palette

Let's take a whirlwind tour of some of the previously unexplored items from the palette, and then we can drag a bunch of them onto a layout and see some of the methods they have that might be useful. We can then implement a mini project to put them all to use.

We have already explored `Button` and `TextView` in the last chapter. Let's take a closer look at a few more widgets.

EditText

The `EditText` widget does what its name suggests. If we make `EditText` available to our users, they will indeed be able to *edit* the *text* in it. We saw this in *Chapter 5 Real-World Layouts*, when we were designing a sign-up form. What we didn't see was how to capture the information from within it or where we would put this text-capturing code.

The next block of code assumes that we have declared an object of the `EditText` type and used it to get a reference to `EditText` in our XML layout. We might write code like the following for a button click, perhaps a submit button for a form, but it could also go anywhere we deem it necessary for our app:

```
String editTextContents = editText.getText()
// editTextContents now contains whatever the user entered
```

We will see this in a real context in the next mini app.

ImageView

We have already put an image onto our layout a couple of times so far, but we have never got a reference to image from our Java code or done anything with it before. The process is exactly the same. Follow the next steps to get a reference to `ImageView` as you would to any other widget:

1. Declare an object
2. Get a reference using the `findViewById` method and a valid `id` property like this:

```
ImageView imageView = (ImageView)
   findViewById(R.id.imageView);
```

Then, we can go on to do some neat things with our image using code like this:

```
// Make the image 50% TRANSPARENT
imageView.setAlpha(.5f);
```

 The odd-looking `f` term simply lets the compiler know that the widget's value is of the type `float`, as required by the `setAlpha` method.

In the preceding code, we used the setAlpha method on imageView. The setAlpha method takes a value between 0 and 1. Completely see-through is 0 and no transparency at all is 1.

 There is also an overloaded setAlpha method that takes an int value from 0 (completely see-through to 255, with no transparency). We can choose whichever value is the most appropriate at the time. If you want a reminder about method overloading, refer to *Chapter 8, Coding in Java Part 2 – Methods*.

We will use some of the ImageView methods in our next mini app.

Radio button and group

RadioButton is used when there are two or more mutually exclusive options for the user to choose from. That is, if you choose one, the other choices cannot be chosen, such as an old-fashioned radio. Take a look at a simple radiogroup with a few RadioButton options in this next image:

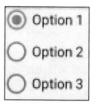

As the user selects an option, the other options will automatically be deselected. We control RadioButton widgets by placing them within RadioGroup in our UI layout. We can, of course, use the visual designer to simply drag a bunch of RadioButtons onto RadioGroup. When we do so, the XML layout looks something like this:

```
<RadioGroup
    android:layout_width="match_parent"
    android:layout_height="match_parent"
    android:layout_alignParentTop="true"
    android:layout_alignParentLeft="true"
    android:layout_alignParentStart="true"
    android:id="@+id/radioGroup">

    <RadioButton
        android:layout_width="wrap_content"
        android:layout_height="wrap_content"
        android:text="Option 1"
```

```
     android:id="@+id/radioButton1"
     android:checked="true" />

  <RadioButton
     android:layout_width="wrap_content"
     android:layout_height="wrap_content"
     android:text="Option 2"
     android:id="@+id/radioButton2"
     android:checked="false" />

  <RadioButton
     android:layout_width="wrap_content"
     android:layout_height="wrap_content"
     android:text="Option 3"
     android:id="@+id/radioButton3"
     android:checked="false" />


  <RadioGroup/>
```

Note that in the previous code, each radio button and radiogroup has an appropriate id property set. We can then get a reference to them, as we might expect, as follows:

```
// Get a reference to all our widgets
RadioGroup radioGroup = (RadioGroup) findViewById(R.id.radioGroup);
RadioButton rb1 = (RadioButton) findViewById(R.id.radioButton1);
RadioButton rb2 = (RadioButton) findViewById(R.id.radioButton2);
RadioButton rbnew3 = (RadioButton) findViewById(R.id.radioButton3);
```

In practice, however, as we will see, we can manage just about everything from the RadioGroup reference alone.

You might be thinking, how do we know when they have been clicked on? Or you may think that keeping track of which one is selected might be awkward. For this, we need some help from the Android API and Java.

Anonymous classes

In the last chapter, we briefly introduced anonymous classes. Here, you will learn a little more about them and see how they can help us. When RadioButton is part of RadioGroup, the visual appearance of all of them is coordinated for us. All we need to do is react when any given radio button is pressed. Of course, as with any other button, we need to know when they have been clicked on.

RadioButton behaves differently than a regular Button, and simply listening for clicks in onClick (after implementing OnClickListener) will not work because RadioButton is not designed that way.

What we need to do is use another Java feature. We need to implement a class, an anonymous class, for the sole purpose of listening for clicks on RadioGroup. The next block of code assumes that we have a reference to RadioGroup called radioGroup:

```
radioGroup.setOnCheckedChangeListener(
   new RadioGroup.OnCheckedChangeListener() {

   @Override
   public void onCheckedChanged(RadioGroup group, int checkedId) {

      // Handle clicks here
   }
   }
);
```

In the preceding code, specifically RadioGroup.OnCheckedChangedListener line from its opening curly brace, {, to the closing curly brace, }, is what is known as an **anonymous** class because it has no name. The actual class code does not run when onCreate is called; it simply prepares the class to handle any clicks on the radiogroup. We will now discuss this in more detail.

> This class is technically known as an **anonymous inner** class because it is inside another class. Inner classes can be anonymous or have names. We will see an inner class with a name in *Chapter 13*, *Handling and Displaying Arrays of Data*.

I remember the first time I saw an anonymous class, and it almost made me want to hide in a cupboard, but it is not as complex as it might look at first.

What the code does is add a listener to radioGroup. This will have very much the same effect as when we implemented View.OnClickListener in *Chapter 10*, *Everything's a Class*; only this time, we are declaring and instantiating a listener class and preparing it to listen to radioGroup while simultaneously overriding the required method, which in this case is onCheckedChanged. This is like the RadioGroup equivalent of onClick.

Let's walk through it. First, we will call the setOnCheckedChangeListener method on our radioGroup class:

```
radioGroup.setOnCheckedChangeListener(
```

We pass in a new anonymous class and the details of its overridden method as the argument:

```
new RadioGroup.OnCheckedChangeListener() {

  @Override
  public void onCheckedChanged(RadioGroup group, int checkedId) {

    // Handle clicks here
  }
}
```

Finally, we have the closing parenthesis of the method and, of course, the semicolon to mark the end of the line. The only reason we present it on multiple lines is to make it more readable. As far as the compiler cares, it could all be lumped together:

```
);
```

If we use the preceding code to create and instantiate a class that listens for clicks to our RadioGroup class, perhaps in the onCreate method, this method will listen and respond for the entire life of the Activity. All you need to learn now is how to handle the clicks in the onCheckedChanged method that we overrode.

Note that one of the parameters of the method that is passed in when radiogroup is pressed is int checkedId. This holds the ID of the currently selected radio button. This is just what we need — almost.

It might be surprising to you that checkedId is int. Android stores all IDs as int even though we declare them with alphanumeric characters, such as radioButton1 or radioGroup. All our human-friendly names are converted to int when the app is compiled. So, how do we know which int element refers to an ID such as radioButton1, or radioButton2, and so on?

What we need to do is get a reference to the actual object that checkedId is referring to. We would do so like this:

```
RadioButton rb = (RadioButton) group.findViewById(checkedId);
```

Now, we can retrieve the familiar ID that we use for the currently selected radio button, for which we now have a reference stored in rb. We do so with the getId method, like this:

```
rb.getId();
```

We could therefore handle `RadioButton` clicks using a `switch` block with `case` for each possible `RadioButton` that could be pressed, and the `rb.getId()` method as the switch block's expression. This next code shows all the contents of the `onCheckedChanged` method that we discussed:

```
// Get a reference to the RadioButton that is currently checked
RadioButton rb = (RadioButton) group.findViewById(checkedId);

// Switch based on the 'friendly' id
switch (rb.getId()) {

  case R.id.radioButton1:
    // Do something here
    break;

  case R.id.radioButton2:
    // Do something here
    break;


  case R.id.radioButton3:
    // Do something here
    break;


}
// End switch block
```

Seeing this block in action in the next working mini app where we can press the buttons for real will make this clearer.

A switch widget

The `Switch` (not to be confused with the lowercase Java keyword, `switch`) widget is just like a `Button` widget, except that it has two possible states that can be read and responded to. An obvious use for the `Switch` widget would be to show and hide something. Remember in our *Java meet UI* app in *Chapter 10, Everything's a Class*, we used a button to show and hide `TextView`. Each time we hid/showed `TextView`, we changed the `Text` property on `Button` to make it plain what would happen if it was clicked again. What might have been more logical for the user and more straightforward for us as programmers would have been to use `Switch`, as pictured in the next figure:

The next code assumes that we already have an object called `mySwitch` with a reference to a `Switch` object in the layout. We could show and hide `TextView` just like we did in our *Java Meet UI* app in *Chapter 10, Everything's a Class*. To listen to and respond to clicks, we again use an anonymous class. This time, however, we use the `CompoundButton` version of `OnCheckedChangeListener` instead of `RadioGroup`.

We need to override the `onCheckedChanged` method, and this method has a Boolean parameter, `isChecked`. The `isChecked` variable simply is false for off and true for on.

Here is how we could more intuitively replace this text hiding/showing code:

```
mySwitch.setOnCheckedChangeListener(
  new CompoundButton.OnCheckedChangeListener() {

    public void onCheckedChanged(
      CompoundButton buttonView, boolean isChecked) {

        if(isChecked){
          // Currently visible so hide it
          txtValue.setVisibility(View.INVISIBLE);

        }else{
          // Currently hidden so show it
          txtValue.setVisibility(View. VISIBLE);
        }
    }
  }
);
```

If the anonymous class code still looks a little odd, don't worry because it will get more familiar the more we use it. And we will do so again now when we look at `CheckBox`.

CheckBox

We used `CheckBox` in our form layout in *Chapter 5, Real-World Layouts*. As with `EditText`, however, we didn't explore how to actually get data from it. With `CheckBox`, we simply detect its state (checked or unchecked) at a given moment, perhaps, when a form's submit button is clicked. This next code gives us a glimpse of how this might happen, again, using an inner class that acts as a listener:

```
myCheckBox.setOnCheckedChangeListener(
    new CompoundButton.OnCheckedChangeListener() {

    public void onCheckedChanged(
```

```
        CompoundButton buttonView, boolean isChecked) {

      if (myCheckBox.isChecked()) {
        // It's checked so do something
      } else {
        // It's not checked do something else
      }

    }
  }
);
```

In the previous code, we assume that myCheckBox has been declared and initialized, and we then use exactly the same type of anonymous class as we did for Switch to detect and respond to clicks.

WebView

This widget can be used as a container for an entire app. We can put the code for complete web pages in our res folder and then manipulate these pages using the JavaScript language from within our apps. It is quite common for an entire app's functionality to be contained within web pages, to just have the Android app present it, and perhaps add a bit of extra functionality via WebView.

Apps that do this, however, rarely achieve the same level of professional look and feel that a true native Android app has because the UI features you are learning about in this book are far more powerful and flexible than those that can be achieved through regular web programming.

We can also use WebView in an app to show the user a web page, but in a way that they don't have to leave our app to open a web browser. This code loads Google in WebView:

```
WebView webView = (WebView) findViewById(R.id.webView);
webView.loadUrl("http://google.com");
```

As usual, the previous Java code assumes that we have a WebView widget in our layout XML with its id property set to webView.

When we use this widget, we need to let the user know that the app will be accessing the Internet and ask for their permission at the time they install the app. We do so by adding the following line to the AndroidManifest.xml file:

```
<uses-permission android:name="android.
  permission.INTERNET"></uses-permission>
```

We will do this for real in the next mini app.

Date & Time

Android devices typically have clocks and calendars. Sometimes, however, we might want to show a clock or have the user pick a date in our app. From the palette, we can select a whole range of useful date and time widgets. Widgets with a strikethrough are deprecated and are generally no longer used:

In our next app, we will use the TextClock widget to show you some of its features.

With all this new information, let's make an app to use the Android widgets more deeply than what we have so far. We will take a quick detour, however, to talk about Android permissions, especially with regard to the latest version of (at the time of writing this) Marshmallow.

Android permissions and Marshmallows

When our apps want to do something that has the potential to cause harm to a user's device or perhaps the user's privacy, Android requires us to deal with it in a specific way, usually by having our app ask permission from the user before we do certain things.

With the introduction of Android Marshmallow at the end of 2015, the way that we had to handle things changed—but only for the new Marshmallow devices.

The current situation, therefore, is that we need to deal with two possible situations: Marshmallow and pre-Marshmallow.

Pre-Marshmallow permissions

Before Marshmallow, if we wanted our app to do something that could potentially cause harm, such as connect to the Internet (our next app will do this), get a GPS location, take pictures, access the address book, and much more, we needed to add a line of code to the AndroidManifest.xml file.

Then, when users install our app from Google Play, a little pop-up warning appears letting them know exactly what potentially harmful operations our app wants to do. Users have to agree that they trust our app or the installation would be aborted.

How this works is outlined in the next steps:

1. We want to add the potentially harmful feature x.

2. We add a permission for the feature x to `AndroidManifest.xml`.

3. The user downloads the app from Google Play and is warned that our app uses the feature x.

4. The user decides whether to let our app use the feature x. If the user does, the app is installed; if the user doesn't, it is not.

 No need for us as developers or the user to ever consider the permission again

But then Marshmallow came along and changed it all.

Marshmallow permissions

Marshmallow does not ask for permissions at the time the app is installed. It asks for permissions when the specific feature that requires the permission is about to be used. This can be considered a good thing or a bad thing for the user, depending on your opinion.

One potential upside is that users can install an app with, for example, two permissions: the permission to access their address book and the permission to make phone calls. This hypothetical example might be an address book app that lets the users add contacts and tap a contact to call them.

With Marshmallow, users will be able to grant a permission to one of the features, for example, access to the address book to allow them to manage their contacts. They could decline the permission to allow the app to make phone calls and be confident that the app will never be responsible for a big phone bill. With the pre-Marshmallow permissions, it is all or nothing.

One downside is that users will more easily install apps that contain features they might not approve of, and not realize until they have wasted some time and potentially missed the 15-minute refund window that Google Play offers. However, I am sure that Google only had user security in mind when they devised this system.

What this means to us as developers is that we will need to not only add permissions to the `AndroidManifest.xml` file for pre-Marshmallow devices, but we will also need to add code in all the right places to handle the Marshmallow permissions at runtime.

The situation is further complicated by the fact that Marshmallow considers some permissions as *dangerous* and others as *normal*. This will add significant complexity to our code.

The permission solution used in this book

It was considered very carefully before starting this book that the amount of coverage that would be necessary to use Marshmallow runtime permissions in the projects of this book would cloud the other learning objectives and provide little immediate benefit to readers who are developers or to our future users. This is especially true as it is unlikely that Marshmallow ownership will reach even 10 percent market share before a new edition of this book is required. In addition to this, there is a very simple workaround to make all our apps compatible with Marshmallow and pre-Marshmallow permissions, and we will see this when we build our first app with a dangerous permission in *Chapter 21, Navigation Drawer and Where It's Snap.*

Now that we have considered permissions, let's build our widget demo app that requires the `android.permission.INTERNET` permission. This is considered a normal permission, so it doesn't require any special handling for Marshmallow devices.

The Widget exploration mini app

We just talked about seven widgets. The `EditText`, `ImageView`, `RadioButton` (and `RadioGroup`), `Switch`, `CheckBox`, `WebView`, and `TextClock` widgets. Let's make a mini app and do something real with each of them. We will also use `Button` as well.

Setting up the widget exploration project and UI

First, we will set up a new project and prepare the UI layout. These quick steps will get all the widgets on the screen and set the `id` properties, ready to grab a reference to them. It will help us to take a look at the target app (as shown in this next figure), which is up and running, before we get started:

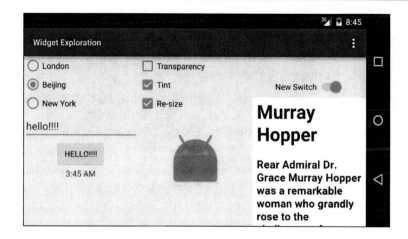

Here is how this app will demonstrate these new widgets:

- The radio buttons will allow the user to change the time displayed on the clock with a choice of three time zones

- The button on the left side, when clicked, will change its text to whatever is currently in the EditText widget

- The three checkboxes will add and remove visual effects from the Android robot image

- Switch will turn on and off WebView, which displays information about an eminent computer scientist

The exact layout positions are not essential, but the id properties specified must match with each other exactly. If you just want to see/use the code, you can find all the files in the Chapter 11/Widget Exploration folder of the download bundle.

1. Create a new project called Widget Exploration, set the **Minimum API** to 17, use a blank Activity and keep all the other settings at their default values. We are using API 17 because one of the features of the TextClock widget requires us to.

2. Let's create a new layout file as we want our new layout to be based on LinearLayout. Right-click on the layout folder in the project explorer and select **Layout resource file** under **New** from the pop-up menu.

3. In the **New resource file** window, enter exploration_layout.xml in the **File name** field and LinearLayout in the **Root element** field. Now, click on **OK**.

4. In the properties window, change the `orientation` property of `LinearLayout` to **horizontal**.

5. Using the drop-down controls above the design view, make sure that you have **Nexus 5** selected in the **Landscape** view.

6. We can now begin to create our layout. Drag and drop three **RelativeLayout** layouts onto the design to create three vertical divisions of our design. Set the **weight** property of each `RelativeLayout` layout in turn to `.33`. We now have three equal vertical divisions just like in the previous figure.

7. Drag **Switch** and then **WebView** from the palette to the right-hand side of `RelativeLayout`. The right-hand side of our layout should now look like as the previous figure.

8. Drag three **CheckBox** widgets, one above the other, and then drag **ImageView** below them onto the central `RelativeLayout` layout. The central column should now look like it does in the previous figure, except that we can't see `ImageView` until we put an appropriate value in its `src` property. We will do this in a few steps' time.

9. Drag **RadioGroup** to the left-hand side of `RelativeLayout` and add three **RadioButton** widgets within **RadioGroup**.

10. Under **RadioGroup**, drag a **PlainText** widget from the **TextFields** category of the palette. Add a **Button** widget to the right-hand side of the **PlainText** widget. Add **TextClock** from the palette to the bottom half of the left-hand side of `RelativeLayout`. You will get a warning about the API level. We can ignore this because we will be running this on an up-to-date Nexus 5 emulator.

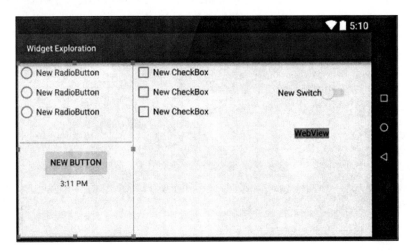

11. Try and tweak your layout so that it resembles the previous image as much as possible. Note that **ImageView** is invisible until we add an actual image to it.

12. Now, add the following properties shown in the following table to the widgets that we just laid out:

Widget Type	Property	Value to set to
RadioGroup	id	radioGroup
RadioButton (top)	id	radioButtonLondon
RadioButton (top)	text	London
RadioButton (top)	checked	true
RadioButton (middle)	id	radioButtonBeijing
RadioButton (middle)	text	Beijing
RadioButton (bottom)	id	radioButtonNewYork
RadioButton (bottom)	text	New York
EditText	id	editText
Button	id	button
TextClock	id	textClock
CheckBox (top)	text	Transparency
CheckBox (top)	id	checkBoxTransparency
CheckBox (middle)	text	Tint
CheckBox (middle)	id	checkBoxTint
CheckBox (bottom)	text	Re-Size
CheckBox (bottom)	id	checkBoxReSize
ImageView	src	@mipmap/ic_launcher
ImageView	id	imageView
Switch	id	switch1
Switch	enabled	true
Switch	clickable	true
WebView	id	webView

We just laid out and set the required properties for our layout. There is nothing that we haven't done before, except that some of the widget types are new to us.

Now, we can get on with using all these widgets in our Java code.

Coding the widget exploration app

As we have `WebView` that will connect to the Internet (to show a web page), we need the user's permission as well. So, we need to add a line to the `AndroidManifest.xml` file. Open it up from the **manifests** folder in the project explorer.

Now, add the following line of code that is highlighted in the position indicated by the highlighted line's context:

```
. . .
<uses-permission android:name="android.permission.INTERNET" />
    <application
        android:allowBackup="true"
. . .
```

Now, let's make sure that our new layout is displayed by changing the call to `setContentView` in `onCreate` so that it looks like this:

```
setContentView(R.layout.exploration_layout);
```

This next block of code looks quite long and sprawling, but all we have done is get a reference to each of the widgets in our layout. When we come to use them, we will discuss the code in more detail.

The only thing that is new in this next block of code is that some of the objects are declared as `final`. This is required as they are going to be used within an anonymous class.

But doesn't final mean that the object can't be changed?

If you remember, back in *Chapter 9*, *Object-Oriented Programming*, we saw that variables declared as final cannot be changed, they are constant. So, how are we going to change the properties of these objects? Remember that objects are reference-type variables. That is, they refer to an object on the heap. They are not an object themselves. We can think of them as holding an address of an object. It is the address that cannot change. We can still use the address to reference the object on the heap and change the actual object as much as we like.

Enter this code just after the call to `setContentView` in the `onCreate` method:

```
// Get a reference to all our widgets

RadioGroup radioGroup = (RadioGroup) findViewById(R.id.radioGroup);
RadioButton rbBeijing = (RadioButton) findViewById
  (R.id.radioButtonBeijing);
```

```
RadioButton rbLondon = (RadioButton) findViewById
  (R.id.radioButtonLondon);
RadioButton rbNewYork = (RadioButton) findViewById
  (R.id.radioButtonNewYork);
final EditText editText = (EditText) findViewById(R.id.editText);
final Button button = (Button) findViewById(R.id.button);
final TextClock tClock = (TextClock) findViewById(R.id.textClock);
final CheckBox cbTransparency = (CheckBox) findViewById
  (R.id.checkBoxTransparency);
final CheckBox cbTint = (CheckBox) findViewById(R.id.checkBoxTint);
final CheckBox cbReSize = (CheckBox) findViewById
  (R.id.checkBoxReSize);

final ImageView imageView = (ImageView) findViewById(R.id.imageView);

Switch switch1 = (Switch) findViewById(R.id.switch1);
final WebView webView = (WebView) findViewById(R.id.webView);
```

Now we can create an anonymous class to listen for and handle clicks on the checkboxes. Each of the next three blocks of code implement an anonymous class for each of the checkboxes in turn. What is different in each of the next three blocks of code, however, is the way in which we respond to a click, and we will discuss each of them in turn.

The first checkbox is labeled **Transparency**, and we use the `setAlpha` method on `imageView` to change how transparent (see-through) it is. The `setAlpha` method takes a floating point value between 0 and 1 as an argument. Here, 0 is invisible and 1 is no transparency at all. So, when this checkbox is checked, we set the alpha to `.1`, so the image is barely visible, and when it is unchecked, we set it to `1`, which is completely visible with no transparency. The `boolean isChecked` parameter of `onCheckedChanged` contains true or false as to whether the checkbox is checked or not.

Add this code after the previous block of code in `onCreate`:

```
/*
  Now we need to listen for clicks
  on the button, the CheckBoxes
  and the RadioButtons
*/

// First the check boxes using an anonymous class
```

```
cbTransparency.setOnCheckedChangeListener(new CompoundButton.
OnCheckedChangeListener()
{
  public void onCheckedChanged(CompoundButton buttonView,
    boolean isChecked)
  {
    if(cbTransparency.isChecked()){
      // Set some transparency
      imageView.setAlpha(.1f);
    }else{
      imageView.setAlpha(1f);
    }


  }
});
```

In the next anonymous class, we handle the checkbox labeled as **Tint**. In the
onCheckedChanged method, we use the setColorFilter method on imageView to
overlay a color layer on the image. When isChecked is true, we layer a color, and
when isChecked is false, we remove it.

The setColorFilter method takes a color in the **alpha, red, green, and blue
(ARGB)** format as an argument. The color is provided by the argb static method of
the Color class. The four arguments of the argb method are, as you might expect,
values for alpha, red, green, and blue. These four values create a color. In our case,
the 150, 255, 0, 0 values creates a strong red tint. And the 0, 0, 0, 0 values
creates no tint at all.

 To understand more about the Color class, check out the Android
developer site at http://developer.android.com/reference/
android/graphics/Color.html, and to understand the RGB
color system more, take a look at the Wikipedia website https://
en.wikipedia.org/wiki/RGB_color_model.

Add this code after the previous block of code in onCreate:

```
// Now the next checkbox
cbTint.setOnCheckedChangeListener(new CompoundButton.
  OnCheckedChangeListener() {
  public void onCheckedChanged(CompoundButton buttonView, boolean
    isChecked) {
    if (cbTint.isChecked()) {
      // Checked so set some tint
      imageView.setColorFilter(Color.argb(150, 255, 0, 0));
    } else {
```

```
      // No tint required
      imageView.setColorFilter(Color.argb(0, 0, 0, 0));
   }


  }
});
```

In the anonymous class that handles the **Resize** labeled checkbox, we use the setScaleX method to resize the robot image. When we call setScaleX(2) and setScaleY(2) on imageView, we will double the size of the image, and setScaleX(1) and setScaleY(1) will return it to normal.

Add this code after the previous block of code in onCreate:

```
// And the last check box
cbReSize.setOnCheckedChangeListener
   (new CompoundButton.OnCheckedChangeListener() {
     public void onCheckedChanged(CompoundButton buttonView,
        boolean isChecked) {
       if (cbReSize.isChecked()) {
         // It's checked so make bigger
         imageView.setScaleX(2);
         imageView.setScaleY(2);
       } else {
         // It's not checked make regular size
         imageView.setScaleX(1);
         imageView.setScaleY(1);
       }
     }
});
```

Now we will handle the three radio buttons. As they are part of RadioGroup, we can handle them much more succinctly than we did the CheckBox objects. Here is how we do it.

First, we make sure that they are clear to start with by calling clearCheck() on radioGroup. Then, we create our anonymous class of the OnCheckedChangedListener type and override the onCheckedChanged method.

This method will be called when any radio button from RadioGroup is clicked. All we need to do is get the id of the RadioButton widget that was clicked on and respond accordingly using a switch statement with the three possible cases, one for each RadioButton widget.

Remember when we first talked about `RadioButton` that the ID supplied in the `checkedId` parameter of `onCheckedChanged` is `int`? This is why we must first create a new `RadioButton` object from `checkedId`:

```
RadioButton rb = (RadioButton) group.findViewById(checkedId);
```

Then, we can call `getId` on the new `RadioButton` widget as the condition for `switch`:

```
switch (rb.getId())
```

Then, in each `case`, we use the `setTimeZone` method with the appropriate Android time zone code as an argument.

 You can see all the Android time zone codes here at `https://gist.github.com/arpit/1035596`.

Add this next code that incorporates everything we just discussed and includes the previous two lines of code. Add it in `onCreate` after the last code that we entered to handle the checkboxes:

```
// Now for the radio buttons
// Uncheck all buttons
radioGroup.clearCheck();

radioGroup.setOnCheckedChangeListener(new RadioGroup.
  OnCheckedChangeListener() {
  @Override
  public void onCheckedChanged(RadioGroup group, int checkedId) {

  RadioButton rb = (RadioButton) group.findViewById
    (checkedId);

    switch (rb.getId()) {

    case R.id.radioButtonLondon:
      tClock.setTimeZone("Europe/London");
      break;

      case R.id.radioButtonBeijing:
      tClock.setTimeZone("CST6CDT");
      break;

    case R.id.radioButtonNewYork:
      tClock.setTimeZone("America/New_York");
```

```
        break;




    }// End switch block
  }
});
```

Now it's time for something a little bit new. In this next block of code, we use an anonymous class to handle the clicks on a regular button. We've called `button.setOnclickListener` as we have before. This time, however, instead of passing `this` as an argument, we've created a brand new class of the `View.OnClickListener` type and overridden `onClick` as the argument, just like we did with our other anonymous classes.

 This method is probably preferable in this situation because there is only one button. If we had lots of buttons, then having `MainActivity` implement `View.OnClickListener` and then overriding `onClick` to handle all clicks in one method would probably be preferable, as we did previously.

In the `onClick` method, we use `setText` to set the `text` property on `button` and the `getText` method of `editText` to get whatever text is currently in the `EditText` widget.

Add this code after the previous block of code in `onCreate`:

```
/*
    Let's listen for clicks on our regular Button.
    We can do this with an anonymous class as well.

*/

button.setOnClickListener(new View.OnClickListener() {
  @Override
  public void onClick(View v) {
    // We only handle one button
    // So no switching required
    button.setText(editText.getText());
  }
});
```

In the next block of code, we use the `loadUrl` method to load up a web page into `webView`:

Next, we will create yet another anonymous class to listen for and handle the changes made to our Switch widget.

When the isChecked variable is true, we show webView, and when it is false, we hide it.

Add this code after the previous block of code in onCreate:

```
// Make the webview display a page
webView.loadUrl("http://www.cs.yale.edu/homes/tap/Files/hopper-story.
  html");

webView.setVisibility(View.INVISIBLE);

switch1.setOnCheckedChangeListener(new CompoundButton.
  OnCheckedChangeListener() {
  public void onCheckedChanged(CompoundButton buttonView,
    boolean isChecked) {
    if(isChecked){
      webView.setVisibility(View.VISIBLE);
    }else{
        webView.setVisibility(View.INVISIBLE);
      }
    }
});
```

Now, we can run our app and try out all the features. The Android emulators can be rotated into the landscape mode by pressing the *Ctrl + F11* keyboard combination on PC or *Ctrl + fn + F11* on Mac.

At the time of writing this, the emulators seem to crash when their orientation is changed using *Ctrl + F11*. So if you have any trouble getting your emulator displayed in the landscape mode, just reconfigure it to startup in the landscape mode. You can do this by clicking on the AVD icon from the toolbar, then clicking on the edit (pencil icon) next to the **Nexus 5** AVD, and selecting **Landscape**. Click on **Finish** and you're ready to run the app.

Try checking the radio buttons to see the time zone change on the clock. Enter different values into `EditText` and then click on the button to see it grab the text and display it on itself.

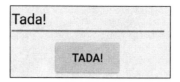

Change what the image looks like with different combinations of checked and unchecked checkboxes and hide and show the web page using the switch widget.

Let's move on to look at another way in which we can significantly enhance our UIs.

Summary

In this chapter, we explored a plethora of widgets, saw how to implement widgets in Java code without any XML layout, used our first anonymous classes to handle clicks on a widget, and put all our new widget prowess into a mini app.

In the next chapter, we will see a totally new UI element that we can't just drag and drop from the palette, but we will still have plenty of help from the Android API. Next up are dialog boxes. We will also make a start on our most significant app so far—the Note To Self, memo, to-do, and personal note app.

12
Having a Dialogue with the User

In this chapter, we will see how to present a user with a pop-up dialog window. We can then put all we know into the first phase of our first app, Note To Self. You will learn about new Android and Java features in this chapter and the next five chapters as well, and we will use your newly acquired knowledge to enhance the Note To Self app each time.

In each chapter, we will also build a selection of mini apps that are separate from this main app. So, this chapter holds the following in store for you:

- How to implement a simple app with a pop-up dialog box
- How to add `DialogFragments` to start the Note To Self app
- How to add resources such as Strings and graphics to a project
- How to use Android naming conventions for the first time to make our code more readable
- How to implement more complex dialog boxes to capture input from the user

Let's get started.

Dialog windows

Often, we will want to show the user some information or perhaps ask for confirmation of an action in a pop-up window. This is known as a **dialog** window. If you quickly scan the palette, you might be surprised to see no mention of dialogs whatsoever.

Dialogs in Android are more advanced than a simple widget or even a layout. They are classes that can contain layouts and widgets of their own.

The best way to create a dialog window in Android is to use the `Fragment` class. Fragments are a wide and vital topic in Android, and we will spend much of the second half of this book exploring and using them.

Creating a neat pop-up dialog for our user to interact with, however, is a great introduction to fragments and not too complicated at all.

The dialog demo mini project – introducing chaining

We previously mentioned that the best way to create a dialog in Android is with the `Fragment` class. In Android, there is another way to create dialogs that is arguably a little bit simpler. The problem with this slightly simpler `Dialog` class is that it is not as well supported in the Activity lifecycle. It is even possible that `Dialog` could accidentally crash the app.

If you were writing an app with one fixed orientation layout that required one simple pop-up dialog, it could be argued that the simpler `Dialog` class should be used. However, as we are aiming to build modern, professional apps with advanced features, we will benefit from ignoring this class. More specifically, we will be using the `DialogFragment` class.

To start the mini project, create a new blank project in Android Studio and call it `Dialog Demo`. As you have come to expect, the completed code for this project is in the `Chapter 12/Dialog Demo` folder of the download bundle.

Create a new class by right-clicking on the folder with the name of your package that contains the `MainActivity.java` file. Select **Java class** under **New** and name it `MyDialog`. Click on **OK** to create the class.

The first thing to do is to change the class declaration in order to extend `DialogFragment`. When you have done so, your new class will look like this:

```
public class MyDialog extends DialogFragment {

    ...
}
```

Now, let's add code to this class, a bit at a time, and see what is happening at each step.

First, we override the onCreateDialog method that will be called when we later show the dialog window via code from MainActivity.

Then, inside the onCreateDialog method, we get our hands on a new class. We declare and initialize an object of the AlertDialog.Builder type that needs a reference to MainActivity that is passed in its constructor. This is why we use getActivity() as the argument. The getActivity method is part of the Fragment class (and therefore, DialogFragment too), and it returns a reference to the Activity that created DialogFragment. In this case, it is our MainActivity class. Add this code to get the builder reference variable ready for use, and then we will see what we can do with it:

```
@Override
    public Dialog onCreateDialog(Bundle savedInstanceState) {

    // Use the Builder class because this dialog has a simple UI
    AlertDialog.Builder builder =
     new AlertDialog.Builder(getActivity());
```

Now, we can use our builder object to do the rest of the work. There is something slightly odd in the next three blocks of code. If you quickly scan the next three blocks, you will note that there is a distinct lack of semicolons, ;. This indicates that these three blocks of code are in fact just one line to the compiler.

What is going on here is something that we have actually seen before in a less pronounced situation. When we create a Toast message and we add a .show() method to the end of it, we are **chaining**, that is, we are calling more than one method, in sequence, on the same object. This is equivalent to writing multiple lines of code; it is just clearer and shorter this way.

In the first of the three blocks that uses chaining, we call builder.setMessage that sets the main message the user will see in the dialog box. Note also that it is fine to have comments in between parts of the chained method calls, as these are ignored entirely by the compiler.

Then, we add a button to our dialog with the .setPositiveButton method, and the first argument sets the text on it to OK. The second argument is an anonymous DialogInterface.OnClickListener class that handles clicks on the button. Note that we are not going to add any code to the onClick method.

Add this code, without any semicolons, of course:

```
// Dialog will have "Make a selection" as the title

builder.setMessage("Make a selection")
```

```
   // An OK button that does nothing

   .setPositiveButton("OK", new DialogInterface.OnClickListener() {

     public void onClick(DialogInterface dialog, int id) {

       // Nothing happening here
     }
   })
```

Next, we call yet another method on the same `builder` object. This time, it's the `setNegativeButton` method. Again, the two arguments set `Cancel` as the text for the button and an anonymous class to listen for clicks. For the purpose of this demo, we are not taking any action in the overridden `onClick` method.

After the call to `setNegativeButton`, we finally see a semicolon marking the end of the line of code. We then code `return builder.create()`. This has the effect of returning to `MainActivity` (which called `onDialogCreate` in the first place), which is our new, fully configured, dialog window. We will see this calling code quite soon.

Add the following code directly after the previous block of code and within the `onCreateDialog` method:

```
   // A "Cancel" button that does nothing
   .setNegativeButton("Cancel", new DialogInterface.OnClickListener() {

     public void onClick(DialogInterface dialog, int id) {

       // Nothing happening here either

     }

   });

   // Create the object and return it
   return builder.create();

}// End onCreateDialog
```

Now, we have our `MyDialog` class that extends `FragmentDialog`; all we have to do for this is declare an object of `MyDialog`, instantiate it, and call its `createDialog` method.

Let's add a button to our layout. Navigate to the **layout_main.xml** tab and then switch to the **Design** tab. Drag a button onto the layout and make sure that its `id` property is set to `button`.

Now, go to the **MainActivity** tab, and we will handle a click on this button using an anonymous class. As we only have one button in the layout, it seems sensible to do things this way.

Note that in the next code, the anonymous class has exactly the same type as that of the class for which we implemented an interface in *Chapter 10, Everything's a Class*. Add this code to the onCreate method.

Just before you do, note also that the only thing that happens in the code is that the onClick method creates a new instance of MyDialog and calls its show method, which, unsurprisingly, will show our dialog window as we configured it in the MyDialog class. The show method requires a reference to FragmentManager (which we get with getFragmentManager); this is the class that tracks and controls all Fragment instances for an Activity. We also pass in an ID (we pass 123). More details about FragmentManager will be revealed when we look more deeply at Fragments, discussed in *Chapter 18, Design Patterns, Fragments, and the Real World*:

```
/*
    Let's listen for clicks on our regular Button.
    We can do this with an anonymous class.
*/

Button button = (Button) findViewById(R.id.button);

button.setOnClickListener(
  new View.OnClickListener() {

    @Override
    public void onClick(View v) {
      // We only handle one button
      // So no switching required
      MyDialog myDialog = new MyDialog();
      myDialog.show(getFragmentManager(), "123");
      // This calls onCreateDialog
      // Don't worry about the strange looking 123
      // We will find out about this in chapter 18
    }
  }
);
```

Now, we can run the app and admire our new dialog window that appears when we click on the button in the main layout. Note that clicking on either of the buttons in the dialog window will close it. This is the default behavior. This next screenshot shows our dialog window in action:

Next, in this chapter, we will make two more classes that implement dialogs as the first phase of our Note To Self app. We will see that a dialog window can have almost any layout we choose, and we don't have to rely on the simple layouts that the `Dialog.Builder` class provided us with in this mini app.

About the Note To Self app

Welcome to the first of the three major apps that we will implement in this book. When we do these projects, we will work on them more professionally than we work on the mini apps. We will use Android naming conventions, string resources, and proper encapsulation.

Sometimes, these things are overkill when you try to learn a new Android/Java topic, but they are really useful and important for real-world projects. It is good to start using them as soon as possible. Then, they become like your second nature, and the quality of our apps will benefit from this. Here is a quick refresher of String resources and Android naming conventions.

Using naming conventions and String resources

In *Chapter 3, Exploring Android Studio*, we talked about using String resources instead of hardcoding text in our layout files. There were a few benefits of doing things this way, but it was also slightly long-winded.

As this is our first real-world project, it would be a good time to do things the right way, so we can get an experience of doing this. If you want a quick refresher on the benefits of String resources, refer to *Chapter 3, Exploring Android Studio*.

Naming conventions are the conventions or rules that are used to name the variables, methods, and classes in our code. Throughout this book, we have somewhat loosely applied the Android naming conventions. As this is our first real-world app, we will be slightly stricter in applying these naming conventions. Most notably, when a variable is a member of a class, we will add a lowercase prefix m to it .

 You can find more information about Android naming conventions and code style at https://source.android.com/source/code-style.html.

In general, throughout the book, we will be fairly relaxed about naming conventions and String resources when learning new things or building mini apps, but we will apply them fairly strictly when building the main apps. There are three such apps (four if you include *Chapter 18, Design Patterns, Fragments, and the Real World*) throughout the book, of which Note To Self is the first.

How to get the Note To Self code

The fully completed app, including all the code and resources, can be found in the Chapter 17/Note to self folder within the download bundle. As we are implementing this app over the next six chapters, it will probably be useful to see the part-completed, runnable app at the end of almost every chapter as well. The part-completed runnable apps and all their associated code and resources can be found in their respective folders:

- Chapter 12/Note to self
- Chapter 14/Note to self
- Chapter 15/Note to self
- Chapter 16/Note to self
- Chapter 17/Note to self

The runnable project for *Chapter 16, UI Animations,* is combined with the new code for *Chapter 17, Sound FX and Supporting Different Versions of Android?*

Be aware that each of these is a separate, runnable project and each is contained within its own unique Java package. This is because then you can easily see the app running, as it would be having completed a given chapter. When copying and pasting the code, be careful not to include the package name because it will likely be different from yours and the code will not compile.

If you are following along and intend to build Note To Self from start to finish, we will simply build a project called `Note To Self`. There is still nothing stopping you, however, from taking a look at the code files of the projects from each chapter if you want to do a bit of copying and pasting at any time. Just don't copy the package directive from the top of a file, and be aware that at a couple of rare points in the instructions, you will be asked to delete/replace the occasional line of code from a previous chapter.

So, even if you are copying and pasting more than you are typing the code, be sure to read the instructions completely and look at the code in the book for extra comments that might be useful.

In each chapter, the code will be presented as if you have completed the last chapter completely, showing code from previous chapters where necessary as context for our new code.

Each chapter will not be solely devoted to the Note To Self app; you will learn about other, usually related, things and build a few mini apps as well. So, when we come to the Note To Self implementation, we will be technically prepared for it.

What we will do and when we will do it

It is worth having a heads-up on when we will implement the different parts of the app:

- In this chapter, we will look into the resources, dialogs, and the `Note` class. We will gather and add to the project all of the String and image resources that we will need throughout the entire project. The image resources are quite important, and for copyright reasons, they are not included in the download bundle. They are, however, free to download from the Android developer site. We will also create two classes that extend `DialogFragment` and create custom layout files, which enable the user to add a new note or view an existing note. We will also see how the dialog windows can communicate with the `MainActivity` class. In addition to this, we will implement a simple class of our own that will represent the structure of the data contained in a note.

- In *Chapter 13, Handling and Displaying Arrays of Data,* we will complete a few mini apps; this will prepare us to add new features to Note To Self in *Chapter 14, Handling and Displaying Notes in Note To Self.*

- In *Chapter 14, Handling and Displaying Notes in Note To Self,* we will use our new-found data handling skills along with a few neat new classes from the Android API to enable all our app's data that is to be shown in a scrolling list.

- In *Chapter 15, Android Intent and Persistence,* none of this data is any good to our user if it disappears when they quit the app or turn the phone off. You will learn and use two strategies to permanently persist data. One strategy is for simple data from the **Settings** screen of the app and the other for the actual app data: the notes.

- In *Chapter 16, UI Animations,* we will add neat animations such as flashing notes when they have been marked important by the user.

- In *Chapter 17, Sound FX and Supporting Different Versions of Android?* we will add a simple sound to our app and the ability to delete notes from the app.

So, what exactly can the user of our new app do?

What the user can do

The following features and screenshots are from the completed app. The app will look slightly different than this at the various stages of development. Where necessary, we will look at more images either as a reminder or to see the slight differences throughout the development process.

The completed app will allow the user to tap a + icon in the action bar of the app to open a dialog window to add a new note. Here is the action bar with the + icon highlighted:

This screenshot shows the dialog window where the user can add a new note:

The user will have a list of all the notes that they have added on the main screen of the app, as shown in this next screenshot. Notice the little icons above some of the notes? Through these, the user can see whether the note is important, an idea, and/or a to-do list.

They will be able to scroll down the list and tap on a note to see it shown in another dialog window that is dedicated to the one note. Here is that dialog window:

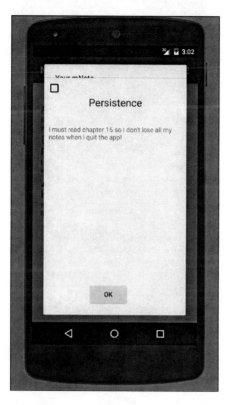

There will also be a **Settings** screen accessible from the menu in the action bar that will allow the user to configure basic settings, such as sound and animation speed. Here is the settings menu option in action:

This is the settings screen itself:

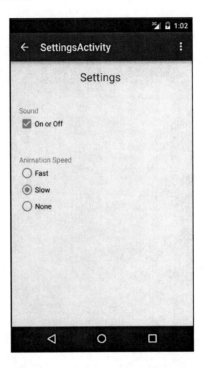

The user will also be able to long-press a note in the list to permanently delete a note when they don't need it any more.

Now that we know exactly what we are going to build, we can go ahead and start implementing it.

Building the project and gathering resources

Let's create our new project now. Create a new project and call it Note to self. Leave the other settings at their default values, including choosing a blank activity.

Downloading the images

Open a web browser and visit the Android developer website, https://www. google.com/design/icons/index.html.

We want to download four icon sets, which are listed as follows:

- An add icon that we will add to the action bar later in this chapter
- An item that looks like a light bulb that we will use for an icon to represent an idea
- An exclamation mark icon that we will use to represent important notes
- A blank checkbox icon that we will use to represent something that the user needs to do

We saw all these icons when we looked at the final appearance of our app.

You can find all these icons at the previous URL in the categories described as follows:

1. Find an image called `add` under the **Content** category. Select **white** (white is the best with a dark default action bar). Click on PNGS to download `add - ic_add_white_24dp`.

2. In the **toggle** category, you will find **check box outline blank**; select the black version of `ic_outline_blank_black_24dp`. Click on PNGS to download it.

3. In the **Alert** category, find **warning** and select the black version of `ic_warning_black_24dp`. Click on PNGS to download it.

4. In the **Image** category, find **wb incandescent** and select the black version of `ic_wb_incandescent_black_24dp`. Click on PNGS to download it.

5. Unzip each of the preceding downloads. In each of the unzipped downloads, we want the full contents of the `Android` folder. Note that within the `Android` folder there is a fairly complicated hierarchy of folders and icons. Here is a figure of the contents of the `incandescent (black) - ic_wb_incandescent_black_24dp/Android` folder as an example:

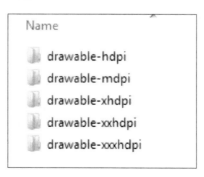

6. Copy and paste all the folders (from inside the `Android` folder) and their contents into the `res` folder in the project explorer. Android Studio will arrange them for us. Note that dragging and dropping does not work. You need to select each of the folders shown in the previous figure, copy them, then select the `res` folder, right-click on it, and select **Paste**.

7. Finally, to ensure that Android Studio has properly prepared and registered all the new files and folders that we just added, from the menu bar, navigate to **Tools | Android | Sync Project with Gradle Files**. Give this process a little time to complete. You can watch the progress of the process in the status bar.

The reason we need this hierarchy of folders with multiple versions of the same image is so that our app can use the appropriately sized icon depending upon the density of the screen on the Android device it is running on.

Here is a screenshot showing the `drawable` folder in the project explorer window after the previous actions. Compare the results in the next figure to your own:

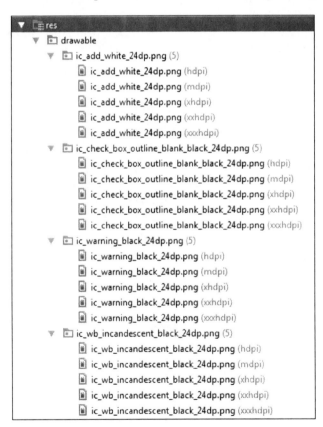

We now have all the images we need for the entire project.

Preparing the String resources

Here, we will create all the String resources that we will refer to from our layout files instead of hardcoding the text property, as we have been doing up until now. Strictly speaking, this is a step that could be avoided; however, if you are looking to make in-depth Android apps sometime in the near future, you will definitely benefit from learning to do things this way.

To get started, open the strings.xml file from the values folder in the project explorer. You will see a few autogenerated resources there. Add the following highlighted string resources that we will use in our app throughout the rest of the project. Add the code before the closing </resources> tag:

```
...
<resources>
    <string name="app_name">Note To Self</string>
    <string name="hello_world">Hello world!</string>
    <string name="action_settings">Settings</string>

    <string name="action_add">add</string>
    <string name="title_hint">Title</string>
    <string name="description_hint">Description</string>
    <string name="idea_checkbox">Idea</string>
    <string name="important_checkbox">Important</string>
    <string name="todo_checkbox">To do</string>
    <string name="cancel_button">Cancel</string>
    <string name="ok_button">OK</string>

    <string name="sound_checkbox">On or Off</string>
    <string name="settings_title">Settings</string>
    <string name="sound_title">Sound</string>
    <string name="amims_title">Animation Speed</string>
    <string name="rb_fast">Fast</string>
    <string name="rb_slow">Slow</string>
    <string name="rb_none">None</string>
</resources>
```

Note that in the preceding code, each string resource has a `name` property, which is unique and distinguishes it from all the others, as well as provides a meaningful and, hopefully, memorable clue as to the actual string value that it represents. It is these name values that we will use to refer to the String that we want to use from within our layout files.

 In later chapters, we will also add more resources in the form of sound and animations.

We will not need to revisit this file for the rest of the app.

Coding the Note class

This is the fundamental data structure of the app. It is a class that we will write ourselves from scratch and has all the member variables we need to represent one user note. In *Chapter 13, Handling and Displaying Arrays of Data*, you will learn some new Java to understand how we can let the user have dozens, hundreds, or thousands of notes.

Create a new class by right-clicking on the folder with the name of your package, the one that contains the `MainActivity.java` file. Select **Java class** under **New** and name it `Note`. Click on **OK** to create the class.

Add the highlighted code to the new `Note` class:

```
public class Note {

    private String mTitle;
    private String mDescription;
    private boolean mIdea;
    private boolean mTodo;
    private boolean mImportant;

}
```

Note that our member variable names are prefixed with m as per the Android convention. Furthermore, as there is no reason for any other class to access these variables directly, they are all declared private.

We will, therefore, require a getter and a setter method for each of our members. Android Studio can quickly do this for us:

1. Right-click below the last member variable declaration, but above the closing curly brace of the class.

2. From the context menu, select **Getter and setter** under **Generate**.

3. As we want to generate getters and setters for all the members, in the **Select fields to generate getters and setters** window, select each of the members individually by holding the *Shift* key and clicking on each of the members in turn. After this step, this window will look like as shown in the next screenshot:

4. Now, click on **OK** and all the getter and setter methods will be generated for us.

Take a look at the code that was just generated, and then we can discuss it. Note that Android Studio has saved us a lot of time by generating many methods. Also note that the names of the methods are imperfect. They have been generated as getmTitle, setmTitle, and so on. We want them to be neater and easier to read. So, quickly modify each of the method names by removing m from between the middle of each method name so that they are like this: getTitle and setTitle.

Here is what our getter and setter methods should look like at this point:

```java
public String getTitle() {
    return mTitle;
}

public void setTitle(String mTitle) {
    this.mTitle = mTitle;
}

public String getDescription() {
    return mDescription;
}

public void setDescription(String mDescription) {
    this.mDescription = mDescription;
}

public boolean isIdea() {
    return mIdea;
}

public void setIdea(boolean mIdea) {
    this.mIdea = mIdea;
}

public boolean isTodo() {
    return mTodo;
}

public void setTodo(boolean mTodo) {
    this.mTodo = mTodo;
}
```

```
public boolean isImportant() {
  return mImportant;
}

public void setImportant(boolean mImportant) {
  this.mImportant = mImportant;
}
```

There is quite a lot of code here but nothing complicated. Each of the methods has `public` access specified so that it can be used by any other class that has a reference to an object of the `Note` type. Furthermore, for each variable, there is a method with the name `get`... and a method of the name `set`.... The getters for the Boolean type variables are named `is`.... This is a logical name if you think about it because the returned answer will be either `true` or `false`.

Each of the getters simply returns the value of the variable and each of the setters sets the value of the variable to whatever value/parameter is passed in to the method.

In fact, we should really enhance our setters a little to do a bit of checking to make sure that the values passed in are within reasonable limits. For example, we might want to set a maximum or minimum length for `String mTtile` and `String mDescription`. We won't do so here, however, as this extraneousness will only serve to cloud the real learning objectives of this project.

Implementing the dialog designs

Now, we will do something that we have done many times before, but for a new reason. As we know, we will have two dialog windows. One for the user to enter a new note and one for the user to view a note of their choice.

We can design the layouts of these two dialog windows in exactly the same way as we have designed all our previous layouts. When we come to create the Java code for the `DialogFragment` classes, we will then see how we incorporate these layouts.

First, let's add a layout for our "new note" dialog:

1. Right-click on the `layout` folder in the project explorer and select **Layout resource file** under **New**. Enter `dialog_new_note` in the **File name** field and `RelativeLayout` in the **Root element** field. Click on **OK** to generate the new layout.

2. Refer to the target design in the next screenshot while following the rest of these instructions:

3. Drag and drop **PlainText** (from the **Text Fields** category) to the very top and on the left-hand side of the layout and then add another one immediately below it. Don't worry about padding and margins for now.

4. Drag and drop three **CheckBox** widgets one below the other. Look at the previous reference image for guidance. Again, don't worry about padding, margins, and so on.

5. Drag and drop two buttons on the layout, the first directly below the last **CheckBox** widget from the previous step and the second button horizontally in line with the first button, but immediately on the right-hand side of the layout.

6. Now, we will quickly tidy up our layout with a few steps, starting with the top widget (**PlainText**). In the **Properties** window, find the **layout margin** property and set **top** to 35dp.

7. Do exactly the same as the previous step for each and every widget in our layout except for the final button. They should all then be nice and uniformly spread out with their new margins, and the final button (on the right-hand side) should just automatically line itself up with the left-hand button, even though we didn't adjust its margin.

8. Click on the **RelativeLayout** root in the **Component Tree** window. Set the **padding all** property to `10dp` to further neaten up our layout by moving all the widgets away from the edges of the screen.

9. Now, we can set up all our `text`, `id`, and `hint` properties. You can do so by using the values from the following table. Remember we are using our string resources for `text` and `hint` properties:

Widget type	Property	Value to set to
Plain Text (top)	id	editTitle
Plain Text (top)	hint	@string/title_hint
Plain Text (Bottom)	id	editDescription
Plain Text (Bottom)	hint	@string/description_hint
Plain Text (Bottom)	inputType	textMultiLine
CheckBox (top)	id	checkBoxIdea
CheckBox (top)	text	@string/idea_checkbox
CheckBox (middle)	id	checkBoxTodo
CheckBox (middle)	text	@string/todo_checkbox
CheckBox (bottom)	id	checkBoxImportant
CheckBox (bottom)	text	@string/important_checkbox
Button (left)	id	btnCancel
Button (left)	text	@string/cancel_button
Button (right)	id	btnOK
Button (right)	text	@string/ok_button

We now have a nice neat layout ready for our Java code to display. Be sure to keep in mind the names of the different widgets because we will see them in action when we write our Java code. The important thing is that our layout looks nice and has an ID for every relevant item, so we can get a reference to it.

Let's layout our dialog to *show the note* to the user:

1. Right-click on the `layout` folder in the project explorer and select **Layout resource file** under **New**. Enter `dialog_show_note` in the **File name** field and `RelativeLayout` in the **Root element** field. Click on **OK** to generate the new layout.

2. Refer to the target design in the next figure while following the rest of these instructions:

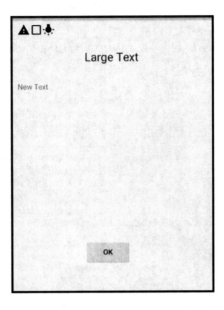

3. First of all, drag and drop three **ImageView** widgets side by side on the top left side of the layout. This is very easy to do if you drag them onto **RelativeLayout** in the component tree.

4. Next, drag and drop a **Large Text** widget just below the images, but in the center.

5. Add **Plain TextView** just below the **Large Text** but immediately (hard) on the left-hand side.

6. Now add a button horizontally in the center and near the bottom of the layout.

7. Click on the **RelativeLayout** root and find the **padding: all** property. Set it to 10dp.

8. Let's quickly configure the properties from the following table:

Widget type	Property	Value to set to
ImageView (left)	id	imageViewImportant
ImageView (left)	src	@drawable/ic_warning_black_24dp
ImageView (center)	id	imageViewTodo
ImageView (center)	src	@drawable/ic_check_box_outline_blank_black_24dp
ImageView (right)	id	imageViewIdea

Widget type	Property	Value to set to
ImageView (right)	src	@drawable/ic_wb_incandescent_black_24dp
Large Text	id	txtTitle
Plain TextView	id	txtDescription
Button	id	btnOK
Button	text	@string/ok_button

Now we have a layout that we can use to show a note to the user. Note that we get to reuse a string resource for our **OK** button. The bigger our apps get, the more beneficial it is to do things this way.

Coding the dialog boxes

Now that we have a design for both our dialog windows (show note and new note), we can use what we know about the FragmentDialog class to implement a class that represents each of the dialog windows that the user can interact with.

We will start with the new note screen.

Coding the DialogNewNote class

Create a new class by right-clicking on the project folder that contains all the .java files and choose **Java class** under **New**. Name the class DialogNewNote.

First, change the class declaration and extend DialogFragment. Also, override the onCreateDialog method, which is where all the rest of the code in this class will go:

```
public class DialogNewNote extends DialogFragment {

  @Override
  public Dialog onCreateDialog(Bundle savedInstanceState) {

    // All the rest of the code goes here

  }
}
```

We temporarily have an error because we need a return statement, but we will get to that in just a moment.

In the next block of code, first we declare and initialize an AlertDialog.Builder object, as we have done before when creating dialog windows. This time, however, we will use this object much less than previously.

Next we initialize a `LayoutInflater` object, which we will use to inflate our XML layout. Inflate simply means to turn our XML layout into a Java object. Once this is done, we can then access all our widgets in the usual way. We can think of `inflater.inflate` replacing `setContentView` for our dialog. And in the second line, we do just that with the `inflate` method.

Add the following code as we just discussed:

```
AlertDialog.Builder builder = new AlertDialog.Builder(getActivity());

LayoutInflater inflater = getActivity().getLayoutInflater();
View dialogView = inflater.inflate(R.layout.dialog_new_note, null);
```

We now have a `View` object called `dialogView`, which contains all the UI elements from our `dialog_new_note.xml` layout file.

Immediately after the previous block of code, we simply get a reference to each of the UI widgets in the usual way. Many of the objects are declared `final` because they will be used in an anonymous class, and as you learned previously, this is required. Remember that it is the reference that is `final` (cannot change), and we can still change the objects on the heap for which they are a reference to.

Add this code just after the previous block of code:

```
final EditText editTitle = (EditText) dialogView.findViewById
    (R.id.editTitle);
final EditText editDescription = (EditText) dialogView.findViewById
    (R.id.editDescription);
final CheckBox checkBoxIdea = (CheckBox) dialogView.findViewById
    (R.id.checkBoxIdea);
final CheckBox checkBoxTodo = (CheckBox) dialogView.findViewById
    (R.id.checkBoxTodo);
final CheckBox checkBoxImportant = (CheckBox) dialogView.findViewById
    (R.id.checkBoxImportant);
Button btnCancel = (Button) dialogView.findViewById(R.id.btnCancel);
Button btnOK = (Button) dialogView.findViewById(R.id.btnOK);
```

In the next code block, we simply set the message of the dialog using `builder`. Then, we write an anonymous class to handle clicks on `btnCancel`. In the overridden `onClick` method, we simply call `dismiss()`, which is a public method of `DialogFragment`, to close the dialog window. This is just what we need when the user clicks on **Cancel**.

Add the following code as we just discussed:

```
builder.setView(dialogView).setMessage("Add a new note");

// Handle the cancel button
btnCancel.setOnClickListener( new View.OnClickListener() {
  @Override
  public void onClick(View v) {
    dismiss();
  }
});
```

Now, we add an anonymous class to handle what happens when the user clicks on the **OK** button (btnOK).

First we create a new Note called newNote. Then we set each of the member variables from newNote to the appropriate contents of the form.

After this, we do something new. We create a reference to MainActivity using the getActivity method, and then, we use that reference to call the createNewNote method in MainActivity. Note that we have not written this method yet. The argument sent in this method is our newly initialized newNote object. This has the effect of sending the users, note back to MainActivity. We will see what we do with this later in this chapter.

Finally, we call dismiss to close the dialog window.

Add this next code after the last block:

```
// Handle the OK button
btnOK.setOnClickListener(new View.OnClickListener() {
  @Override
  public void onClick(View v) {

    // Create a new note
    Note newNote = new Note();

    // Set its variables to match the users entries on the form
    newNote.setTitle(editTitle.getText().toString());
    newNote.setDescription(editDescription.getText().toString());
    newNote.setIdea(checkBoxIdea.isChecked());
    newNote.setTodo(checkBoxTodo.isChecked());
    newNote.setImportant(checkBoxImportant.isChecked());

    // Get a reference to MainActivity
```

```
        MainActivity callingActivity = (MainActivity) getActivity();

        // Pass newNote back to MainActivity
        callingActivity.createNewNote(newNote);

        // Quit the dialog
        dismiss();
      }
    });


    return builder.create();
```

Now, our first dialog's done. We haven't wired it up to appear from the MainActivity class yet, and we need to implement the createNewNote method too. We will do this right after we create the next dialog.

Coding the DialogShowNote class

Create a new class by right-clicking on the project folder that contains all the .java files and choose **Java class** under **New**. Name the class DialogShowNote.

First, change the class declaration, extend FragmentDialog, and override the onCreateDialog method. As most of the code for this class goes in the onCreateDialog method, implement the signature and empty body as shown in the next code snippet, and we will revisit it in a minute. Note that we declare a member variable mNote of the Note type. Also, add the sendNoteSelected method and its one line of code that initializes mNote. This method will be called by MainActivity and it will pass in the Note object the user has clicked on.

Add the code we just discussed and then we can look at and code the details of onCreateDialog:

```
    public class DialogShowNote extends DialogFragment {

        private Note mNote;

        @Override
        public Dialog onCreateDialog(Bundle savedInstanceState) {

          // All the other code goes here


        }
```

```
// Receive a note from the MainActivity
public void sendNoteSelected(Note noteSelected) {
    mNote = noteSelected;
}

}
```

Next up, as usual, we will declare and initialize an instance of `AlertDialog.Builder`. Next, as we did for `DialogNewNote`, we will declare and initialize `LayoutInflater` and then use it to create a `View` object that contains the layout for the dialog. In this case, it is the layout from `dialog_show_note.xml`.

Finally, in the following block of code, we get a reference to each of the UI widgets and set the `text` properties on `txtTitle` and `textDescription` from the appropriate member variables of `mNote`, which was initialized in `sendNoteSelected`.

Add the code we just discussed within the `onCreateDialog` method:

```
AlertDialog.Builder builder = new AlertDialog.Builder(getActivity());

LayoutInflater inflater = getActivity().getLayoutInflater();
View dialogView = inflater.inflate(R.layout.dialog_show_note, null);

TextView txtTitle = (TextView) dialogView.findViewById(R.id.txtTitle);

TextView txtDescription = (TextView) dialogView.findViewById
    (R.id.txtDescription);

txtTitle.setText(mNote.getTitle());
txtDescription.setText(mNote.getDescription());

ImageView ivImportant = (ImageView) dialogView.findViewById
    (R.id.imageViewImportant);

ImageView ivTodo = (ImageView) dialogView.findViewById
    (R.id.imageViewTodo);
ImageView ivIdea = (ImageView) dialogView.findViewById
    (R.id.imageViewIdea);
```

This next code is also in the `onCreateDialog` method. It checks whether the note being shown is important and then shows or hides `ivImportant ImageView` accordingly. We then do exactly the same for `ivTodo` and `ivIdea`.

Add this code after the previous block of code, which is still in the onCreateDialog method:

```
if (!mNote.isImportant()){
   ivImportant.setVisibility(View.GONE);
}

if (!mNote.isTodo()){
   ivTodo.setVisibility(View.GONE);
}

if (!mNote.isIdea()){
   ivIdea.setVisibility(View.GONE);
}
```

All we need to do now is dismiss (close) the dialog window when the user clicks on the **OK** button. This is done with an anonymous class, as we have seen several times before now. The onClick method simply calls the dismiss method to achieve this.

Add this code in the onCreateDialog method after the previous block of code:

```
Button btnOK = (Button) dialogView.findViewById(R.id.btnOK);

builder.setView(dialogView).setMessage("Your Note");

btnOK.setOnClickListener(new View.OnClickListener() {
  @Override
    public void onClick(View v) {
       dismiss();
   }
});

return builder.create();
```

We have two dialog windows that are ready to roll. Now, we just have to add some code to MainActivity to finish the job.

Showing our new dialogs

Add a new temporary member variable just after the MainActivity declaration. This won't be in the final app as it is just so we can test our dialogs:

```
// Temporary code
Note mTempNote = new Note();
```

Now, add this method so that we can receive a new note from the
`DialogNewNote` class:

```
public void createNewNote(Note n){
  // Temporary code
  mTempNote = n;
}
```

Now, to send a note into the `DialogShowNote` method, we need to add a button with
the `button` ID to the `layout_main.xml` layout file.

Just so it is clear as to what this button is for, change its text property to `Show Note`,
drag a button onto `layout_main.xml`, and configure it as we just described.

Just to clarify, this is a temporary button that is used for testing purposes and will
not be in the final app.

Now, in the `onCreate` method, we will set up an anonymous class to handle clicks
on our temporary button. The code in `onClick` does the following:

1.   Creates a new `DialogShowNote` instance called `dialog`.

2.   Calls the `sendNoteSelected` method on `dialog` to pass in our `Note` object,
     `mTempNote`, as a parameter.

3.   Finally, we call `show`, which breathes life into our new dialog.

Add the following code to `onCreate` that we just described:

```
// Temporary code
Button button = (Button) findViewById(R.id.button);
button.setOnClickListener(new View.OnClickListener() {
  @Override
  public void onClick(View v) {

    // Create a new DialogShowNote called dialog
    DialogShowNote dialog = new DialogShowNote();

    // Send the note via the sendNoteSelected method
    dialog.sendNoteSelected(mTempNote);

    // Create the dialog
    dialog.show(getFragmentManager(), "123");
  }
});
```

We can now summon our `DialogShowNote` dialog window at the click of a button.

Adding a + icon to the action bar

Next, we will add a + icon to the action bar and wire it up to display our `DialogNewNote` dialog.

In the `menu` folder, open the `menu_main.xml` file and add the highlighted code just before the closing`</menu>` tag, as shown in the following code for context:

```
<!-- Our add icon will have its own button -->
<item android:id="@+id/action_add"
  android:icon="@drawable/ic_add_white_24dp"
  android:title="@string/action_add"
  app:showAsAction="ifRoom" />

</menu>
```

This will add the icon we downloaded, while gathering our resources previously, to the action bar.

Finally, back in `MainActivity.java`, add this code to the `onOptionsItemSelected` method just before the `return` statement. This will show a new dialog that will add a new note when the + icon is tapped:

```
if (id == R.id.action_add) {
  DialogNewNote dialog = new DialogNewNote();
  dialog.show(getFragmentManager(), "");
  return true;
}
```

We can now run the app. Click on the + icon and add a note. Then, click on the **Show Note** button to see it in a dialog window. Note that if you add a second note, it will overwrite the first because we only have one `Note` object.

Summary

In this chapter, we saw and implemented a common user interface design with dialog windows using the `FragmentDialog` class.

We went a step further when we started the Note To Self app by implementing more complicated dialogs that can capture information from the user. We saw that `DialogFragment` basically enables us to have any UI that we like in a dialog box.

In the next chapter, we will deal with the obvious problem that the user can only have one note, by exploring Java arrays and their close cousin, `ArrayList`.

13
Handling and Displaying Arrays of Data

In this chapter, you will learn about Java arrays that allow us to manipulate a potentially huge amount of data in an organized and efficient manner. We will also use a close Java relation to arrays, ArrayLists and see the differences between them.

Once we are comfortable with handling a large amount of data, we will see what the Android API has that will help us to easily connect our new-found data handling skills to the user interface without breaking a sweat.

The topics in this chapter are as follows:

- A random diversion
- Handling large amount of data with arrays
- A simple array example
- A dynamic array example
- A multidimensional array example
- ArrayLists
- The enhanced `for` loop
- ListViews and BaseAdapter

First, let's take a look at a random diversion

A random diversion

Sometimes in our apps, we will want a random number. There are many possible uses for random numbers, for example, when our app wants to show a random tip of the day, a game that has to choose between scenarios, or a quiz that asks random questions.

The `Random` class is part of the Java API and is fully compatible with our Android apps.

Let's have a look at how we can create random numbers, and later in the chapter, we will put it to practical use. All the hard work is done by the `Random` class. First, we need to create an object of the `Random` type:

```
Random randGenerator = new Random();
```

Then, we use our new object's `nextInt` method to generate a random number between a certain range.

This line of code generates a random number using our `Random` object and stores the result in the `ourRandomNumber` variable:

```
int ourRandomNumber = randGenerator.nextInt(10);
```

The number that we enter for the range starts from 0. So, the preceding line will generate a random number between 0 and 9. If we want a random number between 1 and 10, we just use this:

```
ourRandomNumber ++;
```

We can also use the `Random` object to get other types of random numbers using `nextLong`, `nextFloat`, and `nextDouble`.

We will put the `Random` class to practical use later in the chapter with a quick geography quiz app.

Handling large amount of data with arrays

You might be wondering what happens when we have an app with lots of variables that we need to keep track of. What about our Note To Self app with 100 notes or a high score table in a game with the top 100 scores? We could declare and initialize 100 separate variables, like so:

```
Note note1;
Note note2;
Note note3;
//96 more lines like the above
Note note100;
```

Or, we could begin to handle the high scores scenario like this:

```
int topScore1;
int topScore2;
int topScore3;
//96 more lines like the above
int topScore100;
```

Straight away, this can seem unwieldy, but what about when someone gets a new top score or we want to let our users sort the order their notes are displayed in? Using the high scores scenario, we have to shift the scores in every variable down one place. A nightmare begins. We could handle the high scores as follows:

```
topScore100 = topScore99;
topScore99 = topScore98;
topScore98 = topScore97;
//96 more lines like the above
topScore1 = score;
```

There must be a better way to do this. When we have a whole array of variables, what we need is a Java **array**. An array is a reference variable that holds up to a predetermined fixed maximum number of elements. Each element is a variable with a consistent type.

The following code declares an array that can hold `int` type variables, for example, a high score table or a series of exam grades:

```
int [] intArray;
```

We could also declare arrays of other types, including classes such as `Note`, like this:

```
String [] classNames;
boolean [] bankOfSwitches;
float [] closingBalancesInMarch;
Note [] notes;
```

Each of these arrays would need to have a fixed maximum amount of storage space allocated before they are used. Just like other objects, we must initialize arrays before we use them:

```
intArray = new int [100];
```

The preceding line allocates storage space for up to a maximum of 100 int values. Think of a long aisle of 100 consecutive storage spaces in our variable warehouse. The spaces would probably be labeled as `intArray[0]`, `intArray [1]`, `intArray [2]`, and so on, where each space holds a single `int` value. The slightly surprising thing here is that the storage spaces start off at 0, not 1. Therefore, in an array that is 100 elements *wide*, the storage spaces would run from 0 to 99.

We could actually initialize some of these storage spaces like this:

```
intArray[0] = 5;
intArray[1] = 6;
intArray[2] = 7;
```

However, note that we can only ever put the predeclared type into an array, and the type that an array holds can never change:

```
intArray[3]= "John Carmack"; // Won't compile String not int
```

So, when we have an array of int types, what are each of these int variables called? What are the names of these variables and how do we access the values stored in them? The array notation syntax replaces the name, and we can do anything with a variable in an array that we could do with a regular variable with a name, as shown in the following code:

```
intArray [3] = 123;
```

Here is another example of initializing an array element:

```
intArray[10] = intArray[9] - intArray[4];
```

This declaration also includes assigning the value from an array to a regular variable of the same type, like this:

```
int myNamedInt = intArray [3];
```

Note, however, that myNamedInt is a separate and distinct primitive variable, and any changes to it do not affect the value stored in the intArray reference. It has its own space in the warehouse and is unconnected to the array. To be more specific, the array is on the heap and int is on the stack.

Arrays are objects

We said that arrays are reference variables. Think of an array variable as an address to a group of variables of a given type. Perhaps, using the warehouse analogy, someArray is an aisle number. So, someArray[0], someArray[1], and so on are the aisle numbers followed by their position numbers in the aisle.

Arrays are also objects, that is, they have methods and properties that we can use, for example:

```
int lengthOfSomeArray = someArray.length;
```

Here, we assigned the length of someArray to the int variable called lengthOfSomeArray.

We can even declare an array of arrays. This is an array that, in each of its elements, lurks another array. The declaration is shown as follows:

```
String[][] countriesAndCities;
```

In the preceding array, we could hold a list of cities within each country. Let's not go array crazy just yet though. Just remember that an array holds up to a predetermined number of variables of any predetermined type, and these values are accessed using this syntax:

```
someArray[someLocation];
```

Let's actually use some arrays to try and get an understanding of how to use them in real code and what we might use them for.

A simple array example mini app

Let's make a really simple working array example. You can get the completed code for this example in the downloadable code bundle. It's at `Chapter 13/Simple Array Example/MainActivity.java`.

Create a project with a blank Activity and call it `Simple Array Example`.

First, we declare our array, allocate five spaces, and initialize values to each of the elements. Then, we output each of the values to the logcat console. Add this code to the `onCreate` method just after the call to `setContentView`:

```
// Declaring an array
int[] ourArray;

// Allocate memory for a maximum size of 5 elements
ourArray = new int[5];

// Initialize ourArray with values
// The values are arbitrary as long as they are int
// The indexes are not arbitrary. 0 through 4 or crash!

ourArray[0] = 25;
ourArray[1] = 50;
ourArray[2] = 125;
ourArray[3] = 68;
ourArray[4] = 47;

// Output all the stored values
Log.i("info", "Here is ourArray:");
```

```
Log.i("info", "[0] = " + ourArray[0]);
Log.i("info", "[1] = " + ourArray[1]);
Log.i("info", "[2] = " + ourArray[2]);
Log.i("info", "[3] = " + ourArray[3]);
Log.i("info", "[4] = " + ourArray[4]);
```

Next, we add each of the elements of the array together, just as we do in regular `int` type variables. Note that when we add the array elements together, we are doing so over multiple lines. This is fine as we have omitted a semicolon until the last operation, so the Java compiler treats the lines as one statement. Add the code that we just discussed to `MainActivity.java`:

```
/*
    We can do any calculation with an array element
    As long as it is appropriate to the contained type
    Like this:
*/
int answer = ourArray[0] +
ourArray[1] +
ourArray[2] +
ourArray[3] +
ourArray[4];

Log.i("info", "Answer = " + answer);
```

Run the example and observe the output in the logcat window.

Remember that nothing will happen on the emulator display, as all the output will be sent to our logcat console window in Android Studio. Here is the output:

```
info: Here is ourArray:
info: [0] = 25
info: [1] = 50
info: [2] = 125
info: [3] = 68
info: [4] = 47
info: Answer = 315
```

We declared an array called `ourArray` to hold `int` variables and then allocated space for up to 5 allocations of that type.

Next, we assigned a value to each of the five spaces in our array. Remember that the first space is `ourArray[0]` and the last space is `ourArray[4]`.

Next, we simply printed the value in each array location on the console. From the output, we can see that they hold the value we initialized them to be in the previous step. Then, we added together each of the elements in ourArray and initialized their value to the answer variable. We then printed answer on the console, and we can see that indeed all the values were added together, just as if they were plain old int types, which they are, but just that they are stored in a different manner.

Getting dynamic with arrays

As we discussed at the beginning of all this array discussion, if we need to declare and initialize each element of an array individually, there isn't a huge amount of benefit to an array over regular variables. Let's look at an example of declaring and initializing arrays dynamically.

A dynamic array example

Let's make a really simple dynamic array example. You can get the working project for this example in the download bundle. It is located at Chapter 13/Dynamic Array Example/MainActivity.java.

Create a project with a blank Activity and call it Dynamic Array Example.

Type the following just after the call to setContentView in onCreate. Check whether you can work out what the output is before we discuss it and analyze the code:

```
// Declaring and allocating in one step
int[] ourArray = new int[1000];

// Let's initialize ourArray using a for loop
// Because more than a few variables is a lot of typing!

for(int i = 0; i < 1000; i++){

    // Put the value of ourValue into our array
    // At the position determined by i.
    ourArray[i] = i*5;

    // Output what is going on
    Log.i("info", "i = " + i);
    Log.i("info", "ourArray[i] = " + ourArray[i]);
}
```

Run the example app, remembering that nothing will happen on the screen, as all the output will be sent to our **logcat** console window in Android Studio. Here is the output:

```
info: i = 0
info: ourArray[i] = 0
info: i = 1
info: ourArray[i] = 5
info: i = 2
info: ourArray[i] = 10
```

We removed 994 iterations of the loop for brevity, and the output will be as follows:

```
info: ourArray[i] = 4985
info: i = 998
info: ourArray[i] = 4990
info: i = 999
info: ourArray[i] = 4995
```

First, we declared and allocated an array called `ourArray` to hold up to 1000 `int` values. Note that this time we performed these two steps in one line of code:

```
int[] ourArray = new int[1000];
```

Then, we used a `for` loop that was set to loop 1000 times:

```
(int i = 0; i < 1000; i++){
```

We initialized the spaces in the array, starting at 0 through to 999 with the value of `i` multiplied by 5, like this:

```
ourArray[i] = i*5;
```

Then, to demonstrate the value of `i` and the value held in each position of the array, we output the value of `i` followed by the value held in the corresponding position in the array like this:

```
Log.i("info", "i = " + i);
Log.i("info", "ourArray[i] = " + ourArray[i]);
```

And all this happened 1000 times, producing the output we saw. Of course, we are yet to use this technique in a real-world app, but we will use it soon to make our Note To Self app hold an almost infinite number of notes.

Entering the nth dimension with arrays

We very briefly mentioned that an array can even hold other arrays at each position. And of course, if an array holds lots of arrays that hold lots of some other type, how do we access the values in the contained arrays? And why would we ever need this anyway? Take a look at this next example where multidimensional arrays can be useful.

A multidimensional array mini app

Let's make a really simple multidimensional array example. You can get the working project for this example in the download bundle. It is located at `Chapter 13/ Multidimensional Array Example/MainActivity.java`.

Create a project with a blank Activity and call it `Multidimensional Array Example`.

After the call to `setContentView` in `onCreate`, declare and initialize a two-dimensional array like this:

```
// Random object for generating question numbers
Random randInt = new Random();
// a variable to hold the random value generated
int questionNumber;

// declare and allocate in separate stages for clarity
// but we don't have to
String[][] countriesAndCities;
// Now we have a 2 dimensional array

countriesAndCities = new String[5][2];
// 5 arrays with 2 elements each
// Perfect for 5 "What's the capital city" questions

// Now we load the questions and answers into our arrays
// You could do this with less questions to save typing
// But don't do more or you will get an exception
countriesAndCities [0][0] = "United Kingdom";
countriesAndCities [0][1] = "London";

countriesAndCities [1][0] = "USA";
countriesAndCities [1][1] = "Washington";

countriesAndCities [2][0] = "India";
countriesAndCities [2][1] = "New Delhi";
```

```
countriesAndCities [3][0] = "Brazil";
countriesAndCities [3][1] = "Brasilia";

countriesAndCities [4][0] = "Kenya";
countriesAndCities [4][1] = "Nairobi";
```

Now, we output the contents of the array using a `for` loop and our `Random` object. Note how we've ensured that although the question is random, we can always pick the correct answer. Add this next code after the previous code:

```
/*
 Now we know that the country is stored at element 0
 The matching capital at element 1
 Here are two variables that reflect this
*/
int country = 0;
int capital = 1;

// A quick for loop to ask 3 questions
for(int i = 0; i < 3; i++){
  // get a random question number between 0 and 4
  questionNumber = randInt.nextInt(5);

  // and ask the question and in this case just
  // give the answer for the sake of brevity
  Log.i("info", "The capital of "
    +countriesAndCities[questionNumber][country]);

  Log.i("info", "is "
    +countriesAndCities[questionNumber][capital]);

} // end of for loop
```

Run the example remembering that nothing will happen on the screen, as all the output will be sent to our logcat console window in Android Studio. Here is the output:

```
info: The capital of USA
info: is Washington
info: The capital of India
info: is New Delhi
info: The capital of United Kingdom
info: is London
```

What just happened? Let's go through this chunk by chunk so we know exactly what is going on.

We make a new object of the `Random` type called `randInt`, as shown in the following code, that is ready to generate random numbers later in the program:

```
Random randInt = new Random();
```

And a simple `int` variable to hold a question number is declared as:

```
int questionNumber;
```

And here, we declare our array of arrays called `countriesAndCities`. The outer array holds the arrays:

```
String[][] countriesAndCities;
```

Now, we allocate space within our arrays. The first outer array will now be able to hold 5 arrays and each of the inner arrays will be able to hold 2 Strings.

```
countriesAndCities = new String[5][2];
```

Now, we initialize our arrays so that they hold country names and their corresponding capital city names. Note that with each pair of initializations, the outer array number stays the same, indicating that each country/capital pair is within one inner array (a `String` array). And of course, each of these inner arrays is held in one element of the outer array (which holds arrays), as shown in the following code:

```
countriesAndCities [0][0] = "United Kingdom";
countriesAndCities [0][1] = "London";

countriesAndCities [1][0] = "USA";
countriesAndCities [1][1] = "Washington";

countriesAndCities [2][0] = "India";
countriesAndCities [2][1] = "New Delhi";

countriesAndCities [3][0] = "Brazil";
countriesAndCities [3][1] = "Brasilia";

countriesAndCities [4][0] = "Kenya";
countriesAndCities [4][1] = "Nairobi";
```

To make the upcoming `for` loop clearer, we declare and initialize `int` variables to represent the country and capital names from our arrays. If you glance back at the array initialization, all the country names are held in position `0` of the inner array and all the corresponding capital city names are held at position `1`:

```
int country = 0;
int capital = 1;
```

Now, we set up a `for` loop to run 3 times. Note that this does not simply access the first three elements of our array, it just determines the number of times we go through the loop. We could make it loop one time or a thousand times, the example would still work:

```
for(int i = 0; i < 3; i++){
```

Next, we actually determine which question to ask. Or more specifically, which element of our outer array needs to be accessed. Remember that `randInt.nextInt(5)` returns a number between 0 and 4. Just what we need as we have an outer array with 5 elements: 0 through 4:

```
questionNumber = randInt.nextInt(5);
```

Now, we can ask a question by providing an output of the Strings held in the inner array, which in turn is held by the outer array that was chosen in the previous line by the randomly generated number:

```
Log.i("info", "The capital of "
 +countriesAndCities[questionNumber][country]);

Log.i("info", "is "
 +countriesAndCities[questionNumber][capital]);

}//end of for loop
```

For the record, we will not be using any multidimensional arrays in the rest of this book. So if there is still a little bit of murkiness around these arrays inside arrays, then that doesn't matter. You know they exist, what they can do, and you can revisit them if necessary.

Array out of bounds exceptions

An array out of bounds exception occurs when we attempt to access an element of an array that does not exist. Sometimes, the compiler will catch it for us to prevent the error from making it into a working app. For example, we can declare the array like this:

```
int[] ourArray = new int[1000];
int someValue = 1; // Arbitrary value
ourArray[1000] = someValue;
// Won't compile as compiler knows this won't work.
// Only locations 0 through 999 are valid
```

However, what if we do something like this:

```
int[] ourArray = new int[1000];
int someValue = 1;// Arbitrary value
int x = 999;
if(userDoesSomething){
  x++; // x now equals 1000
}

ourArray[x] = someValue;
/*
  Array out of bounds exception if userDoesSomething evaluates to
  true! This is because we end up referencing position 1000 when the
  array only has positions 0 through 999.
  Compiler can't spot it. App will crash!
*/
```

The only way to avoid this problem is to know the rule. The rule states that arrays start at 0 and go up to their length -1. We can also use clear readable code where it is easy to evaluate what we have done and spot problems more easily.

ArrayLists

`ArrayList` is like a regular Java array on steroids. It overcomes some of the shortfalls of arrays such as having to predetermine its size. It adds some really useful methods to make its data easy to manage, and it uses an enhanced version of a `for` loop, which is clearer to use than a regular `for` loop.

Let's look at some code that uses `ArrayList`:

```
// Declare a new ArrayList called myList to hold int variables
ArrayList<int> myList;

// Initialize the myList ready for use
myList = new ArrayList<int>();
```

In the previous code, we declared and initialized a new ArrayList called myList. We can also do this in a single step as shown in the following code:

```
ArrayList<int> myList = new ArrayList<int>();
```

We have seen nothing especially interesting so far, so let's take a look at what we can actually do with ArrayList. Let's use String ArrayList this time:

```
// declare and initialize a new ArrayList
ArrayList<String> myList = new ArrayList<String>();

// Add a new String to myList in the next available location
myList.add("Donald Knuth");
// And another
myList.add("Rasmus Lerdorf");
// And another
myList.add("Richard Stallman");
// We can also choose 'where' to add an entry
myList.add(1, "James Gosling");

// Is there anything in our ArrayList?
if(myList.isEmpty()){
  // Nothing to see here
}else{
  // Do something with the data
}

// How many items in our ArrayList?
int numItems = myList.size();

// Now where did I put James Gosling?
int position = myList.indexOf("James Gosling");
```

In the previous code, we saw that we can use some really useful methods of the ArrayList class in our ArrayList object. We can add an item (myList.add), add it at a specific location (myList.add(x, value)), check whether ArrayList is empty (myList.isEmpty), see how big the array is (myList.size()), and get the current position of a given item (myList.indexOf).

> There are even more methods in the ArrayList class, and you can read about them at http://docs.oracle.com/javase/7/docs/api/java/util/ArrayList.html. What we have seen so far is enough to complete this book.

With all this functionality, all we need now is a way to handle `ArrayLists` dynamically.

The enhanced for loop

This is what the condition of an enhanced `for` loop looks like:

```
for (String s : myList)
```

The previous example would iterate (step through) all of the items in `myList` one at a time. At each step, `s` would hold the current String.

So, this code would print on the console all our eminent programmers from the previous section's `ArrayList` code sample:

```
for (String s : myList){
  Log.i("Programmer: ","" + s);
}
```

We can also use the enhanced `for` loop with regular arrays too:

```
int [] anArray = new int [];
// We can initialize arrays quickly like this
anArray {0, 1, 2, 3, 4, 5}

for (int s : anArray){
    Log.i("Contents = ","" + s);
}
```

There's another incoming newsflash!

Arrays and ArrayLists are polymorphic

We already know that we can put objects into arrays and `ArrayList`. But being polymorphic means that they can handle objects of multiple different types as long as they have a common parent type, all within the same array or `ArrayList`.

In *Chapter 9, Object-Oriented Programming*, you learned that polymorphism roughly means *different forms*. But what does it mean to us in the context of arrays and `ArrayList`?

Boiled down to its simplest, any subclass can be used as part of the code that uses the super class.

For example, if we have an array of `Animals`, we could put any object that is a type, that is a subclass of `Animal` in the `Animal` array, perhaps, `Cats` and `Dogs`.

This means that we can write code that is simpler and easier to understand and easier to modify or change:

```
// This code assumes we have an Animal class
// And we have a Cat and Dog class that extends Animal
Animal myAnimal =  new Animal();
Dog myDog = new Dog();
Cat myCat = new Cat();
Animal [] myAnimals = new Animal[10];
myAnimals[0] = myAnimal; // As expected
myAnimals[1] = myDog; // This is OK too
myAnimals[2] = myCat; // And this is fine as well
```

Also, we can write code for the super class and rely on the fact that no matter how many times it is subclassed, within certain parameters, the code will still work. Let's continue our previous example:

```
// 6 months later we need elephants
// with its own unique aspects
// As long as it extends Animal we can still do this
Elephant myElephant = new Elephant();
myAnimals[3] = myElephant; // And this is fine as well
```

However, when we remove an object from a polymorphic array, we must remember to cast it to the type we want. This is just like what we do every time we get a reference to a UI element from our XML layout that uses `findViewById`:

```
Cat newCat = (Cat) myAnimals[2];
```

All we just discussed is true for `ArrayLists` as well. Armed with this new toolkit of arrays and `ArrayLists` and the fact that they are polymorphic, we can move on to learn about some more Android classes that we will soon use to enhance our Note To Self app.

ListView and BaseAdapter

In *Chapter 5, Real-World Layouts,* we used ScrollView and we populated it with around 20 TextView widgets, so we could see it scrolling. We could take what we just learned about arrays and ArrayList and create an array of TextViews and use them to populate ScrollView. This sounds like a perfect solution to display excerpts of a note in our Note To Self app.

We could create TextViews dynamically in Java code, set their text property to be the title of a note, and then add TextViews to LinearLayout that is contained in ScrollView. However, this is imperfect.

The problem with displaying lots of widgets

This might seem fine, but what if there were dozens, hundreds, or even thousands of notes? We couldn't have thousands of TextViews in memory because the Android device might simply run out of memory or, at the very least, grind to a halt as it tries to handle the scrolling of such a vast amount of data.

Now consider that we want each note in ScrollView to show an image about the type of note it is—whether it is important, a to-do list, or an idea. How about a small snippet from the description as well.

We would need to devise some really clever code that loads and destroys Note objects, TextViews, and ImageViews from an array. This can be done, but to do it efficiently is far from straightforward.

The solution

Fortunately, this is a problem faced so commonly by mobile developers that the Android API has a solution built in.

We can add a single ListView widget (like ScrollView with boosters) to our UI layout and then interact with it using an **adapter**. We will use the BaseAdapter class, extend it, customize it, and then use it to control the data from ArrayList and display it in ListView.

Let's find out a bit more about how the ListView and BaseAdapter classes work.

How to use ListView and BaseAdapter

To add `ListView` to our layout, we can simply drag and drop it from the palette onto our UI in the usual way. `ListView` will look like this in the UI designer:

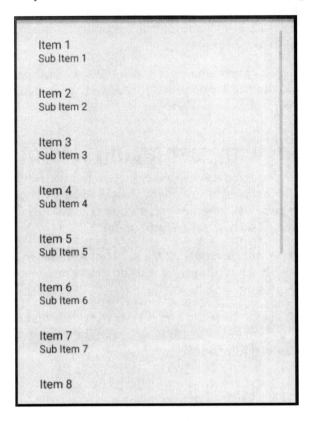

This appearance, however, is more a representation of the possibilities than the actual appearance in an app. If we run the app immediately after adding `ListView`, we just get a blank screen.

The first thing we need to do to make practical use of `ListView` is to decide what each list item will look like. A simple case is implied in the previous figure: an item and a sub item, perhaps, a title and a description.

A list item needs to be defined in its own XML file and then `ListView` can hold multiple instances of a list item.

Of course, none of this explains how we overcome the complexity of managing what data is shown in which list item and how it is retrieved from `ArrayList`.

This data handling is taken care of by our implementation of BaseAdapter. The BaseAdapter class implements the Adapter interface. We don't need to know how Adapter works internally; we just need to override the appropriate methods and then BaseAdapter will do all the work of communicating with ListView.

Wiring up an implementation of BaseAdapter to ListView is certainly more complicated than dragging 20 TextViews onto ScrollView; but once this is done, we can forget about the ListView and it will keep on working.

We need to override four methods and add a little code of our own. Let's take a look at a skeleton of the code that we need to extend BaseAdapter and make it work with our data and ListView.

Here is some sample code that extends and implements BaseAdapter itself:

```
public class MyAdapter extends BaseAdapter {

  List<MyObject> myList = new ArrayList<MyObject>();

  @Override
  public int getCount() {
   return myList.size();
  }

  @Override
  public MyObject getItem(int whichItem) {
   // Simply returns the position of the required item
   return myList.get(whichItem);
  }

  @Override
  public long getItemId(int whichItem) {

   return whichItem;
  }

  @Override
  public View getView(int whichItem, View view, ViewGroup viewGroup) {

   /*
      Prepare a list item to show our data.
      The list item is contained in the
      view parameter. The position of the
      data in our ArrayList is contained
```

```
        in whichItem parameter
    */

    return view;
    }

}
```

At first glance, the preceding code might look slightly complicated, but if we step through it a bit at a time, we will see that it is not as daunting as it might seem.

After the class declaration that extends `BaseAdapter` (of course), we declare and initialize `ArrayList` called `myList`, which holds a list of hypothetical `MyObject` objects. This could easily be changed to hold a list of `Note` objects, for example.

Next, we override the `getCount` method. All this does is return the size of `ArrayList` by calling `myList.size()`. Note that we don't need to use this method ourselves directly.

The next overridden method is `getItem`. This method does no more than return an item from `ArrayList` (`myList`). As such, the return type in the signature matches the type held in `ArrayList`.

The next method `getItemId` is slightly counterintuitive at first glance. It returns a long variable in place of `int` that is passed in. `BaseAdapter` uses this method internally because it needs to distinguish between the `id` property that we give to an item in our list and the internally held `id`. Again, we will not be using this method directly.

Finally, we get to the `getView` method. This is the method that is key to us. This method has a `View` object named `view` as a parameter. This object is the list item that according to what `MyAdapter` (through it's internal workings) has determined needs to be prepared so that it can be displayed to the user. It is here that we can use the techniques you already learned to prepare the list item.

In the `getView` method, we simply, inflate `view`, get a reference to the widgets we want from our list item layout and set the widgets' properties. We have done all these things many times before. We will see this part of the code for real in the next chapter when we enhance our Note To Self app.

So what happens is that the `BaseAdapter` class already handles everything and we just stick our bit of customization in (object type, `ArrayList`, and the `getView` code), and after this, everything is taken care of for us.

Take a look at an outline of the required steps so that we know what to expect when we do this for real. To set the whole thing up and running, we would do the following:

- Add `ListView` to our layout with an appropriate `id` property.
- Create an XML layout to represent a list item.
- Extend `BaseAdapter` as we just discussed.
- Add code in `onCreate` to create an instance of `MyAdapter`, get a reference to `ListView`, and bind it to our adapter instance. Again, we will see this for real in the next chapter.

The only caveats are that we are assuming there is some data in `ArrayList` held by `myAdapter` and we haven't yet got an implementation for our list item.

Let's do all this for real by adding features to our Note To Self app. First, let's take a quick look at inner classes.

Inner classes revisited

As `BaseAdapter` is very closely associated with the Activity that it is created within, it is a perfect candidate to be an inner class. Recall from *Chapter 9, Object-Oriented Programming*, that inner classes are classes declared within another class. Unlike anonymous classes, they must be declared outside the body of any methods of the containing class and have their own name as well. Inner classes can be our own classes or subclasses of a class from the Android API, for example, `BaseAdapter`.

The advantage of an inner class is that it can access all the member variables and methods of its containing class, and we will see in the next chapter how this can be useful. Just note that `BaseAdapter` does not have to be an inner class, it just suits us on this occasion.

FAQ

1. How does a computer which can only make real calculations possibly generate a genuinely random number?

> In reality, a computer cannot create a number that is truly random, but the `Random` class uses a **seed** that produces a number that would stand up as genuinely random under close statistical scrutiny. To find out more about seeds and generating random numbers, take a look at the article at `https://en.wikipedia.org/wiki/Random_number_generation`.

2. Where is the code that manages the creation, showing, hiding, and scrolling of list items and `ListView`?

> It is tucked away in the `BaseAdapter` class and we don't need to know how it works. But if you are curious, you could find out more about it at `http://developer.android.com/reference/android/widget/BaseAdapter.html`.

Summary

In this chapter, we looked at how to use simple Java arrays to store large amount of data with the same type. We also used `ArrayList`, which is like an array with a lot of extra features. Furthermore, we found out that both arrays and `ArrayList` are polymorphic, which means that a single array (or `ArrayList`) can hold multiple different objects as long as they are all derived from the same parent class.

Also, we learned about the `BaseAdapter` class that implements the `Adapter` interface. It allows us to bind together `ListView` and `ArrayList`, allowing the seamless display of data without us (the programmer) having to worry about the complex code that is part of these classes.

In the next chapter, we will put our theory into practice and enhance our Note To Self app.

14
Handling and Displaying Notes in Note To Self

Now that we have thoroughly practiced and theorized data handling and how the Android SDK can help us with `ListView` and `BaseAdapter`, we can begin to stretch our knowledge a little further to make our Note To Self app handle almost unlimited notes.

In this chapter, we will do the following:

- Create a list item layout
- Implement the adapter
- Bind the adapter to `ListView`
- Discuss how we can improve our app

Note To Self continued

Open up the Note To Self app. As a reminder, if you want to see the completed code and working app after completing this chapter, it can be found in the `Chapter 14/ Note to self` folder. As the actions in this chapter require you to jump around between different files, classes, and methods, I encourage you to follow along with the files from the download bundle opened for reference.

Updating onCreate and preparing the UI

Now, let's prepare our UI. To do so, follow these steps:

1. In the `layout_main.xml` file, delete the temporary button with a `button` ID that we added previously for testing purposes.

2. In the `onCreate` method of `MainActivity.java`, we can delete the anonymous class that handles its clicks. In order to do so, delete the code shown next:

```
// Temporary code
Button button = (Button) findViewById(R.id.button);
button.setOnClickListener(new View.OnClickListener() {
  @Override
  public void onClick(View v) {

    DialogShowNote dialog = new DialogShowNote();
    dialog.sendNoteSelected(mTempNote);
    dialog.show(getFragmentManager(), "");
  }
});
```

3. Now, switch back to `layout_main.xml` and drag **ListView** from the palette onto the layout.

4. Set its `id` property to `listView`.

Creating a list item for ListView

Next, let's create a list item to be used within `ListView`. Follow the given steps for the same:

1. Right-click on the `layout` folder and navigate to **New | Layout resource file**. Enter `listitem` in the **Name** field and make the **Root element** field `RelativeLayout`.

2. Take a look at the next screenshot to see what we are trying to achieve:

3. Drag three **ImageView** widgets onto the top-left corner of the layout.

4. It will make the rest of the layout easier to complete if we enter the `src` properties for each of these `ImageView` widgets. So, we might as well add `id` properties while we are doing so. Add the following properties from the table:

Widget type	Property	Value to set to
ImageView (left)	id	imageViewImportant
ImageView (left)	src	@drawable/ic_warning_black_24dp
ImageView (center)	id	imageViewTodo
ImageView (center)	src	@drawable/ic_check_box_outline_blank_black_24dp
ImageView (right)	id	imageViewIdea
ImageView (right)	src	@drawable/ic_wb_incandescent_black_24dp

5. Drag a **LargeText** widget immediately below **ImageViews**, again to the immediate left-hand side of the layout.

6. Now, drag a **Plain TextView** widget immediately below the LargeText widget from the previous step.

7. Follow this table to assign values to the properties:

Widget type	Property	Value to set to
LargeText	id	txtTitle
Plain TextView	id	txtDescription

Now we have ListView and a layout that we can use for each list item. We can go ahead and code our BaseAdapter implementation.

Let's call our new class NoteAdapter. Here is the entire implementation with just the skeleton code for the getView method because it warrants extra discussion and presentation on its own. Add this code within the MainActivity class just before its closing curly brace } because it will be an inner class:

```java
public class NoteAdapter extends BaseAdapter {

  List<Note> noteList = new ArrayList<Note>();

  @Override
  public int getCount() {
    return noteList.size();
  }

  @Override
  public Note getItem(int whichItem) {
    return noteList.get(whichItem);
```

```
    }

    @Override
    public long getItemId(int whichItem) {
      return whichItem;
    }

    @Override
    public View getView(int whichItem, View view, ViewGroup viewGroup)
    {

      // Implement this method next

      return view;
    }
  }
```

The preceding class is nearly identical to the code we discussed previously, except we've called it NoteAdapter. This class holds ArrayList called noteList and the getItem method returns a Note object.

Now, we will look at the code for the getView method. The first thing to note is the parameters that provide us with some useful variables. Most notably, view of the View type and whichItem of the int type.

The view object reference is, in fact, an instance of the list item that is necessary to be displayed as evaluated by BaseAdapter, and whichItem is the position in ArrayList of the Note object that needs to be displayed in it. It seems like BaseAdapter must have read our minds.

All we need to do is write the code to put the data from the Note object into our list item from the listitem.xml layout.

First, we check if (view == null). If it is true, this means that this view has not been inflated to make it ready for use. So, inside the if block we inflate view, which makes all the widgets from listitem.xml available for use in the usual way.

We can then hide any ImageView widgets depending upon the combination of whether the current Note object is TODO, Important, or Idea.

Then, we finally use the setText method on our TextView widgets to display the title and description.

Add the code for the getView method. The entire method including the signature and return statement is shown again for context with the new code highlighted as follows:

```
@Override
public View getView(
    int whichItem, View view, ViewGroup viewGroup) {

    // Implement this method next
    // Has view been inflated already
    if(view == null){

        // If not, do so here
        // First create a LayoutInflater
        LayoutInflater inflater = (LayoutInflater)
        getSystemService(Context.LAYOUT_INFLATER_SERVICE);
        // Now instantiate view using inflater.inflate
        // using the listitem layout
        view = inflater.inflate(R.layout.listitem, viewGroup,false);
        // The false parameter is neccessary
        // because of the way that we want to use listitem

    }// End if

    // Grab a reference to all our TextView and ImageView widgets
    TextView txtTitle = (TextView) view.findViewById(R.id.txtTitle);
TextView txtDescription = (TextView) view.findViewById
    (R.id.txtDescription);
ImageView ivImportant = (ImageView) view.findViewById
    (R.id.imageViewImportant);
ImageView ivTodo = (ImageView) iew.findViewById(R.id.imageViewTodo);
ImageView ivIdea = (ImageView) view.findViewById
    (R.id.imageViewIdea);


    // Hide any ImageView widgets that are not relevant
    Note tempNote = noteList.get(whichItem);

    if (!tempNote.isImportant()){
        ivImportant.setVisibility(View.GONE);
    }

    if (!tempNote.isTodo()){
        ivTodo.setVisibility(View.GONE);
    }

    if (!tempNote.isIdea()){
        ivIdea.setVisibility(View.GONE);
```

```
    }


    // Add the text to the heading and description
    txtTitle.setText(tempNote.getTitle());
    txtDescription.setText(tempNote.getDescription());

    return view;
}
```

Now, we will add one more method to the class. Not an overridden method, one of our own. Just before the closing curly brace } of the NoteAdapter class, add the addNote method. We will call this method when we want to add a Note object to noteList:

```
public void addNote(Note n){

    noteList.add(n);
    notifyDataSetChanged();

}
```

The notifyDataSetChanged method does exactly what the name suggests. It tells NoteAdapter that the data in noteList has changed and that ListView might need to be updated.

Now, in the MainActivity class, modify the createNewNote method that we wrote previously. Add the call to the addNote method that we just wrote inside the NoteAdapter class. The entire method should now look like this:

```
public void createNewNote(Note n){

        mNoteAdapter.addNote(n);

}
```

Now, when DialogNewNote calls createNewNote, createNewNote will pass it straight to the addNote method in the NoteAdapter class, and will be added to ArrayList (noteList). The adapter will be notified of the change as well, which will then trigger the BaseAdapter class to do its work and keep the view up-to-date.

Declare a new NoteAdapter object as a member so that we can access it throughout the class. Add this code just after the opening curly brace, {, of the MainActivity class:

```
private NoteAdapter mNoteAdapter;
```

Delete this temporary member from the last chapter as well:

```
// Temporary code
Note mTempNote = new Note();
```

Next, in the `onCreate` method, we need to initialize `mNoteAdapter`, get a reference to `ListView`, and bind them together:

```
mNoteAdapter = new NoteAdapter();

ListView listNote = (ListView) findViewById(R.id.listView);

listNote.setAdapter(mNoteAdapter);
```

Now, we are really close to being able to use our new features. If you remember, we deleted the temporary button that opened the `DialogShowNote` dialog window. Now, we will click on a list item within `ListView` to open the `DialogShowNote` window instead.

First, we will create a new `AdapterView.OnItemClickListener` anonymous class, set it to `listNote` (`ListView`), and override the `onItemClick` method.

Within this method, we will create a temporary `Note` reference called `tempNote` by calling `mNoteAdapter.getItem(whichItem)`.

Then, we will create a new instance of `DialogShowNote` called `dialog`, send in the temporary `Note` reference using `sendNoteSelected`, and then show the dialog window.

Enter the following code, which we just discussed, just before the closing curly brace, `}`, inside the `onCreate` method:

```
// Handle clicks on the ListView
listNote.setOnItemClickListener(new AdapterView.OnItemClickListener()
{

  @Override
  public void onItemClick(AdapterView<?> adapter, View view, int
    whichItem, long id) {

    /*
      Create  a temporary Note
      Which is a reference to the Note
      that has just been clicked
    */
    Note tempNote = mNoteAdapter.getItem(whichItem);
```

```
            // Create a new dialog window
            DialogShowNote dialog = new DialogShowNote();
            // Send in a reference to the note to be shown
            dialog.sendNoteSelected(tempNote);

            // Show the dialog window with the note in it
            dialog.show(getFragmentManager(), "");

        }
    });
```

You can now run the app and create a whole bunch of notes, view them in the list, and select any note from the list to be shown:

ArrayList reminder
Roses are red violets are blue, ArrayList is handy when arrays just won't do.

Persistence
I must read chapter 15 so I don't lose all my notes when I quit the app!

▲
Happiness
It is not how much we have, but how much we enjoy, that makes happiness.

Here is one of the notes from the list:

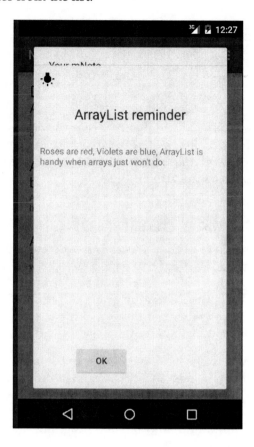

Don't spend too much time on adding new notes, however, because there is a slight problem. Close and restart the app. Uh oh, all the notes are gone!

Improvements in Note To Self

Here are some of the aspects we will fix over the next few chapters.

Persistence

It seems that our `ArrayList`, `BaseAdapter`, and `ListView` combination, while versatile and timesaving, does not persist when the app is quit. In *Chapter 15, Android Intent and Persistence*, we will add the **Settings** menu and look at two separate solutions to save data in a persistent way. One for simple data, such as the **Settings** screen options and one for more complex data, such as the objects in `ArrayList`.

Animation

In *Chapter 16, UI Animations*, we will also add some simple animations to Note To Self that make the user's experience more visually pleasing. We will also experiment with an animation mini app.

Sound FX

The addition of pleasing sounds can enhance an app as well as give audible feedback to the user that the action they just took was successful. In *Chapter 17, Sound FX and Supporting Different Versions of Android* we will add sound to Note To Self, as well as experiment with sounds in a mini app.

Problems with the design of the code

It might seem worthwhile if `noteList` was a class of its own. Actually, it probably should be. It would make a lot of sense to have a class that held `ArrayList` and provided us access to that list with a getter method. Furthermore, it would allow us to put into effect other best practices. As an example, we could ensure that we only ever have one `noteList`, and wherever this `notelist` is accessed from, throughout our app, there would be no danger of creating a second, third, or fourth list.

You have learned many new classes and concepts in the last few chapters, and you will learn a lot more in the next three. Therefore, I thought I would defer the discussion of the Java **singleton**, which helps us achieve all these things, until *Chapter 18, Design Patterns, Fragments, and the Real World*, where we will also discuss **design patterns** that are useful for Android and programming in general.

FAQ

1. I still don't understand how `BaseAdapter` works?

   That's because we haven't really discussed it. The reason we have not discussed the behind-the-scenes details is because we don't need to know them. As long as we override the required methods, as we just saw, everything will work. This is how `BaseAdapter` and most other classes we use are meant to be, the hidden implementation with public methods to expose the necessary functionality.

2. I feel like I *need* to know what is going on inside `BaseAdapter` and other classes as well.

It is true that there are more details for `BaseAdapter` (and almost every class that we use in this book) that we don't have the space to discuss. It is good practice to read the official documentation of the classes you use. You can read more about `BaseAdapter` at `http://developer.android.com/reference/android/widget/BaseAdapter.html`.

Summary

Now that we have added the ability to hold multiple notes, we can work on the list of improvements that we just discussed.

We will start with making the users' notes persist when they quit the app or switch off their device. In addition to this, we will create a settings screen and see how we can make the settings persist as well. We will use different techniques to achieve each of these goals.

15
Android Intent and Persistence

In this chapter, we will look at a couple of different ways to save data to the Android device's permanent storage. Also, for the first time, we will add a second Activity to our app. It often makes sense when implementing a separate "screen," like a settings screen in our app, to do so in a new Activity. We could go to the trouble of hiding the original UI and then showing the new UI, but this would quickly lead to confusing and error-prone code. So, we will see how to add an Activity and navigate the user between them.

In this chapter, we will:

- Learn about Android Intents to switch the Activity and pass data
- Create a settings screen in a new Activity
- Persist the settings screen data using the `SharedPreferences` class
- Learn about JavaScript object notation for serialization
- Explore Java `try-catch-finally`
- Implement saving data in our Note To Self app

Good Intents

The `Intent` class is appropriately named. It is a class that demonstrates the Intent of an Activity from our app. It makes clear Intent and it also facilitates it.

All our apps so far have had just one Activity, but most Android apps are comprised of more than one.

In perhaps its most common use, an `Intent` object allows us to switch between activities. But, of course, activities are classes. So, what happens to their data when we switch between them? Intents handle this problem for us, as well, by allowing us to pass data between activities.

Intents aren't just about wiring up the activities of our app. They also make it possible to interact with other apps. For example, we could provide a link in our app for the user to send e-mail, make a phone call, interact with social media, and open a web page in a browser and have the e-mail, dialer, browser, or relevant social media app do all the work.

There aren't enough pages to really dig deep into interacting with other apps, and we will mainly focus on switching between activities and passing data.

 If you want to know more about the `Intent` class than this chapter has the time to cover, I recommend the book *Learning Android Intents* by Muhammad Usama bin Aftab and Wajahat Karim, published by Packt Publishing (https://www.packtpub.com/application-development/learning-android-intents). The book assumes you already know how to program in Java but has a very gentle learning curve and explores the `Intent` class in vastly greater detail than we have room for in this book.

Throughout the rest of the book, we will occasionally bump into the `Intent` class again and see more of the things it can do.

Switching Activity

Let's say we have an app with two activities, because we will soon. We can assume that, as usual, we have an Activity called `MainActivity`, which is where the app starts, and a second Activity called `SettingsActivity`. This is how we can swap from `MainActivity` to `SettingsActivity`:

```
// Declare and initialize a new Intent object called myIntent
Intent myIntent = new   Intent(this,SettingsActivity.class);

// Switch to the SettingsActivity
startActivity(myIntent);
```

Look carefully at how we initialized the `Intent` object. The `Intent` class has a constructor that takes two arguments. The first is a reference to the current Activity, `this`. And the second parameter is the name of the Activity we want to open, `SettingsActivity.class`. The `.class` on the end of `SettingsActivity` makes it the full name of the Activity, as declared in the `AndroidManifest.xml` file, and we will peek at that when we experiment with Intents shortly.

The only problem is that `SettingsActivity` doesn't share any of the data of `MainActivity`. In a way, this is a good thing because if you need all the data from `MainActivity`, then it is a reasonable indication that switching activities might not be the best way of proceeding with your app's design. It is, however, unreasonable to have encapsulation so thorough that the two activities know absolutely nothing about each other.

Passing data between activities

What if we have a sign-in screen for the user and we want to pass the login credentials to each and every `Activity` of our app? We could do so using Intents.

We can add data to `Intent` like this:

```
// Create a String called username
// and set its value to bob
String username = "Bob";

// Create a new Intent as we have already seen
Intent myIntent = new Intent(this,SettingsActivity.class);

// Add the username String to the Intent
// using the putExtra method of the Intent class
myIntent.putExtra("USER_NAME", username);

// Start the new Activity as we have before
startActivity(myIntent);
```

In `SettingsActivity`, we could then retrieve the string like this:

```
// Here we need an Intent also
// But the default constructor will do
// as we are not switching Activity
Intent myIntent = new Intent();

// Initialize username with the passed in String
String username = intent.getExtra().getStringKey("USER_NAME");
```

In the previous two blocks of code, we switched the Activity in the same way as we have already seen. But before we called `startActivity`, we used the `putExtra` method to load a string into the Intent.

We add data using **key-value pairs**. Each piece of data needs to be accompanied by an `identifier` that can be used in the retrieving Activity to identify and retrieve the data.

The identifier name is arbitrary, but useful/memorable values should be used.

Then, in the receiving Activity, we simply create `Intent` using the default constructor:

```
Intent myIntent = new Intent();
```

And we can then retrieve the data using the `getExtras` method and the appropriate identifier from the key-value pair.

Once we want to start sending more than a few values, then it is worth considering different tactics.

The `Intent` class can help us in sending more complex data than this, but the `Intent` class does have its limits. For example, we wouldn't be able to pass a `Note` object.

We can also save data (complex and simple) to the device's disk, and this is covered later in this chapter. We can even create and use a database dedicated to our app. Databases will be primarily discussed in *Chapter 23, Using SQLite Databases in Our Apps*.

Adding a settings page to the Note To Self app

Now that we are armed with all this knowledge about Android Intents, we can add another screen (Activity) to our Note To Self app.

We will first create a new Activity and see what effect that has on the `AndroidManifest.xml` file. We will then create a layout for our Settings screen and add the Java code to switch from `MainActivity` to the new one. We will, however, defer wiring up our settings screen with Java until we have learned how to save those settings to disk. We will do this later in this chapter and then come back to the settings screen to make the data persist.

First, let's create that new Activity.

Creating SettingsActivity

This will be a screen where the user can turn on or off the sound effects as well as choose the speed of animations. Clearly, our app does not yet have sound and animations, but we can still fully code this screen and see how to save data to the device's permanent storage by following the given steps:

1. In the project explorer, right-click on the folder that contains all your `.java` files and has the same name as your package. From the pop-up context menu, select **New | Activity | Blank Activity**.

2. In the **Activity Name** field, enter `SettingsActivity`.

3. Leave all the other options at their defaults and left-click on **Finish**.

Android Studio has created a new Activity for us and its associated `.java` file. Let's take a quick peek at some of the work that was done behind the scenes for us because it is useful to know what is going on.

Open the `AndroidManifest.xml` file from within the `manifests` folder in the project explorer. Notice the following four lines of code near the end of this file:

```
<activity
    android:name=".SettingsActivity"
    android:label="@string/title_activity_settings" >
</activity>
```

This is how an Activity is **registered** with the operating system. If an Activity is not registered, then an attempt to run it will crash the app. We could create an Activity simply by creating a class that extends the `Activity` class (or `AppCompatActivity`) in a new `.java` file. However, we would then have had to add the previous code ourselves. Also, by using the new Activity wizard, we got both a layout XML file and menu XML file all automatically generated for us.

Designing the Settings screen's layout

We will quickly build a user interface for our **Settings** screen, and the following steps and image should make this straightforward:

1. Open the `activity_settings.xml` file, switch to the **Design** tab, and we will quickly lay out our **Settings** screen.

2. Delete the **Hello world!** widget that was put in automatically.

3. Use this next image as a guide while following the rest of the steps:

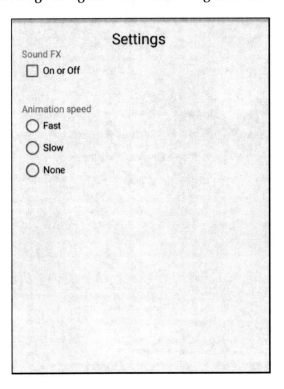

4. Drag and drop a **LargeText** widget onto the center-top of the layout.

5. Drag and drop a **Plain TextView** widget and place it on the left and slightly below the previous widget.

6. Drag and drop a **CheckBox** widget immediately below the previous widget.

7. Drag a **Plain TextView** widget below the previous **CheckBox** widget, and leave a small space as shown in the previous image.

8. Drag and drop a **RadioGroup** widget from the Palette and place it immediately below the widget in the previous step.

9. Drag three **RadioButton** widgets and place them one below the other inside of the **RadioGroup** widget.

10. Use the following table to set the properties on the layout elements we have just added. In case there is any doubt which widget I am referring to in the table, we are working from the top to bottom of the layout:

Widget type	Property	Value to set to
LargeText	text	@string/settings_title
Plain TextView	text	@string/sound_title
CheckBox	text	@string/sound_checkbox
CheckBox	id	checkBoxSound
Plain TextView	text	@string/amims_title
RadioGroup	id	radioGroup
RadioButton (top)	text	@string/rb_fast
RadioButton (top)	id	radioFast
RadioButton (middle)	text	@string/rb_slow
RadioButton (middle)	id	radioSlow
RadioButton (bottom)	text	@string/rb_none
RadioButton (bottom)	id	radioNone

We now have a nice new layout for our **Settings** screen and the id properties are in place, ready for when we wire it up with our Java code later in the chapter.

Enabling the user to switch to the Settings screen

We already know how to switch to SettingsActivity. Also, as we won't be passing any data to it or from it, we can get this working with just two lines of Java.

You might have noticed that in the action bar of our app, there is the menu icon. It is indicated in the following image:

If you tap it, there is already a menu option in there for **Settings**, provided by default when we first created the app. And all we need to do is place our code to switch to SettingsActivity within the onOptionsItemSelected method. Android Studio even provided an if block for us to paste our code into with the assumption we would one day want to add a Settings menu. How thoughtful!

Find the following block of code in the `onOptionsItemSelected` method in `MainActivity.java`:

```
//noinspection SimplifiableIfStatement
if (id == R.id.action_settings) {
  return true;
}
```

Add this code into the `if` block shown previously, just before the `return true` statement:

```
Intent intent = new Intent(this, SettingsActivity.class);
startActivity(intent);
```

You can now run the app and visit the new **Settings** screen by tapping the **Settings** screen's menu option.

To return from `SettingsActivity` to `MainActivity`, you can tap the back button on the device. We will be making this a bit more intuitive for the user later in the chapter in the section *Specifying a parent Activity*.

Persisting data with SharedPreferences

In Android, there are a number of ways to make data persist. By persist, I mean that if the user quits the app, when they come back to it, their data is still available. The correct method to use is dependent upon the app and type of data.

In this book, we will look at three ways to make data persist. For saving our users' settings, we only need a really simple method. After all, we just need to know if they want sound and at which speed they want their animations.

Let's take a look at how we can make our apps save and reload variables to the internal storage of the device. We need to use the `SharedPreferences` class. `SharedPreferences` is a class that provides access to data that can be accessed and edited by all activities of an app. Let's look at how we can use it:

```
// A SharedPreferences for reading data
SharedPreferences prefs;

// A SharedPreferences.Editor for writing data
SharedPreferences.Editor editor;
```

As with all objects, we need to initialize them before we can use them. We can initialize the `prefs` object using the `getSharedPreferences` method and by passing in `String`, which will be used to refer to all the data read and written using this object. Typically, we could use the name of the app as this string. In the next code, `Mode_Private` means that any class, in this app only, can access it:

```
prefs = getSharedPreferences("My App", MODE_PRIVATE);
```

We then use our newly initialized `prefs` object to initialize our `editor` object by calling the `edit` method:

```
editor = prefs.edit();
```

Let's say we wanted to save the user's name that we have in a string called `username`. We can then write the data to the internal memory of the device like this:

```
editor.putString("username", username);
editor.commit();
```

The first argument used in the `putString` method is a label that can be used to refer to the data, and the second is the actual variable that holds the data we want to save. The second line in the previous code initiates the saving process. So, we could write multiple variables to disk like this:

```
editor.putString("username", username);
editor.putInt("age", age);
editor.putBoolean("newsletter-subscriber", subscribed);

// Save all the above data
editor.commit();
```

The preceding code demonstrates that you can save other variable types, and it of course assumes that the `username`, `age`, and `subscribed` variables have previously been initialized with appropriate values.

Once `editor.commit()` is executed, the data is stored. We can quit the app and even turn off the device and the data will persist.

Let's see how we can reload our data the next time the app is run. This code will reload the three values that the previous code saved. We could even declare our variables and initialize them with the stored values:

```
String username =
  prefs.getString("username", "new user");

int age = prefs.getInt("age", -1);
```

```
boolean subscribed =
  prefs.getBoolean("newsletter-subscriber", false)
```

In the previous code, we load the data from disk using the method appropriate for the data type and the same label we used to save the data in the first place. What is less clear is the second argument to each of the method calls. The getString, getInt, and getBoolean methods require a default value as the second parameter. If there is no data stored with that label, it will then return the default value. We could then check for these default values in our code and go about trying to obtain the real values. For example:

```
if (age == -1){
  // Ask the user for his age
}
```

We now know enough to save our users' settings in the Note To Self app.

Making the Note To Self app's settings persist

We have already learned how to save data to the device's memory. As we implement saving users' settings, we will also see again how we handle the CheckBox, RadioGroup, and RadioButton input.

Coding the SettingsActivity class

Most of the action will take place in the SettingsActivity.java file. So, click on the appropriate tab and we will add the code a bit at a time.

First, we need some member variables that will give us a working SharedPreferences and Editor reference. We also want a member variable to represent each of the users' settings options. We need one for sound (boolean for on or off) and int for their preferred animation option (fast, slow, or none). Furthermore, as you will see in the next code, we have three member variables: public, static, and final. These serve several purposes.

As they are final, they cannot be changed, so they are useful for remembering the three possible states the animation option can be set to. This is a lot easier than trying to remember which value represents which animation state. In addition, these variables are static.

Reminder: Static variables persist and are the same throughout multiple instances of a class. They will be accessible in MainActivity as well as SettingsActivity, even when an instance of SettingsActivity does not exist. We will soon see how this is useful.

Add the following member variables to SettingsActivity:

```
private SharedPreferences mPrefs;
private SharedPreferences.Editor mEditor;

private boolean mSound;

public static final int FAST = 0;
public static final int SLOW = 1;
public static final int NONE = 2;

private int mAnimOption;
```

Now, in onCreate, add the highlighted code to initialize mPrefs and mEditor:

```
mPrefs = getSharedPreferences("Note to self", MODE_PRIVATE);
mEditor = mPrefs.edit();
```

Next, still in onCreate, let's get a reference to our checkbox and load up the saved data that represents our user's previous choice for sound. We get a reference to the checkbox in the usual way and based on the value of mSound, we either check or uncheck the box:

```
mSound   = mPrefs.getBoolean("sound", true);

CheckBox checkBoxSound = (CheckBox) findViewById(R.id.checkBoxSound);

if(mSound){
  checkBoxSound.setChecked(true);
}else{
  checkBoxSound.setChecked(false);
}
```

Next, we make an anonymous class to handle any changes to the sound options by detecting taps on the CheckBox class.

Notice the `onCheckedChanged` method has a Boolean parameter, `isChecked`. We add some logging code so we can see what is going on in the console, but the real functionality is simple. Change the status of `mSound` by reversing it, by making it `!` (not) what it was previously. Then, use `Editor` to put the new value into the `sound` key-value pair.

Add the following code to the `onCreate` method that we have just discussed:

```
checkBoxSound.setOnCheckedChangeListener
  (new CompoundButton.OnCheckedChangeListener()
{
  public void onCheckedChanged(
    CompoundButton buttonView, boolean isChecked)
  {
    Log.i("sound = ", "" + mSound);
    Log.i("isChecked = ", "" + isChecked);

    // If mSound is true make it false
    // If mSound is false make it true
    mSound = ! mSound;
    mEditor.putBoolean("sound", mSound);

  }
});
```

Next, let's turn our attention to the `RadioGroup`/`RadioButtons` and the user's preferences for the animation speed. We get the current setting with `mPrefs.getInt` and then we get a reference to `RadioGroup` in the usual way. Then, we clear any `RadioButtons` that might have already been pressed.

We then use a `switch` statement with `mAnimOption` as the argument and check the appropriate button based on the value that we loaded.

Add this new code to `onCreate`:

```
// Now for the radio buttons
mAnimOption = mPrefs.getInt("anim option", FAST);

RadioGroup radioGroup = (RadioGroup) findViewById(R.id.radioGroup);

// Deselect all buttons
radioGroup.clearCheck();

// Which radio button should be selected?
switch(mAnimOption){
```

```
    case FAST:
      radioGroup.check(R.id.radioFast);
      break;

    case SLOW:
      radioGroup.check(R.id.radioSlow);
      break;

    case NONE:
      radioGroup.check(R.id.radioNone);
      break;


  }
```

And now, we can handle clicks on the radio buttons. In the onCheckedChanged method, we use the switch block based on the ID of the just-checked button. In each of the case statements, we assign the appropriate value to mAnimOption and after the switch block, we use the Editor object to put that value away in the appropriate key-value pair.

Add this code to the onCreate method:

```
radioGroup.setOnCheckedChangeListener
  (new RadioGroup.OnCheckedChangeListener() {
@Override
public void onCheckedChanged(RadioGroup group, int checkedId) {
  RadioButton rb = (RadioButton) group.findViewById(checkedId);
  if (null != rb && checkedId > -1) {

    switch (rb.getId()){

      case R.id.radioFast:
        mAnimOption = FAST;
        break;

      case R.id.radioSlow:
        mAnimOption = SLOW;
        break;

      case R.id.radioNone:
        mAnimOption = NONE;
        break;


    }
```

```
    // End switch block

    mEditor.putInt("anim option", mAnimOption);

  }

}
});
```

You might have noticed that at no point in any of that code did we call `mEditor.comit` to actually save the user's settings. We could have placed it after we detected a change to `CheckBox` or `RadioButton`; however, is much simpler to put where it is guaranteed to be called, but only once.

We will use our knowledge of the Activity lifecycle and override the `onPause` method. When the user leaves `SettingsActivity` either to go back to `MainActivity` or to quit the app, `onPause` will be called and the settings will be saved. Add this code to override `onPause` and save the user's settings. Add the code just before the closing curly brace of the `SettingsActivity` class:

```
@Override
protected void onPause() {
  super.onPause();

  // Save the settings here
  mEditor.commit();
}
```

Coding the MainActivity class

Finally, we can add some code to `MainActivity` to load the settings when the app starts or when the user switches back from the **Settings** screen to the main screen.

Add this highlighted code to add some member variables after `NoteAdapter`:

```
private NoteAdapter mNoteAdapter;
private boolean mSound;
private int mAnimOption;
private SharedPreferences mPrefs;
```

At this time, we will override the `onResume` method, initialize our `mPrefs` variable, and load the settings into the `mSound` and `mAnimOption` variables. Now, when we add our sound and animation code in *Chapter 16, UI Animations* and *Chapter 17, Sound FX and Supporting Different Versions of Android*, we will use animations and sound effects at the right time and speed.

Add the overriden `onResume` method as shown next:

```
@Override
protected void onResume(){
  super.onResume();

  mPrefs = getSharedPreferences("Note to self", MODE_PRIVATE);
  mSound  = mPrefs.getBoolean("sound", true);
  mAnimOption = mPrefs.getInt("anim option", SettingsActivity.FAST);
}
```

The user is now able to choose their settings. The app will both save and reload them as necessary.

Specifying a parent Activity

It is not essential but it is good practice (with benefits) to declare a **parent** Activity for new activities. By doing so, we will also enhance our app visually and improve its usability as well.

Open up the `AndroidManifest.xml` file from the `manifests` folder. Add the highlighted line of the following code in the position shown:

```
...
<activity
  android:name=".SettingsActivity"
  android:parentActivityName=".MainActivity"
  android:label="@string/title_activity_settings" >
</activity>
...
```

`SettingsActivity` now officially has `MainActivity` as its parent. Now, we can run the app and see a minor visual enhancement. The user can now use the device's back button or the icon added to the UI upon adding that last bit of code:

Now we have a neat **Settings** screen, and we can permanently save the user's choices. Of course, the big missing link with regard to persistence is that the user's fundamental data, his or her notes, still do not persist.

More advanced persistence

Let's think about what we need to do. We want to save a bunch of notes to the internal storage. Being more specific, we want to store a selection of strings and related Boolean values. These strings and Boolean values represent the user's note title, the note's text, and whether or not it is a to-do, important, or idea.

Given what we already know about the `SharedPreferences` class, at first glance, this might not seem especially challenging until we dig a little deeper into our requirements. What if the user loves our app and ends up with 100 notes? We would need 100 identifiers for the key-value pairs. This is not impossible but is starting to get awkward.

Now, consider that we want to enhance the note app and give the user the ability to add dates to them. Android has a `Date` class that is perfect for this. It would be fairly straightforward to then add neat features like reminders to our app. But when it comes to saving data, all of a sudden, things start to get complicated.

How would we store a date using `SharedPreferences`? It wasn't designed for this. We could convert it to a string when we save it and convert it back again when we load it, but this is far from simple.

And as our app grows in features and our users get more and more notes, the whole persistence thing becomes a nightmare. What we need is a way to save and load objects, actual Java objects. If we can simply save and load objects, including their internal data (strings, Booleans, dates, or anything else), our apps can have any kind of data we can think of to suit our users.

The process of converting data objects into bits and bytes to store on a disk is called **serialization**; the reverse process is called **de-serialization**. Serialization on its own is a vast topic and far from straightforward. Fortunately, as we are coming to expect, there is a class to handle most of the complexity for us.

What is JSON?

JSON stands for **JavaScript Object Notation** and is widely used in fields beyond Android and the Java language. It is perhaps more frequently used for sending data between web applications and servers.

Fortunately, there are JSON classes available for Android that almost entirely hide the complexity of the serialization process. By learning about a few more Java concepts, we can quickly begin to use these classes and start writing entire Java objects to the device storage rather than having to worry ourselves about what primitive types make up the objects.

The JSON classes, compared with other classes we have seen so far, undertake operations that have a higher than normal possibility of failure beyond their control. To find out why this is so and what can be done about it, let's take a look at Java exceptions.

Java exceptions - try, catch, and finally

All this talk of JSON requires us to learn a new Java concept: **exceptions**. When we write a class that performs operations that have a possibility of failure, especially for reasons beyond our control, it is advisable to make this clear in our code so that anyone using our class is prepared for the possibility.

Saving and loading data is one such scenario where failure is possible beyond our control. Think about trying to load data when the SD card has been removed or corrupted. Another instance where code might fail is perhaps when we write code that relies on a network connection—what if the user goes offline part of the way through a data transfer?

Java exceptions are the solution, and the JSON classes use them, so it is a good time to learn about them.

When we write a class that uses code with a chance of failure, we can prepare the users of our class by using exceptions with `try`, `catch`, and `finally`.

We can write methods in our classes using the `throws` Java keyword at the end of the signature. A bit like this, perhaps:

```
public void somePrecariousMethod() throws someException{
  // Risky code goes here
}
```

Now, any code that uses `somePrecariousMethod` will need to **handle** the exception. The way we handle exceptions is by wrapping code in the `try` and `catch` blocks. Perhaps like this:

```
try{
  ...
  somePrecariousMethod();
  ...
```

```
}catch(someException e){
  Log.e("Exception:" + e, "Uh ohh")
  // Take action if possible
}
```

Optionally, we can also add a `finally` block if we want to take any further action after the `try` and `catch` blocks, as shown here:

```
finally{
  // More action here
}
```

In our Note To Self app, we will take the minimum necessary action to handle exceptions and simply output an error to logcat, but you could do things like notify the user, retry the operation, or put into operation some clever back-up plan.

Backing up user data in Note To Self

So, with our newfound insight into exceptions, let's modify our Note To Self code and then we can be introduced to `JSONObject` and `JSONException`.

First, let's make some minor modifications to our `Note` class. Add some more members that will act as the key in a key-value pair for each aspect of our `Note` class:

```
private static final String JSON_TITLE = "title";
private static final String JSON_DESCRIPTION = "description";
private static final String JSON_IDEA = "idea" ;
private static final String JSON_TODO = "todo";
private static final String JSON_IMPORTANT = "important";
```

Now, add a constructor and empty default constructor that receives `JSONObject` and throws `JSONException`. The body of the constructor initializes each of the members that define the properties of a single `Note` object by calling the `getString` or `getBoolean` method of `JSONObject`, passing in the key as an argument. We also provide an empty default constructor, which is required now that we are providing our specialized constructor:

```
// Constructor
// Only used when new is called with a JSONObject
public Note(JSONObject jo) throws JSONException {

  mTitle =  jo.getString(JSON_TITLE);
  mDescription = jo.getString(JSON_DESCRIPTION);
  mIdea = jo.getBoolean(JSON_IDEA);
  mTodo = jo.getBoolean(JSON_TODO);
  mImportant = jo.getBoolean(JSON_IMPORTANT);
```

```
    }
    // Now we must provide an empty default constructor
    // for when we create a Note as we provide a
    // specialized constructor that must be used.
    public Note (){

    }
```

In the next code, we will see how to load the member variables of a given `Note` object into `JSONObject`. This is where the `Note` object's members are packed up as a single `JSONObject` ready for when the actual serialization takes place.

All we need to do is call `put` with the appropriate key and the matching member variable. This method returns `JSONObject` (we will see where in a minute), and it also throws a `JSONException` exception. Add the code we have just discussed:

```
    public JSONObject convertToJSON() throws JSONException{

      JSONObject jo = new JSONObject();

      jo.put(JSON_TITLE, mTitle);
      jo.put(JSON_DESCRIPTION, mDescription);
      jo.put(JSON_IDEA, mIdea);
      jo.put(JSON_TODO, mTodo);
      jo.put(JSON_IMPORTANT, mImportant);

      return jo;
    }
```

Now, let's make a `JSONSerializer` class that will perform the actual serialization and deserialization. Create a new class and call it `JSONSerializer`.

Let's split it up into a few chunks and talk about what we are doing as we code each chunk.

First, we'll incorporate the declaration and a couple of member variables—a string to hold the filename where the data will be saved and a `Context` object that is necessary in Android to write data to a file:

```
    public class JSONSerializer {

        private String mFilename;
        private Context mContext;

      // All the rest of the code for the class goes here

    }// End of class
```

The previous code shows the closing curly brace of the class and all the code that follows, for this class should be entered inside of it. Here is the very straightforward constructor where we initialize the two member variables that are passed in as parameters to the constructor:

```
public JSONSerializer(String fn, Context con){
  mFilename = fn;
  mContext = con;

}
```

Now, we can start coding the real guts of the class. The `save` method is next. It first creates a `JSONArray` object, which is a specialized `ArrayList` for handling JSON objects.

Next, the code uses an enhanced `for` loop to go through all the `Note` objects in `notes` and convert them to JSON objects, using the `convertToJSON` method from the `Note` class that we added previously. Then, we load these converted `JSONObjects` into `jArray`.

Next, the code uses a `Writer` instance combined with an `Outputstream` instance to write the data to an actual file. Notice the `OutputStream` instance needed the `mContext` to be initialized. Add the code we have just discussed:

```
public void save(List<Note> notes)
   throws IOException, JSONException{

  // Make an array in JSON format
  JSONArray jArray = new JSONArray();

  // And load it with the notes
  for (Note n : notes)
    jArray.put(n.convertToJSON());

  // Now write it to the private disk space of our app
  Writer writer = null;
  try {
    OutputStream out = mContext.openFileOutput
      (mFilename, mContext.MODE_PRIVATE);

    writer = new OutputStreamWriter(out);
    writer.write(jArray.toString());
  } finally {
    if (writer != null) {

      writer.close();
    }
  }
}
```

Now, for the de-serialization—loading the data. This time, as we might expect, the method receives no parameters but instead returns ArrayList. An InputStream instance is created using mContext.openFileInput, and our file containing all our data is opened.

We use a while loop to append all the data to a string in addition to our new Note constructor, which extracts JSON data to regular primitive variables to unpack each JSONObject into a Note object and add it to ArrayList, which is returned to the calling code:

```
public ArrayList<Note> load() throws IOException, JSONException{
  ArrayList<Note> noteList = new ArrayList<Note>();
  BufferedReader reader = null;
  try {

    InputStream in = mContext.openFileInput(mFilename);
    reader = new BufferedReader(new InputStreamReader(in));
    StringBuilder jsonString = new StringBuilder();
    String line = null;

    while ((line = reader.readLine()) != null) {

      jsonString.append(line);
    }


    JSONArray jArray = (JSONArray) new JSONTokener
      (jsonString.toString()).nextValue();
    for (int i = 0; i < jArray.length(); i++) {
      noteList.add(new Note(jArray.getJSONObject(i)));
    }
  } catch (FileNotFoundException e) {
    // we will ignore this one, since it happens
    // when we start fresh. You could add a log here.
  } finally {// This will always run
    if (reader != null)
      reader.close();
  }

  return noteList;
}
```

Now, all we need to do is put our new class to work in the MainActivity class or, more specifically, our NoteAdapter class within MainActivity. Add a new member after the NoteAdapter declaration to the NoteAdapter class in MainActivity.java:

```
public class NoteAdapter extends BaseAdapter {

    private JSONSerializer mSerializer;
    List<Note> noteList = new ArrayList<Note>();
    ...
    ...
```

Now, in the same class, we will add a new constructor. In the constructor, we initialize mSerializer by calling the JSONSerializer constructor with the filename and MainActivity.this.getApplicationContext(), which is the Context of the application and is required. We can then use the JSONSerializer load method to load any saved data:

```
public NoteAdapter(){

mSerializer = new JSONSerializer("NoteToSelf.json",
   MainActivity.this.getApplicationContext());

    try {
      noteList = mSerializer.load();
    } catch (Exception e) {
      noteList = new ArrayList<Note>();
      Log.e("Error loading notes: ", "", e);
    }

}
```

Now, add a new method to our NoteAdapter inner class that we can call to save all our users' data. All this new method does is call the save method of the JSONSerializer class, passing in the required list of Note objects:

```
public void saveNotes(){
  try{
    mSerializer.save(noteList);

  }catch(Exception e){
    Log.e("Error Saving Notes","", e);
  }
}
```

Now, just as we did when saving our users' settings, we will override the `onPause` method to save our users' data. Be sure to add this code in the `MainActivity` class and not the inner class we have just been working with:

```
@Override
protected void onPause(){
  super.onPause();

  mNoteAdapter.saveNotes();

}
```

That's it. We can now run the app and add as many notes as we like. `ArrayList` will store them all in our running app, `BaseAdapter` will manage displaying them in `ListView`, and now JSON will take care of loading them from disk and saving them back as well.

FAQ

1. I didn't understand everything in this chapter, so maybe I am not cut out to be a programmer.

    This chapter introduced many new classes, concepts, and methods. If your head is aching a little, that is to be expected. If some of the detail is unclear, don't let it hold you back. Proceed with the next couple of chapters (they are much more straightforward), then revisit this one and especially examine the completed code files.

2. So, how does serialization work in detail?

    Serialization really is a vast topic. It is possible to write apps your whole life and never really need to understand it. It is the type of topic that would be the subject of a computer science degree. If you are curious to know more, have a look at this article: `https://en.wikipedia.org/wiki/Serialization`.

3. What exactly does the data in the file look like when it has been written there?

    The JSON data is in a text format and it is actually possible to view this file. You can use the Android Debug Bridge to "talk" to the emulator. If you are interested, you can see a quick guide for the ADB here: `http://developer.android.com/tools/help/adb.html`. You can then use the `pull` command to get a file from the emulator on to your PC. Or, if you are in a hurry, you can see some sample JSON data, as well as a discussion here: `http://www.w3schools.com/json/json_syntax.asp`.

Summary

At this point in our journey through the Android API, it is worth taking stock of what we know. We can lay out our own UI designs and choose from a fairly wide and diverse range of widgets to allow the user to interact. We can create multiple screens, as well as pop-up dialogs, and we can capture comprehensive user data. Furthermore, we can now make this data persist.

Certainly, there is still a lot more to the Android API to learn, even beyond what this book will teach you, but the point is we know enough now to plan and implement a working app. You could just skip to *Chapter 29, Publishing Apps*, and publish.

If you have the urge to start your own project right away, then my advice is to go ahead and do it. Don't wait until you consider yourself an "expert" or "more ready." Reading this book and, more importantly, implementing the apps will make you a better Android programmer, but nothing will teach you faster than designing and implementing your own app! It is perfectly possible to complete this book and work on your own project simultaneously.

We will spend two more chapters learning about sound and animation, then we will turn to more advanced topics to really make your apps professional.

Next up is how to play sounds in our apps with the Android `SoundPool` class.

16
UI Animations

In this chapter, we will see how to use the `Animation` class to make our UI more mobile and interesting. As we have come to expect, and the `Animation` class is no different, the Android API will allow us to do some quite advanced things with relatively straightforward code.

This chapter can be approximately divided into these topics:

- An introduction to how animations in Android work and are implemented
- An introduction to a new UI widget: **SeekBar**
- A working animated mini app
- Adding simple, pleasing animations to the Note To Self app

First, let's see how do animations in Android work?

Animations in Android

The normal way to create an animation in Android is through XML. We can write XML animations and then load and play them in Java on a specified UI widget. So, for example, we can write an animation that fades in and out five times over 3 seconds and then play that animation on **ImageView** or any other widget. We can think of these XML animations as a script as they define the type, order, and timing of the animation.

Let's explore some of the different properties that we can assign to our animations and how to use them in our Java code, and finally, we can make a neat animated mini app to try it all out.

Designing cool animations in XML

We have learned that XML can also be used to describe animations as well as UI layouts, but let's find out exactly how. We can state properties of an animation that describe the starting and ending appearance of a widget. The XML can then be loaded by our Java code by referencing the name of the XML file that contains it and turning it into a usable Java object, again, like a UI layout.

Let's take a quick look at some of the animation property pairs that we can state in order to create an animation. Straight after we have looked at some XML, we will see how to use it in Java.

Fading in and out

Alpha is the measure of transparency. So, by stating the starting `fromAlpha` values and ending `toAlpha` values, we can fade items in and out. A value of `0.0` is invisible, and the value `1.0` is an object's normal appearance. Steadily moving between the two makes a fading-in effect, as shown in the following code:

```
<alpha
  android:fromAlpha="0.0"
  android:toAlpha="1.0" />
```

Movement

We can move an object within our UI using a similar technique: `fromXDelta` and `toXDelta` can have values set as a percentage of the size of the object that is being animated.

So, the code here would move an object from the left-hand side to the right-hand side by a distance that is equal to the width of the object itself:

```
<translate
  android:fromXDelta="-100%"
  android:toXDelta="0%"/>
```

In addition to this, there are the `fromYDelta` and `toYDelta` properties that can be used to animate the movements up and down.

Scaling or stretching

The `fromXScale` and `toXScale` values will increase or decrease the scale of an object. As an example, the code shown here will change the object that runs the animation from a normal size to invisible:

```
<scale
  android:fromXScale="1.0"
  android:fromYScale="0.0"
/>
```

As another example, we could shrink the object to a tenth of its usual size using `android:fromYScale="0.1"` or make it 10 times as big using `android:fromYScale="10.0"`.

Controlling the duration

Of course, none of these animations would be especially interesting if they just instantly arrived at their conclusion. To make our animations more interesting, we can, therefore, set their duration in milliseconds. A millisecond is one thousandth of a second. We can also make timing easier, especially in relation to other animations by setting `startOffset`, also in milliseconds.

The next code would begin an animation one-third of a second after we started it, and it would take two-thirds of a second to complete:

```
android:duration="666"
android:startOffset="333"
```

Rotating animations

If you want to spin something around, just use `fromDegrees` and `toDegrees`. This next code, predictably, will spin a widget around in a complete circle because, of course, there are 360 degrees in a circle:

```
<rotate android:fromDegrees="360"
  android:toDegrees="0"
/>
```

Repeating animations

Repetition might be important in some animations, for example, a wobble or shake effect, so we can add a `repeatCount` property. In addition, we can specify how the animation is repeated by setting `repeatMode`.

The following code would repeat an animation 10 times, each time reversing the direction of the animation. The `repeatMode` property is relative to the current state of the animation. What this means is that if you, for example, rotated a button from 0 to 360 degrees, the second part of the animation (the first repeat) would rotate the other way from 360 degrees back to 0. The third part of the animation (the second repeat) would again reverse and rotate from 0 to 360 degrees:

```
android:repeatMode="reverse"
android:repeatCount="10"
```

Combining animation properties with a set tag

To combine groups of these effects, we need a `set` tag. This code shows how we can combine all the previous code snippets that we have just seen into an actual XML animation that will be compiled:

```
<?xml version="1.0" encoding="utf-8"?>
<set xmlns:android="http://schemas.android.com/apk/res/android"
...All our animations go here
</set>
```

We still haven't seen any Java code with which we can bring these animations to life. Let's fix that now.

Instantiating animations and controlling them with Java code

This next snippet of Java code shows us how we would declare an object of the type `Animation`, initialize it with an animation contained in an XML file named `fade_in.xml`, and start the animation on `ImageView`. Soon, we will do this in a project and see where to put the XML animations as well:

```
// Declare an Animation object
Animation animFadeIn;

// Initialize it
animFadeIn = AnimationUtils.loadAnimation(getApplicationContext(),
  R.anim.fade_in);

// Get an ImageView from the UI in the usual way
ImageView  (ImageView) findViewById(R.id.imageView);

// Start the animation on the ImageView
imageView.startAnimation(animFadeIn);
```

We already have quite a powerful arsenal of animations and control features for things such as timing, but the Android API gives us a little bit more than this as well.

More animation features

We can listen for the status of animations much like we can listen for clicks on a button. We can also use interpolators to make our animations more life-like and pleasing. Let's look at listeners first.

Listeners

If we implement the `AnimationListener` interface, we can indeed listen to the status of animations by overriding the three methods that tell us when something has occurred. We could then take actions based on these events.

In the following code snippet, `OnAnimationEnd` announces the end of an animation; `onAnimationRepeat` is called each and every time an animation begins a repeat, and perhaps predictably, `onAnimationStart` is called when an animation has started animating. This might not be the same time as when `startAnimation` is called if `startOffset` is set in the animation's XML:

```
@Override
public void onAnimationEnd(Animation animation) {
  // Take some action here

}

@Override
public void onAnimationRepeat(Animation animation) {

  // Take some action here

}

@Override
public void onAnimationStart(Animation animation) {

  // Take some action here

}
```

We will see how `AnimationListener` works in the Animations Demo app, as well as how to put another widget, **SeekBar**, into action.

Animation interpolators

If you can think back to high school, you might remember really exciting lessons about calculating acceleration. If we animate something at a constant speed, then at first glance things might seem OK. If we then compare the animation to another that uses gradual acceleration, then the latter will almost certainly be more pleasing to watch. It is possible that if we were not told that the only difference between the two animations was that one used acceleration and the other didn't, we wouldn't be able to say *why* we preferred it. Our brains are more receptive to things that conform to the norms of the world around us. This is why adding a bit of real-world physics, such as acceleration and deceleration, improves our animations.

The last thing we want to do, however, is start performing a bunch of calculations just to slide a button onto the screen or spin a piece of text in a circle.

This is where interpolators come in. They are animation modifiers that we can set in a single line of code within our XML.

Some examples of interpolators are `accelerate_interpolator` and `bounce_interpolator`, as shown:

```
android:interpolator="@android:anim/accelerate_interpolator"
android:interpolator="@android:anim/cycle_interpolator"/>
```

We will put some interpolators along with some XML animations and the related Java code into action next.

> You can learn more about interpolators and the Android `Animation` class at the developer website, `http://developer.android.com/guide/topics/resources/animation-resource.html`.

The Animations Demo app – introducing SeekBar

That was enough theory, especially with something that should be so visible. Let's build an animation demo app that explores everything that we just discussed and a bit more.

This app involves a little amount of code in lots of different files. So, I have tried to make it plain which code is in which file, so you can keep track of what is going on. This will make the Java code that we write in this mini app more understandable as well.

The app will demonstrate rotations, fades, translations, animation events, interpolations, and controlling duration with **SeekBar**. The best way to explain what **SeekBar** does is to build it and then watch it in action.

Laying out the animation demo

Create a new project called `Animation Demo`, leaving all the settings at their defaults as usual.

Here is how we can lay out the UI for this app:

1. Delete the default **Hello world!** widget.

2. Add **LinearLayout (vertical)**.

3. Inside the layout from the previous step, place **LinearLayout (vertical)** and **RelativeLayout**.

4. Set `layout:weight` on the two layouts that we added in the previous steps to `.3` for `LinearLayout` and `.7` for `RelativeLayout`.

5. Now, set `layout:height` of both to `unset` so that they fill three tenths and seven tenths of the screen, respectively.

6. For **LinearLayout (vertical)**, change its `gravity` property to `center_horizontal`.

7. Add **ImageView** to the inner **LinearLayout (vertical)**. Set the `ImageView src` property to `@mipmap/ic_launcher` to display the Android robot. Of course, you could choose any image that you have added to the `drawable` folder instead.

8. Set the `id` property of `ImageView` to `imageView`.

9. Directly below `ImageView` (still inside `LinearLayout`), add `LargeText`. Set the `id` property to `textStatus` and `layout:margin top` to `10dp`. This should look like this next screenshot:

10. Now, we will add a selection of **SmallButton** widgets to `RelativeLayout`. These are just the same as `Buttons` but with a smaller starting size. The exact positioning is not important, but the exact `id` property values that we add in a few steps time will be essential. Follow this next figure to lay out 12 buttons in `RelativeLayout`:

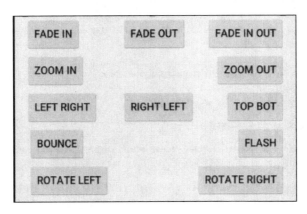

11. Add **SeekBar** on the left-hand side below the buttons. Set the `id` property to `seekBarSpeed`, the `layout:width` property to `250dp`, and the `max` property to `5000`. This means that the **SeekBar** widget will hold a value between `0` and `5000` as it is dragged by the user from left to right. We will see how we can read and use this data soon.

12. Add a plain **TextView** widget just on the right-hand side of **SeekBar** and set its `id` property to `textSeekerSpeed`.

13. The `RelativeLayout` portion of our design should now look like this:

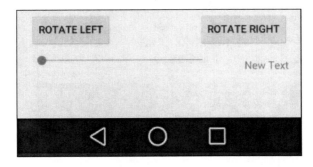

14. Next, add the following `id` properties to the buttons, as identified by the `text` property that is already set:

Existing text property	Value of the ID property to be set
FADE IN	btnFadeIn
FADE OUT	btnFadeOut
FADE IN OUT	btnFadeInOut
ZOOM IN	btnZoomIn
ZOOM OUT	btnZoomOut
LEFT RIGHT	btnLeftRight
RIGHT LEFT	btnRightLeft
TOP BOT	btnTopBottom
BOUNCE	btnBounce
FLASH	btnFlash
ROTATE LEFT	btnRotateLeft
ROTATE RIGHT	btnRotateRight

We will see how to use this newcomer in our UI (**SeekBar**) when we get to coding `MainActivity`.

Coding the XML animations

Right-click on the `res` folder and navigate to **New** | **Android resource directory**. Enter `anim` in the **Directory name** field and click on **OK**.

Now, right-click on the new `anim` directory and navigate to **New** | **Animation resource file**. In the **File name** field, type `fade_in` and then click on **OK**. Delete the entire contents and add this code to create the animation:

```xml
<?xml version="1.0" encoding="utf-8"?>
<set xmlns:android="http://schemas.android.com/apk/res/android"
android:fillAfter="true" >

 <alpha
  android:fromAlpha="0.0"
  android:interpolator="@android:anim/accelerate_interpolator"
  android:toAlpha="1.0" />


</set>
```

Right-click on the `anim` directory and navigate to **New | Animation resource file**. In the **File name** field, type `fade_out` and then click on **OK**. Delete all the contents and add this code to create the animation:

```xml
<?xml version="1.0" encoding="utf-8"?>
<set xmlns:android="http://schemas.android.com/apk/res/android"
android:fillAfter="true" >

 <alpha
  android:fromAlpha="1.0"
  android:interpolator="@android:anim/accelerate_interpolator"
  android:toAlpha="0.0" />

</set>
```

Right-click on the `anim` directory and navigate to **New | Animation resource file**. In the **File name** field, type `fade_in_out` and then click on **OK**. Delete all the contents and add this code to create the animation:

```xml
<?xml version="1.0" encoding="utf-8"?>
<set xmlns:android="http://schemas.android.com/apk/res/android"
  android:fillAfter="true" >

  <alpha
    android:fromAlpha="0.0"
    android:interpolator="@android:anim/accelerate_interpolator"
    android:toAlpha="1.0" />

  <alpha
    android:fromAlpha="1.0"
    android:interpolator="@android:anim/accelerate_interpolator"
    android:toAlpha="0.0" />

</set>
```

Right-click on the `anim` directory and navigate to **New | Animation resource file**. In the **File name** field, type `left_right` and then click on **OK**. Delete all the contents and add this code to create the animation:

```xml
<?xml version="1.0" encoding="utf-8"?>
<set xmlns:android="http://schemas.android.com/apk/res/android">
  <translate

    android:fromXDelta="-500%"
    android:toXDelta="0%"/>
</set>
```

Right-click on the `anim` directory and navigate to **New | Animation resource file**. In the **File name** field, type `right_left` and then click on **OK**. Delete all the contents and add this code to create the animation:

```xml
<?xml version="1.0" encoding="utf-8"?>
<set xmlns:android="http://schemas.android.com/apk/res/android">
  <translate
    android:fillAfter="false"
    android:fromXDelta="500%"
    android:toXDelta="0%"/>
</set>
```

Right-click on the `anim` directory and navigate to **New | Animation resource file**. In the **File name** field, type `top_bot` and then click on **OK**. Delete all the contents and add this code to create the animation:

```xml
<?xml version="1.0" encoding="utf-8"?>
<set xmlns:android="http://schemas.android.com/apk/res/android">
  <translate
    android:fillAfter="false"
    android:fromYDelta="-100%"
    android:toYDelta="0%"/>
</set>
```

Right-click on the `anim` directory and navigate to **New | Animation resource file**. In the **File name** field, type `flash` and then click on **OK**. Delete all the contents and add this code to create the animation:

```xml
<?xml version="1.0" encoding="utf-8"?>
<set xmlns:android="http://schemas.android.com/apk/res/android">
  <alpha android:fromAlpha="0.0"
    android:toAlpha="1.0"
    android:interpolator="@android:anim/accelerate_interpolator"
    android:repeatMode="reverse"
    android:repeatCount="10"/>
</set>
```

Right-click on the `anim` directory and navigate to **New | Animation resource file**. In the **File name** field, type `bounce` and then click on **OK**. Delete all the contents and add this code to create the animation:

```xml
<?xml version="1.0" encoding="utf-8"?>
<set xmlns:android="http://schemas.android.com/apk/res/android"
  android:fillAfter="true"
  android:interpolator="@android:anim/bounce_interpolator">
```

```
<scale
  android:fromXScale="1.0"
  android:fromYScale="0.0"
  android:toXScale="1.0"
  android:toYScale="1.0" />

</set>
```

Right-click on the `anim` directory and navigate to **New | Animation resource file**. In the **File name** field, type `rotate_left` and then click on **OK**. Delete all the contents and add this code to create the animation. Here, we see something new, `pivotX="50%"` and `pivotY="50%"`. This makes the rotating animation central on the widget that will be animated. We can think of this as setting the *pivot* point of the animation:

```
<?xml version="1.0" encoding="utf-8"?>
<set xmlns:android="http://schemas.android.com/apk/res/android">
  <rotate android:fromDegrees="360"
    android:toDegrees="0"
    android:pivotX="50%"
    android:pivotY="50%"
    android:interpolator="@android:anim/cycle_interpolator"/>

</set>
```

Right-click on the `anim` directory and navigate to **New | Animation resource file**. In the **File name** field, type `rotate_right` and then click on **OK**. Delete all the contents and add this code to create the animation:

```
<?xml version="1.0" encoding="utf-8"?>
<set xmlns:android="http://schemas.android.com/apk/res/android">
  <rotate android:fromDegrees="0"
    android:toDegrees="360"
    android:pivotX="50%"
    android:pivotY="50%"
    android:interpolator="@android:anim/cycle_interpolator"/>

</set>
```

Now, we can write the Java code to add our animations to our UI.

Wiring up the Animations Demo app in Java

Open up the `MainActivity.java` file. Now, after the class declaration, we can declare the following member variables for animation:

```
Animation animFadeIn;
Animation animFadeOut;
Animation animFadeInOut;

Animation animZoomIn;
Animation animZoomOut;

Animation animLeftRight;
Animation animRightLeft;
Animation animTopBottom;

Animation animBounce;
Animation animFlash;

Animation animRotateLeft;
Animation animRotateRight;
```

Now, add these member variables for the UI after the previous code:

```
ImageView imageView;
TextView textStatus;

Button btnFadeIn;
Button btnFadeOut;
Button btnFadeInOut;
Button zoomIn;
Button zoomOut;
Button leftRight;
Button rightLeft;
Button topBottom;
Button bounce;
Button flash;
Button rotateLeft;
Button rotateRight;
SeekBar seekBarSpeed;
TextView textSeekerSpeed;
```

Next, we add an `int` member variable that will be used to track the current value/position of **SeekBar**:

```
int seekSpeedProgress;
```

Now, let's call two new highlighted methods from `onCreate` after the call to `setContentView`:

```
@Override
protected void onCreate(Bundle savedInstanceState) {
  super.onCreate(savedInstanceState);
  setContentView(R.layout.activity_main);

  loadAnimations();
  loadUI();


}
```

Now, we will implement the `loadAnimations` method. Although the code in this method is quite extensive, it is also very straightforward. All we are doing is using the `loadAnimation` static method of the `AnimationUtils` class to initialize each of our animation references with one of our XML animations. Note also that for `animFadeIn` animation, we call `setAnimationListener` on it. We will write the methods to listen for events shortly.

Add the `loadAnimations` method:

```
private void loadAnimations(){
  animFadeIn = AnimationUtils.loadAnimation(this, R.anim.fade_in);
  animFadeIn.setAnimationListener(this);
  animFadeOut = AnimationUtils.loadAnimation(this,
    R.anim.fade_out);
  animFadeInOut = AnimationUtils.loadAnimation(this,
    R.anim.fade_in_out);

  animZoomIn = AnimationUtils.loadAnimation(this, R.anim.zoom_in);
  animZoomOut = AnimationUtils.loadAnimation(this,
    R.anim.zoom_out);

  animLeftRight = AnimationUtils.loadAnimation(this,
    R.anim.left_right);
  animRightLeft = AnimationUtils.loadAnimation(this,
    R.anim.right_left);
  animTopBottom = AnimationUtils.loadAnimation(this,
     R.anim.top_bot);

  animBounce = AnimationUtils.loadAnimation(this, R.anim.bounce);
  animFlash = AnimationUtils.loadAnimation(this, R.anim.flash);
```

```
animRotateLeft = AnimationUtils.loadAnimation(this,
   R.anim.rotate_left);
animRotateRight = AnimationUtils.loadAnimation(this,
   R.anim.rotate_right);
}
```

We will discuss and implement the `loadUI` method in three sections. First, let's get a reference to the parts of our XML layout in the usual way:

```
private void loadUI(){

  imageView = (ImageView) findViewById(R.id.imageView);
  textStatus = (TextView) findViewById(R.id.textStatus);

  btnFadeIn = (Button) findViewById(R.id.btnFadeIn);
  btnFadeOut = (Button) findViewById(R.id.btnFadeOut);
  btnFadeInOut = (Button) findViewById(R.id.btnFadeInOut);
  zoomIn = (Button) findViewById(R.id.btnZoomIn);
  zoomOut = (Button) findViewById(R.id.btnZoomOut);
  leftRight = (Button) findViewById(R.id.btnLeftRight);
  rightLeft = (Button) findViewById(R.id.btnRightLeft);
  topBottom = (Button) findViewById(R.id.btnTopBottom);
  bounce = (Button) findViewById(R.id.btnBounce);
  flash = (Button) findViewById(R.id.btnFlash);
  rotateLeft = (Button) findViewById(R.id.btnRotateLeft);
  rotateRight = (Button) findViewById(R.id.btnRotateRight);
```

Now, we will add `ClickListener` for each button. Add this code immediately after the last block within the `loadUI` method:

```
btnFadeIn.setOnClickListener(this);
btnFadeOut.setOnClickListener(this);
btnFadeInOut.setOnClickListener(this);
zoomIn.setOnClickListener(this);
zoomOut.setOnClickListener(this);
leftRight.setOnClickListener(this);
rightLeft.setOnClickListener(this);
topBottom.setOnClickListener(this);
bounce.setOnClickListener(this);
flash.setOnClickListener(this);
rotateLeft.setOnClickListener(this);
rotateRight.setOnClickListener(this);
```

The third and last section of the `loadUI` method sets up an anonymous class to handle the **SeekBar** widget. We could have added this as an interface to `MainActivity` as we did with listening for button clicks and animation events, but with a single **SeekBar** like this, it makes sense to handle it directly.

We will override three methods, as this is required by the interface when implementing `OnSeekBarChangeListener`:

- A method that detects a change in the position of the seek bar called `onProgressChanged`
- A method that detects whether the user has started to change the position called `onStartTrackingTouch`
- A method that detects when the user has finished using the seek bar called `onStopTrackingTouch`

To achieve our goals, we only need to add code to the `onProgressChanged` method, but we must still override them all.

All we do in the `onProgressChanged` method is assign the current value of the **SeekBar** widget to the `seekSpeedProgress` member variable so that it can be accessed from elsewhere. Then, we use this value along with the maximum possible value of **SeekBar**, which is obtained by calling `seekBarSpeed.getMax()`, and output a message to the `textSeekerSpeed` TextView.

Add the code we just discussed into the `loadUI` method:

```
seekBarSpeed = (SeekBar) findViewById(R.id.seekBarSpeed);
textSeekerSpeed = (TextView) findViewById(R.id.textSeekerSpeed);

seekBarSpeed.setOnSeekBarChangeListener(new SeekBar.
OnSeekBarChangeListener() {

 @Override
  public void onProgressChanged(SeekBar seekBar, int value,
    boolean fromUser) {
  seekSpeedProgress = value;
  textSeekerSpeed.setText("" + seekSpeedProgress + " of " +
    seekBarSpeed.getMax());
 }

 @Override
 public void onStartTrackingTouch(SeekBar seekBar) {
 }

 @Override
```

```
  public void onStopTrackingTouch(SeekBar seekBar) {

  }
});

}
```

Now, we need to alter the `MainActivity` class declaration in order to implement two interfaces. In this app, we will be listening for clicks and animation events, so the two interfaces we will be using are `View.OnClickListener` and `Animation.AnimationListener`. Note that to implement more than one interface, we simply separate the interfaces with a comma.

Alter the `MainActivity` class declaration by adding the highlighted code that we just discussed:

```
public class MainActivity extends AppCompatActivity
implements View.OnClickListener, Animation.AnimationListener {
```

Next, we can add and implement the required methods for these interfaces. First, the `AnimationListener` methods: `onAnimationEnd`, `onAnimationRepeat`, and `onaAnimationStart`. We only need to add a little code to two of these methods. In `onAnimationEnd`, we set the `text` property of `textStatus` to STOPPED, and in `onAnimationStart`, we set it to RUNNING. This will demonstrate that our animation listeners are indeed listening and working:

```
@Override
public void onAnimationEnd(Animation animation) {
  textStatus.setText("STOPPED");

}

@Override
public void onAnimationRepeat(Animation animation) {

}

@Override
public void onAnimationStart(Animation animation) {
  textStatus.setText("RUNNING");

}
```

The onClick method is quite long but not complicated. Each case that handles each button from the UI simply sets the duration of an animation based on the current position of the seek bar, sets up the animation so it can be listened to for events, and then starts the animation.

Add the onClick method that we just discussed, and now, we have completed this mini app:

```
@Override
public void onClick(View v) {


switch(v.getId()){
  case R.id.btnFadeIn:
    animFadeIn.setDuration(seekSpeedProgress);
    animFadeIn.setAnimationListener(this);
    imageView.startAnimation(animFadeIn);

    break;

  case R.id.btnFadeOut:

    animFadeOut.setDuration(seekSpeedProgress);
    animFadeOut.setAnimationListener(this);
    imageView.startAnimation(animFadeOut);

    break;

  case R.id.btnFadeInOut:

    animFadeInOut.setDuration(seekSpeedProgress);
    animFadeInOut.setAnimationListener(this);
    imageView.startAnimation(animFadeInOut);

    break;

  case R.id.btnZoomIn:
    animZoomIn.setDuration(seekSpeedProgress);
    animZoomIn.setAnimationListener(this);
    imageView.startAnimation(animZoomIn);

    break;

  case R.id.btnZoomOut:
    animZoomOut.setDuration(seekSpeedProgress);
    animZoomOut.setAnimationListener(this);
```

```
        imageView.startAnimation(animZoomOut);

        break;



    case R.id.btnLeftRight:
      animLeftRight.setDuration(seekSpeedProgress);
      animLeftRight.setAnimationListener(this);
      imageView.startAnimation(animLeftRight);

        break;

    case R.id.btnRightLeft:
      animRightLeft.setDuration(seekSpeedProgress);
      animRightLeft.setAnimationListener(this);
      imageView.startAnimation(animRightLeft);

        break;

    case R.id.btnTopBottom:
      animTopBottom.setDuration(seekSpeedProgress);
      animTopBottom.setAnimationListener(this);
      imageView.startAnimation(animTopBottom);

        break;

    case R.id.btnBounce:
      /*
        Divide seekSpeedProgress by 10 because with
        the seekbar having a max value of 5000 it
        will make the animations range between
        almost instant and half a second
        5000 /  10 = 500 milliseconds
      */
      animBounce.setDuration(seekSpeedProgress / 10);
      animBounce.setAnimationListener(this);
      imageView.startAnimation(animBounce);

        break;

    case R.id.btnFlash:
      animFlash.setDuration(seekSpeedProgress / 10);
      animFlash.setAnimationListener(this);
      imageView.startAnimation(animFlash);
```

```
          break;

      case R.id.btnRotateLeft:
        animRotateLeft.setDuration(seekSpeedProgress);
        animRotateLeft.setAnimationListener(this);
        imageView.startAnimation(animRotateLeft);

          break;

      case R.id.btnRotateRight:
        animRotateRight.setDuration(seekSpeedProgress);
        animRotateRight.setAnimationListener(this);
        imageView.startAnimation(animRotateRight);

          break;
    }


  }
```

Now, run the app. Move the seek bar to roughly the center so that the animations run for a reasonable amount of time. After this, the app will look as follows:

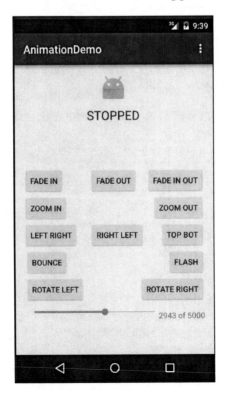

Now, click on the **ZOOM IN** button:

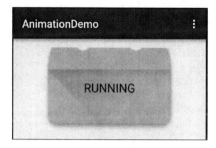

Notice how the text on the Android robot changes from **RUNNING** to **STOPPED** at the appropriate time. Now, click on one of the **ROTATE** buttons:

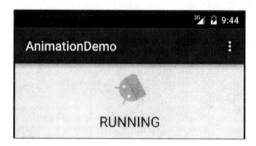

Most of the other animations don't do themselves justice in a screenshot, so be sure to try them all out for yourself.

Now, let's add some simple animations to our Note To Self app.

Adding animations to Note To Self

The completed code for this chapter is in the usual place: Chapter 16/Note to self. Note, however, that the code also includes the minor additions that we will make in the next chapter.

Defining the animations in XML

First, let's define two animations in XML that we can use. A **FADE IN** animation, which is the normal behavior when a note appears in the list and a flash, which will be the behavior that can be tweaked from the settings screen. If the note is important, the user will be able to set it to either flash fast, flash slow, or not flash at all.

Right-click on the res folder and navigate to **New | Android resource directory**. Enter anim in the **Directory name** field and click on **OK**.

Now, right-click on the new `anim` directory and navigate to **New | Animation resource file**. In the **File name** field, type `fade_in` and then click on **OK**. Delete all the contents and add this code to create the animation:

```
<set xmlns:android="http://schemas.android.com/apk/res/android">
  <alpha
    android:fromAlpha="0.0"
    android:toAlpha="1.0"
    android:duration="500"
    android:interpolator="@android:anim/accelerate_interpolator">
  </alpha>
</set>
```

Now, right-click on the new `anim` directory and navigate to **New | Animation resource file**. In the **File name** field, type `flash` and then click on **OK**. Delete all the contents and add this code to create the animation:

```
<?xml version="1.0" encoding="utf-8"?>
<set xmlns:android="http://schemas.android.com/apk/res/android">
  <alpha android:fromAlpha="0.0"
    android:toAlpha="1.0"
    android:interpolator="@android:anim/accelerate_interpolator"
    android:repeatMode="reverse"
    android:repeatCount="infinite"/>
</set>
```

Our XML animations are ready, so let's add the Java code.

Controlling the animations in Java

Add these highlighted member variables to `MainActivity` just after the class declaration:

```
public class MainActivity extends AppCompatActivity {

    Animation mAnimFlash;
    Animation mFadeIn;

    ...
```

Now, let's initialize these animations based on the user's current settings. The best place to do this is in `onResume` because that is where we load the settings, and it is guaranteed to run every time `MainActivity` is run, whether that is because the app has just started or because the user is just returning from the settings screen (perhaps having just changed the settings). Add this code just after the code that loads the settings that we implemented in the previous chapter. The next listing shows the entire `onResume` method. The new code to add is highlighted here:

```
@Override
protected void onResume(){
```

```
super.onResume();

mPrefs = getSharedPreferences("Note to self", MODE_PRIVATE);
mSound  = mPrefs.getBoolean("sound", true);
mAnimOption = mPrefs.getInt("anim option", SettingsActivity.FAST);

mAnimFlash = AnimationUtils.
  loadAnimation(getApplicationContext(), R.anim.flash);
mFadeIn = AnimationUtils.loadAnimation(getApplicationContext(),
  R.anim.fade_in);

// Set the rate of flash based on settings
if(mAnimOption == SettingsActivity.FAST){

  mAnimFlash.setDuration(100);
  Log.i("anim = ",""+ mAnimOption);
  }else if(mAnimOption == SettingsActivity.SLOW){

  Log.i("anim = ",""+ mAnimOption);
    mAnimFlash.setDuration(1000);
  }

mNoteAdapter.notifyDataSetChanged();
}
```

Now, we just need to apply the appropriate animation to the appropriate part of our UI. We can do so in the NoteAdapter inner class in the getView method, just after we initialize tempNote with the details of the note we are currently dealing with. We are then in a position to call isImportant to make a decision about which animation to play. I have included the line before the new code and the line after the new code as well as highlighted the new code to show exactly where this code goes:

```
...
Note tempNote = noteList.get(whichItem);

// To animate or not to animate
if (tempNote.isImportant() && mAnimOption !=
  SettingsActivity.NONE ) {

  view.setAnimation(mAnimFlash);

}else{
  view.setAnimation(mFadeIn);
}

if (!tempNote.isImportant()){
...
```

If you run Note To Self now, you will be able to see the nice FADE IN animations as well as the flashing animations on any note that the user has labeled as important. And, of course, you can change the speed of the flashing animation or switch it off completely from the settings screen. That's it for animation in Note To Self.

FAQ

1. We know how to animate widgets now, but what about shapes or images that I create myself?

    `ImageView` can hold any image you like. Just add the image to the `drawable` folder and then set the appropriate `src` property on the `ImageView`. You can then animate whatever image is being shown in the `ImageView` widget.

2. What if I want more flexibility than this, more like a drawing app or even a game?

    To implement this kind of functionality, you will need to learn another general computing concept (**threads**) as well as some more Android classes (such as `Paint`, `Canvas`, and `SurfaceView`). You will learn how to draw anything from a single pixel to shapes, and then how to move them around the screen in *Chapter 28, Threads, Touches, Drawing, and a Simple Game*.

Summary

Now, we have another app-enhancing trick up our sleeves, and we have seen that animations in Android are quite straightforward. We design an animation in XML and add the file to the `anim` folder. Next, we get a reference to the animation in XML with an `Animation` object in our Java code.

We can then use a reference to a widget in our UI and set an animation to it using `setAmimation` and passing in the `Animation` object. We actually commence the animation by calling `startAnimation` on the reference to the widget.

In this chapter, we also saw that we can control the timing of animations as well as listen for animation events.

Is it me or is it a little quiet around here?

17

Sound FX and Supporting Different Versions of Android

In this chapter, you will learn how to load and play **sound effects** (**FX**) on Android. As the sound part of the Android API has recently been updated, this is also a good opportunity to look at a strategy for supporting different versions of Android. Throughout the book, we have been writing apps that run on 95% of devices by default, but there are times when we want to support more devices. Also, it is useful to be able to future-proof our apps a bit when we know that the code we write will eventually not work on new devices. This chapter includes the following topics:

- How to code for different versions of Android in the same app
- How does the `SoundPool` class work
- The sound FX mini app
- How to add sound to the Note To Self app

Supporting multiple versions of Android

Most of the time throughout this book, we haven't paid any attention to supporting older Android devices because it did not seem worthwhile. The main reason being that all the up-to-date parts of the API we have been using work on such a high percentage of devices (in excess of 95%). Unless you intend to carve out a niche in apps for ancient Android relics, this seems like a sensible approach. With regard to playing sounds, however, there have been some fairly recent modifications to the Android API.

Actually, this isn't immediately a big deal because devices newer than this can still use the old parts of the API. However, it is good practice to specifically handle these differences in compatibility because eventually, one day, the older parts might not work on newer versions of Android.

The main reason for discussing this here is that the slight differences in pre- and post-android Lollipop sound handling give us a good excuse to see how we can deal with things like this in our code.

In this chapter, we will see how we can make our app compatible with the very latest devices and the pre-Lollipop devices as well.

The class we will be using to make some noise is the SoundPool class. First, let's look at some simple code to detect the current Android version.

Detecting the current Android version

We can determine the current version of Android using the static variables of the Build.Version class, SDK_INT, and we can determine whether it is newer than a specific version by comparing it to that version's appropriate variable, Build. VERSION_CODES, as shown in the following code snippet. If this explanation was a bit mouthful, just look at how we determine whether the current version is equal to or newer (greater) than Lollipop:

```
if (Build.VERSION.SDK_INT >= Build.VERSION_CODES.LOLLIPOP) {

  // Lollipop or newer code goes here

} else {

  // Code for devices older than lollipop here

}
```

Now, let's see how to make some noise with Android devices that are newer and older than Lollipop.

The SoundPool class

The SoundPool class allows us to hold and manipulate a collection of sound FX—literally, a pool of sounds. The class handles everything from decompressing a sound file, such as .wav or .ogg, to keeping an identifying reference to it via an integer ID, and of course, playing the sound. When the sound is played, it is done so in a nonblocking manner that does not interfere with the smooth running of our app or our users' interactions with it.

The first thing we need to do is add the sound effects to a folder called `assets` in the `main` folder. Next, in our Java code, we declare an object of the type `SoundPool` and an `int` identifier for each and every sound effect that we intend to use. We also declare another `int` identifier called `nowPlaying`, which we can use to track the sound that is currently playing, and we will see how to do this shortly. Take a look at the following code snippet:

```
// create an identifier
SoundPool sp;
int nowPlaying =-1;
int idFX1 = -1;
```

Now, we will look at the two different ways in which we initialize `SoundPool` depending upon the version of Android that the device is using.

Building SoundPool the new way and the old way

The new way involves us using an `AudioAttributes` object to set the attributes of the pool of sound we want. We use chaining and the `Builder` method of this class to initialize the `AudioAttributes` object to let it know that it will be used for user interface interaction with `USAGE_ASSISTANCE_SONIFICATION`. We will also use `CONTENT_TYPE_SONIFICATION`, which lets the class know that it is to be used for responsive sounds, for example, a user button click or similar tasks.

Now, we can initialize `SoundPool` (`sp`) itself by passing in the `AudioAttributes` object (`audioAttributes`) and the maximum number of simultaneous sounds we likely want to play:

```
// Instantiate a SoundPool dependent on Android version
if (Build.VERSION.SDK_INT >= Build.VERSION_CODES.LOLLIPOP) {

  // The new way
  // Build an AudioAttributes object
  AudioAttributes audioAttributes = new AudioAttributes.Builder()
  .setUsage(AudioAttributes.
    USAGE_ASSISTANCE_SONIFICATION)
    .setContentType(AudioAttributes.CONTENT_TYPE_SONIFICATION)
    .build();

  // Initialize the SoundPool
  sp = new SoundPool.Builder()
  .setMaxStreams(5)
  .setAudioAttributes(audioAttributes)
  .build();
}
```

The `else` block of code shown here will, of course, contain the code for the old way of doing things. No need for an `AudioAttributes` object; we simply need to initialize `SoundPool` (`sp`) by passing in the number of simultaneous sounds. The final parameter is for sound quality, and passing zero is all that we need to do. This is much simpler than the new way but also less flexible with regard to the choices we can make:

```
else {
   // The old way
   sp = new SoundPool(5, AudioManager.STREAM_MUSIC, 0);
}
```

Now that we have sound effects in the `assets` folder and a `SoundPool` object built in one way or another, we can go ahead and load up (decompress) the sound files in our `SoundPool` class.

Loading sound files into memory

As we often do with methods that load or save files to disks, we are required to wrap our code in `try-catch` blocks. This makes sense because reading a file can fail for reasons beyond our control and as we are forced to do so, because the method that we use throws an exception and the code that we write will not be compiled otherwise.

Inside the `try` block, we declare and initialize an object of the `AssetManager` and `AssetFileDescriptor` types.

`AssetFileDescriptor` is initialized here using the `openFd` method of the `AssetManager` object, which actually decompresses the sound file. We then initialize our ID (`idFX1`) at the same time as we load the contents of `AssetFileDescriptor` into `SoundPool`. The `catch` block simply outputs a message to the console to let us know if something has gone wrong. Note that this code is the same regardless of the Android version:

```
try{

   // Create objects of the 2 required classes
   AssetManager assetManager = this.getAssets();
   AssetFileDescriptor descriptor;

   // Load our fx in memory ready for use
   descriptor = assetManager.openFd("fx1.ogg");
   idFX1 = sp.load(descriptor, 0);
}catch(IOException e){

   // Print an error message to the console
   Log.e("error", "failed to load sound files");
}
```

Now, we are ready to make some noise.

Playing a sound

At this point, there is a sound effect in our `SoundPool` class and we have an ID by which we can refer to it.

This code is the same regardless of how we built the `SoundPool` object, and this is how we play the sound. Note that we initialize the `nowPlaying` variable with the return value from the same method that actually plays the sound. The following code, therefore, simultaneously plays a sound and loads the value of the ID that is being played into `nowPlaying`. We will see how this will be useful when we make a real mini app to play some sounds:

```
nowPlaying = sp.play(idFX1, volume, volume, 0, repeats, 1);
```

The parameters of the `play` method are: the ID of the sound effect, the left-hand side speaker volume, the right-hand side speaker volume, the priority over other sounds, the number of times to repeat the sound, and the rate/speed at which it is played (`1` is the normal rate).

Just one more quick thing before we make the real app.

Stopping a sound

It is also very simple to stop a sound when it is still playing with the `stop` method. Note that there might be more than one sound effect playing at any given time, so the stop method requires the ID of the sound effect to stop:

```
sp.stop(nowPlaying);
```

Now, we will go ahead and make some noise for real at the same time as we try out a UI widget that we haven't used yet.

Introducing the Spinner widget

Of course, with all this talk of sound FX we need some actual sound files. You can download sound FX from various free websites, and you can also buy premium sound effects as well. The sound effects for this app are supplied in the download bundle and are in the `assets` folder of the `Chapter 17/Sound Demo` folder. But you might like to make your own.

Making sound FX

There is an open source app called Bfxr that allows us to make our own sound FX. Here is a guide to making your own sound FX very fast using Bfxr. Grab a free copy from www.bfxr.net.

Follow the simple instructions on the website to set it up. Try out a few of these things to make cool sound FX.

 This is a seriously condensed tutorial. You can do so much with Bfxr. To learn more, read the tips on the website at the previous URL.

1. Run Bfxr, as shown:

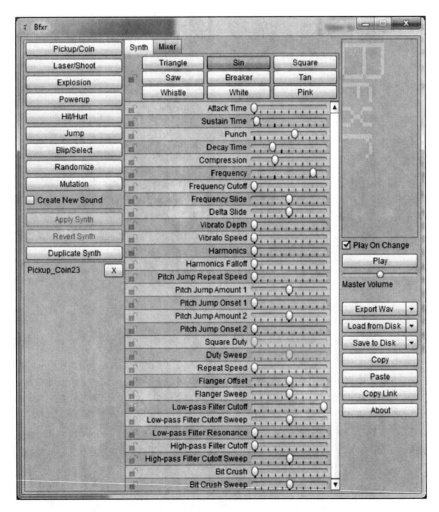

2. Try out all the preset types, as shown in the next screenshot, which generate a random sound of that type. When you have a sound that is close to what you want, move to the next step:

3. Use the sliders to fine tune the pitch, duration, and other aspects of your new sound, as shown in the following figure:

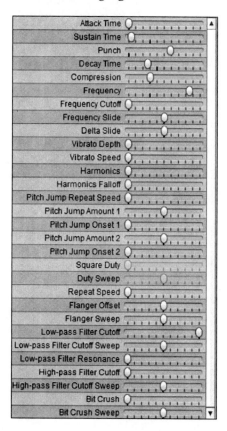

4. Save your sound by clicking on the **Export Wav** button. Despite the text of this button, we can save the sound in formats other than `.wav` too:

5. Android works very well with sounds in the OGG format, so when you're asked to name your file, use the `.ogg` extension at the end of the filename.

6. Repeat steps 2 to 5 to create three cool sound FX. Name them `fx1.ogg`, `fx2.ogg`, and `fx3.ogg`. We use the `.ogg` file format as it is more compressed than formats such as WAV. When you have your sound files ready, we can proceed with the app.

Laying out Sound Demo UI

I will describe the parts of the project that we are getting used to a little more tersely than the previous projects. Every time there is a new concept, however, I will be sure to explain it in full. I guess you will be just fine dragging a few widgets onto `RelativeLayout` and changing their `text` properties.

With this in mind, complete the following steps. If you have any problems at all, you can copy or view the code in the `Chapter 17/Sound Demo` folder of the download bundle:

1. Create a new project, call it `Sound Demo`, and choose **Blank Activity**. Leave all the other settings at their defaults and delete the **Hello world!** widget.

2. In this order, drag **Spinner**, **SeekBar**, and four **Buttons** from the palette and onto the layout while arranging them and setting their `text` properties, as shown in the next screenshot:

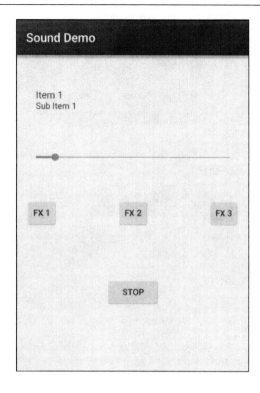

3. Use the following table to set the widget's properties that we will need in our Java code:

Widget	Property to be changed	Value to set
Spinner	id	spinner
Spinner	spinnerMode	dropdown
Spinner	options	@array/spinner_ options
SeekBar	id	seekBar
SeekBar	max	10
Button (FX 1)	id	btnFX1
Button (FX 2)	id	btnFX2
Button (FX 3)	id	btnFX3
Button (STOP)	id	btnStop

Next, add the following highlighted code to the `strings.xml` file in the `values` folder. We used the array of string resources named `spinner_options` for the `options` property in the previous step. It will represent the options that can be chosen from our **Spinner** widget:

```
<resources>
    <string name="app_name">Sound Demo</string>

    <string name="hello_world">Hello world!</string>
    <string name="action_settings">Settings</string>

    <string-array name="spinner_options">
        <item>0</item>
        <item>1</item>
        <item>3</item>
        <item>5</item>
        <item>10</item>
    </string-array>
</resources>
```

Run the app now, and you will not initially see anything new. If you click on the Spinner widget, however, then you will see the options from our string array called `spinner_options`. We will use the spinner to control the number of times a sound effect repeats itself when played, as shown in the following screenshot:

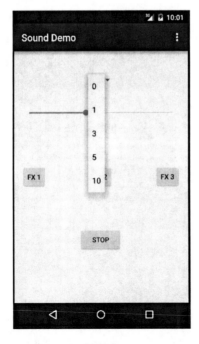

Let's write the Java code to make this app work, including how we interact with our spinner.

Using your operating system's file browser, go to the app\src\main folder of the project and add a new folder called assets.

There are three sound files ready-made for you in the Chapter 17/SoundDemo/ assets folder of the download bundle. Place these three files into the assets directory you just created or use the ones you've created yourself. The important thing is that their filenames must be fx1.ogg, fx2.ogg, and fx3.ogg.

Coding the Sound Demo app

To code the Sound Demo app, we first add a few member variables for our SoundPool, sound FX IDs, and nowPlaying int as previously discussed, and we will also add float to hold a value for the volume between 0 (silent) and 1 (full volume relative to the current volume of the device). We will also add int called repeats, which unsurprisingly holds the value of the number of times we will repeat a given sound FX:

```
SoundPool sp;

int idFX1 = -1;
int idFX2 = -1;
int idFX3 = -1;
int nowPlaying = -1;

float volume = .1f;
int repeats = 2;
```

Now, in onCreate, we can get a reference and set a click listener for our buttons in the usual way:

```
Button buttonFX1 = (Button) findViewById(R.id.btnFX1);
buttonFX1.setOnClickListener(this);

Button buttonFX2 = (Button) findViewById(R.id.btnFX2);
buttonFX2.setOnClickListener(this);

Button buttonFX3 = (Button) findViewById(R.id.btnFX3);
buttonFX3.setOnClickListener(this);

Button buttonStop = (Button) findViewById(R.id.btnStop);
buttonStop.setOnClickListener(this);
```

Still, in `onCreate`, we can initialize `SoundPool` (`sp`) based on the version of Android that the device is using:

```
// Instantiate our sound pool dependent
// upon which version of Android
if (Build.VERSION.SDK_INT >= Build.VERSION_CODES.LOLLIPOP) {
  AudioAttributes audioAttributes = new AudioAttributes.Builder()
  .setUsage(AudioAttributes.USAGE_ASSISTANCE_SONIFICATION)
  .setContentType(AudioAttributes.CONTENT_TYPE_SONIFICATION)
  .build();

  sp = new SoundPool.Builder()
  .setMaxStreams(5)
  .setAudioAttributes(audioAttributes)
  .build();
} else {
  sp = new SoundPool(5, AudioManager.STREAM_MUSIC, 0);
}
```

Next, we load each sound FX in turn and initialize our IDs with a value that points to the related sound FX that we loaded into `SoundPool`. The whole thing is wrapped in a `try-catch` block as required:

```
try{
  // Create objects of the 2 required classes
  AssetManager assetManager = this.getAssets();
  AssetFileDescriptor descriptor;

  // Load our fx in memory ready for use
  descriptor = assetManager.openFd("fx1.ogg");
  idFX1 = sp.load(descriptor, 0);

  descriptor = assetManager.openFd("fx2.ogg");
  idFX2 = sp.load(descriptor, 0);

  descriptor = assetManager.openFd("fx3.ogg");
  idFX3 = sp.load(descriptor, 0);


  }catch(IOException e){
    // Print an error message to the console
    Log.e("error", "failed to load sound files");
}
```

Then, we see how we are going to handle SeekBar. As you probably have come to expect, we will use an anonymous class. We will use OnSeekBarChangeListener and override the onProgressChanged, onStartTrackingTouch, and onStopTrackingTouch methods.

We only need to add code to the onProgressChanged method. Within this method, we simply change the value of our volume variable and then use the setVolume method on our SoundPool object, passing in the currently playing sound FX and the volume of the left and right channels of sound:

```
// Now setup the seekbar
SeekBar seekBar = (SeekBar) findViewById(R.id.seekBar);


seekBar.setOnSeekBarChangeListener(new SeekBar.
  OnSeekBarChangeListener() {

  @Override
  public void onProgressChanged(SeekBar seekBar, int value,
    boolean fromUser) {
    volume = value / 10f;
    sp.setVolume(nowPlaying, volume, volume);
  }

  @Override
  public void onStartTrackingTouch(SeekBar seekBar) {
  }

  @Override
  public void onStopTrackingTouch(SeekBar seekBar) {

  }
});
```

After SeekBar comes Spinner and yet another anonymous class which is used to handle user interaction. We use AdapterView.OnItemSelectedListener to override the onItemSelected and onNothingSelected methods.

All our code goes in the onItemSelected method, which creates a temporary String named temp and then uses the Integer.ValueOf method to convert String to int, which we can use to initialize the repeats variable:

```
// Now for the spinner
Spinner spinner = (Spinner) findViewById(R.id.spinner);
spinner.setOnItemSelectedListener(new AdapterView.
  OnItemSelectedListener() {
```

```
@Override
public void onItemSelected(AdapterView<?> parentView,
  View selectedItemView, int position, long id) {
  String temp = String.valueOf(spinner.getSelectedItem());
  repeats = Integer.valueOf(temp);
}

@Override
public void onNothingSelected(AdapterView<?> parentView) {

}

});
```

That's everything from onCreate. Now, change the class declaration to implement View.OnClickListener, as highlighted in the next code:

```
public class MainActivity extends
  AppCompatActivity implements View.OnClickListener{
```

Now, implement the onClick method. Quite simply, there is a case statement for each button. There is a case to play each of our three sound FX, set the volume and set the number of times to repeat a sound. Note that the return value for each call to play is stored in nowPlaying. When the user clicks on the **STOP** button, we simply call stop with the current value of nowPlaying, causing the most recently started sound FX to stop, as shown in the following code:

```
@Override
public void onClick(View v) {
  switch (v.getId()){
  case R.id.btnFX1:
    sp.stop(nowPlaying);
    nowPlaying = sp.play(idFX1, volume, volume, 0, repeats, 1);
    break;

  case R.id.btnFX2:
    sp.stop(nowPlaying);
    nowPlaying = sp.play(idFX2, volume, volume, 0, repeats, 1);
    break;

  case R.id.btnFX3:
    sp.stop(nowPlaying);
    nowPlaying = sp.play(idFX3, volume, volume, 0, repeats, 1);
    break;
```

```
    case R.id.btnStop:
        sp.stop(nowPlaying);
        break;
    }
}
```

We can now run the app. Make sure that the volume on your device is turned up if you can't hear anything. Here is a screenshot of the sound demo app:

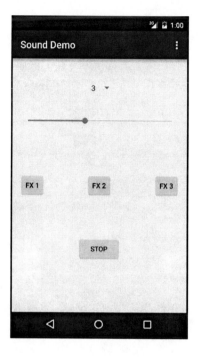

Click on the appropriate button for the sound FX you want to play. Change the volume and the number of times it is repeated and, of course, try stopping it with the **STOP** button.

Also note that you can repeatedly tap on multiple play buttons when a sound FX is already playing, and the sounds will be played simultaneously up to the maximum number of streams (5) that we've set. However, this shows a slight inadequacy with regard to the way we handle stopping sounds, as the stop button will only stop the most recently started sound.

Sound FX touches to Note To Self

As it has become customary over the last few chapters, we will use our new-found knowledge to add an enhancement to our Note To Self app. This chapter will be the last time we do this, however, before we move on to new coding pastures.

Using your operating system's file browser, go to the app\src\main folder of the project and add a new folder called assets.

There is a sound file called beep.ogg ready-made for you in the Chapter 17/Note To Self/assets folder of the download bundle. Of course, you can make your own sound FX using Bfxr if you prefer.

Place the file into the assets directory that you just created.

Now, we can add some Java code to play the beep sound each time a note from the list is selected.

First, let's add a couple of new member variables to the MainActivity class:

```
public class MainActivity extends AppCompatActivity {

    Animation mAnimFlash;
    Animation mFadeIn;

    int mIdBeep = -1;
    SoundPool mSp;

    private NoteAdapter mNoteAdapter;
    private boolean mSound;
    private int mAnimOption;
    private SharedPreferences mPrefs;



    @Override
    protected void onCreate(Bundle savedInstanceState) {
    ...
    ...
```

Now, in onCreate, as we have done in the Sound Demo app, after the call to setContentView, add code to initialize SoundPool in a version-specific manner, as highlighted in this next code:

```
@Override
protected void onCreate(Bundle savedInstanceState) {
    super.onCreate(savedInstanceState);
```

```
    setContentView(R.layout.activity_main);

    // Instantiate our sound pool
    if (Build.VERSION.SDK_INT >= Build.VERSION_CODES.LOLLIPOP) {
      AudioAttributes audioAttributes = new
        AudioAttributes.Builder()
      .setUsage(AudioAttributes.USAGE_MEDIA)
      .setContentType(AudioAttributes.CONTENT_TYPE_SONIFICATION)
      .build();

      mSp = new SoundPool.Builder()
      .setMaxStreams(5)
      .setAudioAttributes(audioAttributes)
      .build();
      } else {
        mSp = new SoundPool(5, AudioManager.STREAM_MUSIC, 0);
      }


      try{
        // Create objects of the 2 required classes
        AssetManager assetManager = this.getAssets();
        AssetFileDescriptor descriptor;

        // Load our fx in memory ready for use
        descriptor = assetManager.openFd("beep.ogg");
        mIdBeep = mSp.load(descriptor, 0);


      }catch(IOException e){
        // Print an error message to the console
        Log.e("error", "failed to load sound files");
      }
  mNoteAdapter = new NoteAdapter();

  ListView listNote = (ListView) findViewById(R.id.listView);

  listNote.setAdapter(mNoteAdapter);
  ...
  ...
```

Now, add this next code that plays a sound in the `onItemClick` method. I have added some context and highlighted the new code to make it plain as to where it goes:

```
...
public void onItemClick(AdapterView<?> adapter, View view,
    int whichItem, long id) {

    if(mSound) {
      mSp.play(mIdBeep, 1, 1, 0, 0, 1);
    }

    Note tempNote = mNoteAdapter.getItem(whichItem);
...
```

That's it. You can now run the Note To Self app and receive a satisfying click each time a note from the list is clicked on.

Deleting a note – introducing OnLongClick

As a final improvement to Note To Self and as an excuse to talk about a neat Android UI feature, we will add the ability to delete a note. Context actions are often chosen in Android apps by long clicking. Long clicking is when the user holds their finger on the device screen rather than simply tapping and removing their finger.

First, let's add a delete note method to the `NoteAdapter` class. Here is the code that removes a `Note` object from the array list and then asks the adapter to update itself and `ListView`:

```
public void deleteNote(int n){

    noteList.remove(n);
    notifyDataSetChanged();

}
```

Now, in `onCreate`, we can prepare `ListView` to accept long clicks and then use an anonymous class to listen and respond to them. This inner class simply calls our new `deleteNote` method. Add this code just before the anonymous class that handles the regular click of `ListView` and just after the call to `setAdapter`. Here, I have included the context and highlighted the new code that is to be added:

```
...
listNote.setAdapter(mNoteAdapter);

// So we can long click it
listNote.setLongClickable(true);

// Now to detect long clicks and delete the note
listNote.setOnItemLongClickListener(new AdapterView.
OnItemLongClickListener() {

  public boolean onItemLongClick(AdapterView<?> adapter,
    View view,
    int whichItem, long id) {

    // Ask NoteAdapter to delete this entry
    mNoteAdapter.deleteNote(whichItem);

  return true;
  }
});

listNote.setOnItemClickListener(new AdapterView.OnItemClickListener()
{
...
```

Now you can long click to delete a note. In an app that we are going to release to real users, we might like to use a popup dialog window to confirm their decision before deleting the note.

FAQ

1. What do I do if I want to play music?

    You can play some music in the background of your app using the `MediaPlayer` class. Here is some sample code to show how simple this can be:

    ```
    // Create a MediaPlayer object
    MediaPlayer mp = new MediaPlayer();
    // Choose where to load the music from
    ```

```
mp.setDataSource(musicFileToLoad);
// Call the prepare method
mp.prepare();
// Play some music
mp.start();
```

Take a look at the official documentation for full details at http://developer.android.com/reference/android/media/MediaPlayer.html.

2. How about if I want to make an actual music playing app where the user can select music from their library to play.

This is also made easy for us by Android. On the Android Studio palette, you can drag a **MediaController** widget, which not only allows your user to control music playback but video as well. Find out how to use this widget on the Android developer site, http://developer.android.com/reference/android/widget/MediaController.html.

Summary

Now we know how to make our apps audible. Most apps we will build in this book are of the type to which you would probably only add a few beeps or buzzes, but when you design your own apps, you might want to go further, and now you can. We also saw how to use yet another useful widget from the palette: **Spinner**.

This chapter concludes the Note To Self app, and it is time to move on to more advanced Android programming. As we will see, more advanced does not necessarily mean more complicated; however, we will see quite a few new topics that will be introduced over the rest of the book.

In the next chapter, we will see how we can start to code even more real-world apps using the Fragment class, and how we can keep our ever-growing code organized with **design patterns**.

18
Design Patterns, Fragments, and the Real World

We have come a long way since the start of the book when we were just setting up Java and Android Studio. Back then, we went through everything step by step. But as we proceeded, we have tried to show you not only how to add x to y or feature a to app b, but we've also tried to enable you to use what you have learned in your own ways so that you can bring your own ideas to life.

This chapter is more about your future apps and is different than anything that we've covered in this book so far. We will look at a number of aspects of Java and Android that you can use as a framework or template to make even more exciting and complex apps at the same time as keeping the code manageable. Furthermore, in this chapter, I will suggest the areas of further study that you can take a look at, which are out of the scope of this book.

You will learn about the following topics in this chapter:

- Patterns and the model-view-controller pattern
- Android design guidelines
- Getting started with real-world designs and handling multiple different devices
- An introduction to Fragments

Let's get started.

Introducing the model-view-controller pattern

MVC refers to the separation of different aspects of our app into distinct parts called **layers**. Android apps commonly use the model-view-controller **pattern**. A pattern is simply a recognized way to structure our code and other application resources, such as layout files, images, databases, and so on. Patterns are useful to us because by conforming to a pattern, we can be more confident that we are doing things right and are less likely to have to undo lots of hard work because we have coded ourselves into an awkward situation.

There are many patterns in computer science, but an understanding of MVC will be enough to create some really professional Android apps.

We have actually been partly using MVC already, so let's take a look at each of the three layers in turn.

The model

The model refers to the data that drives our app and any logic/code that specifically manages it and makes it available to the other layers. For example, in our Note To Self app, the Note class along with its getters, setters, and JSON code was the data and logic.

The view

The view of the Note To Self app referred to all the widgets in all the different layouts. Anything the user can see or interact with on screen is typically part of the view. And as you can probably remember, the widgets actually came from the View class hierarchy of the Android API.

The controller

The controller is the bit in between the view and model. It interacts with both and also keeps them separate. It contains what is known in geek language as the application logic. If a user clicks on a button, the application layer decides what to do about it. When the user clicks on **OK** to add a new note, the application logic listens for the interaction on the view layer. It captures the data contained in the view and passes it to the model layer. Almost...

The imperfections of Note To Self revisited

Actually, as mentioned before, we did not use a strict MVC pattern in that app. If you remember, the `ArrayList` of notes was actually held in the `Activity` class. In our next app, we will see how to improve our adherence to the MVC pattern with the use of a specially designed Java class, the singleton. The singleton is not yet another class type such as, inner, anonymous, static, interface, and so on. It is simply a way in which we can design and code a regular class in order to make our code more adherent to the MVC pattern and therefore more manageable as it becomes more complex, more potentially reusable in the future, and more understandable to other developers who might get involved with the project.

So, why did we do it *wrong* in our Note To Self app? For simplicity. When designing the Note To Self app, we knew that it was never going to be a big or complex project, and it was never going to be worked on simultaneously by more than one developer. It simply served the purpose of learning about aspects of Android and not cramming yet more concepts (MVC and singleton) into the list of things to know before achieving anything meaningful. Having said that, we were about 95% *right* in the design of Note To Self.

So in summary, the Note To Self app is a great demonstration of MVC, and we just need to see how we can tweak things a little in future apps because it will benefit us as our apps get more complicated. The reason we use the MVC pattern is because by separating our code into classes and then our classes into the MVC layers, we can enhance the goals of object-oriented design and use proven techniques.

This whole thing might seem like overkill and an unnecessary complication at first, but even in the context of this beginners programming book, we will reap the benefits of conformity with it. So, this is why it is worth introducing all these concepts as fast as possible—but not too fast.

Design patterns are a huge topic. There are many different design patterns, and if you want a beginner-friendly introduction to the topic in general, I would recommend you read *Head First Design Patterns* by O'Reilly Media. If you want to really dive into the world of design patterns, then you can try reading *Design Patterns: Elements of Reusable Object-Oriented Software*, which is recognized as a kind of design pattern Oracle, but is more difficult to read.

As we progress through *Chapter 19, Using Multiple Fragments,* and *Chapter 20, Paging and Swiping,* we will steadily introduce Java that we need to conform more closely to the MVC pattern. We will also begin to utilize more of the object-oriented programming aspects that we discussed, but haven't fully benefited from so far. We will do this step by step.

Android design guidelines

App design is a vast topic. It is a topic that we could only begin if it is taught in a book of its own. Also, like programming, you can only start to get good at app design with constant practice, review, and improvement.

So, what exactly do I mean by design? I am talking about where you put the widgets on the screen, which widgets, what color should they be, how big should they be, how to transition between screens, the best way to scroll a page, when and which interpolators to use, what screens should your app be divided into, and much more.

This book will hopefully leave you well qualified so that you are able to *implement* all your choices of the preceding questions and many more besides them. This book unfortunately doesn't have the space and the author probably doesn't have the skill to teach you how to *make* these choices.

You might be wondering, what should I do? Keep making apps and don't let the lack of design experience and knowledge stop you! Even release your apps on the app store. Keep in mind, however, that there is an entire other topic, design, that needs some attention if your apps are going to truly be world class.

In medium-sized development companies, the designer is rarely also the programmer, and even very small companies will often outsource the design of their app (or designers might outsource the coding).

Designing is both art and science, and Google has demonstrated that they recognize this with really high-quality support for both existing designers and aspiring new designers.

I highly recommend you visit and bookmark this page: `http://developer.android.com/design/index.html`. It is quite detailed and comprehensive, and it is totally focused on Android. It also has a digital ton of resources in the form of images, color palettes and guidelines.

Make understanding the design principles your short term goal. Make improving your actual design skills an ongoing task. Visit and read design focused websites and try and implement the ideas that you find exciting.

Most important of all, however, don't wait until you are a design expert to make apps. Keep bringing your ideas to life and publish them. Make it a point to make each app a little better designed than the last.

We will see in the coming chapters, and have seen already, that the Android API makes a whole bunch of super-stylish UI available to us that we can take advantage of with very little code. These go a long way to making your apps look like they have been designed by a professional.

Real-world apps

So far, we have designed one fairly significant app and a dozen or more mini apps. Some we designed for tablets, but we designed most of them on the Nexus 5 phone. Also, most of the screenshots in this book have been on the Nexus 5 emulator.

Of course, in the real world, our apps need to work well on any device and must be able to handle what happens when in either portrait or landscape view (on all devices).

Furthermore, it is often not enough for our apps to just work and look OK on different devices. Often, our apps will need to *behave* differently and appear with a significantly different UI based on whether the device is a phone, a tablet, or in the landscape/portrait orientation.

 Android has supported apps for large screen TV's for some time now, and in 2015, it introduced the Wear API to build apps for Android watches. We will not be covering these two most-extreme cases in this book.

Take a look at this screenshot of the BBC news app running on an Android phone in the portrait orientation. Look at the basic layout, but also note that the categories of news (**TOP STORIES**, **WORLD**, and **UK**) are all visible and allow the user to scroll down so that they can see more categories or swipe to the left or right between the stories within each category.

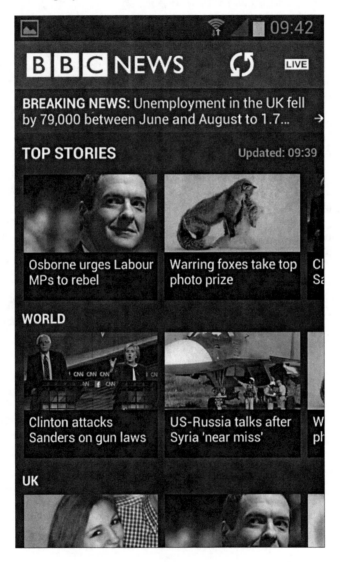

We will see how we can implement a swiping/paging UI using the `ImagePager` and `FragmentPager` classes in *Chapter 20, Paging and Swiping*. For now, the purpose of the diagram is not so much to show you the specific UI features, but to allow you to compare it with the next screenshot. Look at the exact same app running on a tablet in the landscape orientation:

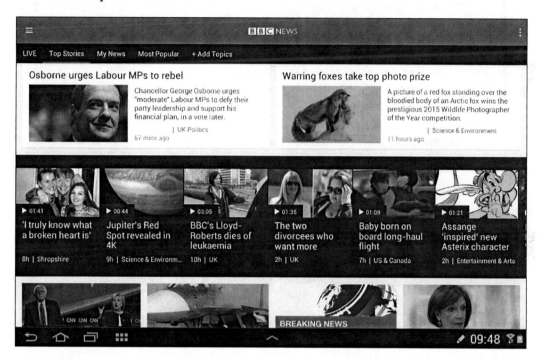

Note that the stories (data layer) are identical, but the layout (the view layer) is very different. The user is not only given the option to select categories from a menu of tabs at the top of the app, but they are also invited to add their own tabs through the **+ Add Topics** option.

The point of this image, again, is not so much the specific UI or even how we might implement one like it, but more that they are so different they could easily be mistaken for totally different apps.

Android allows us to design real-world apps like these, where not only is the layout different for varying device types/orientations/sizes, but so is the behavior. The Android secret weapon that makes this possible is `Fragments`.

Google says

A Fragment represents a behavior or a portion of user interface in an activity. You can combine multiple Fragments in a single activity to build a multipane UI and reuse a Fragment in multiple activities.

You can think of a Fragment as a modular section of an activity, which has its own lifecycle, receives its own input events, and which you can add or remove while the activity is running (sort of like a subactivity that you can reuse in different activities).

A Fragment must always be embedded in an activity, and the Fragment's lifecycle is directly affected by the host activity's lifecycle.

We can design multiple different layouts in different XML files, and we will do so soon. We can also detect things such as device orientation and screen resolution in code so that we can then make decisions about layouts dynamically.

Let's try this out and then we will take a look at Fragments.

The device detection mini app

To make this app, create a new project and call it Device Detection. Delete the default **Hello world!** widget. Drag **Button** onto the top of the screen and set its **onClick** property to detectDevice. We will code this method in a minute.

Drag two **LargeText** widgets onto the layout and set their **id** properties to txtOrientation and txtResolution, respectively. You should now have a layout that looks something like this:

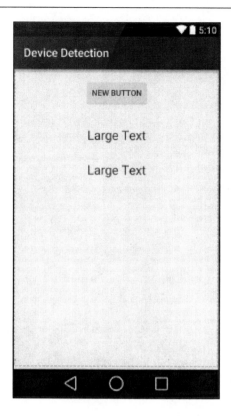

Add the following members just after the MainActivity class declaration to hold references to our two TextView widgets:

```
private TextView txtOrientation;
private TextView txtResolution;
```

Now, in the onCreate method of MainActivity, just after the call to setContentView, add this code:

```
// Get a reference to our TextView widgets
txtOrientation = (TextView) findViewById(R.id.txtOrientation);
txtResolution = (TextView) findViewById(R.id.txtResolution);
```

After `onCreate`, add the method that handles our button click and runs our detection code:

```
public void detectDevice(View v){

    // What is the orientation?
    Display display = getWindowManager().getDefaultDisplay();
    txtOrientation.setText("" + display.getRotation());

    // What is the resolution?
    Point xy = new Point();
    display.getSize(xy);
    txtResolution.setText("x = " + xy.x + " y = " + xy.y);


}
```

Now, run the app. On some computers, the emulator is prone to crashing when it is rotated. If necessary, test this on a real device:

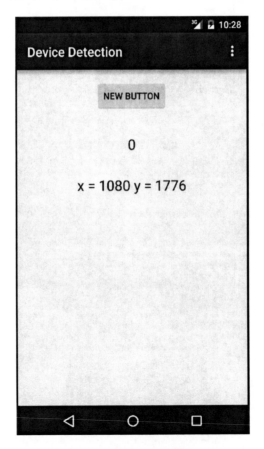

Rotate the device to landscape (use *Ctrl + F11* on PC or *Ctrl + fn + F11* on Mac). Now, click on the **NEW BUTTON** button, as shown here:

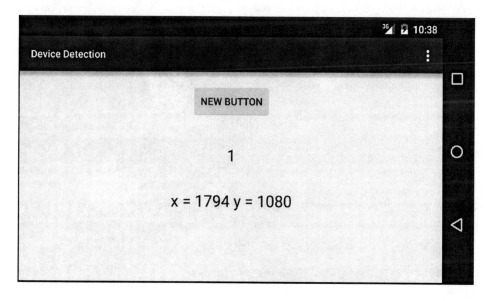

If the 0 and 1 results are less than obvious regarding the device orientation, they refer to the `public static final` variables of the `Surface` class, where `Surfcae.ROTATION_0` equals `0` and `Surface.ROTATION_180` equals `1`.

And we could switch based on the results of these detection tests and load up different layouts.

Android makes this simpler than this for us by allowing us to add specific layouts into folders with configuration qualifiers.

Configuration qualifiers

We have already seen configuration qualifiers such as `layout-large` or `layout-xhdpi` in *The Android Studio guided tour* section from *Chapter 3, Exploring Android Studio*. Here, we will refresh and expand our understanding of them.

We can begin to remove the reliance on the controller layer to influence the app layout by using configuration qualifiers. There are configuration qualifiers for size, orientation, and pixel density. To take advantage of a configuration qualifier, we simply design a layout in the usual way that is optimized for our preferred configuration and then place that layout in a folder with a name that Android recognizes as being of that particular configuration.

So, if we want to have a different layout for landscape and portrait, we would create a folder called `layout-land` in the `res` folder and place our specially designed layout within it. When the device is in the portrait position, the regular layout from the `layout` folder would be used, and when it is in landscape, the layout from the `layout-land` folder would be used.

If we are designing for different sizes of screen, we place layouts into folders with the following names:

- `layout-small`
- `layout-normal`
- `layout-large`
- `layout-xlarge`

If we are designing for screens with different pixel densities, we can place XML layouts into folders with names like these:

- The `layout-ldpi` layout for low DPI devices
- The `layout-mdpi` layout for medium DPI devices
- The `layout-hdpi` layout for high DPI devices
- The `layout-xhdpi` layout for extra high DPI devices
- The `layout-xxhdpi` layout for extra, extra high DPI devices
- The `layout-xxxhdpi` layout for extra, extra, extra high DPI devices
- The `layout-nodpi` layout for devices with a DPI that you have not otherwise catered for
- The `layout-tvdpi` layout for TVs

What exactly qualifies as a low, high, or extra high DPI can be researched at the link in the next information box. The point here is the principle, and we will do something practical with this knowledge in the next mini app.

You might also remember that we added icons of different sizes into folders with names such as `drawable-mdpi` and `drawable-hdpi` when we started the Note To Self app in *Chapter 12, Having a Dialogue with the User*. This was because Android would use different graphics based upon the screen density of the device our app is being run on.

It is worth pointing out that what we have just discussed is a long way from the whole story regarding the configuration qualifiers, and as with design, it is worth putting this on your list of things to study further.

As so often, the Android developer site has lots of detailed information on handling layouts for different devices. Try out `http://developer.android.com/guide/practices/screens_support.html` for more information.

Let's try out some device qualifiers now.

Using configuration qualifiers – mini app

Create a new project and call it `Configuration Qualifiers` and follow the next steps:

1. Right-click on the `res` folder in the project explorer and navigate to **New | Android resource directory**. Type `layout-land` and click on **OK**.

 If you don't see your new directory in the project explorer, you need to change the view of the project explorer through its drop-down selector at the top of the project explorer window. Click on the drop-down selector and choose **Project**.

2. In the `layout_main.xml` file, change the text of the default **TextView** widget from `Hello world` to `Hello portrait!`.

3. Right-click on the `layout-land` folder and navigate to **New | Layout resource**. Name the file `layout_main.xml`. Add a single **Plain TextView** widget and change the `text` property to `Hello landscape!`.

4. Run the app and rotate the device between landscape and portrait orientations. Note that the OS automatically uses the appropriate version of `layout_main.xml`.

If we got a reference to `TextView` (or any other widget) in our Java code, the same exact code would work as long as the `id` values in the different layouts were the same.

Effectively, we have two different layouts controlled by the same Java code.

The configuration qualifier's summary

What the last two mini apps and our discussion on configuration qualifiers have shown us is certainly very useful in a number of situations. Unfortunately, however, configuration qualifiers and detecting attributes in code only solve the problem in the view layer of our MVC pattern. As discussed in the *Real-world apps* section, our apps sometimes need to have a different *behavior* as well as layout. This perhaps implies multiple branches of our code in the controller layer and perhaps summons nightmarish visions of having huge great if or switch blocks with different code for each different scenario.

Fortunately, this is not how it's done. For such situations (actually for most apps), Android has **Fragments**.

Fragments

Fragments will likely become a staple of almost every real app you make. They are so useful; there are so many reasons to use them; and once you get used to them, they are so simple. There is almost no reason not to use them.

Fragments are reusable elements of an app just like any class, but as mentioned previously, they have special features, such as the ability to load their own view as well as having their very own lifecycle methods that make them perfect to achieve the goals that we've discussed in the *Real-world apps* section.

Let's dig a bit deeper into Fragments one feature at a time.

Fragments have a lifecycle too

We can set up and control Fragments very much like we do Activities, by overriding the appropriate lifecycle methods.

onCreate

In the onCreate method, we can initialize variables and do almost all the things we would typically do in the Activity onCreate method. The big exception to this is initializing our UI.

onCreateView

In this method, we will, as the name suggests, get a reference to any of our UI widgets, set up anonymous classes to listen for clicks, and do more besides these tasks, as you will soon see.

onAttach and onDetach

These methods are called just before the Fragment is actually put into use/taken out of use.

onStart, onPause, and onStop

In these methods, we can take certain actions such as creating or deleting objects or saving data, just like we did with their counterparts that were based on Activity.

 There are other Fragment lifecycle methods as well, but we know enough to start using Fragments already. If you want to study the details of the fragment lifecycle, you can do so on the Android developer website at `http://developer.android.com/guide/components/fragments.html`.

This is all very well, but we need a way to create our Fragments in the first place and be able to call these methods at the right time.

Managing Fragments with FragmentManager

The `FragmentManager` class is part of `Activity`. We use it to initialize `Fragment`, add Fragments to the Activities layout, and to end `Fragment`. We actually briefly saw `FragmentManager` earlier when we initialized some `FragmentDialog`. It is very hard to learn much about Android without bumping into the Fragment class just as it is tough to learn much about Java without OOP. The highlighted code here shows how we used `FragmentManager` (which is already a part of the Activity) that was passed in as an argument to create the pop-up dialog:

```
button.setOnClickListener(new View.OnClickListener() {
  @Override
  public void onClick(View v) {

    // Create a new DialogShowNote called dialog
    DialogShowNote dialog = new DialogShowNote();

    // Send the note via the sendNoteSelected method
    dialog.sendNoteSelected(mTempNote);

    // Create the dialog
    dialog.show(getFragmentManager(), "123");
  }
});
```

At the time when we used the previous code, I had asked you not to concern yourself with the arguments of the method call. The second argument of the method call is an ID for Fragment. We will see how to use FragmentManager more extensively as well as use the Fragment ID.

FragmentManager does exactly what its name suggests. What is important here is that Activity only has one FragmentManager, but it can take care of many fragments; just what we need to have multiple behaviors and layouts within a single app.

FragmentManager also calls the various lifecycle methods of the fragments it is responsible for. This is distinct from the Activity lifecycle methods that are called by Android, yet closely related because FragmentManager calls many of the Fragment lifecycle methods *in response to* the Activity lifecycle methods being called. As usual, we don't need to worry too much about when and how as long as we respond appropriately in each situation.

Fragments are going to be a fundamental part of many, if not all, of our future apps. As we did with naming conventions, string resources, and encapsulation, however, we will not use fragments for simple learning purposes or mini apps when they would be overkill. The exception to this will, of course, be when we are learning about or making mini apps to specifically demonstrate fragments.

In addition, there will be a few fragment-based mini apps where we will focus on just the fragment-related code in order to understand it properly.

Our first working Fragment mini app

Let's build a Fragment in its simplest possible form so that we can understand what is going on before in later chapters we start producing Fragments all over the place.

I urge all readers to go through and actually build this project. There is a lot of jumping around from file to file and just reading alone can make it seem more complex than it really is. You can copy and paste the code from the download bundle but please also follow the steps and create your own projects and classes. Fragments are not too tough but their implementation, like there name suggests is a little fragmented.

Create a new project called `Simple Fragment` using the same default settings as always. Note that there is the option to create a project with `Fragment`, but you will learn more about them by doing things from scratch.

Switch to `activity_main.xml` and delete the default **Hello world!** widget. Now, make sure that the `RelativeLayout` root is selected by clicking on it in the **Component Tree** window. Change its **id** property to `fragmentHolder`. We will now be able to get a reference to this layout in our Java code, and as the `id` property implies, we will be adding a Fragment to it.

Now, we will create a layout that will define our Fragment's appearance. Right-click on the `layout` folder and navigate to **New | Layout resource file**. In the **File name** field, type `fragment_layout` and click on **OK**.

Add a single **Button** widget anywhere on the layout and make its **id** property `button`.

Now that we have a simple layout for our fragment to use, let's write some Java code to make the actual fragment.

Note that you can create a `Fragment` by simply dragging and dropping one from the palette, but doing things this way is much less flexible and controllable. Also, flexibility and control are the big benefits to fragments, as we will see throughout this chapter. By creating a class that extends `Fragment`, we can make as many fragments from it as we like.

In the project explorer, right-click on the folder that contains the `MainActivity` file. From the context menu, navigate to **New | Java class**. In the **Name** field, type `SimpleFragment` and click on **OK**.

Note that there are options to create `Fragment` classes in various precoded states to implement `Fragment` more quickly, but at the moment, they will slightly cloud the learning objectives of this mini app.

In our new `SimpleFragment` class, change the code to extend Fragment. As you type the code, you will be asked to choose a specific `Fragment` class to import, as shown in the next screenshot:

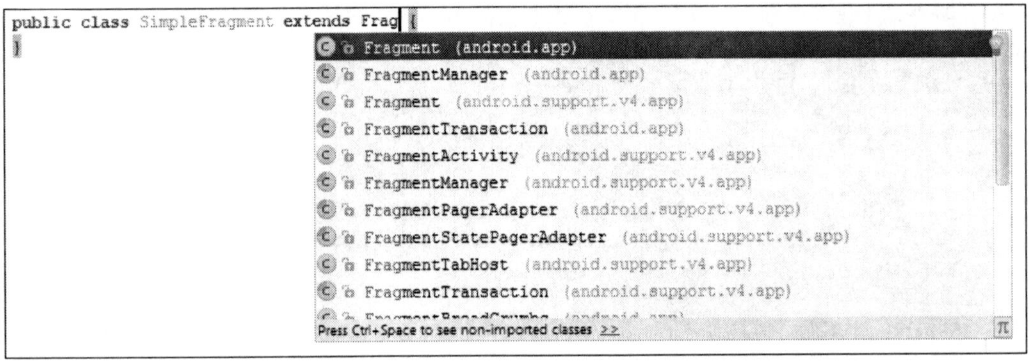

Choose the top option (as shown in the previous screenshot), which is a regular `Fragment` class.

Now, add a single `String` variable called `myString` and a `Button` variable called `myButton` as members and override the `onCreate` method. Inside the `onCreate` method, initialize `myString` to `Hello from SimpleFragment`. Our code so far (excluding the package declaration) will look exactly like this next code:

```java
import android.app.Fragment;
import android.os.Bundle;

public class SimpleFragment extends Fragment {

  // member variables accessible from anywhere in this fragment
  String myString;
  Button myButton;

  @Override
  public void onCreate(Bundle savedInstanceState){
    super.onCreate(savedInstanceState);

    myString = "Hello from SimpleFragment";
  }
}
```

In the previous code, we created a member variable called `myString`, and then in the `onCreate` method, we initialized it. This is very much like we do for our previous apps when we only use Activity. The difference, however, is that we did not set the view or attempt to get a reference to our `Button` member variable, `myButton`.

When using Fragment, we need to do this in the `onCreateView` method. Let's override this now and see how we set the view and get a reference to our Button.

Add this code to the `SimpleFragment` class after the `onCreate` method:

```
@Override
public View onCreateView(LayoutInflater inflater,
  ViewGroup container, Bundle savedInstanceState) {

  View view = inflater.inflate
    (R.layout.fragment_layout, container, false);

  myButton = (Button) view.findViewById(R.id.button);

  return view;
}
```

To understand the previous block of code, we must first look at the `onCreateView` method signature. First, note that the start of the method states that it must return an object of the type `View`:

```
public View onCreateView...
```

Next, we have the three arguments. Let's look at the first two now:

```
(LayoutInflater inflater, ViewGroup container,...
```

We need `LayoutInflater` as we cannot call `setContentView` because `Fragment` provides no such method. In the body of `onCreateView`, we use the `inflate` method of `inflater` to inflate our layout contained in `fragment_layout.xml` and initialize view (an object of the type `View`) with the result.

We use `container` that was passed in to `onCreateView` as an argument in the `inflate` method. The `container` variable is a reference to the layout in `activity_main.xml`.

It might seem obvious that `activity_main.xml` is the containing layout, but as we will see later in the chapter, the `ViewGroup container` argument allows *any* `Activity` with *any* layout to be the container for our fragment. This is exceptionally flexible and makes our `Fragment` code reusable to a significant extent. The third argument that we pass into `inflate` is `false`, which means that we don't want our layout to be immediately added to the containing layout. We will do this soon from another part of the code.

The third argument of `onCreateView` is `Bundle savedInstanceState`, which is there to help us maintain the data that our fragments hold. We will see this in action in *Chapter 22, Capturing Images*.

Now that we have an inflated layout contained in `view`, we can use this to get a reference to `Button` like this:

```
myButton = (Button) view.findViewById(R.id.button);
```

And we can also use it as the return value to the calling code, as required:

```
return view;
```

Now, we can add an anonymous class to listen for clicks on our button in the usual manner. In the `onClick` method, we display a pop-up `Toast` message to demonstrate that everything is working as expected. Add this code just before the `return` statement in `onCreateView` as highlighted in this next code:

```
@Override
public View onCreateView(LayoutInflater inflater,
  ViewGroup container, Bundle savedInstanceState) {

  View view = inflater.inflate(R.layout.fragment_layout,
    container, false);

  myButton = (Button) view.findViewById(R.id.button);

  myButton.setOnClickListener(new View.OnClickListener() {
    @Override
    public void onClick(View v) {

      Toast.makeText(getActivity(),myString ,
        Toast.LENGTH_SHORT).show();
    }
  });

  return view;
}
```

As a reminder, the `getActivity()` call that is used as an argument in `makeText` gets a reference to the Activity that contains Fragment. This is required to display a `Toast` message. We also used `getActivity` in our classes based on `FragmentDialog` in the Note To Self app.

We can't run our mini app just yet, as it will not work because there is one more step that we need to complete. We need to create an instance of `SimpleFragment` and initialize it appropriately. This is where `FragmentManager` will get introduced.

This next code creates a new `FragmentManager` by calling `getFragmentManager`. It creates a new Fragment based on our `SimpleFragment` class by using `FragmentManager` and passing in the ID of the layout (within the Activity) that will hold it.

Add this code in the `onCreate` method of `MainActivity.java` just after the call to `setContentView`:

```
// Get a fragment manager
FragmentManager fManager = getFragmentManager();

// Create a new fragment using the manager
// Passing in the id of the layout to hold it
Fragment frag = fManager.findFragmentById(R.id.fragmentHolder);

// Check the fragment has not already been initialized
if(frag == null){

  // Initialize the fragment based on our SimpleFragment
  frag = new SimpleFragment();
  fManager.beginTransaction()
  .add(R.id.fragmentHolder, frag)
  .commit();

}
```

Now, run the app and gaze in wonder at our clickable button that took two layouts and two complete classes for us to create as shown in the following screenshot:

I think we need a fragment reality check to answer a few questions like, why!

Fragment reality check

So, what does this Fragment stuff really do for us? Our first `Fragment` mini app would have exactly the same appearance and functionality had we not bothered with Fragment at all. In fact, using Fragment has made the whole thing more complicated! Why would we want to do this?

We kind of know the answer to this already, but it just isn't especially clear based on what we have seen so far. We know that Fragment or fragments can be added to the layout of an Activity. We know that a Fragment not only contains its own layout (view), but also its very own code (controller), which although hosted by Activity, the Fragment is virtually independent.

Our quick mini app only showed one Fragment in action, but we could have an Activity that hosts two or more fragments. We can then effectively have two almost-independent controllers displayed on a single screen. This sounds like it could be useful.

What is most useful about this, however, is that when the Activity starts, we can detect attributes of the device that our app is running on, perhaps a phone or tablet or in the portrait or landscape orientation. We can then use this information to decide to display either just one or two of our fragments simultaneously.

This not only helps us achieve the kind of functionality discussed in the *Real-world apps* section at the start of the chapter, but it also allows us to do so using the exact same `Fragment` code for both possible scenarios! This really is the essence of fragments. We can create a complete app by pairing up both functionality (controller) and appearance (view) into a bunch of fragments that we can reuse in different ways, almost without care.

It is, of course, possible to foresee a few stumbling blocks, so take a look at these FAQs.

FAQ

1. As each Fragment is an entirely separate class, how will they communicate with each other?

   We will solve this problem with a practical use of Java that you have already learned about—interfaces—along with some other tools as well, starting in the next chapter.

2. The other missing link is that, if all these fragments are fully functioning independent controllers, then you need to learn a bit more about how we would implement our model layer. If we simply have `ArrayList`, like with Note To Self, where will it go? How would we share it between fragments (assuming both fragments need access to the same data)?

   There is an entirely more elegant solution that we can use to create a model layer (both the data itself and the code to maintain the data). We can use the Java **singleton,** and we will do so in the next chapter.

Summary

Now that we have a broad understanding of what Fragments are for and how we can begin to use them, we can start to go deeper into how they are used. In the next chapter, we will complete a couple of apps that will enable us to finally implement the data layer of our apps as they are meant to and to create a simple app that uses multiple layouts, multiple fragments, and our new data layer. At the same time, we will see another type of adapter that is used to link our UI to our data layer.

19
Using Multiple Fragments

Now that we have discussed the principals of MVC as well as seen how to implement a Fragment, we can take things a stage further. You will learn how to separate the data layer using a Java singleton and then we will see how Fragments can communicate with each other.

Once we have achieved both of these things, we can implement our first multi-Fragment, orientation-aware app that will put everything we know so far into practice.

 In this chapter, to save digital ink, I will stop giving specific instructions on how to make classes and layout files. As a reminder, to create a new class, right-click on the folder that contains all the .java files and navigate to **New** | **Class**. Type the name and click on **OK**. To create a new layout file, right-click on the **layout** folder and navigate to **New** | **Resource layout file**.

In short, we will do the following in this chapter:

- Explore Java singletons to implement the data layer
- Implement inter-Fragment communication with a Java interface
- Build an address book app with two Fragments that behave differently between the landscape view and the portrait view

Using singletons for the model layer

A singleton, as the name suggests, is a class where there can only be one instance of that class. If you think about data storage, this makes sense. If you have more than one place to store the same set of data, it is possible, if not highly likely, that at some point you will attempt to store or retrieve something inconsistently.

Think about having two identical sets of folders to manage your e-mails. If you have two (or more) folders marked as Urgent, how will you know where to store that urgent e-mail. And when you need to check if you have any urgent emails, you will need to check both. What if you forget and only check one?

Also, consider a shopping app, where the user browses from page to page and each page is, perhaps, a separate Fragment/Activity. If they add something to the cart on more than one page, they could end up with two separate carts instead of one with both the items in it.

When we are making straightforward apps, it is possible that we could survive without using singletons. But as our apps quickly become more complicated, it will be very easy to find our data storage solution, literally all over the place.

If it's starting to sound like singletons might be complicated, be reassured that they are quite straightforward. In software engineering, the singleton pattern is simply a design pattern that restricts the instantiation/creation of a class to one object. This is useful when exactly one object is needed to coordinate actions across the system. Note that our singleton will be accessible throughout the entire app but not to other apps.

The other thing that our singleton design will ensure is that the data persists for the entire life of the app and is available throughout the classes (including fragments) of the app.

This makes sense for us because although there are ways to communicate between classes, some of which we have already seen, if the data is fundamental to the app, it should be easily available throughout.

Let's review our requirements. We need a class that can only have one instance, but this one instance must be available to all throughout the life of the app at the same time as controlling how its data is accessed.

Take a look at this block of code for example:

```
public class Movie{
  private String mTitle;
  private boolean mOnLoan;

  public void setTitle(String title){
    mTitle = title;
  }

  public String getTitle(){
    return mTitle;
```

```
  }

  public void setLoanStatus(boolean loanStatus){
    mOnLoan = loanStatus;

  }

  public boolean getLoanStatus(){
    return mLoanStatus;
  }
}
```

In the previous code, we have a simple class called Movie with two private members: mTitle and mOnLoan. The two variables would hold the tile of a movie and the status whether it is currently out on loan or not. This could be a useful class for an app to manage a movie rental store or perhaps a personal movie collection. The code also has two getters and two setters that are used to check and change the value of these two private member variables, which would otherwise be inaccessible from outside the class.

The class is public, so any part of our app can create instances of the class in order to manipulate data of the Movie type. The trick is how our app obtains these instances, and this is where the singleton comes in handy. Take a look at this next code block as an example:

```
public class RentalStore {

  // I am instantiating an instance of myself - weird!
  // This is the only RentalStore that will ever exist
  private static RentalStore ourInstance = new RentalStore();

  private ArrayList <Movie> mMovies;

  // Anyone who wants my one and only instance will
  // need to use this method
  public static RentalStore getInstance() {
    return ourInstance;
  }

  // Here is the constructor and it is private
  // So only this class itself can ever instantiate it
  private RentalStore() {
    mMovies = new ArrayList<Movie>();
  }
```

```
    // Anyone can get the list of movies though
    public ArrayList <Movie> getMovies(){

        return mMovies;
    }
}
```

The previous code might look complicated, but when we break it down, it really isn't. First, look at the constructor (the method with the same name as the class). The `RentalStore` constructor method is private. Since we have provided a default constructor that is `private`, it might at first seem that it is now impossible to ever instantiate `RentalStore`.

Just before the constructor, we have a `public static` method called `getInstance`. Recall that in *Chapter 9, Object-Oriented Programming*, we discussed that a `static` method can be called *without* an instance of the class. Look again at the `getInstance` method and note that its return type is `RentalStore`. This means that any code anywhere in our app can call the `getInstance` method and receive a `RentalStore` instance.

Now, look at the body of `getInstance`, and it does indeed return `ourInstance`, which was instantiated just after the class declaration.

This means that *nobody* can ever instantiate `RentalStore`, but *everybody* can get a reference to the one and only `RentalStore` stored in our singleton.

Furthermore, the class has a public method `getMovies` that returns `ArrayList` of all the `Movie` objects that have been created so that they can do what they like to the movies in it—as long as it is allowed by the getters and setters of the `Movie` class. This is a kind of data paradox. Complete freedom with complete control! Any code that does anything to any movie in `ArrayList` or adds or removes anything to/from `ArrayList` is guaranteed to be working on exactly the same set of data as any other part of our app that does so.

We could go on to add more features to our singleton, perhaps, to add getters and setters and to control exactly what can and can't be done to `ArrayList` instead of simply handing `ArrayList` to the calling code. This discussion has taken the concept of a singleton far enough for the purpose of the next few apps.

We can now go about using `RentalShop` in our code like this:

```
RentalShop myRentalShop = RentalShop.getInstance();
```

We can then get hold of the list of movies like this:

```
ArrayList <Movie> myMovies = myRentalShop.getMovies();
```

We can now do whatever we like within the constraints of the Movie class. And if later on in our code, probably in another Activity or Fragment, we have code like this, we can be confident that the code is working on exactly the same set of data as the code in the other Activity or Fragment:

```
RentalShop someRentalShop = RentalShop.getInstance();
ArrayList <Movie> myMovies = someRentalShop.getMovies();
```

Inter-Fragment communications – interfaces revisited

The main point of Fragments is that they have flexibility and reusability. If you remember, back in *Chapter 12*, *Having a Dialogue with the User*, when we were passing Note to and from a Fragment dialog, we added a method to Fragment and then called this method from the instance of the dialog in order to pass in the correct note that is to be shown. And when we added a new note in a dialog, we used getActivity() to get a reference to MainActivity in order to return the new note to be added to ArrayList of notes. Here is the code as a reminder:

```
// Get a reference to MainActivity
MainActivity callingActivity = (MainActivity) getActivity();

// Pass newNote back to MainActivity
callingActivity.createNewNote(newNote);
```

The problem with this is that it assumes that the communication is with an Activity called MainActivity.

Although this works in the Note To Self scenario, it is inflexible because this means that our fragments can only be used in Activities that have the correct methods, or that fragments must have the right methods so that our Activities can be called.

This didn't bother us much in the Note To Self app, but when we will be showing different combinations of fragments on different Activities, then we need a uniform way to communicate, and we need a way to guarantee/force our code that uses our Fragments, to be aware of this communication method.

Interfaces are the solution! Recall that in *Chapter 9*, *Object-Oriented Programming*, we saw that an interface is a class in which all the methods have no body and all the methods are abstract by default. So any class that implements the interface must override all its methods using the correct name and parameters.

Take a look at the code in this interface. It has one method, `onListItemSelected`. It takes a `Movie` object as an argument, but this argument could, of course, be whatever we want it to be and there could be more than one argument:

```
public interface ActivityComs {

    void onListItemSelected(Movie movie);
}
```

We can then declare an instance of the interface within any `Fragment` that needs to communicate:

```
private ActivityComs mActivityComs;
```

We can then override the Fragments `onAttach` method and initialize it like the next block of code. Note that `onAttach` receives `Activity` as a parameter. This is the parent `Activity` where `Fragment` is created. So, provided `Activity` implements the interface, when we call the interfaces method from `Fragment`, we will be calling the overridden method in `Activity`. Seeing this in action is the best way to understand this and we will soon. Here is the overridden `onAttach` method in `Fragment`:

```
@Override
public void onAttach(Activity activity) {
  super.onAttach(activity);

  /*
    activity is a ActivityComs but must
    still be explicitly cast to the type
  */
  mActivityComs = (ActivityComs)activity;
}
```

In the `onDetach` method, we can render it harmless like this:

```
@Override
public void onDetach() {
  super.onDetach();

  /*
    Set the reference to null.
    Now there is no active reference
    the garbage collector will clean it up
  */
  mActivityComs = null;
}
```

And most importantly, we can, of course, call its one and only method on the event that we want the communication to take place on, most likely a click, perhaps on an item in `ListView`, as shown in the next code snippet. Remember that this code is still taking place within `Fragment`, and we will see the `Activity` code afterwards:

```
public void onListItemClick(ListView l, View v, int position, long id)
{

  Movie movie =
    ((MovieListAdapter)getListAdapter()).getItem(position);

  mActivityComs.onListItemSelected(movie);
}
```

The previous code assumes that we have an adapter called `MovieListAdapter`. It creates a new `Movie` object and calls `onListItemSelected` on the interface, passing in the new `Movie` object as an argument. So, if the `Activity` that created `Fragment` has implemented `ActivityComs`, the new `Movie` object will be passed into the overridden `onListItemSelected` method in `Activity`.

The last piece of the puzzle takes place in the related `Activity` when we first implement the interface:

```
public class MainActivity extends AppCompatActivity implements
  ActivityComs{
```

And then, we must override the method to handle the data that is passed in:

```
public void onListItemSelected(Movie movie) {

  // Do whatever you want with the Movie
}
```

As we will see in the `Address book` app, and as implied in the previous block of code, we still need to decide what exactly we will do with the passed-in data.

We can do something with the data right there in the `Activity` or pass it to another `Fragment` using the `onCreate` method's `Bundle`.

It makes sense that these bundles be configured (packed with data) in the same place and in the same method of the interface so that the `Bundle` passed into a new `Activity` that we know is destined for a particular Fragment in the end, will be managed from the same place.

We will see this happen in the Address book app very soon, but you will probably be pleased to hear that once we have prepared data in Bundle and passed it to the appropriate Activity, Fragments can also receive and unpack these Bundle packages in the same way as implied by the signature of the onCreate method, as shown:

```
public void onCreate(Bundle savedInstanceState)
```

We can now put all our new information about Fragment, interfaces, singleton and a new trick, configuration qualifiers all together in our next app to create a true dual fragment app that behaves differently depending upon whether the device is in landscape or portrait orientation.

In this next app, we will not save data to a disk or add new data via the UI, as this could be almost copy pasted from the Note To Self app with minor amendments to cater for names and addresses instead of notes.

The dual-Fragment address book mini app

The app will show a list of names and allow the user to tap on a name so that it displays the address. What is new about this app is that when we compare it to the Note To Self app, it will behave differently depending upon whether it is in the portrait or landscape orientation.

When in the portrait orientation, tapping on a name will cause a new Activity to open and display the address. When in the landscape mode, tapping on a name will cause the address to be shown on the right-hand side of the screen in the same Activity. This next image clarifies this visually:

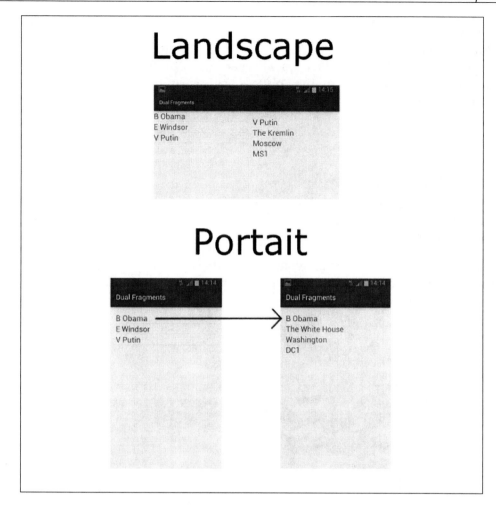

This is the kind of behavior a user might expect from a mobile app. The best part is that it doesn't matter whether the user is in the portrait or landscape orientation, the exact same Java code and XML layout will be used for both the list and the detail parts. We will, of course, achieve this feat by using Fragments.

Getting started

Create a new blank project called `Dual Fragment`. This mini app has us jumping between files and directories. I have made every effort to ensure that the exact location in which the action is taking place is made clear. If there is any doubt about exactly what goes where, be sure to refer to the code in the download bundle in the `Chapter 19/Dual Fragments` folder. Every file or folder that we either need to create or amend is in there.

Alias resources

First, you will learn a new trick that is a more flexible, although slightly more complicated, method of determining which layout file is used depending upon the device orientation.

The project explorer window has a number of different layout options. Some are very subtly different, and for this next part of the mini app, it is really important that you are using the right layout as we will be creating new directories.

Click on the drop-down **Project** list and make sure that the **Project** option is selected. It might have been already, but if it isn't, this next part won't work. The next screenshot makes this step clear:

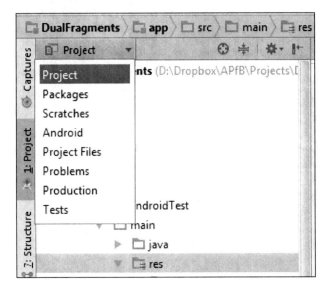

First, we will use an Android trick known as **alias resources**.

Follow this tutorial through to the end. It will be clearer as to exactly what we are achieving as we implement the final steps:

1. Right-click on **res/values** and navigate to **New | Values resource file**. In the **File name** field, enter `refs` and then click on **OK**.

2. In the new `refs.xml` file that we just created, add the highlighted code that is shown next:

```xml
<?xml version="1.0" encoding="utf-8"?>
<resources>
 <item name = "activity_dualfragment" type= "layout">
    @layout/activity_main
 </item>
</resources>
```

What we have just done will make more sense when we implement the next step as well.

3. Right-click on the **res** folder and navigate to **New | Android resource directory**. Now, enter `values-land` in the **Directory name** field.

4. Right-click on the directory that you just created and navigate to **New | Values resource file**. In the **File name** field, enter `refs` and then click on **OK**.

5. Now in the new `refs` file that is in the **values-land** directory, add the highlighted line of code shown here:.

```xml
<?xml version="1.0" encoding="utf-8"?>
<resources>
 <item name = "activity_dualfragment" type= "layout">
    @layout/activity_main_land
 </item>
</resources>
```

6. Right-click on the layout folder and navigate to **New | Layout resource file**. In the **File name** field, type `activity_main_land`.

Very quickly, for the sake of testing, add **Plain TextView** to `activity_main_land` and change its `text` property to `Landscape`. In `activity_main`, add **Plain TextView** and change its `text` property to `Portrait`.

We can now update the call to `setContentView` in the `onCreate` method of `MainActivity` so that it looks like this:

```
@Override
protected void onCreate(Bundle savedInstanceState) {
  super.onCreate(savedInstanceState);

  setContentView(R.layout.activity_dualfragment);
}
```

This `setContentView` line of code passes the `activity_dualfragment` alias and not either of the actual layout files. The two `refs.xml` files each contain an alias for `activity_dualfragment` that will ensure that a different layout file is used depending upon which orientation the device is in. So when the device is in the landscape orientation, `activity_main_land` will be loaded as the view, and when the device is in the portrait orientation, `activity_main` will be used.

> We could have just as easily added a folder named `layout_land` and added our landscape layout there. We didn't have to use aliases. Using aliases, however, is more flexible as the number of potential layouts grow as it allows us to use the same layout for multiple different devices/orientations. For example, what if we decide to use the `activity_main_land` layout on tablets that are over 1,000 pixels wide, even when they are in the portrait orientation? Aliases would give us this flexibility without duplicating the `activity_main_land` file and creating a maintenance problem where we need to remember to update the file in two different places.

Run the app and try it now. Note that as you rotate the device, a new layout is loaded. This one for the landscape orientation:

This one for the portrait orientation:

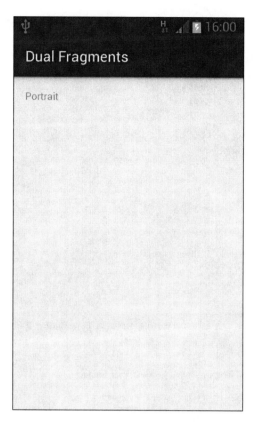

Our app now shows a different layout between different orientations using resource aliases. Soon, we will add to these layouts so that it either holds two fragments for landscape (a list and the details) or holds one Fragment for portrait (just the list).

Before we can make much progress, we need a class to store a single name and address.

The NameAndAddress class

Create a new class and call it NameAndAddress. We implement Serializable as this is required by ArrayAdapter, which will act as our adapter between ListView and our data. We will see this in action soon. We will see that ArrayAdapter saves us a mountain of code at the expense of a slight loss in flexibility.

Add this code for the `NameAndAddress` class:

```java
public class NameAndAddress implements Serializable{

    private String mName;
    private String mAddress1;
    private String mAddress2;
    private String mZipCode;

    public NameAndAddress(String name,
        String address1,
        String address2,
        String zipCode){

        mName = name;
        mAddress1 = address1;
        mAddress2 = address2;
        mZipCode = zipCode;
    }
}
```

We need a getter method for each member, so you can use *one* of these three methods:

1. Type the next code block.
2. Copy and paste it from the download bundle.
3. Right-click below the last line of code and navigate to **Generate | Getters**. Then, highlight all the members and click on **OK**. This generates getter methods with names such as `getmName` that you will need to tidy up the names to match the more friendly method names that we will be using, such as `getName`, as per the next code block.

Here is the code that needs to be added to the `NameAndAddress` class using the method of your choice:

```java
public String getName() {
    return mName;
}


public String getAddress1() {
    return mAddress1;
}


public String getAddress2() {
```

```
        return mAddress2;
    }


    public String getZipCode() {
      return mZipCode;
    }
```

Next, we can implement the logic of our model layer, and, of course, we will do so with a singleton class. Right-click on the folder with our `MainActivity.java` file in it. Now, navigate to **New | Java class**. Type `AddressBook` in the **Name** field and click on the **Kind** drop-down menu and choose **Singleton**. Android Studio will give us a template for our singleton class called `AddressBook`. Here is the generated code:

```
public class AddressBook {
    private static AddressBook ourInstance = new AddressBook();

    public static AddressBook getInstance() {
        return ourInstance;
    }

    private AddressBook() {
    }
}
```

Now, we can add our code to make it our own. We will require an `ArrayList` member that will hold all the instances of our `NameAndAddress` class. We will call this `mNamesAndAddresses` and initialize it in the private constructor. We also need a public getter method so that it returns a reference to `ArrayList`. We will call this method `getBook`. Here is the next phase of the `AddressBook` class in which the new code that we just discussed is highlighted:

```
public class AddressBook {
  private static AddressBook ourInstance = new AddressBook();

  private ArrayList <NameAndAddress> mNamesAndAddresses;

  public static AddressBook getInstance() {
    return ourInstance;
  }

  private AddressBook() {
    mNamesAndAddresses = new ArrayList<NameAndAddress>();
  }
```

```
    public ArrayList <NameAndAddress> getBook(){

        return mNamesAndAddresses;
    }
}
```

As this will not be a fully functioning app, we need to cheat a bit by creating some dummy data for us to play around with. We know that the constructor will only be called once, so let's add a few names and addresses by adding the highlighted code into the constructor after we initialize ArrayList, as shown in the next code snippet:

```
private AddressBook() {
    mNamesAndAddresses = new ArrayList<NameAndAddress>();

    // Some hardcoded dummy data

    // Create a new entry
    NameAndAddress tempEntry = new NameAndAddress("B Obama",
        "The White House",
        "Washington",
        "DC1");

    // Add it to the ArrayList
    mNamesAndAddresses.add(tempEntry);

    // Create a new entry
    tempEntry = new NameAndAddress("E Windsor",
        "Buckingham Palace",
        "London",
        "SW1A 1AA");

    // Add it to the ArrayList
    mNamesAndAddresses.add(tempEntry);

    // Create a new entry
    tempEntry = new NameAndAddress("V Putin",
        "The Kremlin",
        "Moscow",
        "MS1");

    // Add it to the ArrayList
    mNamesAndAddresses.add(tempEntry);
}
```

With the model layer taken care of and our controller already determining which layout should be used based upon the orientation of the device, we can now move on to creating the `Fragment` that will handle the list of names.

Create a new Java class in the usual manner and call it `AddressListFragment`. Amend the code so that it extends `ListFragment`. Make sure when you're given the choice, import `android.app.ListFragment`.

Here is what the code in `AdressListFragment` should look like:

```
import android.app.ListFragment;

public class AddressListFragment extends ListFragment {
}
```

Now, add the `ArrayList` member that will be managed by `ArrayAdapter`, which will be bound to `ListFragment`. Note that `ArrayList` will hold a copy of what is in our model layer but does not replace it.

In addition, add the overridden `onCreate` method. In `onCreate`, we also create and initialize an instance of `AddressListAdapter`, for which we will code the class in a moment.

All the contents of the class so far are shown in the following code where the new parts that we just discussed are highlighted:

```
public class AddressListFragment extends ListFragment {

  private ArrayList<NameAndAddress> mNamesAndAddresses;

  @Override
  public void onCreate(Bundle savedInstanceState) {
    super.onCreate(savedInstanceState);

    mNamesAndAddresses = AddressBook.getInstance().getBook();
    AddressListAdapter adapter = new AddressListAdapter
      (mNamesAndAddresses);
    setListAdapter(adapter);


  }
}
```

Now, we can add an inner class to `AddressListFragment` that extends `ArrayAdapter` and will bind `ListView` to our data. Most of the code should look like a simplified version of when we extended `BaseAdapter`. We use `getView`, inflate `list_item.xml`, and add a name to it from the appropriate `NameAndAddress` object.

However, you might be curious as to why we don't need to bother with `getCount`, `getItem`, or `getItemID`. This is because `ArrayAdapter` itself extends `BaseAdapter` and handles these things for us.

Add this inner class to `AddressListFragment`:

```java
private class AddressListAdapter extends ArrayAdapter<NameAndAddress>
{

  /*
     This simple constructor lets the ArrayAdapter
     super class
     know what data to use. Notice we didn't need to bind
     the data in onCreate.

     Neither do we need to override getCount,
     getItem or  getItemId
     It is all handled by ArrayAdapter because it is a more
     specialized version of Base Adapter
  */
  public AddressListAdapter(ArrayList<NameAndAddress>
    namesAndAddresses) {
    super(getActivity(), R.layout.list_item, namesAndAddresses);
  }


  @Override
  public View getView(int whichItem, View view,
    ViewGroup viewGroup) {

    if (view == null) {

      LayoutInflater inflater = (LayoutInflater)
        getActivity().getLayoutInflater();
      view = inflater.inflate(R.layout.list_item, null);
    }

      // We also have this super-handy getItem method
      NameAndAddress tempNameAndAddress = getItem(whichItem);
```

```
        TextView txtName = (TextView)
          view.findViewById(R.id.txtName);
        txtName.setText(tempNameAndAddress.getName());

      return view;
    }
  }
```

Now, we need to create a layout for our list item called `list_item.xml`. Create a new layout resource file called `list_item` in the `layout` folder in the usual way, drag a single **Plain TextView** widget onto the layout, and give the `id` property the value `txtName`.

While dealing with layouts, we need to modify our `activity_main` and `activity_main_land` layout files. The former so that it contains a single `Fragment` and the latter so that it contains two Fragments side by side. We will now set the IDs that we will use to place the Fragments.

In `activity_main.xml`, delete the **portrait TextView** widget and add `FrameLayout` from the `Containers` category of the palette. Set its `id` property to `listFragmentHolder`. Here is the code that you should now have in `activity_main.xml`. Check whether you have the same code as the following that we just discussed:

```xml
<RelativeLayout
xmlns:android="http://schemas.android.com/apk/res/android"
  xmlns:tools="http://schemas.android.com/tools"
    android:layout_width="match_parent"
  android:layout_height="match_parent"
    android:paddingLeft="@dimen/activity_horizontal_margin"
    android:paddingRight="@dimen/activity_horizontal_margin"
    android:paddingTop="@dimen/activity_vertical_margin"
    android:paddingBottom="@dimen/activity_vertical_margin"
    tools:context=".MainActivity"
    android:id="@+id/layout">

<FrameLayout
  android:layout_width="match_parent"
  android:layout_height="match_parent"
  android:layout_alignParentTop="true"
  android:layout_alignParentLeft="true"
  android:layout_alignParentStart="true"
  android:id="@+id/listFragmentHolder"></FrameLayout>
</RelativeLayout>
```

Switch to the `activity_main_land.xml` file and delete the **landscape TextView** widget.

Change the existing **LinearLayout** to set the `orientation` property to `horizontal`. Drag two FrameLayouts to the layout and set both their `width` properties to `unset` and both their `layout_weight` properties to `.5`. Set the `id` property of the left-hand side `FrameLayout` to `listFragmentHolder` and the `id` property of the right-hand side `FrameLayout` to `detailFragmentHolder`.

To be absolutely certain that you have the correct code for `activity_main_land.xml`, you can compare it to this listing. Just copy and paste the code if necessary:

```
<?xml version="1.0" encoding="utf-8"?>
<LinearLayout
xmlns:android="http://schemas.android.com/apk/res/android"
   android:orientation="horizontal" android:layout_width="match_parent"
   android:layout_height="match_parent">

<FrameLayout
   android:layout_width="wrap_content"
   android:layout_height="match_parent"
   android:id="@+id/listFragmentHolder"
   android:layout_weight=".5"></FrameLayout>

<FrameLayout
   android:layout_width="wrap_content"
   android:layout_height="match_parent"
   android:id="@+id/detailFragmentHolder"
   android:layout_weight=".5">


</FrameLayout>
</LinearLayout>
```

The `activity_main_land` layout should now look like as shown in the next screenshot in the designer. Remember that you can switch between the landscape and portrait view in the designer, but that whichever way you view the layout in the designer, it will still work properly in the app. The designer is unaware of what our Java code or aliases will do:

We are making good progress. At this point, we can run the app, and our slightly short and somewhat unlikely list of names from our address book will be displayed in both the portrait and landscape orientation.

The landscape view might not be exactly what we expect because the list side expands to fill the entire screen as the detail side is currently empty. But our two different layouts both use the same AddressListFragment class, which doesn't need a layout file itself because ListView is supplied with ListFragment.

Now, we need to handle what happens when a list item is clicked. We already know how to handle list-item clicks, but we have a few small problems:

- If a list item is clicked on in the landscape view, we need to show the appropriate details in the detail pane (on the right-hand side)

- If a list item is clicked on in the portrait view, we need a whole new Activity to show the detail (albeit still in an instance from the same Fragment)

Whichever of the preceding is the case, the detail view is a different class. So, we need to somehow communicate with that class. Before we look at the solution, which we have already discussed in the *Inter-Fragment communications – interfaces revisited* section earlier in this chapter, it is worth pointing out that we haven't created this class yet.

It is worth dealing with the communication issue first, however. We need an efficient way for AddressListFragment to communicate with MainActivity so that MainActivity can populate the detail pane (if in the landscape orientation) or start a new Activity to show a detail pane (if in the portrait orientation).

We will first code a solution to the communication issue. Then, we will create AddressDetailFragment that can be used in both our dual-Fragment landscape layout as well as a new Activity that we will call PortraitDetailActivity, which will be for the devices that are held in the portrait orientation.

Creating the communication interface

This code will be surprisingly straight forward and nearly identical to the one we discussed in the *Inter-Fragment communications – interfaces revisited* section earlier in this chapter. The only difference is that we will see exactly where and how to implement the interface, and the onListItemClicked method will be fully coded to see how it either starts a new Activity with the Fragment detail in it or repopulates/renews the existing Fragment detail when it is in the landscape orientation.

I will show you the code and then we will discuss where and how to use the code again to try and reinforce what we are doing:

```
public interface ActivityComs {

    void onListItemSelected(int pos);
}
```

We will create an interface (the one we just saw) with a single method. We will then make MainActivity implement this interface, and it will then be forced to override the onListItemSelected method.

The AddressListFragment class can then call the method when a list item is clicked on and pass the appropriate NameAndAddress reference as well as its position in ArrayList. We will see why both the pieces of data are used.

MainActivity can then handle either starting a new Activity (when in the portrait orientation) or just passing the data onto DetailFragment directly (when in the landscape orientation).

Right-click on the folder that contains all our .java files and navigate to **New | Class**. Type ActivityComs in the **Name** field and select **Interface** from the drop-down list named **Kind**. Then, click on **OK** and code the new interface exactly as shown in the previous block of code.

Next, we need to create an instance of this interface in the AddressListFragment class as a member. Add this member just after the class declaration, as highlighted in the next snippet:

```
public class AddressListFragment extends ListFragment {

    private ActivityComs mActivityComs;

    private ArrayList<NameAndAddress> mNamesAndAddresses;
```

Now, we need to initialize the member as a reference to MainActivity but cast to the type ActivityComs, and we do this in the overridden onAttach method. Then, we need to use it in the onListItemClick method, and finally, we need to delete the reference by setting it to null in the onDetach method. Add these three methods to the AddressListFragment class, as shown in the next code snippet:

```
@Override
public void onAttach(Activity activity) {
  super.onAttach(activity);

  /*
    activity is a ActivityComs but must
    still be explicitly cast to the type
  */
  mActivityComs = (ActivityComs)activity;
}

@Override
public void onDetach() {
  super.onDetach();
  mActivityComs = null;
}

public void onListItemClick(ListView l,
  View v, int position, long id) {
  // pass the position to MainActivity

  mActivityComs.onListItemSelected(position);
}
```

Now, change the class declaration in MainActivity.java to implement our new interface:

```
public class MainActivity extends ActionBarActivity implements
  ActivityComs{
```

Now, we need to implement the `onListItemClicked` method within the `MainActivity` class. We will do this in one go so that we don't need to keep coming back to this method. Study this code carefully as we will go through it in a minute. Add the `onListItemClicked` method to `MainActivity`:

```
public void onListItemSelected(int position) {

    // Is there a layout with an id that matches the detail container?
    if (findViewById(R.id.detailFragmentHolder) == null) {
        // If not we need to start a new activity

        Intent i = new Intent(this, PortraitDetailActivity.class);

        // We can't pass an object in an intent.
        // Neither do we want to.
        // So we pass its position in the array list
        i.putExtra("Position", position);
        startActivity (i);

    } else {
        // Fragment already exists

        FragmentManager fManager= getFragmentManager();
        FragmentTransaction fTransaction= fManager.beginTransaction();

        Fragment fragOld =
            fManager.findFragmentById(R.id.detailFragmentContainer);
        Fragment fragNew =
            AddressDetailFragment.newInstance(position);

        if (fragOld != null) {
            fTransaction.remove(fragOld);
        }

        fTransaction.add(R.id.detailFragmentContainer, fragNew);
        fTransaction.commit();
    }
}
```

We will now examine this code in three parts.

Explaining the structure of the onListItemSelected method

In the previous code, we first check whether there is an appropriate Fragment holder for the `Fragment` details. If there isn't, it implies that we are in the portrait orientation, and if there is, we are in the landscape. Here is the structure of the preceding `if-else` block with the functional code stripped out for now:

```
// Is there a layout with an id that matches the detail container?
if (findViewById(R.id.detailFragmentHolder) == null) {
  // If not we need to start a new activity

  ...

} else {
  // Fragment already exists

  ...
}
```

If `findViewById(R.id.detailFragmentHolder)` equates to `null`, then `detailFragmentHolder` cannot exist and the appropriate part of `if-else` is accessed.

Let's look at the code in each part now.

Explaining the code that starts a new Activity

Now, we can explain the following code that handles the situation when we need a new `Activity` to host the detail Fragment. We simply create a new `Intent`, load the position of `NameAndAddress` in `ArrayList`, and then start the `Activity`. Remember that all the data is held in our singleton, and we don't need to worry about passing the actual details, just the position:

```
Intent i = new Intent(this, PortraitDetailActivity.class);

// We can't pass an object in an intent
// So we pass its position in the array list
i.putExtra("Position", position);
startActivity (i);
```

We will see exactly what happens when `PortraitDetailActivity` is started when we implement it. Now, we will see how the existing Fragment is updated.

Explaining the code when the detail Fragment is already present

Now, you can learn about the code that handles the situation when the detail Fragment already exists. Here is the code in question again, piece by piece.

First, we get a reference to `FragmentManager` and then begin a transaction:

```
FragmentManager fManager= getFragmentManager();
FragmentTransaction fTransaction= fManager.beginTransaction();
```

Second, we get a reference to the existing `Fragment` and create a new one. Note that we pass in the position of `NameAndAddress` so that it is displayed in the constructor:

```
Fragment fragOld =
    fManager.findFragmentById(R.id.detailFragmentContainer);
Fragment fragNew = AddressDetailFragment.newInstance(position);
```

Now, we check whether the old Fragment actually exists, and if it does, we remove/destroy it:

```
if (fragOld != null) {
  fTransaction.remove(fragOld);
}
```

Finally, we add the new Fragment in the usual manner:

```
fTransaction.add(R.id.detailFragmentContainer, fragNew);
fTransaction.commit();
```

We are close to running this project now.

What do we need to do?

Now, to make the previous code work, we need to do the following:

1. Create a new class called `AddressDetailFragment` that takes `int` in its constructor.

2. Create a suitable layout for `AddressDetailFragment`.

3. Create a new `Activity` class called `PortraitDetailActivity` to host `AddressDetailFragment` when the device is in the portrait orientation.

4. Create a simple layout for `PortraitDetailActivity` that has a single `FrameLayout` in it with an `id` property of `detailFragmentHolder`.

The next three sections will deal with these points.

Creating the AddressDetailFragment class and layout

Create a new class and call it `AddressDetailFragment`. Amend the class declaration and add two new members that can hold the entire collection of `NameAndAdress` objects as well as a single object for whatever the current one is. Add code so that the new class looks like this:

```
public class AddressDetailFragment extends Fragment {

    private ArrayList<NameAndAddress> mNamesAndAddresses;

    private NameAndAddress mCurrentNameAndAddress;

}
```

Now, add the `onCreate` method that gets an `AddressBook` instance from our singleton. Then, we chain `getArguments` and `getInt` to get the position of the `NameAndAdress` object that we want.

Now, override `onCreate` with this code:

```
@Override
public void onCreate(Bundle savedInstanceState) {
    super.onCreate(savedInstanceState);

    mNamesAndAddresses = AddressBook.getInstance().getBook();

    // Get the position from the Bundle
    // using the constant string
    int position = (int)getArguments().getInt("Position");

    // Initialize with the current name and address
    mCurrentNameAndAddress = mNamesAndAddresses.get(position);


}
```

Before we move on, you may probably be wondering where `getArguments()`. `getInt` magically acquired the position of the `NameAndAddress` object that we need? The answer is that it is placed there in the `newInstance` method. Here is how we add values into the `Bundle`.

Now, add the `newInstance` method, as shown in the following code snippet:

```
public static AddressDetailFragment newInstance(int position) {
    Bundle args = new Bundle();
    args.putInt("Position", position);

    AddressDetailFragment frag = new AddressDetailFragment();
    frag.setArguments(args);

    return frag;
}
```

Next, we override the `onCreateView` method to inflate and initialize our simple UI that consists of four `TextView` widgets that have their text properties initialized with the appropriate values from the current `NameAndAddress` object:

```
@Override
public View onCreateView(LayoutInflater inflater, ViewGroup
    container, Bundle savedInstanceState) {

    View view = inflater.inflate(R.layout.detail_fragment,
        container, false);

    TextView txtName = (TextView)
        view.findViewById(R.id.txtName);
    TextView txtAddress1 = (TextView)
        view.findViewById(R.id.txtAddress1);
    TextView txtAddress2 = (TextView)
        view.findViewById(R.id.txtAddress2);
    TextView txtZip = (TextView) view.findViewById(R.id.txtZip);

    txtName.setText(mCurrentNameAndAddress.getName());
    txtAddress1.setText(mCurrentNameAndAddress.getAddress1());
    txtAddress2.setText(mCurrentNameAndAddress.getAddress2());
    txtZip.setText(mCurrentNameAndAddress.getZipCode());

    return view;
}
```

Now, we need to actually make that layout for `AddressDetailFragment`. Create a new layout called `detail_fragment` in the usual way.

Drag four **TextView** widgets with the following `id` properties: from top to bottom, the `id` properties are, `txtName`, `txtAddress1`, `txtAddress2`, and `txtZip`.

The finished result will look like as shown in this screenshot:

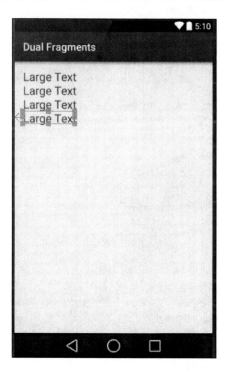

To make the preceding layout absolutely clear, here is the XML layout code. If you are uncertain in any way, copy and paste this code into the detail_fragment layout file:

```
<RelativeLayout xmlns:android="http://schemas.android.com/apk/res/
android"
  xmlns:tools="http://schemas.android.com/tools"
    android:layout_width="fill_parent"
  android:layout_height="fill_parent"
    android:paddingLeft="@dimen/activity_horizontal_margin"
  android:paddingRight="@dimen/activity_horizontal_margin"
  android:paddingTop="@dimen/activity_vertical_margin"
  android:paddingBottom="@dimen/activity_vertical_margin"
    tools:context=".MainActivity"
  android:id="@+id/layout">


<TextView
  android:layout_width="match_parent"
  android:layout_height="wrap_content"
  android:textAppearance="?android:attr/textAppearanceLarge"
```

```
            android:text="Large Text"
            android:id="@+id/txtName"
            android:layout_alignParentTop="true"
            android:layout_alignParentLeft="true"
            android:layout_alignParentStart="true" />

        <TextView
            android:layout_width="wrap_content"
            android:layout_height="wrap_content"
            android:textAppearance="?android:attr/textAppearanceLarge"
            android:text="Large Text"
            android:id="@+id/txtAddress1"
            android:layout_below="@+id/txtName"
            android:layout_alignParentLeft="true"
            android:layout_alignParentStart="true" />

        <TextView
            android:layout_width="wrap_content"
            android:layout_height="wrap_content"
            android:textAppearance="?android:attr/textAppearanceLarge"
            android:text="Large Text"
            android:id="@+id/txtAddress2"
            android:layout_below="@+id/txtAddress1"
            android:layout_alignParentLeft="true"
            android:layout_alignParentStart="true" />

        <TextView
            android:layout_width="wrap_content"
            android:layout_height="wrap_content"
            android:textAppearance="?android:attr/textAppearanceLarge"
            android:text="Large Text"
            android:id="@+id/txtZip"
            android:layout_below="@+id/txtAddress2"
            android:layout_alignParentLeft="true"
            android:layout_alignParentStart="true" />
    </RelativeLayout>
```

All we need to do now is add a hosting `Activity` for when the detail Fragment is viewed in the portrait orientation.

Coding PortraitDetailActivity and the layout

First, we need a very simple layout. To get a simple layout, follow the given steps:

1. Create a layout called `activity_portrait_layout`.

2. Add a single `FrameLayout`.

3. Set its `id` property to `detailFragmentHolder`.

Now, we can create a new `Activity` called `PortraitDetailActivity`. Do so by right-clicking on the folder that contains all the Java files. Navigate to **New | Activity | Blank Activity**. This is almost the same as creating a new class and then adding the `extends...` code to turn it into an `Activity`. The difference of doing things this way is that Android Studio will also add the new `Activity` to the `AndroidManifest.xml` file for us, which saves us a few minute's work.

In the `PortraitDetailActivity` `onCreate` method, which is the only method in this class that we need to concern ourselves with, we do the following:

1. First, we get a reference to `FragmentManager` and begin a transaction.

2. Second, we get a reference to the existing `Fragment` and create a new reference. Now, we check whether the old Fragment actually exists, and if it does, we remove/destroy it.

3. Then, we extract the single `int` variable that was passed in by `MainActivity`. Finally, we add the new `Fragment` in the usual manner, passing in the position of the `NameAndAdress` object that is to be shown.

4. Add the overridden `onCreate` method shown next that we just discussed:

```
@Override
protected void onCreate(Bundle savedInstanceState) {
  super.onCreate(savedInstanceState);
  setContentView(R.layout.activity_portrait_detail);

  // Get a fragment manager
  FragmentManager fManager = getFragmentManager();

  // Create a new fragment using the manager
  // Passing in the id of the layout to hold it
  Fragment frag =
    fManager.findFragmentById(R.id.detailFragmentHolder);

  // Pass the Bundle onto the fragment
  int position = 0;
  Bundle extras = getIntent().getExtras();
  if (extras != null) {
```

```
          position = extras.getInt("Position");
      }



      // Check the fragment has not already been initialized
      if(frag == null){

        frag   = AddressDetailFragment.newInstance(position);



        fManager.beginTransaction()
        .add(R.id.detailFragmentHolder, frag)
        .commit();
      }
  }
```

We can now run our app in the portrait orientation and see the list:

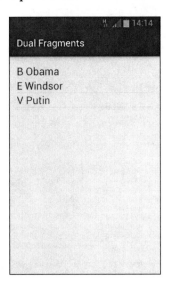

Tap on an item to see the details open up in a new Activity:

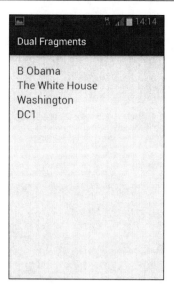

Tap the back button, rotate the device to landscape, and tap on **V Putin** to see our two Fragments displayed side by side:

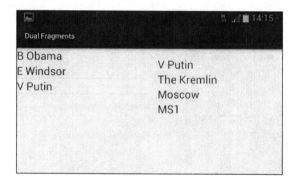

Let's think about when we should use Fragments and when we shouldn't by looking at some frequently asked questions.

FAQ

1. When should I use Fragments?

   Hopefully, you have learned enough in this chapter to realize that using Fragments further enhances reusability and encapsulation of our code, and whenever we implement anything more than just a single, simple UI, it is well worth the overhead to use Fragments.

2.   Any other times I should use Fragments?

Further consider that even the most simple of apps can evolve. If your simple single-screen app for phones only, suddenly needs to be ported for tablets, you will need to refactor everything to use Fragments. This is always harder than using Fragments from the start.

3.   So are you saying that I should always use Fragments?

Probably, yes! Unless you have an extremely compelling case not too. However, in this book, to learn new ideas, such as capturing an image on an Android device or displaying the users' location in Google maps, we will do so without Fragments getting in the way of the new code.

Summary

Potentially, this was one of the most complicated apps we have built. If it is at all unclear exactly what happened, the way to overcome this is to break it into pieces (or fragments).

Each Fragment has a class and a layout. The Fragment with the list communicates with the `Activity` via the interface, and the Activity either loads a new (detail) Fragment into itself (when in landscape) or starts a new `Activity` that loads the same (detail) `Fragment` when in the portrait orientation. All the data is tucked away in our singleton and can be basically forgotten about because it can only ever be instantiated once, and it is guaranteed that any class changing or reading the data will do so from the same instance.

Certainly, there may be some aspects of the code or principles from this chapter that may be still unclear to you but with repeated use, you can make them like second nature.

In the next chapter, we are not going to increase the complexity any further. So if all these Fragments and interfaces are not totally clear, it doesn't matter. We will revisit these concepts one at a time over the course of the rest of the book at the same time as we investigate more about the Android API.

If you have ever wanted to make one of those cool swiping UIs like the Angry Birds level-selection menu where you can swipe from screen to screen, then the next chapter is for you. And as you might expect, we will get a bit more familiar with Fragments while we are at it.

20
Paging and Swiping

Paging is the act of moving from page to page, and on Android, we do this by swiping a finger across the screen. The current page transitions in a direction and speed to match the finger movement. It is a useful and practical way to navigate around an app, but perhaps even more than this, it is an extremely satisfying visual effect for the user. Also, as with `ListView`, we can selectively load just the data required for the current page, and perhaps the data for the previous and next pages.

In the next screenshot, you can see the calendar app on the Nexus 5 emulator paging between months. Be sure to launch an emulator and give it a try if you are unsure how paging and swiping works:

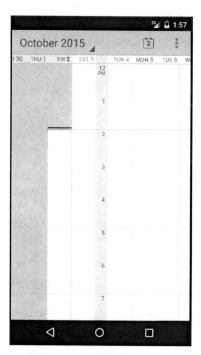

In the next figure, we can see the famous Angry Birds level-selection menu showing swiping/paging in action:

The Android API, as you would have come to expect by now, has some solutions through which you can achieve paging in a quite simple manner.

In this chapter, you will learn to:

- Achieve paging and swiping with images like you might do in a photo gallery app.
- Implement paging and swiping with Fragments, which will give our app the potential to offer our users the ability to swipe their way through a selection of user interfaces. This will give our apps enormous potential.

We will not be adding paging/swiping to the Where it's snap app, but let's build two paging mini apps: one with images and one with Fragments.

Building an image gallery/slider app

The first thing we should do is add the six images that we will have in our gallery to the drawable folder. But we want to do things a bit differently here. You can find these images in the Chapter 20/Image Slider/drawable-xhdpi folder of the download bundle. The following is a representation of these images:

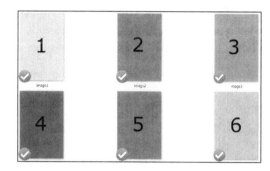

Create a new folder called drawable-xhdpi in the res folder by right-clicking on the **res** folder and navigating to **New | Android resource directory**. Name the directory drawable-xhdpi and click on **OK**.

Add the images to the folder that you just created or, of course, you could add more interesting images, perhaps some photos you have taken.

The reason we do things this way is because of the way a few modern Android devices handle images. We already know that in an ideal situation, we should provide images for the whole range of different screen densities and place them in their appropriate folders. To do so for this demonstration would be overkill; in fact, depending upon the exact project, it is sometimes overkill in a real app as well.

It is because the manufacturers of some modern phones want their devices to look great, they make them automatically scale-up in size any images it thinks might not already be high quality. The effect of this is that any images we place in the regular drawable folder are likely to be supersized by these devices with high-density screens.

This often has the effect of causing the devices to run out of memory and crash. By placing the images in the drawable-xhdpi folder, we avoid this problem because the device assumes that the image doesn't need to be scaled up. Also, devices with lower density screens will happily use the images from the drawable-xhdpi folder as well.

Implementing the layout

For a simple image-paging app, we use the `PagerAdapter` class. We can think of this to be like `BaseApater`, as it will handle the display of an array of images in a `ViewPager` widget. This is much like how `BaseAdapter` handles the display of the contents of `ArrayList` in `ListView`. All we need to do is override the appropriate methods.

To implement an image gallery with `PagerAdapter`, we first need `ViewPager` in our main layout. So you can see precisely what is required here is the actual XML code for `layout_main.xml`. Edit `layout_main.xml` so that it looks exactly like this:

```
<RelativeLayout
  xmlns:android=
  "http://schemas.android.com/apk/res/android"
  android:layout_width="fill_parent"
  android:layout_height="fill_parent" >

  <android.support.v4.view.ViewPager
  android:id="@+id/pager"
  android:layout_width="wrap_content"
  android:layout_height="wrap_content" />

</RelativeLayout>
```

The slightly unusually named class `android.support.v4. view.ViewPager` is the class that makes this functionality available in Android versions that were released before `ViewPager`.

The same manner in which we needed a layout to represent a list item, we need a layout to represent an item; in this case, an image in our pager. Create a new layout file in the usual way and call it `pager_item.xml`. It will have a single **ImageView** widget with an ID of `ImageView`.

Use the visual designer to achieve this or copy the following XML into `pager_item.xml`:

```
<RelativeLayout
  xmlns:android=
  "http://schemas.android.com/apk/res/android"
  android:layout_width="fill_parent"
  android:layout_height="fill_parent"
  android:gravity="center"
  android:padding="10dp" >

  <ImageView
```

```
        android:id="@+id/imageView"
        android:layout_width="match_parent"
        android:layout_height="match_parent"/>

    </RelativeLayout>
```

Now, we can make a start with our `PagerAdapter` class.

Coding the PagerAdapter class

Next, we need to extend `PagerAdapter` so that it handles images. Create a new class called `ImagePagerAdapter` and make it extend `PagerAdapter`.

Add the following imports to the top of the `ImagePagerAdapter` class. We normally rely on using the shortcut *Alt + Enter* to add imports. We are doing things slightly differently this time because there are a few very similarly named classes that will not suit our objectives.

Add the following imports to the `ImagePagerAdapter` class:

```
import android.content.Context;
import android.support.v4.view.PagerAdapter;
import android.support.v4.view.ViewPager;
import android.view.LayoutInflater;
import android.view.View;
import android.view.ViewGroup;
import android.widget.ImageView;
import android.widget.RelativeLayout;
```

Here is the class declaration with the `extends...` code added as well as a couple of member variables. These variables are the `Context` object that we will put to use shortly and an `int` array called `images`. The reason for having an `int` array for images is because we will store `int` identifiers for images. We see how this works in a few code blocks time. The last member variable is `LayoutInflater`, which as you can probably guess will be used to inflate each of the instances of `pager_item.xml`.

Extend `PagerAdapter` and add the member variables we just discussed:

```
public class ImagePagerAdapter extends PagerAdapter {

    Context context;

    int[] images;
    LayoutInflater inflater;

}
```

Now, we need a constructor that sets up `ImagePagerAdapter` by receiving `Context` from `MainActivity` as well as the `int` array for the images and to initialize the member variables with them.

Add the highlighted constructor method to the `ImagePagerAdapter` class:

```
public class ImagePagerAdapter extends PagerAdapter {

  Context context;

  int[] images;
  LayoutInflater inflater;

  public ImagePagerAdapter(Context context,  int[] images) {
    this.context = context;
    this.images = images;
  }


}
```

Now, we must override the required methods of `PagerAdapter`. Immediately after the previous code, add the overridden `getCount` method, which simply returns the number of image IDs in the array. This method is used internally by the class:

```
@Override
public int getCount() {

  return images.length;
}
```

Now, we must override the `isViewFromObject` method that just returns `boolean` that is dependent upon whether the current `View` is the same or associated with the current `Object` that is passed in as a parameter. Again, this is a method that is used internally by the class. Immediately after the previous code, add this overridden method:

```
@Override
public boolean isViewFromObject(View view, Object object) {
  return view == object;
}
```

Now, we must override the `instantiateItem` method, and this is where we get most of the work that concerns us done. First, we declare a new `ImageView` object and then we initialize our `LayoutInflater` member. Next, we use `LayoutInflater` to declare and initialize a new `View` from our `pager_item.xml` layout file.

After this, we get a reference to ImageView inside the pager_item.xml layout. We can now add the appropriate image as the content of ImageView is based on the position parameter of the instantiateItem method and the appropriate ID from the images array.

Finally, we add the layout to PagerAdapter with addView and return from the method.

Now, we will add the method we just discussed here:

```
@Override
public Object instantiateItem(ViewGroup container, int position) {


    ImageView image;

    inflater = (LayoutInflater)
      context.getSystemService(Context.LAYOUT_INFLATER_SERVICE);
    View itemView = inflater.inflate(R.layout.pager_item,
      container,false);

    // get reference to imageView in pager_item layout
    image = (ImageView) itemView.findViewById(R.id.imageView);

    // Set an image to the ImageView
    image.setImageResource(images[position]);

    // Add pager_item layout as the current page to the ViewPager
    ((ViewPager) container).addView(itemView);

    return itemView;
}
```

The last method we must override is destroyItem, which the class can call when it needs to remove an appropriate item based on the value of the position parameter.

Add the destroyItem method after the previous code and before the closing curly brace of the ImagePagerAdapter class:

```
@Override
public void destroyItem(ViewGroup container, int position,
  Object object) {
  // Remove pager_item layout from ViewPager
  ((ViewPager) container).removeView((RelativeLayout) object);

}
```

As we saw when coding `ImagePagerAdapter`, there is very little to it. Just a case of properly implementing the `instantiateItem` method and putting straightforward overridden methods that the `PagerAdapter` class uses to help make things work smoothly behind the scenes.

Coding the MainActivity class

Finally, we can code our `MainActivity` class. As with the `ImagePagerAdapter` class, for clarity, add the following import statements manually to the `MainActivity.java` class before the class declaration, as shown in the next code snippet:

```
import android.support.v4.view.PagerAdapter;
import android.support.v4.view.ViewPager;
import android.support.v7.app.AppCompatActivity;
import android.os.Bundle;
import android.view.Menu;
import android.view.MenuItem;
```

Now, we need a few member variables. Unsurprisingly, we need `ViewPager`, which will be used to get a reference to `ViewPager` in our layout, as well as a `ImagePagerAdapter` reference for the class that we have just coded. We also need an `int` array to hold an array of image IDs:

```
public class MainActivity extends AppCompatActivity {

    ViewPager viewPager;
    PagerAdapter adapter;

    int[] images;

    @Override
    public void onCreate(Bundle savedInstanceState) {
        super.onCreate(savedInstanceState);
    ...
```

All the rest of the code goes in `onCreate`. We initialize our `int` array with each of the images that we added to the `drawable-xhdpi` folder.

We initialize `ViewPager` in the usual way with the `findViewByID` method. We also initialize `ImagePagerAdapter` by passing in a reference to `MainActivity` and the `images` array, as required by the constructor that we coded previously. Finally, we bind the adapter to the pager with `setAdapter`.

Add the highlighted code in the `onCreate` method:

```
@Override
public void onCreate(Bundle savedInstanceState) {
  super.onCreate(savedInstanceState);

  setContentView(R.layout.activity_main);

  // reference the images and put them in our array
  images = new int[] { R.drawable.image1,
    R.drawable.image2,
    R.drawable.image3,
    R.drawable.image4,
    R.drawable.image5,
    R.drawable.image6 };

  // get a reference to the ViewPager in the layout
  viewPager = (ViewPager) findViewById(R.id.pager);

  // Initialize our PagerAdapter
  adapter = new ImagePagerAdapter(MainActivity.this, images);

  // Bind the PagerAdapter to the ViewPager
  viewPager.setAdapter(adapter);

}
```

Now, we are ready to run the app.

Running the gallery app

Run the app in the usual way on either the emulator or a real device. Using a real device instead of the emulator will be more satisfying because you will be able to use a real swiping motion with your finger instead of a simulated swipe(drag) with the mouse. In this screenshot, we can see the first image from our `int` array:

Swipe a little to the right-hand side and left-hand side to see the smooth pleasing manner in which the images transition:

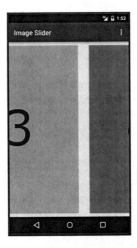

Now, we will build an app with almost identical functionality except that each page in the pager will be a `Fragment`, which could have any or all of the functionality that a regular `Fragment` can have because they are regular `Fragment`s.

Building a Fragment pager/slider app

We can put complete Fragments as pages in `PagerAdapter`. This is quite powerful because as we know, a Fragment can have a lot of functionality, even a full-fledged UI.

To keep the code short and straightforward, we will add a single `TextView` to each `Fragment` layout, just to demonstrate that the pager is working. When we see how easy it is to get a reference to `TextView`, however, it should be clear as to how we could easily add any layout that we have learned about so far and then let the user interact with it.

The first thing we will do is build the content for the slider. In this case, of course, the content is `Fragment`. We will build one simple class called `SimpleFragment` and one really simple layout called `fragment_layout`.

This implies that each slide will be identical in appearance, but we will use the `Fragment` ID passed in by `FragmentManager` at the instantiation as the text for the one and only `TextView`. This way, when we flip/swipe through Fragments, it will be clear that each `Fragment` is a new distinct instance.

When we see the code that loads Fragments from a list, it will be simple to design completely different Fragment classes, as we have done before, and use these different classes for some or all the slides. Each of these classes could, of course, also use a different layout as well.

Coding the SimpleFragment class

As with the Image Slider app, it is not straightforward exactly which classes need to be autoimported by Android Studio. We use the classes that we do because they are all compatible with each other and it is possible that if you let Android Studio suggest which classes to import, Android Studio will get it 'wrong'. The project files are in the Chapter 20/Fragment Pager folder.

Create a new project called Fragment Slider and leave all the settings at the default values.

Now, create a new class called SimpleFragment, make it extend Fragment, and add the import statements and one member variable, as shown in the following snippet:

```
import android.os.Bundle;
import android.support.v4.app.Fragment;
import android.view.LayoutInflater;
import android.view.View;
import android.view.ViewGroup;
import android.widget.TextView;

public class SimpleFragment extends Fragment {

    // Holds the fragment id passed in when created
    public static final String MESSAGE = "";

}
```

We have to add two methods. The first of which is newInstance, which we will call from MainActivity to set up and return a reference to Fragment. The next code does what we have seen before. It creates a new instance of the class, but it also puts a String into the Bundle object that will eventually be read from the onCreate method. The String that is added to Bundle is that which is passed in the one-and-only parameter of this newInstance method.

Add the newInstance method to the SimpleFragment class:

```
// Our newInstance method which we call to make a new Fragment
public static SimpleFragment newInstance(String message)
{
```

```
    // Create the fragment
    SimpleFragment fragment = new SimpleFragment();

    // Create a bundle for our message/id
    Bundle bundle = new Bundle(1);
    // Load up the Bundle
    bundle.putString(MESSAGE, message);
    // Call setArguments ready for when onCreate is called
    fragment.setArguments(bundle);
    return fragment;
}
```

In the final method for our `SimpleFragment` class, we need to override `onCreateView`, where, as usual, we will get a reference to the layout that was passed in, and load up `fragment_layout` as the layout.

Then, the first line of code unpacks the String from `Bundle` using `getArguments`. `getString` and the `MESSAGE` identifier of the key-value pair.

Add the `onCreateView` method that we just discussed:

```
@Override
public View onCreateView(LayoutInflater inflater, ViewGroup container,
    Bundle savedInstanceState) {

    // Get the id from the Bundle
    String message = getArguments().getString(MESSAGE);

    // Inflate the view as normal
    View view = inflater.inflate(R.layout.fragment_layout,
        container, false);

    // Get a reference to textView
    TextView messageTextView = (TextView)view.findViewById(R.id.textView);

    // Display the id in the TextView
    messageTextView.setText(message);

    // We could also handle any UI
    // of any complexity in the usual way
    // ..
    // ..

    return view;
}
```

Let's also make a super simple layout for `Fragment`, which will, of course, contain `TextView` that we have just been using.

fragment_layout

`fragment_layout` is the simplest layout we have ever made. Right-click on the **layout** folder and navigate to **New | Resource layout file**. Name the file `fragment_layout` and click on **OK**. Now, add a single `TextView` and set its `id` property to `textView`.

We can now code the `MainActivity` class that handles `FragmentPager` and brings our `SimpleFragment` instances to life.

Coding the MainActivity class

This class consists of two main parts. First, the changes we will make to the overridden `onCreate` method, and second, the implementation of our inner class and its overridden methods of `FragmentPagerAdapter`.

To code this class, we first add the following imports and a single member variable that will be the instance of our implementation of `FragmentPagerAdapter` and `SimpleFragmentPagerAdapter`:

```
import android.support.v4.app.Fragment;
import android.support.v4.app.FragmentManager;
import android.support.v4.app.FragmentPagerAdapter;
import android.support.v4.view.ViewPager;
import android.support.v7.app.AppCompatActivity;
import android.os.Bundle;
import android.view.Menu;
import android.view.MenuItem;
import java.util.ArrayList;
import java.util.List;

public class MainActivity extends AppCompatActivity {

    SimpleFragmentPagerAdapter pageAdapter;

    @Override
    public void onCreate(Bundle savedInstanceState) {
        super.onCreate(savedInstanceState);
        setContentView(R.layout.activity_main);

    }
```

Next, in the onCreate method, we create a List for Fragments and then create and add three instances of SimpleFragment, passing in a numerical identifier that is to be packed away in Bundle.

Then, we initialize SimpleFragmentPagerAdapter (that we will code soon), passing in our list of Fragments.

We get a reference to ViewPager with findViewByID and bind our adapter to it with setAdapter.

Now, add the highlighted code to the onCreate method of MainActivity:

```
@Override
public void onCreate(Bundle savedInstanceState) {
  super.onCreate(savedInstanceState);
  setContentView(R.layout.activity_main);

  // Initialize a list of three fragments
  List<Fragment> fragmentList = new ArrayList<Fragment>();

  // Add three new Fragments to the list
  fragmentList.add(SimpleFragment.newInstance("1"));
  fragmentList.add(SimpleFragment.newInstance("2"));
  fragmentList.add(SimpleFragment.newInstance("3"));

  pageAdapter = new SimpleFragmentPagerAdapter
    (getSupportFragmentManager(), fragmentList);

  ViewPager pager = (ViewPager)findViewById(R.id.pager);
  pager.setAdapter(pageAdapter);

}
```

Now, we will add our inner class, SimpleFragmentPagerAdapter. All we do is add List for Fragments as a member variable and a constructor that initializes it with the passed-in List.

Then, we override the getItem and getCount methods, which are used internally in the same way as we used them in the last project, except this time, we use the methods of List instead of the size of the array.

Add the following inner class that we just discussed to the MainActivity class:

```
private class SimpleFragmentPagerAdapter extends
  FragmentPagerAdapter {
  // A List to hold our fragments
  private List<Fragment> fragments;
```

```
// A constructor to receive a fragment manager and a List
public SimpleFragmentPagerAdapter(FragmentManager fm,
    List<Fragment> fragments) {
    // Call the super class' version
    // of this constructor
    super(fm);
    this.fragments = fragments;
}

// Just two methods to override
// to get the current position of
// the adapter and the size of the List

@Override
public Fragment getItem(int position) {
    return this.fragments.get(position);
}

@Override
public int getCount() {
    return this.fragments.size();
}
}
```

The last thing we need to do is add the layout for `MainActivity`.

The activity_main layout

Implement the `activity_main` layout by copying the following code. It contains a single widget, `ViewPager`, and it is important that it is from the `android.support.v4.view` hierarchy so that it is compatible with the other classes that we use in this project.

Amend the code in the `layout_main.xml` file that we just discussed:

```
<RelativeLayout xmlns:android="http://schemas.android.com/apk/res/
    android"
    xmlns:tools="http://schemas.android.com/tools" android:layout_
      width="match_parent"
    android:layout_height="match_parent" android:paddingLeft="@dimen/
      activity_horizontal_margin"
    android:paddingRight="@dimen/activity_horizontal_margin"
    android:paddingTop="@dimen/activity_vertical_margin"
    android:paddingBottom="@dimen/activity_vertical_margin"
      tools:context=".MainActivity">

    <android.support.v4.view.ViewPager
```

```
        android:id="@+id/pager"
        android:layout_width="wrap_content"
        android:layout_height="wrap_content" />

    </RelativeLayout>
```

Let's see our **Fragment** slider in action now.

Running the Fragment slider app

Run the app and you can swipe your way, to the left or the right, through the Fragments in the slider. The next image shows the visual effect produced by FragmentPagerAdapter when the user tries to swipe beyond the final Fragment in List:

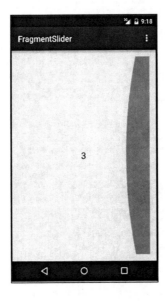

Summary

In this chapter, we saw that we can use pagers for simple image galleries or to swipe through complex pages of an entire UI; however, we demonstrated this with a very simple TextView.

In the next chapter, we will look at another really cool UI element that is used in many of the latest Android apps, probably because it looks great and is a real pleasure, as well as extremely practical to use. Let's take a look at NavigationDrawer.

21

Navigation Drawer and Where It's Snap

In this chapter, we will start the Where it's snap project, and we will talk more about the features that it will have later. The project will be discussed right up until *Chapter 27, Going Local – Hola!* where it is completed, but we won't only be working on this app.

Where it's snap will feature a navigation drawer as a means of allowing the users to access the features and screens of the app, and this will be the main focus of this chapter.

In this chapter, we will:

- Introduce the navigation drawer
- Look at the features of the Where it's snap project
- Get started on the Where it's snap project, including implementing its navigation drawer

Let's take a look at this extremely cool UI pattern.

Introducing the navigation drawer

What's so great about navigation drawer. Well, the first thing that might catch your eye is that it can be made to look extremely stylish. Take a look at this next figure , which shows off a navigation drawer in action in the Google Play app:

To be honest, right from the start, our navigation drawer is not going to be as fancy as the one in the Google Play app. However, the same functionality will be present in our app.

What else is neat about the navigation drawer is the way that it slides to hide/reveal itself when required. It is because of this behavior that it can be of a significant size, making it extremely flexible with regard to the options that can be put on it. When the user is finished with it, it completely disappears like a drawer.

I suggest that you open up the Google Play app now and see how it works, if you haven't already.

You can slide your thumb/finger from the left-hand side edge of the screen and the drawer will slowly slide out. You can, of course, slide it away again in the opposite direction.

While the navigation drawer is open, the rest of the screen is slightly dimmed, as seen the previous figure, helping the users to focus on the navigation options offered.

You can also tap anywhere off of the navigation drawer while it is open, and it will slide itself away, leaving the entire screen clear for the rest of the app.

The drawer is also opened by tapping on the menu icon in the top-left corner, as highlighted in the next screenshot:

We can also tweak and refine the behavior of the navigation drawer, as we will see toward the end of the chapter, by overriding a few more lifecycle methods that are called at just the right time.

Here, we will see the `onPostCreate` and `onConfigurationChanged` methods. Let's see what we will do with our Where it's snap app, and then, we can get on with implementing a navigation drawer.

The Where it's snap app

Where it's snap will be our most-advanced app! It will have the following features:

- It will show a list of photos by their titles.
- It will offer the alternative of a list of tags, which when clicked takes you to a list of titles with that matching tag.
- It will allow the user to take photos with the device camera and assign a title as well as related tags.
- All of the data required (titles and tags) will be stored in a database. You will learn about databases in *Chapter 23, Using SQLite Databases in Our Apps*, and we will add a database functionality to Where it's snap in *Chapter 24, Adding a Database to Where It's Snap*.

- When the user taps on a photo's title in a list, he/she will see that photo and also be offered the option of showing a Google map of the location the photo was taken at.

- We will also see how to make this app multilingual (Spanish and English). Hola!

As with the Note To Self app, we will do things as correctly as possible and use string resources and Android naming conventions in our code.

We will build this app over the course of the next six chapters. As we explore and practice new features of the Android API, we will then utilize them by improving or adding features to Where it's snap.

The first thing we will do is prepare the project's resources and implement a navigation drawer. This will be the fundamental part of the UI for this project.

The project files that represent a runnable version of this app, as it is at the end of this chapter, can be found in the download bundle in the `Chapter 21/Where its snap 1` folder.

Create a new project called `Where Its Snap` and accept all the default settings as usual.

To handle Marshmallow runtime permissions, as discussed in *Chapter 11, Widget Mania* in the *Android permissions and marshmallows*, we need to set the target API to 22.

To do this, select **Android** from the drop-down list at the top of the project explorer. Now, double-click on the **build.gradle (module: app)** option that is near the bottom of the project explorer window.

Change the highlighted line of code to make sure that `targetSdkVersion` is set to 22, as shown in the following code snippet:

```
defaultConfig {
  applicationId "com.gamecodeschool.whereitssnap"
  minSdkVersion 15
  targetSdkVersion 22
  versionCode 1
  versionName "1.0"
}
```

Now, we can add the resources that we will need in the next six chapters.

Preparing the resources

In this section, we will prepare the String resources. For this, open up the `strings.xml` file from the `res` folder. We will not need to come back to this file for the entire project. Some of the resources might look a little odd and indeed may not be used right away, but if you look back at the features of the project, it will be quite easy to guess where these String resources will eventually be used. We will, however, create another `strings.xml` file in *Chapter 27, Going Local – Hola!* when we make our app multilingual.

As well as some regular String resources, there is a `string-array` element with the `name` property set to `nav_drawer_items`. We will shortly see how in our Java code we can use this just like a regular Java array, like the ones we discussed in *Chapter 13, Handling and Displaying Arrays of Data*.

Modify the contents of the `strings.xml` file so that they are the same as the next code:

```xml
<resources>
  <string name="app_name">Where It's Snap</string>

  <string name="action_settings">Settings</string>
  <string name="drawer_open">Open navigation drawer</string>
  <string name="drawer_close">Close navigation drawer</string>

  <string name="enter_photo_title">Enter photo title</string>

  <string name="tag1">Tag 1</string>
  <string name="tag2">Tag 2</string>
  <string name="tag3">Tag 3</string>

  <string name="capture">Capture</string>
  <string name="save">Save</string>

  <string name="tags">Tags</string>
  <string name="titles">Titles</string>
  <string name="show_map">Show Map</string>

  <!-- These are the items in our Navigation drawer -->
  <string-array name="nav_drawer_items">
    <item >Titles</item>
    <item >Tags</item>
    <item >Capture</item>
  </string-array>

</resources>
```

We are now nearly ready to implement our navigation drawer. Before we do, let's add some empty placeholder Fragments that we can use for each of the options of the drawer.

Placeholder code for three Fragments

As we know from our plan, there are four Fragments: image capture, title list, tag list, and showing a picture.

The first three are directly accessible from the main navigation drawer UI. For these three Fragments, we will quickly create placeholder classes and layouts so that we can get MainActivity wired up. Then, over the coming chapters, we will add the real functionality and layouts.

Two of these three Fragments (titles view and tags view) will be a list of clickable options, and so, using ListFragment seems like a good choice. The third (the image capture view) will be much more like a regular layout; so, Fragment is the best choice.

Let's go ahead and quickly create these classes.

Create a new class and call it TitlesFragment. Amend the code so that it looks exactly like the next code, where we extend ListFragment and implement a basic onCreate method ready in the project for later use:

```
public class TitlesFragment extends ListFragment {

    @Override
    public void onCreate(Bundle savedInstanceState) {
        super.onCreate(savedInstanceState);

    }

}
```

Now, for the tags list view, create a new class and call it TagsFragment. Amend the code so that it looks exactly like the next code, where we extend ListFragment and implement a basic onCreate method that is ready for later use in the project:

```
public class TagsFragment extends ListFragment {

    @Override
    public void onCreate(Bundle savedInstanceState) {
        super.onCreate(savedInstanceState);
```

```
    }

  }
```

Now, for the Fragment that will eventually allow the user to take a photo as well as add a title and tags to it.

Create a new class and call it `CaptureFragment`. Amend the code so that it looks exactly like the next code, where we extend Fragment and implement a basic version of `onCreate` and `onCreateView` ready for later use in the project.

Here is the code for `CaptureFragment.java`:

```
public class CaptureFragment extends Fragment{

  @Override
  public void onCreate(Bundle savedInstanceState){
    super.onCreate(savedInstanceState);

  }

  @Override
  public View onCreateView(LayoutInflater inflater,
    ViewGroup container,Bundle savedInstanceState) {

    //Inflate the layout file then get all necessary references
    View view = inflater.inflate
      (R.layout.fragment_capture, container, false);

    return view;
  }

}
```

> The reason the two classes previous to `CaptureFragment` didn't need an `onCreateView` method was because `ListFragment` has `ListView` built in, and will have its functionality and appearance handled by an array adapter later in the project.

Now, we also need to create a placeholder layout for `fragment_capture.xml` to get rid of the error caused by referencing `R.id.fragment_capture` in the previous code.

Right-click on the `layout` folder and navigate to **New | Layout resource file**. Name it `fragment_capture` and click on **OK**.

Finally, drag a single `TextView` onto the layout and set its `text` property to `Capture`.

We can now write code in `MainActivity.java` to bring these Fragments to life. However, they are currently just blank, apart from the single `TextView` that we just added to `fragment_capture.xml`.

Coding the MainActivity class and layout

Let's add a really simple, but totally new, layout that will define the appearance of our app. Unsurprisingly, the layout will have our navigation drawer in it.

The code for the layout that follows in a moment looks long and complicated, but on close inspection, it is just `DrawerLayout` within a regular `RelativeLayout`. Then, within `DrawerLayout` is `RelativeLayout` that has an id of `fragmentHolder`. This `RelativeLayout` is where we will swap our various Fragments in and out. Then, still within `DrawerLayout`, we have `ListView`. It is this `ListView` that will hold all the options of navigation drawer.

Note that the `id` property of `ListView` is `navList`. We will see exactly how we use this `id` property to make it come to life (slide in and out) shortly.

Also, note that we set the `width` property of `ListView` to `200dp`. Feel free to play with this and make it wider or narrower as you like.

As neither of the previous UI elements (`RelativeLayout` and `ListView`) have been given any relative layout instructions, they will both start in the top-left corner and fill the entire screen, with the exception that `ListView` will only be `200dp` wide. Also, because `ListView` is declared after `RelativeLayout`, which will hold our Fragments, it will be on the top. This is exactly what we need.

Here is the code for `activity_main.xml` that we just discussed. Edit `activity_main.xml` so that it looks exactly like this:

```
<RelativeLayout xmlns:android=
  "http://schemas.android.com/apk/res/android"
  xmlns:tools="http://schemas.android.com/tools"
    android:layout_width="match_parent"
  android:layout_height="match_parent"
    tools:context=".MainActivity">

  <android.support.v4.widget.DrawerLayout
    xmlns:android="http://schemas.android.com/apk/res/android"
    xmlns:tools="http://schemas.android.com/tools"
    android:id="@+id/drawerLayout"
    android:layout_width="match_parent"
```

```
        android:layout_height="match_parent">

    <!-- For our fragments-->
    <RelativeLayout
        android:layout_width="match_parent"
        android:layout_height="match_parent"
        android:paddingLeft="@dimen/activity_horizontal_margin"
        android:paddingRight="@dimen/activity_horizontal_margin"
        android:paddingTop="@dimen/activity_vertical_margin"
        android:paddingBottom="@dimen/activity_vertical_margin"
            tools:context=".MainActivity"
        android:background="#ffffffff"
        android:id="@+id/fragmentHolder">


    </RelativeLayout>

    <!-- Side navigation drawer UI -->
    <ListView
        android:id="@+id/navList"
        android:layout_width="200dp"
        android:layout_height="match_parent"
        android:layout_gravity="left|start"
        android:background="#ffeeeeee"/>

    </android.support.v4.widget.DrawerLayout>

</RelativeLayout>
```

Now, we can get on with coding `MainActivity.java` itself. As with many of the files in this project, it will evolve as we progress. The following code is the minimum requirement to get the navigation drawer working and load up our Fragments.

First, we need to add some imports, and these need to be just the right classes and as with our paging apps in the last chapter, Android Studio doesn't always suggest the best class to import.

Furthermore, we need a few member variables, which are as follows:

- `ListView`: This will hold the navigation options.
- `DrawerLayout`: This is our navigation drawer.
- `ArrayAdapter`: This is used to bind our array (from `strings.xml`) to `ListView`.

- `ActionBarDrawerToggle`: This enables us to bring the menu icon in the action bar to life and interact with `DrawerLayout` to open and close it. We will do so by calling its methods, and `ActionBarDrawerToggle` will handle all the complexity as well as provide a neat animation on the menu icon.
- `String`: This will be used to hold the title of our app.

Add the imports and member variables that we just discussed through this code snippet:

```
package com.gamecodeschool.whereitssnap1;

import android.app.Fragment;
import android.app.FragmentManager;
import android.content.res.Configuration;
import android.os.Bundle;
import android.support.v4.view.GravityCompat;
import android.support.v4.widget.DrawerLayout;
import android.support.v7.app.AppCompatActivity;
import android.support.v7.app.ActionBarDrawerToggle;
import android.util.Log;
import android.view.Menu;
import android.view.MenuItem;
import android.view.View;
import android.widget.AdapterView;
import android.widget.ArrayAdapter;
import android.widget.ListView;


public class MainActivity extends AppCompatActivity {

  private ListView mNavDrawerList;
  private DrawerLayout mDrawerLayout;
  private ArrayAdapter<String> mAdapter;
  private ActionBarDrawerToggle mDrawerToggle;
  private String mActivityTitle;

  @Override
  protected void onCreate(Bundle savedInstanceState) {
    super.onCreate(savedInstanceState);
    setContentView(R.layout.activity_main);

    // We will come back here in a minute!
  }
```

```
// ...
// Usual auto-generated methods
// ...

}
```

We are now in a position to think about how to handle Fragments. As we are dealing with more and more varied range of Fragments, let's create a method that we can call to specifically handle switching between Fragments.

Switching between Fragments

Next, right after `onCreate`, we will add a method called `switchFragment` that will handle switching between our Fragments when the user taps on an option in the navigation drawer UI.

Notice how the method takes a single `int` called `position`. We then declare a Fragment called `fragment` and set it to `null`. Then, we initialize a String called `fragmentID` as an empty string. We will use this same null `Fragment` object and empty String regardless of which navigation option the user chooses. What will vary, however, is how we initialize it.

The initialization is handled using `switch` and `position` as the argument. We have three `case` statements: `0`, `1`, and `2`. These values represent `TitlesFragment`, `TagsFragment`, and `CaptureFragment` respectively.

For each case, we initialize `fragment` with the appropriate type of the `Fragment` class and set the `fragmentID` String to a similarly appropriate value, as we will soon need to be able to detect the currently displayed Fragment.

Note also that for `TitlesFragment`, we also create `Bundle`. At present, `Bundle` has no function. We add it here so that we don't need to amend this method later. It will eventually pass in the tag that a user has clicked on in order to help `TitlesFragment` show an appropriate list of related titles.

Add the first part of the `switchFragment` method that we just discussed:

```
private void switchFragment(int position) {

  Fragment fragment = null;
  String fragmentID ="";
  switch (position) {
    case 0:
      fragmentID = "TITLES";
      Bundle args = new Bundle();
```

```
            args.putString("Tag", "_NO_TAG");
            fragment = new TitlesFragment();
            fragment.setArguments(args);
            break;

        case 1:
            fragmentID = "TAGS";
            fragment = new TagsFragment();
            break;

        case 2:
            fragmentID = "CAPTURE";
            fragment = new CaptureFragment();
            break;

        default:
            break;
    }


    // More code goes here next

}
```

In the next block of code, which completes the method we started in the previous block, we create a new `FragmentManager` as usual. After this, we call `beginTransaction` that is chained with the `replace` method, which handles the destruction of the existing `Fragment`, at the same time as using our newly initialized Fragment and ID, held in `fragment` and `fragmentID` respectively.

The last line of code will shut the drawer in order to fully reveal the newly selected option/Fragment.

Add the highlighted code to the `switchFragment` method at the point indicated by the comment that is highlighted in the following code:

```
private void switchFragment(int position) {

    ...

    // More code goes here next

    FragmentManager fragmentManager = getFragmentManager();
    fragmentManager.beginTransaction()
        .replace(R.id.fragmentHolder, fragment,
        fragmentID).commit();
```

```
// Close the drawer
mDrawerLayout.closeDrawer(mNavDrawerList);

}
```

Setting up the drawer

Next, we will create a single method that will do everything to actually set up a navigation drawer. The method is called setupDrawer, and we will write code to call it from onCreate soon.

Here is how it works. We initialize mDrawerToggle at the same time as we create a new ActionBarDrawerToggle reference.

Within it, we handle the following two key events:

- The event when the drawer is opened
- The event when the drawer is closed

The onDrawerOpened method first calls the parent method and then sets the title of the action bar. When the drawer is open, we want to encourage the user to make a selection. We do so by setting the title as Make selection. Finally, in this method, the call to invalidateOptionsMenu causes the action bar to be redrawn.

In the onDrawerClosed method, we again start by calling the parent method. Again, we set the title of the action bar, but this time, we use the mActivityTitle String, and we will see exactly how this is configured in the onCreate method later in this chapter.

The last two lines in this class are called when the instance is created and sets up mDrawerToggle and then passes it in setDrawerListener, which has the combined effect of animating the menu button on the left-hand side of the action bar as the drawer is toggled between open and closed.

The following screenshot shows the drawer toggle when the drawer is closed:

This next screenshot shows the drawer toggle when the drawer is open:

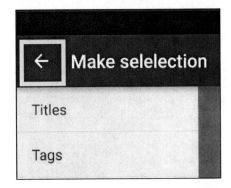

We will be able to see this for real near the end of this chapter, including how a neat animation morphs between the preceding two highlighted states.

Add the `setupDrawer` method that we just discussed right after the `switchFragment` method in `MainActivity.java`:

```
private void setupDrawer() {

  mDrawerToggle = new ActionBarDrawerToggle
    (this, mDrawerLayout, R.string.drawer_open,
    R.string.drawer_close) {

    // Called when drawer is opened
    public void onDrawerOpened(View drawerView) {
      super.onDrawerOpened(drawerView);

      getSupportActionBar().setTitle("Make selection");

      // triggers call to onPrepareOptionsMenu
      invalidateOptionsMenu();
    }

    // Called when drawer is closed
    public void onDrawerClosed(View view) {
      super.onDrawerClosed(view);

      getSupportActionBar().setTitle(mActivityTitle);

      // triggers call to onPrepareOptionsMenu
      invalidateOptionsMenu();
    }
```

```
    };

    mDrawerToggle.setDrawerIndicatorEnabled(true);
    mDrawerLayout.setDrawerListener(mDrawerToggle);
}
```

Next, we override the `onPostCreate` and `onConfigurationChanged` methods and call `syncState` and `onConfigurationChanged` on `mDrawerToggle`.

We have not seen `onPostCreate` or `onConfigurationChanged` before, and there are not that many situations where we need to use them.

As the names suggests, they are called after `onCreate` and after a configuration change of the Activity, respectively.

We use them here so that if the application goes into the background or if the device gets rotated, the app will use `onPostCreate` and `onConfigurationChanged` to make sure that it remembers the state of the drawer and the toggle, and keeps them both in sync.

Add these two overridden methods to the `MainActivity` class:

```
@Override
protected void onPostCreate(Bundle savedInstanceState) {
    super.onPostCreate(savedInstanceState);

    mDrawerToggle.syncState();
}

@Override
public void onConfigurationChanged(Configuration newConfig) {
    super.onConfigurationChanged(newConfig);

    mDrawerToggle.onConfigurationChanged(newConfig);
}
```

Handling the back button

There are just two more areas to pay attention to before we can turn our attention to `onCreate` and get all this code working.

The `onBackPressed` method is an overridden method that is called when the back button is pressed. It is useful to apply this method to add a functionality because we can make the app behave a little more as the user might expect.

The first `if` statement detects whether the drawer is open, and if it is, it closes it. The `else` block is more nuanced and this is what it does.

If you are on the home screen of an app and you tap on the back button, you probably expect it to quit. If you are on the second screen of an app and you tap on the back button, you probably expect to go back to the first screen.

The `else` block achieves this by creating a temporary `Fragment` reference, `f`, and using the `f instanceof TitleFragment` condition, which returns true if `TitlesFragment` is currently the type in `fragmentHolder`. As the title's screen is effectively our home screen, when this condition is true the app quits by calling `finish`, followed by `System.exit(0)`.

If, on the other hand, any other Fragment is present, then we can assume that the user wants to go back a screen, so we call our `switchFragment` method with 0 as the argument to load `TitlesFragment`.

Enter the code for the `onBackPressed` method:

```
@Override
public void onBackPressed() {

  // Close drawer if open
  if (mDrawerLayout.isDrawerOpen(GravityCompat.START)) {

    //drawer is open so close it
    mDrawerLayout.closeDrawer(mNavDrawerList);

  }else {

    // Go back to titles fragment
    // Quit if already at titles fragment
    Fragment f = getFragmentManager().
      findFragmentById(R.id.fragmentHolder);
    if (f instanceof TitlesFragment) {

      finish();
      System.exit(0);

    }else{

      switchFragment(0);

    }

  }
}
```

Now, add the highlighted code to the onOptionsItemSelected method, which will ensure that our drawer toggle is handled correctly each time it is pressed:

```
@Override
public boolean onOptionsItemSelected(MenuItem item) {


    int id = item.getItemId();

    //noinspection SimplifiableIfStatement
    if (id == R.id.action_settings) {
      return true;
    }

    // Activate the navigation drawer toggle
    if (mDrawerToggle.onOptionsItemSelected(item)) {
      return true;
    }

    return super.onOptionsItemSelected(item);
}
```

Finally, in onCreate, we can put all the other pieces of our code together.

First, we get a reference to ListView by calling findViewByID. Then, we get a reference to DrawerLayout in the same way.

Next, we use the getTitle().toString() method and assign the result to mActivityTitle. The effect of this is that the title of our app is now held in mActivityTitle.

Add the first part of the new code that we just discussed, as highlighted, in the onCreate method:

```
@Override
protected void onCreate(Bundle savedInstanceState) {
    super.onCreate(savedInstanceState);
    setContentView(R.layout.activity_main);

    // We will come back here in a minute!
    mNavDrawerList = (ListView) findViewById(R.id.navList);
```

```
mDrawerLayout = (DrawerLayout)findViewById(R.id.drawerLayout);
mActivityTitle = getTitle().toString();

// We will finish off this method next
// From here

}
```

Now, we will discuss the last part of the code that goes in the onCreate method from where we just left it.

We create a String array by calling getResources.getStringArray and passing in the name of our array in the strings.xml file.

After this, we initialize ArrayAdapter (with the previous array) and set it as the adapter for ListView.

Look at these two lines of code (don't add them yet):

```
getSupportActionBar().setDisplayHomeAsUpEnabled(true);
getSupportActionBar().setHomeButtonEnabled(true);
```

They enable the drawer control in the action bar that we previously configured when we initialized our drawer in the setupDrawer method.

Lastly, we create an anonymous class to handle clicks on ListView, and we simply call switchFragment with the appropriate position (whichItem) that was clicked.

Add the highlighted code that we discussed just after the code that we added previously into the onCreate method:

```
@Override
protected void onCreate(Bundle savedInstanceState) {
  super.onCreate(savedInstanceState);

  ...

  // We will finish off this method next
  // From here


  // Initialize an array with our titles from strings.xml
  String[] navMenuTitles = getResources().
    getStringArray(R.array.nav_drawer_items);
  // Initialize our ArrayAdapter
  mAdapter = new ArrayAdapter<String>
    (this, android.R.layout.simple_list_item_1, navMenuTitles);
  // Set the adapter to the ListView
```

```
mNavDrawerList.setAdapter(mAdapter);

setupDrawer();

getSupportActionBar().setDisplayHomeAsUpEnabled(true);
getSupportActionBar().setHomeButtonEnabled(true);

mNavDrawerList.setOnItemClickListener
  (new AdapterView.OnItemClickListener() {

  @Override
  public void onItemClick(AdapterView<?> adapter,
    View view, int whichItem, long id) {

    switchFragment(whichItem);

  }
});

switchFragment(0);
}
```

That's it for our navigation drawer, and we can run the project so far. Now, we can see the loading data animation provided by default in `ListView` from `TitlesFragment` and `ListFragment`:

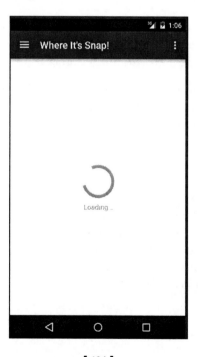

When we drag from the left-hand edge of the screen, the drawer slides open:

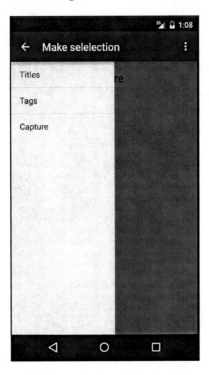

Notice the behavior of the drawer when the back key is pressed. This is because of the code that we added in `onBackPressed`. You can also swipe the drawer away or tap/click on the left-pointing arrow in the action bar.

Note that if you tap on **Capture** in the navigation drawer, you will see the single `TextView` with the word "Capture" from the `fragment_capture` layout, indicating that our Fragments are indeed switching themselves around as intended.

Summary

Now, we have a working Activity that happily swaps different Fragments in and out of `RelativeLayout` with an `id` property of `fragmentHolder`. Of course, these Fragments don't actually do anything, and we will begin to put this right in the next chapter when we see how to use the device's camera to take pictures. We will then proceed to expand on what we know to add a picture capture function within the `CaptureFragment` class of Where it's snap.

22
Capturing Images

In this chapter, we will see how we can harness the Android `Intent` class to add the otherwise complicated functionality with ease. Although this is a short chapter, it is surprising how much we can get done in these few pages. We will not only build a very quick mini app with the image capture functionality, but we will also add this functionality to the Where it's snap app. At the same time, we will see how Android stores images that are captured by the camera and how we interact with them. In this chapter, we will:

- Look at how to capture an image from a camera with the `Intent` class
- Put this knowledge to work in a camera mini app
- Code the Where it's snap capture Fragment

Capturing images using the camera

Android provides two ways to write apps that use a camera:

- One way is to write a camera app from scratch and utilize any or all of the features of any camera that the device may have. This is a big topic and is usually only used when the app is designed to add some kind of a new camera functionality.
- The other way is to use the existing camera app to do the work for us.

We will be cheating (in a good way) by using the existing camera app of the device (option 2). We can do this using the `Intent` class that we first saw in *Chapter 15, Android Intent and Persistence*.

By carefully constructing the argument passed into the constructor of the `Intent` class, we can get other apps to do work for us. We will see the code to capture an image, but the same simple techniques can be used to send an e-mail, post a message on social media platforms, play media, and much more besides this.

To have an `Intent` class launch the camera app, we will build an `Intent` class with `android.provider.MediaStore.ACTION_IMAGE_CAPTURE`.

All we need to do is construct an `Intent` class like this:

```
Intent intent = new Intent(android.provider.
  MediaStore.ACTION_IMAGE_CAPTURE);
```

After we have done this, we start an Activity using our new `Intent` object, but unlike in *Chapter 15, Android Intent and Persistence*, where we called `startActivity`, this time we call `startActivityForResult` so that the new Activity knows we want a result (some data) handed back to our Activity.

We would start the `Intent` class like this:

```
startActivityForResult(cameraIntent, CAMERA_REQUEST);
```

And then, we can capture the result (hopefully, a picture) in the `onActivityResult` method, which is the method that Android will call in these situations. We would do so with the help of the following code:

```
Bitmap photo = (Bitmap) data.getExtras().get("data");
```

In the preceding code, we created a new `Bitmap` (image) object and assigned the returned data to it. There are a few caveats and missing pieces to the preceding explanation, and they are best demonstrated rather than explained. Let's see how to make all this work in a quick mini app.

When we come to code the image capture functionality of the Where it's snap app, we will take things even further.

The capturing images mini app

Create a new project and call it `Simple Photo`. You can leave all the settings at their defaults as usual.

To handle Marshmallow runtime permissions, as discussed in *Chapter 11, Widget Mania* in the *Android permissions and Marshmallows* section, we need to set the target API to 22.

To do this, select **Android** from the drop-down list at the top of the project explorer. Now, double-click on the **build.gradle (module: app)** option from the bottom of the project explorer window.

Change the highlighted line of code so that `targetSdkVersion` is set to 22, as shown in the following code:

```
defaultConfig {
    applicationId "com.gamecodeschool.simplephoto"
    minSdkVersion 15
    targetSdkVersion 22
    versionCode 1
    versionName "1.0"
}
```

Now, we need to ask for the users' permission to use the camera.

Adding the camera permission to the manifest

The first thing we need to do is edit the `AndroidManifest.xml` file. The reason for this is that we need to ask the users' permission to access their camera. When we add a permission to the `AndroidManifest.xml` file, it triggers the user to be notified of our app's intention to use their camera and asks their permission at install time. Also, we can add the use of a camera as a feature so that our app would be hidden from users with devices that don't have a camera at all.

Fortunately, adding the camera permission and feature is easy. Open the `AndroidManifest.xml` file from the `manifests` folder in the project explorer. Add the highlighted lines shown in the next code:

```
<?xml version="1.0" encoding="utf-8"?>
<manifest xmlns:android=
    "http://schemas.android.com/apk/res/android"
    package="com.gamecodeschool.simplephoto" >

    <application
        android:allowBackup="true"
        android:icon="@mipmap/ic_launcher"
        android:label="@string/app_name"
        android:theme="@style/AppTheme" >

    <activity
        android:name=".MainActivity"
        android:label="@string/app_name" >
        <intent-filter>
            <action android:name="android.intent.action.MAIN" />

            <category android:name=
                "android.intent.category.LAUNCHER" />
```

```
      </intent-filter>
    </activity>

    </application>

    <uses-permission android:name="android.permission.CAMERA" />
    <uses-feature android:name="android.hardware.camera" />

  </manifest>
```

Now, we can deal with the layout.

Defining a simple layout

This layout is really basic. When we add the picture capture functionality into Where it's snap later this chapter, we will spend a bit more time and effort laying out the capture Fragment:

```
<LinearLayout xmlns:android=
  "http://schemas.android.com/apk/res/android"
  android:orientation="vertical"
  android:layout_width="fill_parent"
  android:layout_height="fill_parent">

  <Button android:id="@+id/button1"
    android:layout_width="wrap_content"
    android:layout_height="wrap_content"
    android:text="Take picture"/>

  <ImageView android:id="@+id/imageView1"
    android:layout_height="wrap_content"
    android:layout_width="wrap_content"/>

</LinearLayout>
```

The preceding layout has `Button` with an `id` property of `button1` and `ImageView`, to place the newly captured image, with an `id` property of `imageView1`.

Now, we can move on to coding Java in `MainActivity`.

Coding the MainActivity class

First, we need to add two member variables:

- We have `final int` called `CAMERA_REQUEST`. When we start a new Activity and expect some data back, we must send an ID for the request. It is good practice to use a `final` variable because when we receive data in `onActivityResult`, we need to be certain that it is the camera data that we are dealing with. Any time we call `startActivityForResult`, the reply comes back to `onActivityResult`. We will see how we can verify that we are actually dealing with the data we think we are. In this simple app, it is a foregone conclusion that we will be receiving data from the camera app, but as our apps get more complex, this will not always be the case.

- `ImageView` will be used to display the returned `Bitmap`.

Add the two highlighted member variables:

```
public class MainActivity extends AppCompatActivity {

    private static final int CAMERA_REQUEST = 123;
    private ImageView imageView;

    @Override
    protected void onCreate(Bundle savedInstanceState) {
        super.onCreate(savedInstanceState);
        setContentView(R.layout.activity_main);
    }
}
```

Next, in the `onCreate` method, we get a reference to `ImageView` and `Button` in our layout.

Then, we code an anonymous class to listen for clicks on `Button`. Note that the `onClick` method creates the new `Intent` class, which we discussed earlier, as well as calls `startActivityForResult` and passes in the `Intent` class along with our `id` property, `CAMERA_REQUEST`.

Now, add the code that we just discussed to the `onCreate` method. It is highlighted in this next code listing:

```
    @Override
    protected void onCreate(Bundle savedInstanceState) {
        super.onCreate(savedInstanceState);
        setContentView(R.layout.activity_main);

        imageView = (ImageView)this.findViewById(R.id.imageView1);
        Button photoButton = (Button) this.findViewById(R.id.button1);
```

```
photoButton.setOnClickListener(new View.OnClickListener() {

    @Override
    public void onClick(View v) {
        Intent cameraIntent = new Intent
          (android.provider.MediaStore.ACTION_IMAGE_CAPTURE);
        startActivityForResult(cameraIntent, CAMERA_REQUEST);
    }
});
}
```

Finally, we can add the all-important `onActivityResult` method that captures the result (a photo) from the `Intent` class, which is passed in as a parameter. Notice the `int requestCode` parameter here, this should match the `id` property that we sent into `startActivityForResult`. Also, notice `resultCode`, which is also `int`.

We use an `if` statement to test for two things:

- Is this the data that we think it is (`requestCode == CAMERA_REQUEST`)?
- Is there actually some appropriate data at all within the `Intent` class (`resultCode == RESULT_OK`)?

It is possible that the Activity failed; it is also possible that the users changed their mind and did not take a picture. The `if` statement handles these possibilities.

If all is well, the execution enters the body of the `if` statement and we declare and initialize a new `Bitmap` from the `Intent` class and then use the `setImageBitmap` method to display it on `ImageView`.

Add the `onActivityResult` method that we just discussed:

```
protected void onActivityResult
    (int requestCode, int resultCode, Intent data) {

    if (requestCode == CAMERA_REQUEST && resultCode == RESULT_OK) {

        Bitmap photo = (Bitmap) data.getExtras().get("data");
        imageView.setImageBitmap(photo);
    }
}
```

We are now ready to test our mini app.

Running the Simple Photo app

If you are running this app on the emulator, then now would be a good time to slightly change the emulator's configuration to increase compatibility.

To do this, click on the AVD Manager icon in the menu bar of Android Studio. Click on the pencil icon to edit the emulator. Click on the **Advanced Settings** button. Find the **Camera** section. And set both the **Front** and **Back** options to **Emulated**.

Run the app and click on the **TAKE PICTURE** button. You will see that the default camera app for your device has opened. You can take a picture with all of the same options that you have when taking a photo under normal circumstances. When you have taken a photo, however, you are offered the option to save or discard the image:

If you choose to discard it (by clicking on the cross icon), then when `onActivityResult` is called, `resultCode == RESULT_OK` will be `false`, and the code in the body of the `if` statement will not be executed.

If you choose to save it (by clicking on the tick icon), however, then the picture you took will be displayed in ImageView, as expected:

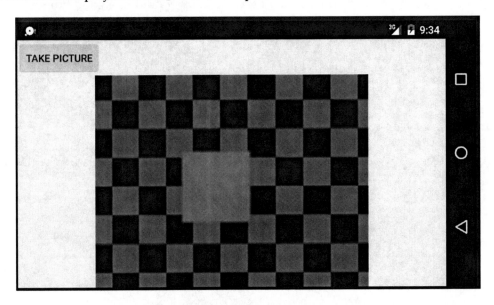

The previous two figures look slightly odd. They show how the emulator deals with using the camera. If you run this on a real device, you will be able to take a real picture.

Let's add this kind of functionality to Where it's snap, but let's take things a little further too.

Where it's snap – coding the capture Fragment

Now we can add the capture functionality to the Where it's snap app. We will implement the functionality of capturing an image from the camera as well as allow the user to add a title and tags for the image. We will not, however, add any functionality to save any of this data, as you will first want to learn about databases before we do.

In preparation to save the data, however, we will meet the Android Uri and File classes, which allow us to identify and locate the photos that the user captures.

The completed app, as it is at the end of this chapter, can be found in Chapter 22/ Where Its Snap 2.

We will first add a layout that `CaptureFragment` will use, and we will then add some code, some of which should look fairly familiar by now, in order to capture an image. The next two chapters will then look at databases to save and show all our data.

Creating the layout for the capture Fragment

You can add all the String resources and `id` properties manually if you like, but the fastest way to proceed is to copy the next code into the `capture_fragment.xml` file. Be sure to review the code, however, and make a mental note of the `id` properties, as this will make it easier for you to follow along when we code the `CaptureFragment` class shortly.

Add this code to the `capture_fragment.xml` file:

```xml
<?xml version="1.0" encoding="utf-8"?>
<RelativeLayout xmlns:android=
  "http://schemas.android.com/apk/res/android"
  android:orientation=
    "vertical" android:layout_width="match_parent"
  android:layout_height="match_parent">

  <Button
    android:layout_width="wrap_content"
    android:layout_height="wrap_content"
    android:text="@string/capture"
    android:id="@+id/btnCapture"
    android:layout_marginBottom="28dp"
    android:layout_alignParentBottom="true"
    android:layout_alignParentLeft="true"
    android:layout_alignParentStart="true"
    android:layout_marginLeft="25dp"
    android:layout_marginStart="25dp" />

  <ImageView
    android:layout_width="150dp"
    android:layout_height="150dp"
    android:id="@+id/imageView"
    android:src="@mipmap/ic_launcher"
    android:layout_below="@+id/editTextTitle"
    android:layout_centerHorizontal="true" />

  <Button
    android:layout_width="wrap_content"
    android:layout_height="wrap_content"
```

```
            android:text="@string/save"
            android:id="@+id/btnSave"
            android:layout_alignTop="@+id/btnCapture"
            android:layout_alignParentRight="true"
            android:layout_alignParentEnd="true"
            android:layout_marginRight="22dp"
            android:layout_marginEnd="22dp" />

    <EditText
        android:layout_width="wrap_content"
        android:layout_height="wrap_content"
        android:id="@+id/editTextTitle"
        android:hint="@string/enter_photo_title"
        android:layout_alignParentTop="true"
        android:layout_centerHorizontal="true" />

    <EditText
        android:layout_width="wrap_content"
        android:layout_height="wrap_content"
        android:id="@+id/editTextTag1"
        android:hint="@string/tag1"
        android:layout_marginBottom="121dp"
        android:layout_above="@+id/btnCapture"
        android:layout_alignLeft="@+id/btnCapture"
        android:layout_alignStart="@+id/btnCapture" />

    <EditText
        android:layout_width="wrap_content"
        android:layout_height="wrap_content"
        android:id="@+id/editTextTag2"
        android:hint="@string/tag2"
        android:layout_alignTop="@+id/editTextTag1"
        android:layout_alignLeft="@+id/editTextTag1"
        android:layout_alignStart="@+id/editTextTag1"
        android:layout_marginTop="59dp" />

    <EditText
        android:layout_width="wrap_content"
        android:layout_height="wrap_content"
        android:id="@+id/editTextTag3"
        android:hint="@string/tag3"
        android:layout_above="@+id/btnCapture"
        android:layout_alignLeft="@+id/btnCapture"
        android:layout_alignStart="@+id/btnCapture" />

</RelativeLayout>
```

Take a look and make sure that your layout looks as shown in the next figure. However, it doesn't have to be exact, the `id` properties do, and for the coding we do in *Chapter 27, Going Local – Hola!* to work correctly, we need to use the string resources (as in the preceding code) and not hardcode anything:

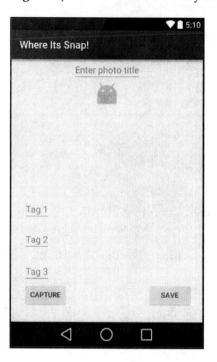

Coding the capture Fragment

Most of this code will be quite straight forward because of the preparation we have done, but I will point out all the new code as it arises.

First, we have to add some more permissions to the `AndroidManifest.xml` file. Open it up now and add the highlighted lines in the next code listing:

```xml
<?xml version="1.0" encoding="utf-8"?>
<manifest xmlns:android=
  "http://schemas.android.com/apk/res/android"
  package="com.gamecodeschool.whereitssnap2" >

  <uses-permission android:name=
    "android.permission.WRITE_EXTERNAL_STORAGE" />

  <application
    android:allowBackup="true"
```

```
      android:icon="@mipmap/ic_launcher"
      android:label="@string/app_name"
      android:theme="@style/AppTheme" >
      <activity
        android:name=".MainActivity"
        android:label="@string/app_name" >
        <intent-filter>
          <action android:name="android.intent.action.MAIN" />

          <category android:name="android.intent.category.
            LAUNCHER" />
        </intent-filter>
      </activity>
    </application>

  </manifest>
```

As we will soon see, we will be creating our own file, which will be used to save the photo. This is why we need the WRITE_EXTERNAL_STORAGE permission.

Now, add the four highlighted member variables to the CaptureFragment class:

```
public class CaptureFragment extends Fragment{

    private static final int CAMERA_REQUEST = 123;
    private ImageView mImageView;

    // The filepath for the photo
    String mCurrentPhotoPath;

    // Where the captured image is stored
    private Uri mImageUri = Uri.EMPTY;

    @Override
    public void onCreate(Bundle savedInstanceState){
      super.onCreate(savedInstanceState);

    }
```

In the onCreateView method, which is shown next, we get a reference to each of our UI widgets, ImageView, both the Button widgets, and the four EditText.

We then add an anonymous class to listen for the user clicking on the **Capture** button. In the onClick method, we use the same code as we did in the onClick method in our mini app. The only difference this time is that the action is taking place in onCreateView instead of onCreate, as required when dealing with a Fragment.

In addition, we create a new file for our image by calling the `createImageFile` method that we will write soon. After this, we use the `Uri.fromFile` method to get a URI, which points to our newly created file. We will talk more about what URIs are in *Chapter 24, Adding a Database to Where It's Snap* when we use them to store images in our database. For now, we can think of them as a link to the image.

Note that we then use the `putExtra` method to add this same `Uri` to the `Intent` class. This has the effect of telling the camera app to make this `Uri` point to the place where the image is saved. In effect, we now have a link to the image that will be captured.

Note that the next code does not handle the **Save** button. We will do this when you learn how to handle the data in a couple of chapters.

Add the code that we just discussed to `onCreateView`:

```
@Override
public View onCreateView(LayoutInflater inflater,
    ViewGroup container,Bundle savedInstanceState) {

    // Inflate the layout file then get all necessary references
    View view = inflater.inflate(R.layout.fragment_capture,
        container, false);

    mImageView = (ImageView)view.findViewById(R.id.imageView);
    Button btnCapture = (Button)view.findViewById(R.id.btnCapture);
    Button btnSave = (Button)view.findViewById(R.id.btnSave);

    final EditText mEditTextTitle =
        (EditText)view.findViewById(R.id.editTextTitle);
    final EditText mEditTextTag1 =
        (EditText)view.findViewById(R.id.editTextTag1);
    final EditText mEditTextTag2 =
        (EditText)view.findViewById(R.id.editTextTag2);
    final EditText mEditTextTag3 =
        (EditText)view.findViewById(R.id.editTextTag3);


    // Listen for clicks on the capture button
    btnCapture.setOnClickListener(new View.OnClickListener() {

        @Override
        public void onClick(View v) {

            Intent cameraIntent =
                new Intent(MediaStore.ACTION_IMAGE_CAPTURE);
```

```
         File photoFile = null;
         try {
           photoFile = createImageFile();
         } catch (IOException ex) {
           // Error occurred while creating the File
           Log.e("error", "error creating file");


         }
         // Continue only if the File was successfully created
         if (photoFile != null) {
           mImageUri = Uri.fromFile(photoFile);
           cameraIntent.putExtra(MediaStore.EXTRA_OUTPUT,
             Uri.fromFile(photoFile));
           startActivityForResult(cameraIntent, CAMERA_REQUEST);
         }



       }
    });

    return view;
}
```

Next, let's write that new `createImageFile` method. The full details of this method are somewhat convoluted, but they do need to be.

All we are really doing is creating a new file. This could have been done in a single line of code. The reason our code is much more verbose than one line is because we use `SimpleDateFormat` and its related classes and methods to create a unique filename to be sure that our file doesn't get repeated as the user takes more and more pictures.

Then, we use `getExternalStoragePublicDirectory` to get a location to create the file.

Note that the last thing the method does is return the `File` reference to the calling code:

```
    private File createImageFile() throws IOException {
      // Create an image file name
      String timeStamp = new SimpleDateFormat
        ("yyyyMMdd_HHmmss").format(new Date());
      String imageFileName = "JPEG_" + timeStamp + "_";
      File storageDir = Environment.getExternalStoragePublicDirectory(
        Environment.DIRECTORY_PICTURES);
      File image = File.createTempFile(
        imageFileName,  // filename
```

```
    ".jpg",          // extension
    storageDir       // folder
  );

  // Save for use with ACTION_VIEW Intent
  mCurrentPhotoPath = "file:" + image.getAbsolutePath();
  return image;
}
```

Now, add the `onActivityResult` method into the `CaptureFragment` class to set the captured `Bitmap` image to `ImageView`:

```
@Override
public void onActivityResult
  (int requestCode, int resultCode, Intent data) {
  if (requestCode == CAMERA_REQUEST &&
    resultCode == Activity.RESULT_OK) {

    try {

      mImageView.setImageURI(Uri.parse(mImageUri.toString()));
    }catch(Exception e){
      Log.e("Error","Uri not set");
    }

  }else{
    mImageUri = Uri.EMPTY;
  }
}
```

We also need to override `onDestroy` so that we can clean up after ourselves. This next code gets Bitmap from the drawable, and by calling its chained `getBitmap()`. `recycle()` methods, we can prevent the possibility of the app running out of memory:

```
public void onDestroy(){
  super.onDestroy();

  // Make sure we don't run out of memory
  BitmapDrawable bd = (BitmapDrawable) mImageView.getDrawable();
  bd.getBitmap().recycle();
  mImageView.setImageBitmap(null);
}
```

Now, we can test the image capturing functionality.

Testing the capture Fragment

Run the Where it's snap app and tap on **Capture** in the navigation drawer. You can now add tags and a title and capture an image:

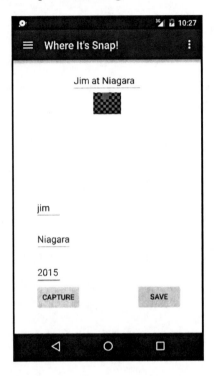

Of course, we have the slight issue that none of our users' data is saved.

Summary

In this chapter, we saw how to use other apps installed on our users' device to get data from them. Specifically, we learned to get an image from the camera app, but we also know that we can use similar techniques with many other apps; however, this is beyond the scope of this beginners guide.

In the next two chapters, you will first learn the necessary techniques and then we will implement a way to save the users' data using an **SQLite database**. Databases are a very efficient way to store data in our apps. Certainly, there would be nothing wrong with using JSON in this app, just as we did in *Chapter 15, Android Intent and Persistence*, but we will see some advantages of using a database as the project proceeds. The least of which will be the ability to easily sort our data, as well as upgrade/update the structure of the data.

23
Using SQLite Databases in Our Apps

If we are going to make apps that offer our users significant features, then almost certainly we are going to need a way to manage, store, and filter significant amounts of data.

It is possible to efficiently store very large amounts of data with JSON, but when we need to use this data selectively, instead of simply restricting ourselves to the options of "save everything" and "load everything", we need to think about which other options are available.

A good computer science course would probably teach the algorithms necessary to handle sorting and filtering our data, but the efforts involved to do this would be quite extensive. Also, what are the chances of us coming up with a solution that is as good as one offered by the people who provide us with the Android API?

As always, it makes sense for us to use the solutions provided in the Android API. As we have seen, JSON and SharedPreferences classes have their place, but at some point, we need to move on to using real databases for real-world solutions. Android uses the SQLite database management system, and as you would expect, there is an API to make this as easy as possible.

In this chapter, we will do the following:

- Find out exactly what a database is
- Learn what SQL and SQLite are
- Learn the basics of the SQL language
- Take a look at the Android SQLite API
- Build a SQLite mini app

Database 101

Let's answer a whole bunch of database-related questions and then we can get started with making apps that use SQLite. So, what is a database?

What is a database?

A database is both a place of storage and the means to retrieve, store, and manipulate data. It helps to visualize a database before learning how to use it. The actual structure of the internals of a database varies greatly depending upon the database in question. SQLite actually stores all its data in a single file.

It will aid our comprehension greatly; however, if we visualize our data as if it were in a spreadsheet or sometimes, multiple spreadsheets, our database, just like a spreadsheet, will be divided into multiple columns that represent different types of data and rows that represent entries in the database.

Think about a database with names and exam scores. Take a look at the following visual representation of this data to understand how a database would look:

_ID	name	score
1	Bart	23
2	Lisa	100
3	Jim	66

Note, however, that there is an extra column of data here: an **_ID** column. We will talk more about this as we proceed. This single spreadsheet-like structure is called a **table**. As mentioned before, there might be, and often are, multiple tables in a database. Each column of the table will have a name that can be referred to when we speak about the database.

What is SQL?

SQL stands for **Structured Query Language**. It is the syntax that is used to get things done with the database.

What is SQLite?

SQLite is the name of the entire database system that is favored by Android, and it has its own version of SQL. The reason the SQLite version of SQL needs to be slightly different than some other versions is because the database has different features.

The SQL syntax primer that follows will be focused on the SQLite version.

The SQL syntax primer

Before you learn how to use SQLite with Android, you first need to learn the basics of how to use SQLite in general in a platform-neutral context.

Let's look at some example SQL code that could be used on an SQLite database directly, without any Java or Android classes, and then we can more easily understand what our Java code will doing later.

The SQLite example code

SQL has keywords much like Java that cause things to happen. Here is a flavor of some of the SQL keywords that we will be using soon:

- **INSERT**: This allows us to add data to the database
- **DELETE**: This allows us to remove data from the database
- **SELECT**: This allows us to read data from the database
- **WHERE**: This allows us to specify the parts of the database that match a specific criteria that we want to insert, delete, or select data from
- **FROM**: This is used to specify a table or column name in a database

 There are many more SQLite keywords than this, and for a full list of keywords, take a look at https://sqlite.org/lang_keywords.html.

In addition to keywords, SQL has **types**. A few examples of SQL types are as follows:

- `integer`: This is just what we need to store whole numbers
- `text`: This is perfect for storing a simple name or address
- `real`: This is used for large floating point numbers

 There are many more SQLite types than this, and for a full list of types, take a look at https://www.sqlite.org/datatype3.html.

Let's look at how we can combine these types with the keywords to create tables and add, remove, modify, and read data using full SQLite statements.

Creating a table

It would be a perfectly decent question to ask why we don't create a new database first. The reason for this is that every app has access to an SQLite database by default. The database is private to that app. Here is the statement that we would use to create a table within that database. I have highlighted a few parts to make the statement clearer:

```
create table StudentsAndGrades
  _ID integer primary key autoincrement not null,
  name text not null,
  score int;
```

The previous code creates a table called StudentsAndGrades with a row id of the integer type that will be automatically increased (incremented) each time a row of data is added.

The table will also have a name column that will be of the text type and cannot be blank (not null).

It will also have a score column that will be of the int type. Also note that the statement is completed by a semicolon.

Inserting data into the database

Here is how we might insert a new row of data into that database:

```
INSERT INTO StudentsAndGrades
  (name, score)
  VALUES
  ("Bart", 23);
```

The previous code added a row to the database. After the preceding statement, the database will have one entry with the 1, "Bart", and 23 values for the _ID, name, and score columns.

Here is how we might insert another new row of data into that database:

```
INSERT INTO StudentsAndGrades
  (name, score)
  VALUES
  ("Lisa", 100);
```

The previous code added a new row of data with the 2, "Lisa", and 100 values for the _ID, name, and score columns.

Our spreadsheet-like structure would now look as shown in this next figure:

_ID	name	score
1	Bart	23
2	Lisa	100

Retrieving data from the database

Here is how we would access all the rows and columns from our database:

```
SELECT * FROM StudentsAndGrades;
```

The previous code asks for every row and column. The * symbol can be read as **all**.

We can also be a little more selective as this code demonstrates:

```
SELECT score FROM StudentsAndGrades
  where name = "Lisa";
```

The previous code would only return 100, which, of course, is the score associated with the name Lisa.

Updating the database structure

We can even add new columns after the table has been created and data has been added. This is simple as far as the SQL is concerned but can cause some issues with regard to users' data on already published apps. We will explore this problem more in *Chapter 26, Upgrading SQLite – Adding Locations and Maps*. The next statement adds a new column called age that is of the int type:

```
ALTER TABLE StudentsAndGrades
  ADD
  age int;
```

There are many more data types, keywords, and the ways to use them than we have seen so far. We will see many of them in the two database-driven apps that we will build. This was just a taste. Next, let's look at the Android SQLite API, and now we will begin to see how we can use our new SQLite skills.

The Android SQLite API

There are a number of different ways in which the Android API makes it fairly easy for us to use our app's database. The first class we need to get familiar with is SQLiteOpenHelper.

SQLiteOpenHelper and SQLiteDatabase

The SQLiteDatabase class is the class that represents the actual database. The SQLiteOpenHelper class, however, is where most of the action takes place. This class will enable us to get access to a database and initialize an instance of SQLiteDatabase.

In addition, the SQLiteOpenHelper class, which we will extend in our forthcoming mini app, has two methods to override. First, it has an onCreate method, which is called the first time a database is used, and therefore it makes sense that we place our SQL in this method to create our table structure.

The other method we must override is onUpgrade, which, as you can probably guess, is called when we upgrade our database (ALTER its structure). Exactly how this works is best explained with a practical example, which we will see in a few chapter's time.

Building and executing queries

As our database structures get more complex and as our SQL knowledge grows, our SQL statements will get quite long and awkward. The potential for errors is high.

The way in which we will help overcome the problem of complexity is by building our queries from parts into a String. We can then pass this String to the method (we will see this soon) that will execute the query for us.

Furthermore, we will use final strings to represent things such as table and column names so that we can't get in a muddle with them.

For example, we could declare the following members that would represent the table names and column names from the earlier fictitious example. Note that we will also give the database itself a name and have a string for that too:

```
private static final String DB_NAME = "MyCollegeDB";
private static final String TABLE_S_AND_G = " StudentsAndGrades";

public static final String TABLE_ROW_ID = "_id";
public static final String TABLE_ROW_NAME = "name";
public static final String TABLE_ROW_SCORE = "score";
```

As you can see in the preceding code, we will benefit from accessing the string outside the class as well because we declare it public.

We could then build a query like this next example. The following example adds a new entry to our hypothetical database and incorporates our Java variables into the SQL statement:

```
String name = "Divij";
int score = 94;

// Add all the details to the table
String query = "INSERT INTO " + TABLE_S_AND_G + " (" +
    TABLE_ROW_NAME + ", " +
    TABLE_ROW_SCORE + ") " +
    "VALUES (" +
    "'" + name + "'" + ", " +
    score +
    ");";
```

Note that in the previous code, the regular Java variables `name` and `score` are highlighted. The previous String called `query` is now the SQL statement that is exactly equivalent to the following code:

```
INSERT INTO StudentsAndGrades (
  name, score)
  VALUES ('Divij',94);
```

It is not essential to completely grasp the previous two blocks of code in order to proceed with learning Android programming. But if you want to build your own apps and construct SQL statements that do exactly what you need, it *will* help to do so. Why not study the previous two blocks of code in order to discern the difference between the pairs of double quote marks " that are the parts of the String joined together with +, the pairs of single quote marks ' that are part of the SQL syntax, the regular Java variables, and the distinct semicolons from the SQL statement in the String and Java.

Throughout the typing of the query, Android Studio prompts us the names of our variables, making the chances of an error much less likely even though it is more verbose than simply typing the query.

Now, we can use the classes that we introduced previously to execute the query:

```
// This is the actual database
private SQLiteDatabase db;

// Create an instance of our internal CustomSQLiteOpenHelper class
```

```
CustomSQLiteOpenHelper helper =
  new CustomSQLiteOpenHelper(context);

// Get a writable database
db = helper.getWritableDatabase();

// Run the query
db.execSQL(query);
```

When adding data to the database, we will use `execSQL`, as in the previous code, and when getting data from the database, we will use the `rawQuery` method, as shown in the next code snippet:

```
Cursor c = db.rawQuery(query, null);
```

Note that the `rawQuery` method returns an object of the `Cursor` type.

> There are several different ways in which we can interact with SQLite, and they each have their advantages and disadvantages. Here, we have chosen to use raw SQL statements, as it is entirely transparent as to what we are doing and at the same time, we will be reinforcing our knowledge of the SQL language. Refer to the next tip if you want to know more.

Database cursors

In addition to the classes that give us access to the database and the methods that allow us to execute our queries, there is the issue of exactly how the results that we get back from our queries are formatted.

Fortunately, there is the `Cursor` class. All our database queries will return objects of the `Cursor` type. We can use the methods of the `Cursor` class to selectively access the data returned from the queries like we've used in this code:

```
Log.i(c.getString(1), c.getString(2));
```

The previous code would output to logcat the two values stored in the first two columns of the result that the query returned. It is the `Cursor` object itself that determines which row of our returned data we will currently read.

We can access a number of methods of the `Cursor` object including the `moveToNext` method, which unsurprisingly would move `Cursor` to the next row that is ready for reading:

```
c.moveToNext();
```

```
/*
   This same code now outputs the data in the
   first and second column of the returned
   data but from the SECOND row.
*/

Log.i(c.getString(1), c.getString(2));
```

On some occasions, we will be able to bind `Cursor` to a part of our UI (such as `ListView`) and just leave everything to the Android API. We will see this when we add a database to the Where it's snap app in the next chapter.

There are many more useful methods of the `Cursor` class, some of which we will see soon.

 This introduction to the Android SQLite API really only scratches the surface of its capabilities. We will bump into a few more methods and classes as we proceed further. It is, however, worth studying further if your app idea requires complex data management. If you want to know more, I recommend you read *Android Database Programming, Jason Wei, Packt Publishing*, which you can find at `https://www.packtpub.com/application-development/android-database-programming`.

Now, we can see how all this theory comes together and how we will structure our database code in an actual working mini app.

The database mini app

In this section, we will put into practice everything that you have learned so far and create a mini database that enables us to add, delete, search, and select data.

First, let's create a new project with all the settings at their default values and call it `Database`. The code for this mini app is in the download bundle of the `Chapter 23/Database` folder.

Implementing the layout

Create the layout by copying and pasting the next block of XML code. There is nothing new or complicated in the code, but be sure to review it to make a mental note of the various `id` properties on the `EditText` and `Button` widgets because it will make understanding the Java code simpler.

Add this XML to the `layout_main.xml` file:

```xml
<RelativeLayout xmlns:android=
  "http://schemas.android.com/apk/res/android"
    xmlns:tools="http://schemas.android.com/tools"
      android:layout_width="match_parent"
    android:layout_height="match_parent" android:paddingLeft=
      "@dimen/activity_horizontal_margin"
    android:paddingRight="@dimen/activity_horizontal_margin"
    android:paddingTop="@dimen/activity_vertical_margin"
    android:paddingBottom="@dimen/activity_vertical_margin"
      tools:context=".MainActivity">

    <EditText
        android:layout_width="wrap_content"
        android:layout_height="wrap_content"
        android:id="@+id/editName"
        android:hint="Type a name"
        android:layout_alignParentTop="true"
        android:layout_centerHorizontal="true" />

    <EditText
        android:layout_width="wrap_content"
        android:layout_height="wrap_content"
        android:id="@+id/editAge"
        android:hint="Type their age"
        android:layout_below="@+id/editName"
        android:layout_alignLeft="@+id/editName"
        android:layout_alignStart="@+id/editName" />

    <Button
        android:layout_width="wrap_content"
        android:layout_height="wrap_content"
        android:text="INSERT"
        android:id="@+id/btnInsert"
        android:layout_below="@+id/editAge"
        android:layout_toRightOf="@+id/editSearch"
        android:layout_toEndOf="@+id/editSearch"
        android:layout_marginTop="24dp" />

    <Button
        android:layout_width="wrap_content"
        android:layout_height="wrap_content"
        android:text="DELETE"
        android:id="@+id/btnDelete"
```

```
        android:layout_above="@+id/btnSearch"
        android:layout_alignParentRight="true"
        android:layout_alignParentEnd="true"
        android:layout_marginBottom="40dp" />

    <Button
        android:layout_width="wrap_content"
        android:layout_height="wrap_content"
        android:text="SELECT *"
        android:id="@+id/btnSelect"
        android:layout_alignParentBottom="true"
        android:layout_alignRight="@+id/editName"
        android:layout_alignEnd="@+id/editName" />

    <Button
        android:layout_width="wrap_content"
        android:layout_height="wrap_content"
        android:text="Search"
        android:id="@+id/btnSearch"
        android:layout_above="@+id/btnSelect"
        android:layout_alignLeft="@+id/btnDelete"
        android:layout_alignStart="@+id/btnDelete"
        android:layout_marginBottom="32dp" />

    <EditText
        android:layout_width="wrap_content"
        android:layout_height="wrap_content"
        android:id="@+id/editSearch"
        android:hint="name to search"
        android:layout_alignBottom="@+id/btnSearch"
        android:layout_alignParentLeft="true"
        android:layout_alignParentStart="true" />

    <EditText
        android:layout_width="wrap_content"
        android:layout_height="wrap_content"
        android:id="@+id/editDelete"
        android:hint="name to delete"
        android:layout_alignBottom="@+id/btnDelete"
        android:layout_alignParentLeft="true"
        android:layout_alignParentStart="true"
        android:focusableInTouchMode="true" />

</RelativeLayout>
```

Here is the completed layout in the Android Studio designer:

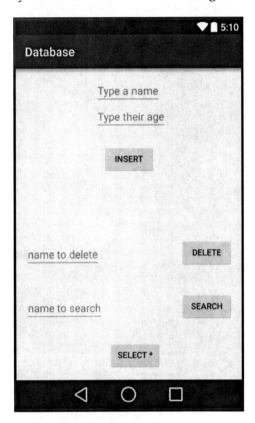

Coding the database class

We will create a class that manages our database by implementing
`SQLiteOpenHHelper`. It will also define a few `final` Strings to represent the names
of the table and its columns. Furthermore, it will supply a bunch of helper methods
that we can call to perform all the necessary queries. Where necessary, these helper
methods will return a `Cursor` object that we can use back in `MainActivity` to
display the data that we have retrieved. It would be trivial then to add new helper
methods should our app need to evolve.

Create a new class called `DataManager` and add the following member variables:

```
public class DataManager {

    // This is the actual database
    private SQLiteDatabase db;
```

```
/*
    Next we have a public static final string for
    each row/table that we need to refer to both
    inside and outside this class
*/

public static final String TABLE_ROW_ID = "_id";
public static final String TABLE_ROW_NAME = "name";
public static final String TABLE_ROW_AGE = "age";

/*
    Next we have a private static final strings for
    each row/table that we need to refer to just
    inside this class
*/

private static final String DB_NAME = "address_book_db";
private static final int DB_VERSION = 1;
private static final String TABLE_N_AND_A =
    "names_and_addresses";
}
```

Next, we add the constructor that will create an instance of our custom version of
SQLiteOpenHelper. We will actually implement this class as an inner class soon. The
constructor also initializes the db member, which is our SQLiteDatabase reference.

Add the following constructor that we just discussed to the DataManager class:

```
public DataManager(Context context) {
    // Create an instance of our internal
    //CustomSQLiteOpenHelper class
    CustomSQLiteOpenHelper helper =
        new CustomSQLiteOpenHelper(context);

    // Get a writable database
    db = helper.getWritableDatabase();
}
```

Now, we can add the helper methods that we will access from MainActivity. First,
the insert method that executes an INSERT SQL query based on the name and age
parameters that are passed into the method.

Add the insert method to the DataManager class:

```
// Here are all our helper methods
```

```
// Insert a record
public void insert(String name, String age){

    // Add all the details to the table
    String query = "INSERT INTO " + TABLE_N_AND_A + " (" +
        TABLE_ROW_NAME + ", " +
        TABLE_ROW_AGE + ") " +
        "VALUES (" +
        "'" + name + "'" + ", " +
        "'" + age + "'" +
        ");
        ";

    Log.i("insert() = ", query);

    db.execSQL(query);

}
```

This next method called `delete` will delete a record from the database if it has a matching value in the `name` column to that of the one passed in the `name` parameter. It achieves this using the SQL DELETE keyword.

Add the `delete` method to the `DataManager` class:

```
// Delete a record
public void delete(String name){

    // Delete the details from the table if already exists
    String query = "DELETE FROM " + TABLE_N_AND_A +
        " WHERE " + TABLE_ROW_NAME +
        " = '" + name + "';";

    Log.i("delete() = ", query);

    db.execSQL(query);

}
```

Next, we have the `selectAll` method that also does as its name suggests. It achieves this with a SELECT query using the * parameter, which is equivalent to specifying all the columns individually. Also note that the method returns `Cursor`, which we will use in the `MainActivity` class.

Add the `selectAll` method to the `DataManager` class:

```
// Get all the records
public Cursor selectAll() {
  Cursor c = db.rawQuery("SELECT *" +" from " +
      TABLE_N_AND_A, null);

  return c;
}
```

Now, we add a `searchName` method, which has a String parameter for the name the user wants to search for. It also returns `Cursor`, which will contain all the entries that were found. Note that the SQL statement uses SELECT, FROM, and WHERE to achieve this:

```
// Find a specific record
public Cursor searchName(String name) {
  String query = "SELECT " +
      TABLE_ROW_ID + ", " +
      TABLE_ROW_NAME +
      ", " + TABLE_ROW_AGE +
      " from " +
      TABLE_N_AND_A + " WHERE " +
      TABLE_ROW_NAME + " = '" + name + "';";

  Log.i("searchName() = ", query);

  Cursor c = db.rawQuery(query, null);


  return c;
}
```

Finally, for the `DataManager` class, we create an inner class that will be our implementation of `SQLiteOpenHelper`. It is a barebones implementation, and over the course of a few chapters, we will make a more advanced implementation that also handles the task of upgrading the database for our Where it's snap app.

We have a constructor that receives a `Context` object, the database name, and the database version. We will see how the database version is useful in *Chapter 26, Upgrading SQLite – Adding Locations and Maps*.

We also override the `onCreate` method, which has the SQL statement that creates our database table with the _ID, name, and age columns.

The `onUpgrade` method is left intentionally blank for this mini app.

Add the `inner` `CustomSQLiteOpenHelper` **class** to the `DataManager` **class:**

```
// This class is created when our DataManager is initialized
private class CustomSQLiteOpenHelper extends SQLiteOpenHelper {
  public CustomSQLiteOpenHelper(Context context) {
    super(context, DB_NAME, null, DB_VERSION);
  }

  // This method only runs the first time the database is created
  @Override
  public void onCreate(SQLiteDatabase db) {

    // Create a table for photos and all their details
    String newTableQueryString = "create table "
        + TABLE_N_AND_A + " ("
        + TABLE_ROW_ID
        + " integer primary key autoincrement not null,"
        + TABLE_ROW_NAME
        + " text not null,"
        + TABLE_ROW_AGE
        + " text not null);";


    db.execSQL(newTableQueryString);

  }

  // This method only runs when we increment DB_VERSION
  // We will look at this in chapter 26
  @Override
  public void onUpgrade(SQLiteDatabase db,
  int oldVersion, int newVersion) {

  }

}
```

Now, we can add code to use our new `DataManager` class.

Coding MainActivity

Make `MainActivity` implement `View.OnClickListener` so that it can listen for button clicks. Also, add the following members for each of the `EditText` and `Button` widgets. Note also that we declare an object of the `DataManager` type.

Amend the `MainActivity` class as we just discussed so that it matches the following code:

```
public class MainActivity extends AppCompatActivity
    implements View.OnClickListener{

    // For all our buttons and edit text
    Button btnInsert;
    Button btnDelete;
    Button btnSelect;
    Button btnSearch;

    EditText editName;
    EditText editAge;
    EditText editDelete;
    EditText editSearch;

    // This is our DataManager instance
    DataManager dm;

    @Override
    protected void onCreate(Bundle savedInstanceState) {
        super.onCreate(savedInstanceState);
        setContentView(R.layout.activity_main);
    }
    ...
    ...
```

Now, we add code to `onCreate` that initializes `DataManager` (`dm`) by calling its constructor, gets a reference to all the `EditText` and `Button` widgets in the layout, and sets a listener for each of the buttons.

Add the highlighted code to the `onCreate` method:

```
@Override
protected void onCreate(Bundle savedInstanceState) {
  super.onCreate(savedInstanceState);
  setContentView(R.layout.activity_main);

  dm = new DataManager(this);

  // get a reference to the UI item
  btnInsert = (Button) findViewById(R.id.btnInsert);
  btnDelete = (Button) findViewById(R.id.btnDelete);
  btnSelect = (Button) findViewById(R.id.btnSelect);
  btnSearch = (Button) findViewById(R.id.btnSearch);
```

```
    editName = (EditText) findViewById(R.id.editName);
    editAge = (EditText) findViewById(R.id.editAge);
    editDelete = (EditText) findViewById(R.id.editDelete);
    editSearch = (EditText) findViewById(R.id.editSearch);

    // Register MainActivity as a listener
    btnSelect.setOnClickListener(this);
    btnInsert.setOnClickListener(this);
    btnDelete.setOnClickListener(this);
    btnSearch.setOnClickListener(this);
}
```

Now, add a method that will print out the contents of our `Cursor` returned by some of our `DataManager` methods. The `moveToNext` method returns `true` or `false` depending upon whether there is another row of data in `Cursor`. So, wrapping it as the condition for a `while` statement will make sure that all the returned entries are read and output to the logcat.

Add the `showData` method to `MainActivity`:

```
// Output the cursor contents to the log
public void showData(Cursor c){

  while (c.moveToNext()){
    Log.i(c.getString(1), c.getString(2));
  }
}
```

Now, we can implement the overridden `onClick` method to handle all the buttons. Note how the `R.id.btnSearch` case of the `switch` statement calls the appropriate method of the `DataManager` class with the appropriate `EditText` contents by chaining the `getText` and `toString` methods directly within the `showData` method call. The effect of this is to pass the returned `Cursor` object to the `showData` method with only one line of code.

The `R.id.btnInsert` and `R.id.btnDelete` cases simply pass the contents of the appropriate `EditText` widgets to the `insert` and `delete` methods of the `DataManager` class respectively.

Add the `onClick` method to the `MainActivity` class:

```
@Override
public void onClick(View v){

  switch (v.getId()){
    case R.id.btnInsert:
      dm.insert(editName.getText().toString(),
```

```
        editAge.getText().toString());

      break;

    case R.id.btnSelect:
      showData(dm.selectAll());
      break;

    case R.id.btnSearch:
      showData(dm.searchName(editSearch.getText().toString()));
      break;

    case R.id.btnDelete:
      dm.delete(editDelete.getText().toString());
      break;

    }

  }
```

Let's take a look at the app in action.

Running the mini app

Add a few names and ages to the database by typing a name and an age followed by tapping **INSERT**, as shown in the following screenshot:

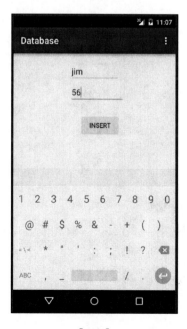

After you have added a few names, try tapping the **SELECT** button and then check the output in the logcat window:

```
I/bob:  42
I/jim:  56
I/Ed:  22
I/Divij:  23
I/Merwyn:  24
```

Click on **SEARCH**, passing in the name you are searching for. Note that just the rows matching the search term are returned:

Finally, type a name in EditText next to the **DELETE** button and then tap on the **DELETE** button:

Now, click on **SELECT** and we can see that "bob" is no longer part of the database:

```
I/delete() =:  DELETE FROM names_and_addresses WHERE name = 'bob';
I/jim:  56
I/Ed:  22
I/Divij:  23
I/Merwyn:  24
```

Let's review what we have done in this chapter.

Summary

We covered a lot in this chapter. You learned about databases and, in particular, the database of Android apps, SQLite. We practiced the basics of communicating with a database using the SQL language.

We saw how the Android API helps us use a SQLite database, and we implemented our first working app with a database.

In the next chapter, we will use a more advanced DataManager class, and we will also use it within the Where it's snap app to save all our user's titles, tags, and photos.

24
Adding a Database to Where It's Snap

In this chapter, we will be entirely focused on using all we know about fragments, interfaces, and SQLite in order to add significant functionality to Where it's Snap.

We will cover the following tasks:

- Building a new class to represent a photo
- Creating a `DataManager` class to handle our database, including a selection of helper methods to make the appropriate queries
- Enabling the saving of photos into the database from the `FragmentCapture` class
- Coding an interface to handle communications
- Coding `TagsFragment` to show a list of tags and sending a tag to `MainActivity` when one is clicked
- Coding `TitlesFragment` to show a list of titles either based upon a specific tag or the entirety of `wis_tables_photos`
- Coding the `MainActivity` class to handle the communications of the fragments via the interface

As usual, the files for all of the above are in the download bundle in the `Chapter 24/Where Its Snap 3` folder.

The Photo class

The first new thing we need is a class to hold the data structure of a photo.

We will need the class to have four string members for the title and three tags. This is quite straightforward. The photo itself, however, is worth further discussion. We have seen in *Chapter 22, Capturing Images*, that we actually capture a bitmap from the camera. It is possible to store images directly in a database, but we can probably be more efficient than this while at the same time keeping our code a lot simpler.

When the camera app in an Android device takes a photo, it saves it in internal storage already. If there was a way to refer to this image in storage, then we could just store the location in our database and then load up the image from the regular internal storage when we need it.

Such a location is known as a **URI**. In a somewhat simplified way, we can think of a URI as a file path or address (like a web address) that points to a page, image, or other resource type. There is even a `Uri` class in the Android API to make things easier for us.

 So, what exactly is a URI? **URI** stands for **Uniform Resource Identifier,** and it is used to identify a resource in a computer system or network. If you want to know the full details of how URIs work (and you have a fair bit of spare time), then take a look at this Wikipedia article: `https://en.wikipedia.org/wiki/Uniform_Resource_Identifier`.

In addition to our member variables, we will also need to add getter and setter methods so we can keep the members `private` and still offer access to them.

Create a new class, call it `Photo`, and add the following members and getter and setter methods that we have discussed:

```
import android.net.Uri;

public class Photo {

    private String mTitle;
    private Uri mStorageLocation;
    private String mTag1;
    private String mTag2;
    private String mTag3;


    public String getTitle() {
```

```
      return mTitle;
   }

   public void setTitle(String title) {
      this.mTitle = title;
   }

   public Uri getStorageLocation() {
      return mStorageLocation;
   }

   public void setStorageLocation(Uri storageLocation) {
      this.mStorageLocation = storageLocation;
   }


   public String getTag1() {
      return mTag1;
   }

   public void setTag1(String tag1) {
      this.mTag1 = tag1;
   }

   public String getTag2() {
      return mTag2;
   }

   public void setTag2(String tag2) {
      this.mTag2 = tag2;
   }

   public String getTag3() {
      return mTag3;
   }

   public void setTag3(String tag3) {
      this.mTag3 = tag3;
   }
}
```

Now, we can get started on our DataManager class.

Handling the SQLite database

Create a new class called `DataManager`. We need an `SQLiteDatabase` object and a whole bunch of `final` string members for the table and column names.

All the code that we will add first to our `DataManager` is straightforward, but it is worth pointing out that we will actually have two tables in this database. One called `wis_table_photos` will have a column for each of the member variables of our `Photo` class.

Another called `wis_table_tags` will have just two columns, `autoincrement _ID` and a `tag` column.

The `wis_table_photos` table will have a row of data for each and every photo the user takes. The `tags` column will only have a row for each new/unique tag that the user enters. So, if the user has more than one photo with the "Barbados" or "2016" tag, it will only appear once in the `wis_table_tags` table but will appear with each and every photo that uses it in the `wis_table_photos` table.

This way, it will be possible to show the user a list of all the unique tags they have added, and when they tap on a tag, it will present them with a list of all the photos that have been tagged with this tag.

It would probably help clarify the usage of all the strings in the code that follow to have a spreadsheet eye view to help visualize our two tables:

wis_table_photos

_id	image_title	image_uri	tag1	tag2	tag 3
1	Dave in the pool	/external/ima	2016	Barbados	Fun
2	Sarah on the beach	/external/ima	2015	Barbados	Pretty
3	My new car	/external/ima	2016	UK	Sad

In the previous image, you can see that the `wis_table_photos` table has all the data that the user might enter represented for each row. If you look at the next image, (`wis_table_tags`) however, you can see that each tag is only stored once. How we manage to insert data to achieve this and how we manage to select data will become clear as we proceed.

wis_table_tags

_id	tag
1	Barbados
2	2015
3	2016
4	Fun
5	Pretty
6	UK
7	Sad

Remember from the previous chapter that we declare the member `public` where it is useful to refer to them directly from another class. They are also `static` because we do not need new instances should we end up with more than one `DatabaseManager` instance.

You might be wondering where the MVC pattern and our separate data layer that can only be instantiated once corresponds to this `DataManager` class. It works because all our strings are `static` and are therefore the same instance across multiple instances of `DataManager`. When we call `getWriteableDatabase`, the OS will always return the same database, so it is not possible that we will ever end up with multiple out-of-sync databases, and the same database is automatically accessible from any activity of our app.

Add the member variables we have just discussed that we will use to build our database queries:

```
public class DataManager {

  // This is the actual database
  private SQLiteDatabase db;

  /*
    Next we have a public static final string for
    each row/table that we need to refer to both
    inside and outside this class
  */

  public static final String TABLE_ROW_ID = "_id";
  public static final String TABLE_ROW_TITLE = "image_title";
  public static final String TABLE_ROW_URI = "image_uri";
```

```
/*
  Next we have a private static final strings for
  each row/table that we need to refer to just
  inside this class
*/

private static final String DB_NAME = "wis_db";
private static final int DB_VERSION = 1;
private static final String TABLE_PHOTOS = "wis_table_photos";
private static final String TABLE_TAGS = "wis_table_tags";
private static final String TABLE_ROW_TAG1 = "tag1";
private static final String TABLE_ROW_TAG2 = "tag2";
private static final String TABLE_ROW_TAG3 = "tag3";
public static final String TABLE_ROW_TAG =
  "tag";// For the tags table

}
```

Now, let's add the constructor for our `DataManager`. It simply instantiates a `CustomSQLiteHelper` that we will code soon and then uses it to initialize `db`, just as we saw in the previous chapter.

Add the constructor to the `DataManager` class:

```
public DataManager(Context context) {
  // Create an instance of our internal
  //CustomSQLiteOpenHelper class
  CustomSQLiteOpenHelper helper =
    new CustomSQLiteOpenHelper(context);

  // Get a writable database
  db = helper.getWritableDatabase();
}
```

We will now be introduced to our first helper method called `addPhoto`. It takes a `Photo` object parameter and then adds all the values as a new row using the getter methods of the `Photo` class, among an `INSERT` query into the `wis_table_photos` table.

This next code is only the first part of the `addPhoto` method. We will look at the second part next.

Add the `addPhoto` method to the `DataManager` class:

```
// Here are all our helper methods
public void addPhoto(Photo photo){
```

```
// Add all the details to the photos table
String query = "INSERT INTO " + TABLE_PHOTOS + " (" +
    TABLE_ROW_TITLE + ", " +
    TABLE_ROW_URI + ", " +
    TABLE_ROW_TAG1 + ", " +
    TABLE_ROW_TAG2 + ", " +
    TABLE_ROW_TAG3 +
") " +
"VALUES (" +
    "'" + photo.getTitle() + "'" + ", " +
    "'" + photo.getStorageLocation() + "'" + ", " +
    "'" + photo.getTag1() + "'" + ", " +
    "'" + photo.getTag2() + "'" + ", " +
    "'" + photo.getTag3() + "'" +
");";

Log.i("addPhoto()", query);

db.execSQL(query);
```

Next, still in `addPhoto`, we execute three queries, one for each tag, and `INSERT` them into the `wis_table_tags` table, but notice the highlighted `WHERE NOT EXISTS` clause in the SQL that we build. This ensures that we only add a tag if it has not been added already.

Complete the `addPhoto` method by adding this code:

```
// Add any NEW tags to the tags table

query = "INSERT INTO " + TABLE_TAGS + "(" +
    TABLE_ROW_TAG + ") " +
    "SELECT '" + photo.getTag1() + "' " +
    "WHERE NOT EXISTS ( SELECT 1 FROM " +
    TABLE_TAGS +
    " WHERE " + TABLE_ROW_TAG + " = " +
    "'" + photo.getTag1() + "');";

db.execSQL(query);

query = "INSERT INTO " + TABLE_TAGS + "(" +
    TABLE_ROW_TAG + ") " +
    "SELECT '" + photo.getTag2() + "' " +
    "WHERE NOT EXISTS ( SELECT 1 FROM " +
    TABLE_TAGS +
    " WHERE " + TABLE_ROW_TAG + " = " +
```

```
          "'" + photo.getTag2() + "');";

   db.execSQL(query);

   query = "INSERT INTO " + TABLE_TAGS + "(" +
      TABLE_ROW_TAG + ") " +
      "SELECT '" + photo.getTag3() + "' " +
      "WHERE NOT EXISTS ( SELECT 1 FROM " +
      TABLE_TAGS +
      " WHERE " + TABLE_ROW_TAG + " = " +
      "'" + photo.getTag3() + "');";

   db.execSQL(query);

}// End addPhoto
```

Now, we have a really simple query to get all the titles from the `wis_table_photos` table. Note that we return `Cursor`, which contains the data from the query.

Add the `getTitles` method to the `DataManager` class:

```
public Cursor getTitles() {
   Cursor c = db.rawQuery("SELECT " + TABLE_ROW_ID + ",
      " + TABLE_ROW_TITLE + " from " + TABLE_PHOTOS, null);
   c.moveToFirst();

   return c;
}
```

Now we begin to see how we will selectively filter the titles we display to the user. The `getTitlesWithTag` method returns `Cursor` with photo titles but only if they contain a specific tag that was passed in to the method.

Add the `getTitlesWithTag` method to the `DataManager` class:

```
public Cursor getTitlesWithTag(String tag) {
   Cursor c = db.rawQuery("SELECT " + TABLE_ROW_ID + ", " +
      TABLE_ROW_TITLE + " from " +
      TABLE_PHOTOS + " WHERE " +
      TABLE_ROW_TAG1 + " = '" + tag + "' or " +
      TABLE_ROW_TAG2 + " = '" + tag + "' or " +
      TABLE_ROW_TAG3 + " = '" + tag + "';"
      , null);

   c.moveToFirst();

   return c;
}
```

This method returns all the columns of a photo with a specific `_id` value.

Add the `getPhoto` method to the `DataManager` class:

```
public Cursor getPhoto(int id) {

  Cursor c = db.rawQuery("SELECT * from " +
    TABLE_PHOTOS +
    " WHERE " +
    TABLE_ROW_ID + " = " + id, null);

  c.moveToFirst();

  return c;
}
```

The next method returns all the tags, which is just what we will need for our `TagsFragment` class.

Add the `getTags` method to the `DataManager` class:

```
public Cursor getTags(){
  Cursor c = db.rawQuery("SELECT " + TABLE_ROW_ID + ",
    " + TABLE_ROW_TAG + " from " + TABLE_TAGS, null);
  c.moveToFirst();

  return c;
}
```

Finally, we get to our inner class, `CustomSQLiteOpenHelper`, which extends `SQLiteOpenHelper`. As in the last chapter, we have the same simple constructor, but the `onCreate` method builds and executes two queries to create both of our required tables.

The `onUpgrade` method will be left blank until *Chapter 26, Upgrading SQLite – Adding Locations and Maps*.

Add the `CustomSQLiteOpenHelper` class as an inner class of `DataManager`:

```
// This class is created when our DataManager is initialized
private class CustomSQLiteOpenHelper extends SQLiteOpenHelper {
  public CustomSQLiteOpenHelper(Context context) {
    super(context, DB_NAME, null, DB_VERSION);
  }

  // This method only runs the first time the database is created
  @Override
```

```
    public void onCreate(SQLiteDatabase db) {

        // Create a table for photos and all their details
        String newTableQueryString = "create table "
                + TABLE_PHOTOS + " ("
                + TABLE_ROW_ID
                + " integer primary key autoincrement not null,"
                + TABLE_ROW_TITLE
                + " text not null,"
                + TABLE_ROW_URI
                + " text not null,"
                + TABLE_ROW_TAG1
                + " text not null,"
                + TABLE_ROW_TAG2
                + " text not null,"
                + TABLE_ROW_TAG3
                + " text not null" + ");";

        db.execSQL(newTableQueryString);

        // Create a separate table for tags
        newTableQueryString = "create table "
                + TABLE_TAGS + " ("
                + TABLE_ROW_ID
                + " integer primary key autoincrement not null,"
                + TABLE_ROW_TAG
                + " text not null" + ");";

        db.execSQL(newTableQueryString);
    }
    // This method only runs when we increment DB_VERSION
    @Override
    public void onUpgrade(SQLiteDatabase db,
        int oldVersion, int newVersion) {
    }
}
```

Now that we have implemented our DataManager class and all its helper methods, we can put them to use and enhance the features of Where it's Snap.

Saving a new photo from the capture fragment

Open up the `CaptureFragment.java` file in the editor.

We need to add a new member variable for the `CaptureFragment` class to hold our new `DataManager` class instance.

Add the new highlighted member variable to `CaptureFragment`, which we have just discussed:

```java
public class CaptureFragment extends Fragment{

    private static final int CAMERA_REQUEST = 123;
    private ImageView mImageView;

    // Where the captured image is stored
    private Uri mImageUri = Uri.EMPTY;

    // Where to save the image
    String mCurrentPhotoPath;

    // A reference to our database
    private DataManager mDataManager;

    @Override
    public void onCreate(Bundle savedInstanceState){
        super.onCreate(savedInstanceState);

    }
```

Now, we can initialize the `DataManager` instance by adding this highlighted line of code to the `onCreate` method in `CaptureFragment`:

```java
@Override
public void onCreate(Bundle savedInstanceState) {
    super.onCreate(savedInstanceState);

    mDataManager =
        new DataManager(getActivity()
        .getApplicationContext());
}
```

Since our `DataManager` is coded and ready for use and we have an initialized instance of it, we can go ahead and implement the **SAVE** button. We already have a reference to all of the relevant **EditText** widgets as well as the **Button** widget via `btnSave`.

We can finish the job of saving our data in `onCreateView` by implementing an anonymous class to handle the button click. Inside the `onClick` method, we step through the following tasks:

- First, check that `mImageUri` has been initialized with `if(mImageUri != null)`.

- Next, check that the `mImageUri` member is not empty with `if (!mImageUri.equals(Uri.EMPTY))`.

- Assuming we have a photo to save, we enter the `if` block and declare a new `Photo` object.

- Store the user's title by calling `setTitle` and passing in the contents of the `mEditTextTitle` **EditText** widget.

- Store the URI by calling `setStorageLocation` and passing in `mImageUri`.

- Capture the user's values for each of the tags in three strings, and then use the appropriate setters of the `Photo` class to store them in the `Photo` object.

- The last thing we do inside the `if` block is to use our `DataManager` instance to call `addPhoto`, and of course, we pass in our just-constructed `Photo` object. The `DataManager` class will add all the data into the required tables.

- At the end of the `if` block, we have an `else` block that delivers a pop-up message to the user if he or she tries to save a photo that doesn't exist or if it is successful.

Add the highlighted code in `onCreateView`, which we have just discussed, right after the code that handles the **CAPTURE** button:

```
// Listen for clicks on the capture button
btnCapture.setOnClickListener(new View.OnClickListener() {
  . . .
  . . .
});// End capture button handling

// Listen for clicks on the save button
btnSave.setOnClickListener(new View.OnClickListener() {

  @Override
  public void onClick(View v) {
    if(mImageUri != null){
      if(!mImageUri.equals(Uri.EMPTY)) {
        // We have a photo to save
```

```
                    Photo photo = new Photo();
                    photo.setTitle(mEditTextTitle.getText().toString());
                    photo.setStorageLocation(mImageUri);

                    // What is in the tags
                    String tag1 = mEditTextTag1.getText().toString();
                    String tag2 = mEditTextTag2.getText().toString();
                    String tag3 = mEditTextTag3.getText().toString();

                    // Assign the strings to the Photo object
                    photo.setTag1(tag1);
                    photo.setTag2(tag2);
                    photo.setTag3(tag3);

                    // Send the new object to our DataManager
                    mDataManager.addPhoto(photo);
                    Toast.makeText(getActivity(), "Saved", Toast.LENGTH_LONG).
                        show();
                }else {
                    // No image
                    Toast.makeText(getActivity(), "No image to save", Toast.
                        LENGTH_LONG).show();
                }
            }else {
                // Uri not initialized
                Log.e("Error ", "uri is null");
            }


        }
    });

    return view;
}// End onCreateView
```

We could run the app at this point and actually begin to save photos to our database. The problem, of course, is that we don't yet have any way to see the list of available tags, photo titles, or any of the photos themselves.

Before TitlesFragment can respond to clicks and show a photo, we need a fragment to show those photos. So, let's code a fragment to view photos.

Displaying a photo from the database

Let's start by building a simple layout that our soon-to-be-built fragment can use.

Preparing the View layout

Create a new layout by right-clicking on the `layout` folder and choosing **New |
Resource layout file**, naming it `fragment_view`, and left-clicking **OK**.

This image is what we are aiming for, but there is also an unseen `ImageView`
covering the entire layout:

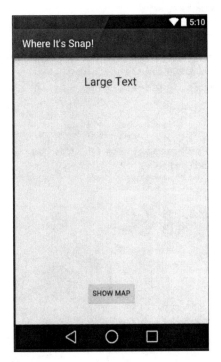

To achieve this layout, add the following XML code to the `fragment_view.xml` file. I
have highlighted a few points worth noting that we will discuss:

```xml
<?xml version="1.0" encoding="utf-8"?>
<RelativeLayout xmlns:android=
  "http://schemas.android.com/apk/res/android"
  android:orientation="vertical"
    android:layout_width="match_parent"
  android:layout_height="match_parent">

  <ImageView
```

```
    android:layout_width="match_parent"
    android:layout_height="match_parent"
    android:id="@+id/imageView"
    android:layout_gravity="center_horizontal" />

<Button
    android:layout_width="wrap_content"
    android:layout_height="wrap_content"
    android:text="@string/show_map"
    android:id="@+id/buttonShowLocation"
    android:layout_alignParentBottom="true"
    android:layout_centerHorizontal="true"
    android:layout_marginBottom="35dp" />

<TextView
    android:layout_width="wrap_content"
    android:layout_height="wrap_content"
    android:textAppearance="?android:attr/textAppearanceLarge"
    android:text="Large Text"
    android:id="@+id/textView"
    android:layout_alignParentTop="true"
    android:layout_centerHorizontal="true"
    android:layout_marginTop="33dp" />

</RelativeLayout>
```

Notice that the **ImageView** widget's `layout_width` and `layout_height` properties are set to `match_parent` to fill the screen.

Notice there is a button (`buttonShowLocation`) that uses a string resource to set its text. This button is ready for *Chapter 26, Upgrading SQLite – Adding Locations and Maps*, after we have learned to handle GPS locations and upgrade a database.

Also notice the `id` properties of the three widgets in order to better follow what happens when we code our new `Fragment` class.

Coding the ViewFragment class

Create a new class called `ViewFragment`. Now, we need to add some members and have our new class extend the `Fragment` class. We have a `Cursor` member ready to use the data that we will grab from the database. We also have an `ImageView` member, which, unsurprisingly, will be used to get a reference to the **ImageView** widget in our layout.

Amend the `ViewFragment` class to match the next code as we have just discussed:

```
public class ViewFragment extends Fragment {

  private Cursor mCursor;
  private ImageView mImageView;
}
```

Now, we continue by adding the overridden `onCreate` method. First, we declare and initialize a new `int` variable called `position` from the `Bundle` passed into `onCreate`. From the `getInt` method, we can see that we are getting some data that was loaded as a key-value pair with a key of `Position`. Of course, we haven't written any code to actually send this data yet, but we will later in the chapter.

Next, we declare and instantiate a `DataManager` object so we can talk to the database, and then we initialize our `Cursor` member by calling the `DataManager` method `getPhoto` and passing in the `position` variable, whose value we extracted from `Bundle` a moment ago.

So now that we have `Cursor` with `Photo` in it, we can see how to display it, and then we can see how we pass in the position.

Code the `onCreate` method in the `ViewFragment` class as we have just discussed:

```
@Override
public void onCreate(Bundle savedInstanceState) {
  super.onCreate(savedInstanceState);

  // Where is the photo object we want to show?
  int position = getArguments().getInt("Position");

  // Load the appropriate photo from db
  DataManager d = new DataManager
    (getActivity().getApplicationContext());
  mCursor = d.getPhoto(position);

}
```

As usual, when we want to initialize the view of a regular `Fragment`, we do so in the `onCreateView` method. Here is how the next block of code works.

We inflate the view as we have done several times before. Then, we get a reference to our **TextView**, **Button**, and **ImageView** widgets. We will not, however, be doing anything with **Button** just yet.

Then, we see how we access the data in Cursor to set **TextView** with the title of the photo and **ImageView** with the image.

Notice that we can identify the correct column in the returned data (in Cursor) by using the public static strings from our DataManager class. The DataManager.TABLE_ROW_TITLE string is the column name for the photo's title, and the DataManager.TABLE_ROW_URI string is, of course, the column name that holds the URI.

We can also see that Cursor has some useful methods that allow us to use the names of the columns to extract the data. They are getString and getColumnIndex.

Add the onCreateView method we have just been talking about into the ViewFragment class:

```
public View onCreateView(LayoutInflater inflater,
  ViewGroup container, Bundle savedInstanceState) {

  View view = inflater.inflate(R.layout.fragment_view,
    container, false);
  TextView textView  = (TextView)
    view.findViewById(R.id.textView);
  Button buttonShowLocation = (Button)
    view.findViewById(R.id.buttonShowLocation);

  // Set the text from the tile column of the data.
  textView.setText(mCursor.getString
    (mCursor.getColumnIndex(DataManager.TABLE_ROW_TITLE)));

  mImageView = (ImageView) view.findViewById(R.id.imageView);

  // Load the image into the TextView via the URI
  mImageView.setImageURI(Uri.parse(mCursor.getString
    (mCursor.getColumnIndex(DataManager.TABLE_ROW_URI))));


  return view;
}
```

Finally, for the ViewFragment class, we need to override the onDestroy method. We do so to make sure that as the user views multiple images (which could be quite large with high-quality cameras on devices these days), we call recycle on the image we loaded with Uri and set the source of ImageView to null. This has the effect of freeing up RAM memory and prevents the device from eventually running out and crashing.

Actually, the device probably won't run out of memory, but the amount of memory the OS is prepared to allocate for our app probably will.

Add the `onDestroy` method we have just discussed to the `ViewFragment` class:

```
public void onDestroy(){
    super.onDestroy();

    // Make sure we don't run out of memory
    BitmapDrawable bd = (BitmapDrawable) mImageView.getDrawable();
    bd.getBitmap().recycle();
    mImageView.setImageBitmap(null);
}
```

Now, the app has somewhere to show the photo connected to any titles that are clicked on by the user. It will also need a way of communicating with our new `ViewFragment` before it can do so. So, let's create an interface to do just that.

Coding the communications interface

We know that `TitlesFragment` needs a way to communicate with `ViewFragment`, but also `TagsFragment` needs a way of telling `TitlesFragment` which tag it would like to use for the criteria to search for database entries with the matching tag.

This same interface will handle all this work. `MainActivity` can then implement the interface and handle the inter-fragment communication.

Create a new class called `ActivityComs` and code it into our interface by editing it to exactly the code shown next:

```
public interface ActivityComs {

    void onTitlesListItemSelected(int pos);

    void onTagsListItemSelected(String tag);
}
```

We now have two methods we can use for communicating between our `Fragment` classes and `MainActivity`. One (`onTitlesListItemSelected`) will pass in an `int` to represent the `_id` of the row in our database of the required `Photo` object. The other (`onTagsListItemSelected`) will pass a string that is the tag to be searched for and matched against rows in the `wis_table_photos` table.

We will handle this in three stages:

1. First, we will add the required code to `TitlesFragment`.
2. Next, we will add the code to `TagsFragment`.
3. Finally, we will tie the whole thing together and implement the interface in `MainActivity`.

As we will be dipping in and out of existing methods as well as writing new ones, if you get disoriented in any way, simply open up the relevant files in the `Chapter 24/Where Its Snap 3` folder where you can see all the code we add in this chapter complete in the appropriate places.

Coding TitlesFragment

We are really close to being able to actually show a photo in our Photos app. We need to load a list of photo titles from our database into `ListView`, provided by `ListFragment`, and handle what happens when the user clicks on a list item.

Some of the code in here won't make complete sense until we finish coding `MainActivity`, which will, of course, handle the communication between `TitlesFragment` and `ViewFragment`, as well as `TagsFragment` and `TitlesFragment`.

Let's add two new members to `TitlesFragment` — a `Cursor` member to load some data into and an instance of our new interface.

Add the two highlighted member variables where shown:

```
public class TitlesFragment extends ListFragment {

    private Cursor mCursor;
    private ActivityComs mActivityComs;


    @Override
    public void onCreate(Bundle savedInstanceState) {
        super.onCreate(savedInstanceState);
    }
```

Next, in the `onCreate` method, we do the following:

- Get a string to represent the tag from `Bundle`, using `getArguments`. `getString` to search for in the database.
- Get an instance of `DataManager`.

- If `TitlesFragment` receives a tag to search for, it will only show the photo titles with that matching tag, but if it receives no tag, it will show all the titles. With this in mind, the `if` block either loads the `Cursor` object up with data using `getTitles` or `getTitlesWithTag`.

- Next, we create an instance of `SimpleCursorAdapter`. A cursor adapter is just like an array adapter, except it uses a `Cursor` object. `SimpleCursorAdapter` is perfect for displaying straightforward data in a `ListView` from `Cursor`. The slightly intimidating list of arguments its constructor takes is not as bad as it looks. The important arguments are a layout for each list item for **ListView**. `list_item_1` is provided by default; we don't need to create it. Next is `Cursor` containing the data, following that is the way to identify the data within the cursor, and we pass the column name from the table.

- Then, we call `setListAdapter` to set our new `SimpleCursorAdapter` as the adapter for `ListView`.

> To learn more about `SimpleCursorAdapter`, check out the Android developer site: `http://developer.android.com/reference/android/widget/SimpleCursorAdapter.html`.

Add the following highlighted code to `onCreate` that we have just discussed:

```
@Override
public void onCreate(Bundle savedInstanceState) {
  super.onCreate(savedInstanceState);

  // Get the tag to search for
  String tag = getArguments().getString("Tag");

  // Get an instance of DataManager
  DataManager d = new DataManager
    (getActivity().getApplicationContext());


  if(tag == "_NO_TAG"){
    // Get all the titles from the database
    mCursor = d.getTitles();
  }else{
    // Get all the titles with a specific related tag
    mCursor = d.getTitlesWithTag(tag);
  }
```

```
// Create a new adapter
SimpleCursorAdapter cursorAdapter =
  new SimpleCursorAdapter(getActivity(),
android.R.layout.simple_list_item_1, mCursor,
new String[] { DataManager.TABLE_ROW_TITLE },
new int[] { android.R.id.text1 }, 0 );

// Attach the adapter to the ListView
setListAdapter(cursorAdapter);
}
```

Now, we can handle what happens when the user taps on a title in `ListView`. We implement the `onListItemClick` method, and all we need is the `position` parameter of this method in order to do our work.

We use the `moveToPosition` method on our `Cursor` and pass in `position` to set the cursor to the right place for the next line of code.

We then declare and initialize an `int` variable called `dBID` with the value of the `_id` column from the database with this line of code:

```
int dBID = mCursor.getInt(
  mCursor.getColumnIndex(
  DataManager.TABLE_ROW_ID));
```

Finally, we can call the `onTitlesListItemSelected` method of our interface to pass the appropriate `_id` value to `MainActivity`.

Add the `onListItemClick` method we have just discussed to `TitlesFragment`:

```
public void onListItemClick(ListView l, View v,
  int position, long id) {

  // Move the cursor to the clicked item in the list
  mCursor.moveToPosition(position);

  // What is the database _id of this item?
  int dBID = mCursor.getInt(
    mCursor.getColumnIndex(
    DataManager.TABLE_ROW_ID));

  // Use the interface to send the clicked _id
  mActivityComs.onTitlesListItemSelected(dBID);
}
```

Of course, we haven't initialized our `mActivityComs` member yet, and we do so the same way we did in *Chapter 19, Using Multiple Fragments,* and set it to `null` the same way also.

Add the final two methods to achieve this at the appropriate times:

```
@Override
public void onAttach(Activity activity) {
  super.onAttach(activity);
  mActivityComs = (ActivityComs)activity;
}

@Override
public void onDetach() {
  super.onDetach();
  mActivityComs = null;
}
```

We can now code `TagsFragment` to communicate with `TitlesFragment` via `MainActivity`.

Coding TagsFragment

All the `TagsFragment` class needs to do is display a list of tags from the appropriate table and when the user clicks one, let `MainActivity` know via the `ActivityComs` interface.

Add the `ActivityComs` interface as a new member variable as highlighted in the following code:

```
public class TagsFragment extends ListFragment {

  private ActivityComs mActivityComs;

  @Override
  public void onCreate(Bundle savedInstanceState) {
    super.onCreate(savedInstanceState);

  private ActivityComs mActivityComs;

  @Override
  public void onCreate(Bundle savedInstanceState) {
    super.onCreate(savedInstanceState);
  }
}
```

As we have seen upon just coding `TitlesFragment`, the next code allows us to:

- Get access to the database
- Get the list of tags from `wis_table_tags`
- Set up `SimpleCursorAdapter` and bind it to `ListView`

Add the highlighted code we have just discussed to the `onCreate` method:

```
@Override
public void onCreate(Bundle savedInstanceState) {
  super.onCreate(savedInstanceState);

  DataManager d = new DataManager
    (getActivity().getApplicationContext());
  Cursor c = d.getTags();

  // Create a new adapter
  SimpleCursorAdapter cursorAdapter =
    new SimpleCursorAdapter(getActivity(),
  android.R.layout.simple_list_item_1, c,
  new String[] { DataManager.TABLE_ROW_TAG },
  new int[] { android.R.id.text1 }, 0);

  // Attach the Cursor to the adapter
  setListAdapter(cursorAdapter);
}
```

Now, to handle the touches. This code does the following:

- Retrieves a `Cursor` object from `SimpleCursorAdapter` by chaining `getAdapter` and `getCursor` and then casting the result as a `SimpleCursorAdapter`
- Creates a string based on the tag that was just clicked
- Passes the string to `MainActivity` using the `onTagsListItemSelected` method of the interface

Add the `onListItemClick` method that we have discussed:

```
public void onListItemClick(ListView l, View v,
  int position, long id) {

  // What tag has just been clicked?
  Cursor c = ((SimpleCursorAdapter)l.getAdapter()).getCursor();
  c.moveToPosition(position);
```

```
    String clickedTag = c.getString(1);
    // 1 is the position of the string
    Log.e("clickedTag = ", " " + clickedTag);

    mActivityComs.onTagsListItemSelected(clickedTag);
}
```

Now, we need to handle the creation and destruction of our `ActivityComs` instance with the usual two methods, as shown next:

```
@Override
public void onAttach(Activity activity) {
    super.onAttach(activity);
    mActivityComs = (ActivityComs)activity;
}

@Override
public void onDetach() {
    super.onDetach();
    mActivityComs = null;
}
```

We are nearly there. Let's write some code in `MainActivity`.

Coding the fragment communications in MainActivity

We just need to implement the `ActivityComs` interface and add an instance of our `DataManager` class. Then, we'll handle the two methods of the interface, and we are good to go.

Implement the interface and add an instance of `DataManager` as shown highlighted in the next code:

```
public class MainActivity extends
  ActionBarActivity implements ActivityComs{

    private ListView mNavDrawerList;
    private DrawerLayout mDrawerLayout;
    private ArrayAdapter<String> mAdapter;
    private ActionBarDrawerToggle mDrawerToggle;
    private String mActivityTitle;

    public DataManager dataManager;
```

Initialize the `DataManager` instance by adding the highlighted line of code
in `onCreate`:

```
@Override
protected void onCreate(Bundle savedInstanceState) {
    super.onCreate(savedInstanceState);
    setContentView(R.layout.activity_main);

    dataManager = new DataManager(getApplicationContext());

    // We will come back here in a minute!
    mNavDrawerList = (ListView)findViewById(R.id.navList);
    mDrawerLayout = (DrawerLayout)findViewById(R.id.drawerLayout);
    mActivityTitle = getTitle().toString();
    ...
```

Now, we will code the `onTagsListItemSelected` method. Here, we put the passed
in string that represents a tag into `Bundle` and pass it in to the new instance of
`TitlesFragment`. We have seen already how `TitlesFragment` deals with this string.

Implement the required `onTagsListItemSelected` method of the interface
as discussed:

```
public void onTagsListItemSelected(String clickedTag){
    // We have just received a String for the TitlesFragment

    // Prepare a new Bundle
    Bundle args = new Bundle();

    // Pack the string into the Bundle
    args.putString("Tag", clickedTag);

    Create a new instance of TitlesFragment
    TitlesFragment fragment = new TitlesFragment();

    // Load the Bundle into the Fragment
    fragment.setArguments(args);

    // Start the fragment
    FragmentManager fragmentManager = getFragmentManager();
    fragmentManager.beginTransaction().replace
        (R.id.fragmentHolder, fragment, "TAGS").commit();

    // update selected item and title, then close the drawer
    mNavDrawerList.setItemChecked(1, true);
```

```
        mNavDrawerList.setSelection(1);
        mDrawerLayout.closeDrawer(mNavDrawerList);


    }
```

In the `onTitlesListItemSelected` method, we have received `int`, which represents the `_id` of a row in the `wis_table_photos` table that needs to be shown to the user in the `ViewFragment`.

The code adds `int` to `Bundle` and then adds `Bundle` to `Fragment` before starting `Fragment`.

Implement the `onTitlesListItemSelected` method of the interface:

```
// Open ViewFragment with the photo indicated by position
public void onTitlesListItemSelected(int position) {

    // Load up the bundle with the row _id
    Bundle args = new Bundle();
    args.putInt("Position", position);

    // Create the fragment and add the bundle
    ViewFragment fragment = new ViewFragment();
    fragment.setArguments(args);

    // Start the fragment
    if (fragment != null) {
        FragmentManager fragmentManager = getFragmentManager();
        fragmentManager.beginTransaction().
            replace(R.id.fragmentHolder, fragment, "VIEW").commit();

        // update selected item and title, then close the drawer
        mNavDrawerList.setItemChecked(1, true);
        mNavDrawerList.setSelection(1);
        //setTitle(navMenuTitles[position]);
        mDrawerLayout.closeDrawer(mNavDrawerList);
    } else {
        // error in creating fragment
        Log.e("MainActivity", "Error in creating fragment");
    }


}
```

That was a code-heavy chapter, but now we have the pleasure of seeing our app in action.

Running the app so far

Add a selection of photos, tags, and titles to the database, and run your app. You will see the following:

On the **Tags** screen, click on a tag to see a list of photo titles that contain that tag:

Click on a title to see the photo in `ViewFragment`:

Summary

That is probably the most code-intensive chapter so far. It is possible that every detail of how this works isn't totally clear. The way to make things more clear is to build the project piece by piece. It might also help to refer back to *Chapter 19, Using Multiple Fragments*, for a refresher on interfaces.

If there are a few cloudy parts to your knowledge, this doesn't have to stop you from moving on because the rest of the book will still provide lots more Android API goodness that is not dependent on having mastered this chapter.

Next, we will look at how to integrate GPS locations and Google Maps into our apps.

25
Integrating Google Maps and GPS Locations

In this chapter, we are going global and even briefly into space. We will see how the Android API works with the **GNSS (Global Navigation Satellite System)** to provide location data. We can then use this data to plot a position on Google Maps.

In this chapter, we will:

- Learn the very basics of GPS
- Build a GPS mini app
- Learn about Google Maps
- Connect with the Google Maps server to get map data

Let's start with a quick overview of GPS.

Global Positioning System

GPS is one of those technologies that never fails to amaze you when you sit and think about how it works. When you also consider that a phone you can put in your pocket is capable of using it too, it is even more mind-numbingly extraordinary.

 Warning: If you were born after 1990, you might not understand the previous paragraph and probably think that GPS is quite dull.

The system works with 27 satellites in space known as the GNSS. Out of these, 24 of the satellites are active and three are a backup. Each satellite orbits the Earth every 12 hours constantly broadcasting the changing position data.

By performing calculations on data from at least three of these satellites, our device can provide us with a location in the world in longitude and latitude. Oversimplifying a little (ok, oversimplifying quite a lot), these are the degrees from the poles and equator. They are extremely precise values, as we will see, and therefore accurate potentially to five meters.

As we already know from *Chapter 1*, *The First App*, all the complexity is hidden from us by the Android API, and we can now build a super-simple app to see GPS in action.

Where in the world – the GPS mini app

Create a new project and call it `Where in the world`.

To handle Marshmallow runtime permissions, as discussed in *Chapter 11*, *Widget Mania* in the *Android permissions and Marshmallows* section, we need to set the target API to 22.

To do this, select **Android** from the drop-down list at the top of the project explorer. Now, double-click on the **build.gradle (module: app)** option from near the bottom of the project explorer window.

Make sure to change the highlighted line of code too so that `targetSdkVersion` is set to `22`, as shown in this code snippet:

```
defaultConfig {
    applicationId "com.gamecodeschool.whereitssnap3"
    minSdkVersion 15
    targetSdkVersion 22
    versionCode 1
    versionName "1.0"
}
```

Now, we can add the required permissions to the `AndroidManifest.xml` file.

Open the file and add the three permissions as highlighted in the next code:

```xml
<?xml version="1.0" encoding="utf-8"?>
<manifest xmlns:android=
  "http://schemas.android.com/apk/res/android"
  package="com.gamecodeschool.whereintheworld" >
  <uses-permission android:name=
    "android.permission.ACCESS_FINE_LOCATION" />
  <uses-permission android:name=
    "android.permission.ACCESS_COARSE_LOCATION" />
  <uses-permission android:name="android.permission.INTERNET" />
  <application
    android:allowBackup="true"
    android:icon="@mipmap/ic_launcher"
    android:label="@string/app_name"
    android:theme="@style/AppTheme" >
    <activity
      android:name=".MainActivity"
      android:label="@string/app_name" >
      <intent-filter>
        <action android:name="android.intent.action.MAIN" />

        <category android:name=
          "android.intent.category.LAUNCHER" />
      </intent-filter>
    </activity>
  </application>

</manifest>
```

Now, we can get on with the app for real.

Where in the world – implementing a simple layout

To create the layout, copy and paste the following XML code into `layout_main.xml`:

```xml
<LinearLayout xmlns:android=
  "http://schemas.android.com/apk/res/android"
  android:layout_width="match_parent"
  android:layout_height="match_parent"
  android:orientation="vertical" >

  <TextView
    android:id="@+id/txtLat"
    android:layout_width="wrap_content"
    android:layout_height="wrap_content"
```

```
      android:text="Lat ?"
      android:textSize="40dip"
      android:layout_gravity="center_horizontal"
      android:layout_marginTop="20dp">
  </TextView>

  <TextView
      android:id="@+id/txtLong"
      android:layout_width="wrap_content"
      android:layout_height="wrap_content"
      android:text="Long ?"
      android:textSize="40dip"
      android:layout_gravity="center_horizontal"
      android:layout_marginTop="100dp">
  </TextView>

  <TextView
      android:id="@+id/txtSource"
      android:layout_width="wrap_content"
      android:layout_height="wrap_content"
      android:text="Source ?"
      android:textSize="40dip"
      android:layout_gravity="center_horizontal"
      android:layout_marginTop="100dp">
  </TextView>

</LinearLayout>
```

As you can see, the layout is just three **TextView** widgets with their id properties set to txtLat, txtLong, txtSource respectively from top to bottom. The result is shown in the next screenshot:

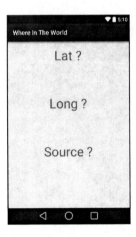

Now, let's add some Java to MainActivity.java.

Coding the Where in the world mini app

Most of the functionality we require is provided by the `LocationListener` interface and its methods. Make `MainActivity` implement `LocationListener` and add the member variables for our UI, a String, and a new class, `LocationManager`, as highlighted in this code:

```
public class MainActivity extends
   Activity implements LocationListener {

   private TextView txtLat;
   private TextView txtLong;
   private TextView txtSource;
   private LocationManager locationManager;
   private String provider;

   @Override
   public void onCreate(Bundle savedInstanceState) {
     super.onCreate(savedInstanceState);
     setContentView(R.layout.activity_main);

   }
...
```

Now, in `onCreate`, we can perform the following tasks:

- Get a reference to all the `TextView` widgets in the UI
- Initialize `LocationManager` by calling `getSystemService` and casting the result accordingly
- Declare and initialize a `Criteria` instance
- Initialize our member String (`provider`) by calling the `locationManager.getBestProvider` method
- Declare and initialize a `Location` object by calling `getLastKnownLocation` on our `LocationManager` object
- Finally, after checking whether the `location` reference is not `null`, set the text on the `txtSource` widget and call `onLocationChanged`

Add the code that we just discussed into the `onCreate` method, as shown in the next code snippet:

```
@Override
public void onCreate(Bundle savedInstanceState) {
  super.onCreate(savedInstanceState);
  setContentView(R.layout.activity_main);
```

```
txtLat = (TextView) findViewById(R.id.txtLat);
txtLong = (TextView) findViewById(R.id.txtLong);
txtSource = (TextView) findViewById(R.id.txtSource);

// Initialize locationManager
locationManager = (LocationManager)
  getSystemService(Context.LOCATION_SERVICE);


Criteria criteria = new Criteria();
provider = locationManager.getBestProvider(criteria, false);
Location location = locationManager.
  getLastKnownLocation(provider);

// Initialize the location
if (location != null) {
  txtSource.setText("Source = " + provider);
  onLocationChanged(location);
}
}
```

Now, we start and stop listening for GPS location updates by calling `requestLocationUpdates` in `onResume` and calling `removeUpdates` in `onPause`.

The `requestLocationUpdates` method takes four arguments. The first is the provider that was established and saved in our `provider` variable. The second is the minimum number of milliseconds between updates, and the third is the minimum change in location in meters. So, the user only has to move slightly to prompt another update as we pass in 1 meter. The final argument needs to be a reference to `LocationListener`. As our `MainActivity` class implements `LocationListener`, it is indeed `LocationListener`, so we pass in `this`.

Now, whenever there are GPS updates, they will be sent to `MainActivity`, and we will implement all the necessary methods in a minute.

Add the two overridden methods that we just discussed:

```
// Start updates when app starts/resumes
@Override
protected void onResume() {
  super.onResume();
  locationManager.requestLocationUpdates
    (provider, 500, 1, this);
}

// pause the location manager when app is paused/stopped
```

```
@Override
protected void onPause() {
    super.onPause();
    locationManager.removeUpdates(this);
}
```

Now, all we need to do is add the required methods of the `LocationListener` interface.

In `onLocationChanged`, we get the latitude and longitude by calling `getLatitude` and `getLongitude`. Note that we store the result in a variable of the `double` type, which is just what we need for very precise fractions. Then, we update our **TextView** widgets.

In `onStatusChanged`, `onProviderEnabled`, and `onProviderDisabled`, we update the **TextView** widget that displays our provider.

Add the `LocationListener` methods that we just discussed:

```
@Override
public void onLocationChanged(Location location) {
    double lat = location.getLatitude();
    double lng = location.getLongitude();
    txtLat.setText(String.valueOf(lat));
    txtLong.setText(String.valueOf(lng));
    txtSource.setText("Source = " + provider);
}

@Override
public void onStatusChanged(String provider,
    int status, Bundle extras) {
    txtSource.setText("Source = " + provider);

}

@Override
public void onProviderEnabled(String provider) {
    txtSource.setText("Source = " + provider);

}

@Override
public void onProviderDisabled(String provider) {
    txtSource.setText("Source = " + provider);
}
```

We are now ready to test the app.

Running the Where in the world mini app

If GPS is enabled and has a connection, you will see the precise details of where you are; otherwise, the source for the location could be your wireless network or your mobile network. The former will be disconnected when you move too far away, and the latter could be a very long way off. Mine was around 60 miles off with the GPS switched off.

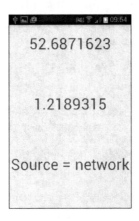

If you have a connection and walk around a bit, you will see the values of latitude and longitude change.

Of course, in real life, a bunch of numbers isn't especially helpful when you're trying to find your way around. It would be better if we could plot our GPS location on a map.

The Google Maps mini app

Create a new project and call it `Simple Map`. As we will be using a fairly new API, on the **Target Android Devices** screen, select **API 19 Android 4.4(KitKat)** in the **Minimum SDK** field. Also, on the **Add an Activity to mobile** screen, select the **Google Maps Activity** option. We will see that this will save us some work as well as provide us with some helpful information to get our app up and running with less complexity.

 Of course, you will also need a device with Android 4.4 or a later version to run this mini app. Furthermore, this app won't run on an emulator.

There are a couple of ways to use Google Maps. We can use an Intent to open the Google Maps app a bit like we did with the camera app, or we can connect directly to the Google Map's servers, which gives us the flexibility of making a better featured app.

We are going to use the second method that we discussed to get map data on our app by directly connecting to Google Map's servers. We will use the simpler, but less flexible, method via an Intent and the Google Maps app when we enhance the Where it's snap app in the next chapter.

So, how do we connect to the Google Maps servers? It has to be complicated. Fortunately not; as we have come to expect, there are a couple of classes to handle all the hard stuff for us. There is a little bit of work involved before we can get coding, however.

Preparing to connect to Google Maps

There are two main stages to get started. First we will see how to get an API key that our app will use to communicate with the servers and second we must make the app.

First, let's get an API key.

Acquiring an API key

To get an API key, you first need a Google account. If you use Gmail or Google+, then you already have one. If not, you can get one for free at `https://accounts.google.com`.

In the `values` folder of the project explorer, find the `google_maps_api.xml` file that Android Studio created for you. It might already be open in the editor.

In this file, there is a link to the **Google Developers Console** website where we obtain our API key. Android Studio has been very helpful as it generated this link. More than this, within the link, all the details about our app that we would otherwise have to search for and that are required to obtain the key, are encoded. The location of the link within the file is highlighted in the following screenshot. I have obscured a few details as they are specific to my account. Yours will be in exactly the same place, but with different specific values:

Copy the link from your google_maps_api.xml file identified in the previous screenshot and paste it into your web browser. You will see this next screen then. Agree with the terms of service and click on **Agree and continue**:

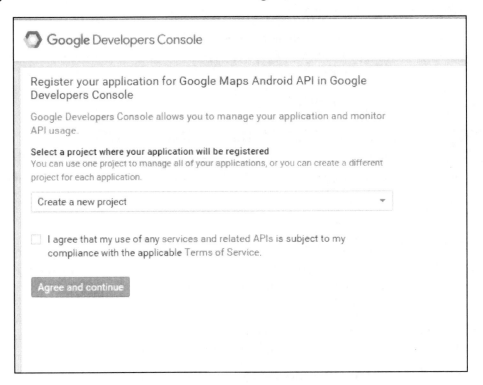

You will now see this next screen. Click on **Go to credentials**:

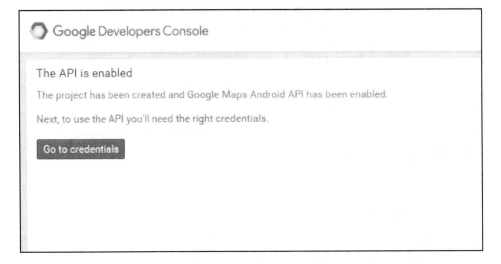

Now, click on the **Create** button as shown in the next screenshot:

You will be shown your new API key in a pop-up window, as shown in this screenshot:

Copy the API key into the `<string>` element in the `google_maps_api.xml` file, as shown in the next screenshot:

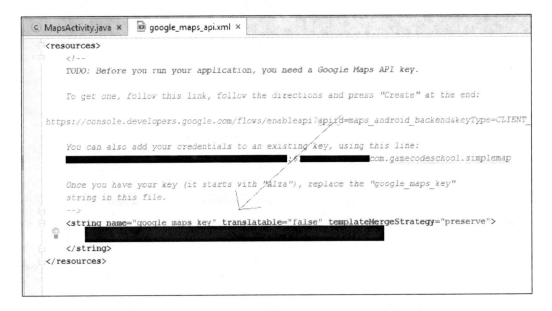

You can always get the key again by logging into your developer console and navigating to **APIs and auth | Credentials** from the left-hand side main menu.

Now that we have an API key, we just need to check whether we have the latest APIs installed and ready for our code to use.

Installing the Google Play services API

From the Android Studio menu, navigate to **Tools | Android | SDK Manager**. Click on the **SDK Tools** tab as indicated in the next screenshot:

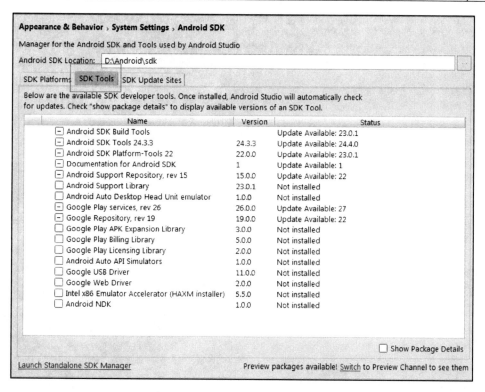

Find the line that starts with **Google Play Services**. If the checkbox by this line is empty, then it needs to be installed. If it has a dash, then it needs updating. If it has a tick, then you are good to skip to the section titled *Coding the maps_activity layout*.

If you have a blank checkbox or a dash, then click on the checkbox until it has a green tick in it, as shown in this figure:

Now, click on **OK**. Next, you will be prompted for a confirmation in the **Confirm Change** pop-up window:

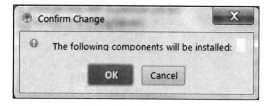

Click on **OK** and wait for the downloading and installation to complete.

Coding the maps_activity layout

Edit the `maps_activity.xml` layout file so that it is exactly the same as this code snippet:

```
<fragment xmlns:android=
  "http://schemas.android.com/apk/res/android"
  xmlns:tools="http://schemas.android.com/tools"
  android:layout_width="match_parent"
  android:layout_height="match_parent"
  android:id="@+id/map"
  tools:context=".MapsActivity"
  android:name="com.google.android.gms.maps.SupportMapFragment" />
```

The preceding code snippet is actually `Fragment` with an `id` property of `map`.

Coding MapsActivity

As we need to be sure that we've imported exactly the right classes, amend your imports to be the same as the next code and create a new `SupportMapFragment`, as shown in the next code snippet. Also, note that the code already implements `OnMapReadyCallback`:

```
import android.os.Bundle;
import android.support.v4.app.FragmentActivity;
import com.google.android.gms.maps.CameraUpdateFactory;
import com.google.android.gms.maps.GoogleMap;
import com.google.android.gms.maps.OnMapReadyCallback;
import com.google.android.gms.maps.SupportMapFragment;
import com.google.android.gms.maps.model.LatLng;
import com.google.android.gms.maps.model.MarkerOptions;

public class MapsActivity extends
  FragmentActivity implements OnMapReadyCallback {
  @Override
  protected void onCreate(Bundle savedInstanceState) {
    super.onCreate(savedInstanceState);
    setContentView(R.layout.activity_maps);
    SupportMapFragment mapFragment =
      (SupportMapFragment) getSupportFragmentManager()
        .findFragmentById(R.id.map);
    mapFragment.getMapAsync(this);


  }
```

Now, in the `onMapReady` method, we will put a pin at Silicon Valley, California.

For this, we use a LatLng object that holds both a latitude and longitude, and we pass the coordinates of Silicon Valley into the LatLng constructor.

Next, we call the addMarker method to add a marker to that location and then the moveCamera method to change the view to make the marker central on the screen:

```
@Override
public void onMapReady(GoogleMap map) {
  // Add a marker in Silicon Valley
  // 37.3876° N, 123.0575° W
  LatLng siliconValley = new LatLng(37.3876,238.0575);
  map.addMarker(new MarkerOptions().position
    (siliconValley).title("Silicon Valley"));
  map.moveCamera(CameraUpdateFactory.newLatLng(siliconValley));
}
```

The app will now connect to the Google servers and get the required map data.

Running the Simple Map app

Remember to run the app on a real device with Android 4.4 or a later version. In addition, your device's Google apps will need to be up-to-date for this app to run. Here is a screenshot from a Samsung Galaxy S4 phone:

Summary

It is true that the Maps API has a lot more to offer than we have had room to explore here. It is also true that once you are connected to the Google servers and have `SupportMapFragment` and its map object, you can quickly do more.

Take a look at the Google Maps page on the Google developer website at `https://developers.google.com/maps/documentation/android-api/` and check how to add some more functionality of your own.

In the next chapter, we will do a bit more location and map coding and at the same time learn how to upgrade/add features to our SQLite database, even after the app has been published.

26
Upgrading SQLite – Adding Locations and Maps

Now that we know how GPS and Google Maps work together, we will look at another approach to using them. To achieve this, we will need to make minor modifications throughout the app, but we will see how to do this and still allow the existing users to keep their data.

In this chapter, we will:

- Update our database code, which will result in the users of our app getting an updated database
- Add code to the Photo class to handle location information about where in the world a photo was taken
- Upgrade the code in CaptureFragment and ViewFragment to give the functionality we are aiming for

Adding locations and maps to Where it's Snap

We want to add a feature to our app where the user can click on the **SHOW MAP** button while viewing a photo, and the app will then show a map with the location of where the photo was taken in the world.

We have a good insight into this already from the previous chapter, when we viewed a specific GPS location on Google Maps.

The functionality we need to add and the issues we need to overcome are as follows:

- To capture and store the location each time a photo is taken
- When the **SHOW MAP** button is clicked on, we launch a map screen of that location
- Change the `Photo` class and database structures to store GPS locations
- Modify `DataManager` and helper methods to store and retrieve the extra bit of data
- Add the Google Maps functionality to the **SHOW MAP** button

Initially, in the context of simply developing an app, this might seem straightforward. Now, imagine that our app is already published. We have a million users with lots of photos already stored in their database. If we simply update our app with new helper methods and a new database structure that holds GPS locations, then all the users' existing data will be lost.

Fortunately, SQLite and the supporting Android API are designed around this problem. What we will do now is we will step through and update the Where it's Snap database, `Photo` class, and helper methods and we will add the map functionality as well.

 If you were adding features to an unreleased app, you could simply update the database structure, the `Photo` class, and so on. We are inventing this problem for ourselves just for the sake of learning about this real-world situation.

Updating the database

We need to update the database, not delete the existing one and create a new one.

We have two scenarios to deal with:

- The existing users of our app need an update (not replacement) to their existing database so that they can keep all their current data
- New users installing our app for the first time need the new database

To cater for the first scenario, the SQL keyword we need is `ALTER`. Also, we need to put our code and SQL into the `onUpgrade` method of the `CustomSQLiteOpenHelper` class in our `DataManager` class.

How will we trigger the upgrade in devices that already have the app installed? All we need to do is increment the version of the database. In our case, this is held in the DB_VERSION int. Each time an instance of the CustomSQLiteOpenHelper class is instantiated, it checks the version held in the DB_VERSION int against the actual version of the *current* database on the device. The point at which this check occurs is when we call the super class constructor from our constructor, which is highlighted in the next code snippet:

```java
public CustomSQLiteOpenHelper(Context context) {
    super(context, DB_NAME, null, DB_VERSION);
}
```

This code is already part of our app. All we need to do to get started is increment the version.

Now that we know what we need to do, we can go ahead and update the database structure (for new and existing users), increment the database version, and add code in onUpgrade (for the existing users).

Adding member variables to represent location data

First, add two more public static final String variables to our DataManager class so that they represent our new fields, as highlighted in the next code:

```java
public static final String TABLE_ROW_ID = "_id";
public static final String TABLE_ROW_TITLE = "image_title";
public static final String TABLE_ROW_URI = "image_uri";

// New with version 2
public static final String TABLE_ROW_LOCATION_LAT = "gps_location_
lat";
public static final String TABLE_ROW_LOCATION_LONG = "gps_location_
long";

/*
  Next we have a private static final strings for
  each row/table that we need to refer to just
  inside this class
*/...
```

Updating the database version

The next step will cause the onUpgrade method to be called for any users whose current database is at version 1. Edit the value of DB_VERSION in the DataManager class, as highlighted in the following code:

```
/*
  Next we have a private static final strings for
  each row/table that we need to refer to just
  inside this class
*/

private static final String DB_NAME = "wis_db";
private static final int DB_VERSION = 2;
private static final String TABLE_PHOTOS = "wis_table_photos";
private static final String TABLE_TAGS = "wis_table_tags";
private static final String TABLE_ROW_TAG1 = "tag1";
private static final String TABLE_ROW_TAG2 = "tag2";
private static final String TABLE_ROW_TAG3 = "tag3";
...
```

Adding code in onUpgrade to upgrade the database for existing users

Now, we can add code to execute the altered SQL in the onUpgrade method. In the onUpgrade method, we add code that uses ALTER in two separate queries, uses our two new Strings, and adds in the columns to the structure. Remember that this code only runs when the database on the device of the user has a version number lower than that held in DB_VERSION. In the last step, we incremented DB_VERSION, so this next method will run once for all existing users.

Add the code that we just discussed to the onUpgrade method:

```
// This method only runs when we increment DB_VERSION
@Override
public void onUpgrade(SQLiteDatabase db, int oldVersion, int
newVersion) {

  // Update for version 2
  String addLongColumn = "ALTER TABLE " +
      TABLE_PHOTOS +
      " ADD " +
      TABLE_ROW_LOCATION_LONG +
      " real;";
```

```
db.execSQL(addLongColumn);

String addLatColumn = "ALTER TABLE " +
    TABLE_PHOTOS + " ADD " +
    TABLE_ROW_LOCATION_LAT +
    " real;";

db.execSQL(addLatColumn);

}
```

Updating the database creation code in onCreate for new users

Of course, some users will be completely new to our app and may have never used it when the database was at version 1. When they install our app for the first time, onUpgrade won't run, so we need to alter the code that creates the database to add the extra fields there as well.

We simply modify our create table statement in the overridden onCreate method of our SQLiteOpenHelper class and add in the two new real columns.

Amend the code in onCreate that we just discussed to be the same as this next code:

```
// This method only runs the first time the database is created
@Override
public void onCreate(SQLiteDatabase db) {

  // Create a table for photos and all their details
  String newTableQueryString = "create table "
      + TABLE_PHOTOS + " ("
      + TABLE_ROW_ID
      + " integer primary key autoincrement not null,"
      + TABLE_ROW_TITLE
      + " text not null,"
      + TABLE_ROW_URI
      + " text not null,"
      + TABLE_ROW_LOCATION_LAT
      + " real,"
      + TABLE_ROW_LOCATION_LONG
      + " real,"
      + TABLE_ROW_TAG1
      + " text not null,"
      + TABLE_ROW_TAG2
```

```
        + " text not null,"
        + TABLE_ROW_TAG3
        + " text not null" + ");";

    db.execSQL(newTableQueryString);

    // Create a separate table for tags
    newTableQueryString = "create table "
        + TABLE_TAGS + " ("
        + TABLE_ROW_ID
        + " integer primary key autoincrement not null,"
        + TABLE_ROW_TAG
        + " text not null" + ");";

    db.execSQL(newTableQueryString);
}
```

Updating the addPhoto method to handle GPS coordinates

Now, we need to make the following minor changes to our helper method that stores a photo to make sure that it handles the two extra columns.

Amend the addPhoto helper method as shown in the following code:

```
// Here are all our helper methods
public void addPhoto(Photo photo){

    // Add all the details to the photos table
    String query = "INSERT INTO " + TABLE_PHOTOS + " (" +
        TABLE_ROW_TITLE + ", " +
        TABLE_ROW_URI + ", " +
        TABLE_ROW_LOCATION_LAT + ", " +
        TABLE_ROW_LOCATION_LONG + ", " +
        TABLE_ROW_TAG1 + ", " +
        TABLE_ROW_TAG2 + ", " +
        TABLE_ROW_TAG3 +
        ") " +
        "VALUES (" +
        "'" + photo.getTitle() + "'" + ", " +
        "'" + photo.getStorageLocation() + "'" + ", " +
        photo.getGpsLocation().getLatitude() + ", " +
        photo.getGpsLocation().getLongitude() + ", " +
        "'" + photo.getTag1() + "'" + ", " +
```

```
        "'" + photo.getTag2() + "'" + ", " +
        "'" + photo.getTag3() + "'" +
        ");";

    Log.i("addPhoto()", query);

    db.execSQL(query);

    // Add any NEW tags to the tags table
    ...
    ...
```

That's all the changes that are needed for the `DataManager` class.

Updating the Photo class

We need to add one new member as well as a getter and setter method into the
`Photo` class. The new member is of the type `Location` that stores both the latitude
and longitude. Add the highlighted part of the next code:

```
private String mTitle;
private Uri mStorageLocation;
private Location mGpsLocation;
private String mTag1;
private String mTag2;
private String mTag3;

public Location getGpsLocation() {
  return mGpsLocation;
}

public void setGpsLocation(Location mGpsLocation) {
  this.mGpsLocation = mGpsLocation;
}

public String getTitle() {
  return mTitle;
}
}
    ...
    ...
```

The updated `Photo` class is ready for use.

Updating CaptureFragment

This will be a breeze because we have already seen most of the code that we need in the previous chapter.

Make `CaptureFragment` implement `LocationListener` and add the highlighted member variables:

```
public class CaptureFragment extends Fragment
    implements LocationListener {

    private static final int CAMERA_REQUEST = 123;
    private ImageView mImageView;

    // The filepath for the photo
    String mCurrentPhotoPath;

    // Where the captured image is stored
    private Uri mImageUri = Uri.EMPTY;

    // A reference to our database
    private DataManager mDataManager;

    // For the Location
    private Location mLocation = new Location("");
    private LocationManager mLocationManager;
    private String mProvider;
```

In the `onCreate` method, let's get the location in the usual way. Add the highlighted code to find it:

```
@Override
public void onCreate(Bundle savedInstanceState) {
    super.onCreate(savedInstanceState);

    mDataManager = new DataManager
        (getActivity().getApplicationContext());

    // Initialize mLocationManager
    mLocationManager = (LocationManager)
        getActivity().getSystemService(Context.LOCATION_SERVICE);
    Criteria criteria = new Criteria();
    mProvider = mLocationManager.getBestProvider(criteria, false);
}
```

Now, we can update the class that listens for clicks on the **SAVE** button in the `onCreateView` method to use our new setter method in the `Photo` class, as shown in the following code:

```
// Listen for clicks on the save button
btnSave.setOnClickListener(new View.OnClickListener() {

  @Override
  public void onClick(View v) {
    if(mImageUri != null){
      if(!mImageUri.equals(Uri.EMPTY)) {

        // We have a photo to save

        Photo photo = new Photo();
        photo.setTitle(mEditTextTitle.getText().toString());
        photo.setStorageLocation(mImageUri);

        // Set the current GPS location
        photo.setGpsLocation(mLocation);

        // What is in the tags
        String tag1 = mEditTextTag1.getText().toString();
        String tag2 = mEditTextTag2.getText().toString();
        String tag3 = mEditTextTag3.getText().toString();

        // Assign the strings to the Photo object
        photo.setTag1(tag1);
        photo.setTag2(tag2);
        photo.setTag3(tag3);

        // Send the new object to our DataManager
        mDataManager.addPhoto(photo);
        Toast.makeText(getActivity(),
          "Saved", Toast.LENGTH_LONG).show();
      }else {
        // No image
        Toast.makeText(getActivity(),
          "No image to save", Toast.LENGTH_LONG).show();
      }
    }else {
      // No image
      Toast.makeText(getActivity(),
        "No image to save", Toast.LENGTH_LONG).show();
    }
  }
});
```

And of course, we must override the necessary methods of the `LocationListener` interface. We don't use all these next three methods, but we must still override them as this is required by the interface. Add the following methods to the `CaptureFragment` class:

```
@Override
public void onLocationChanged(Location location) {
  // Update the location if it changed
  mLocation = location;
}

@Override
public void onStatusChanged(String provider,
    int status, Bundle extras) {

}

@Override
public void onProviderEnabled(String provider) {

}

@Override
public void onProviderDisabled(String provider) {

}
```

Just as we did in the Where in the World mini app, we must start and stop the updates in the `onResume` and `onPause` methods. If we don't call `requestLocationUpdates`, then we will never get any updates, and if we don't call `removeUpdates`, the device will go on communicating and receiving updates even when our Activity has ended:

```
// Start updates when app starts/resumes
@Override
public void onResume() {
  super.onResume();

  mLocationManager.requestLocationUpdates
    (mProvider, 500, 1, this);

}

// pause the location manager when app is paused/stopped
@Override
```

```
public void onPause() {
  super.onPause();

  mLocationManager.removeUpdates(this);
}
```

That's the `CaptureFragment` class ready to go.

Updating ViewFragment

Now, let's move on to `ViewFragment`. We will be using an `Intent` class to launch the built-in Google Maps app but with a pin to mark the location the photo was taken at.

The GPS location is already in the `Photo` object and we just need to do the following:

- Capture the latitude and longitude in `Double` variables
- Build a String from these values that will represent the URI that we need to create the `Intent` object
- Create the `Intent` class
- Start a Google Maps `Activity` passing in the `Intent` class

Of course, all this takes place inside the class that handles the button clicks for **SHOW MAP**.

Add the highlighted code that we just discussed to handle what happens when the user clicks on the **SHOW MAP** button:

```
public View onCreateView(LayoutInflater inflater, ViewGroup container,
Bundle savedInstanceState) {

  View view = inflater.inflate(R.layout.fragment_view, container,
false);
  TextView textView  = (TextView) view.findViewById(R.id.textView);
  Button buttonShowLocation = (Button) view.findViewById(R.
id.buttonShowLocation);

  textView.setText(mCursor.getString(mCursor.
getColumnIndex(DataManager.TABLE_ROW_TITLE)));

  mImageView = (ImageView) view.findViewById(R.id.imageView);
  mImageView.setImageURI(Uri.parse(mCursor.getString(mCursor.
getColumnIndex(DataManager.TABLE_ROW_URI))));
```

```java
buttonShowLocation.setOnClickListener(new View.OnClickListener() {

    @Override
    public void onClick(View v) {

        double latitude = Double.valueOf(mCursor.getString
    (mCursor.getColumnIndex(DataManager.
    TABLE_ROW_LOCATION_LAT)));
double longitude = Double.valueOf(mCursor.getString
    (mCursor.getColumnIndex(DataManager.
    TABLE_ROW_LOCATION_LONG)));

// Create a URI from the latitude and longitude
String uri = String.format(Locale.ENGLISH,
    "geo:%f,%f", latitude, longitude);

        // Create a Google maps intent
        Intent intent = new Intent(Intent.ACTION_VIEW, Uri.parse(uri));

        // Start the maps activity
        getActivity().startActivity(intent);
    }
});


    return view;
}
```

Adding location permissions

The last thing to do before we can try out our near-complete Where it's Snap app is
to add the permissions that let us use the device to get the GPS coordinates.

 These permissions will work fine with Android 6 (Marshmallow)
because of the way we configured our project back in *Chapter 21,
Navigation Drawer and Where It's Snap*. If you want a reminder
about the new Android permissions in Marshmallow, refer
to *Chapter 11, Widget Mania*, which was the first time we used
permissions in this book.

Add the highlighted permissions into the `AndroidManifest.xml` file:

```xml
<?xml version="1.0" encoding="utf-8"?>
<manifest xmlns:android=
  "http://schemas.android.com/apk/res/android"
  package="com.gamecodeschool.whereitsapp" >

  <uses-permission android:name=
    "android.permission.ACCESS_FINE_LOCATION" />
  <uses-permission android:name=
    "android.permission.ACCESS_COARSE_LOCATION" />
  <uses-permission android:name=
    "android.permission.INTERNET" />

  <application
    android:allowBackup="true"
    android:icon="@mipmap/ic_launcher"
    android:label="@string/app_name"
    android:theme="@style/AppTheme" >
    <activity
      android:name=".MainActivity"
      android:label="@string/app_name" >
      <intent-filter>
        <action android:name="android.intent.action.MAIN" />

        <category android:name=
          "android.intent.category.LAUNCHER" />
      </intent-filter>
    </activity>
  </application>

</manifest>
```

We can now run our app.

Testing the new map feature

Run the Where it's Snap app, tap on the **Capture** button, and take a picture. Then, save the picture. Now, navigate back to that picture either by its title or tag and title. Tap on the **SHOW MAP** button:

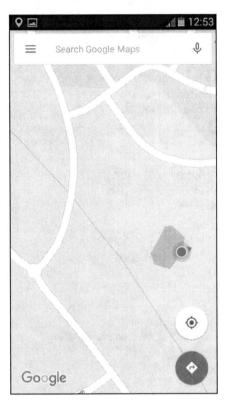

Summary

We are almost done with the Where it's Snap app. In this chapter, we added the locations and maps functionality. We used the Intent class to open the Google Maps app. This made our code simpler and we didn't need to connect to the Google servers (directly) either. Another advantage of this approach is that we didn't have to set the minimum OS version to version 4.4, and therefore, our app caters for a wider range of Android devices.

The final phase for this app will be to make it accessible to users who don't speak English. In the next chapter, we will build a simple app to experiment with adding multiple languages and then we will use what we've learned to make Where it's Snap in Spanish.

27
Going Local – Hola!

This chapter is short and simple, but here you will learn to make your app accessible to millions of potential users. In this chapter, we will see how to add additional languages. This is made really easy because we have been using String resources for the text in our app.

In this chapter, we will:

- Learn the basics by building a very simple app that uses English, Spanish, and French
- Add Spanish to the Where it's Snap app by adding a single text file

The Localization mini app

Create a new project and call it `Localization`. Keep all the project settings at their default values. We don't need to do any Java coding for this project.

Preparing the layout

Edit the `activity_main` layout file by copying and pasting the following code to replace the autogenerated code:

```
<RelativeLayout xmlns:android="http://schemas.android.com/apk/res/
android"
  xmlns:tools="http://schemas.android.com/tools"
    android:layout_width="match_parent"
  android:layout_height="match_parent"
    android:paddingLeft="@dimen/activity_horizontal_margin"
  android:paddingRight="@dimen/activity_horizontal_margin"
  android:paddingTop="@dimen/activity_vertical_margin"
  android:paddingBottom="@dimen/activity_vertical_margin"
    tools:context=".MainActivity">
```

```
    <TextView
      android:layout_width="wrap_content"
      android:layout_height="wrap_content"
      android:textAppearance="?android:attr/textAppearanceLarge"
      android:text="@string/movie_title"
      android:id="@+id/textView"
      android:layout_alignParentTop="true"
      android:layout_alignParentLeft="true"
      android:layout_alignParentStart="true" />

    <TextView
      android:layout_width="wrap_content"
      android:layout_height="wrap_content"
      android:textAppearance="?android:attr/textAppearanceMedium"
      android:text="@string/line_one"
      android:id="@+id/textView2"
      android:layout_below="@+id/textView"
      android:layout_marginTop="35dp"
      android:layout_alignParentRight="true"
      android:layout_alignParentEnd="true" />

    <TextView
      android:layout_width="wrap_content"
      android:layout_height="wrap_content"
      android:textAppearance="?android:attr/textAppearanceMedium"
      android:text="@string/line_two"
      android:id="@+id/textView3"
      android:layout_below="@+id/textView2"
      android:layout_alignLeft="@+id/textView2"
      android:layout_alignStart="@+id/textView2"
      android:layout_marginTop="52dp" />

</RelativeLayout>
```

Preparing the first strings.xml file

To prepare the file, copy and paste the following code in to the `strings.xml` file. These are the String resources that are referred to in the layout that we just coded:

```
<resources>
  <string name="app_name">Localization</string>
  <string name="hello_world">Hello world!</string>
  <string name="action_settings">Settings</string>
  <string name="movie_title">Gone with the wind</string>
```

```
    <string name="line_one">...Rhett,
      if you go, where shall I go? What shall I do?</string>
    <string name="line_two">Frankly, my dear.
      I don't give a damn.</string>
  </resources>
```

Now that all the references in the layout have a matching resource, switch to the **Design** tab to see a couple of **TextView** widgets that contain a couple of famous lines from a movie:

Now, we can add another language.

Making the app multilingual with the second strings.xml file

For this, all we have to do is add another `strings.xml` file into an appropriately named folder with the same name for each resource, but with an appropriate translation. Then, the app will detect the user's preferred language based on the settings of the device on which the app is running.

Make sure that the project explorer is in the **Project** view by clicking on the drop-down list on the top left-side, as shown in the following screenshot:

After this, click on **Project**. We can now add resource folders for as many countries as we like.

Right-click on the res folder and navigate to **New | Android resource directory**. Name the new folder values-es. ES is the country code for Spain. So, this is where an Android device set to the Spanish locale will look for the strings.xml file.

Right-click on the values-es folder and navigate to **New | Android resource file**. Name the file strings.xml. Now, copy and paste the following code:

```
<resources>
  <string name="app_name">Localización</string>
  <string name="movie_title">Lo que el viento se llevó</string>
  <string name="line_one">... Rhett, si te vas,
    dónde iré? ¿Qué debo hacer?</string>
  <string name="line_two">Francamente, querida.
    Me importa un bledo.</string>
</resources>
```

 If you don't provide all the string resources in the second strings.xml file, then the resources from the default will be used.

Adding a third language

To add another language, right-click on the res folder and navigate to **New |
Android resource directory**. Name the new folder values-fr. FR is the country code
for France. So, this is where an Android device set to the French locale will look for
the strings.xml file.

Right-click on the values-fr folder and navigate to **New | Android resource file**.
Name the file strings.xml. Now, copy and paste the following code:

```xml
<resources>
  <string name="app_name">Localisation</string>
  <string name="movie_title">Emporté par le vent</string>
  <string name="line_one">... Rhett, si vous allez,
    où irai-je? Que dois-je faire?</string>
  <string name="line_two">Franchement, ma chère.
    Je ne donne pas une putain.</string>
</resources>
```

If you look at the project explorer window, as shown in the following screenshot,
you can see that Android Studio provides a nice little flag graphic for each of our
translation files:

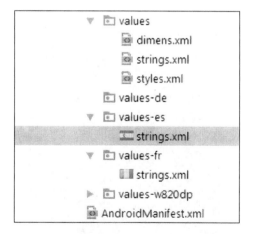

You can even localize different versions of a language. For
example, US or United Kingdom English. The complete
list of codes can be found at http://stackoverflow.
com/questions/7973023/what-is-the-list-of-
supported-languages-locales-on-android. You can
even localize resources such as images and sound. Find out
more about this at http://developer.android.com/
guide/topics/resources/localization.html.

The translations were copy and pasted from Google Translate, so it is very likely that some of the translations are far from accurate. Translating on-the-cheap like this can be a good way to get an app with a basic set of String resources onto devices of users who speak different languages. Furthermore, if you require in-depth translations, perhaps the lines from a movie, you will certainly benefit from having the translation done by human professionals.

The purpose of this exercise is to show you how Android works, and not how to translate.

[My sincere apologies to any Spanish or French speakers who can likely see the limitations of the translations provided here.]

Running the app

Run the app to see it working as normal. Now, we can change the localization settings to see the app in Spanish. Different devices vary slightly in how to do this, but the Nexus 5 emulator can be changed by clicking on the **Custom Locale** app, selecting **es - ES**, and then clicking on the **SELECT 'ES'** button in the bottom-left corner of the screen, as shown in the next screenshot:

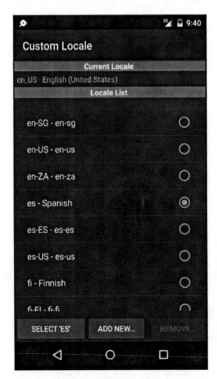

Now, run the app again and you will see the translated string resources in action:

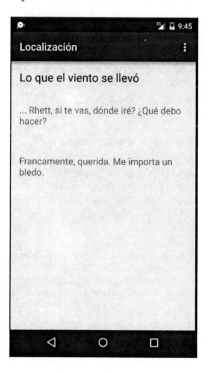

To switch back to English, follow these steps. Run the **Custom Locale** app and select **en-US - en-us**. Then, click on the **SELECT 'EN-US'** button in the bottom-left corner of the screen.

Localizing the Where it's snap app

The final and complete code for Where it's snap can be found in the Chapter 27/ Where Its Snap folder.

Simply add a folder for any languages that you want to add to the app. To add Spanish, right-click on the res folder and navigate to **New | Android resource directory**. Name it values-es. Now, right-click on the folder that we just created and navigate to **New | Android resource file**. Name it strings.xml, and copy and paste the following code into it:

```
<resources>
    <string name="app_name">Donde Es Snap!</string>

    <string name="action_settings">Ajustes</string>
    <string name="drawer_open">Abra</string>
```

```
<string name="drawer_close">Cerca</string>

<string name="enter_photo_title">
   Ingrese título de la foto</string>
<string name="tag1">Tag 1</string>
<string name="tag2">Tag 2</string>
<string name="tag3">Tag 3</string>
<string name="capture">Tomar foto</string>
<string name="save">Guardar</string>

<string name="tags">Tags</string>
<string name="titles">Títulos</string>
   <string name="show_map">Ver mapa</string>

<!-- These are the items in our list -->
<string-array name="nav_drawer_items">
   <item >Títulos</item>
   <item >Tags</item>
   <item >Tomar foto</item>
</string-array>

</resources>
```

You can now switch the device to Spanish, as we did for the last mini app, and run Where it's snap to see it as it would look if somebody in Spain downloaded it from the app store. This next screenshot shows you `CaptureFragment` in action:

Summary

That's it for Where it's snap; we won't be doing anything else with it. Of course, there are lots of improvements that you could make if you wanted to.

You could offer the ability to delete a photo from the database. Perhaps, by a long-press on a title in the `TitlesFragment` class. The facility to edit the tags and title might be useful. You could add an edit button to `ViewFragment` that opens up a new `EditFragment` class.

In the next chapter, we will do something totally new while exploring the concept of threads, touches, and drawing in Android.

28
Threads, Touches, Drawing, and a Simple Game

So far throughout the book, we have concentrated on using the diverse range of UI widgets provided by the Android API. In conventional apps, this is almost always the best way to do things.

For example, why would we want to reinvent a widget that has been designed and refined by experts?

Lots of Android apps, however, are not based on this conventional appearance. Think of the multitude of kids' or artists' drawing apps. And what about the best selling category on Google Play: games?

In this chapter, we will look at and play with the skills and Android classes that are needed to build apps of this type. The topics for this chapter are:

- **Threads**: How to run more than one block of code simultaneously
- **Drawing**: How we use the `Canvas` and `Paint` classes for pixels, lines, shapes, and custom text, including a mini app
- **Screen touches**: Detecting and responding to screen touches that are not on a UI widget
- **Pong**: Combining the first three things to make a retro arcade game

First up is threads.

Threads

So, what is a thread? You can think of threads in Java programming in the same way you think of threads in a story. In one thread of a story, we might have the primary character battling the enemy on the frontline while in another thread, the soldier's family is getting by, day-to-day. Of course, a story doesn't have to have just two threads. We could introduce a third thread; perhaps the story also tells of the politicians and military commanders making decisions. And these decisions then subtly, or not so subtly, affect what happens in the other threads.

Programming threads are just like this. We create parts/threads in our program that control different aspects for us. Threads are especially useful when we need to ensure that a task does not interfere with the main (UI) thread of the app, or if we have a background task that takes a long time to complete and must not interrupt the main thread of execution. We introduce threads to represent these different aspects because of the following reasons:

- They make sense from an organizational point of view
- They are a proven way of structuring a program that works
- The nature of the system we are working on forces us to use them from time to time

In Android, we use threads for all three reasons simultaneously. It makes sense, it works, and we have to use the threads because of the design of the system.

Often, we use threads without knowing about it. This happens because we use classes that use threads on our behalf. `SoundPool` for example, loads sounds in a thread, and `BaseAdapter` sorts our data and loads up our `ListView` in a thread. Threads are also very useful in games, as we will see.

In gaming, think about a thread that is receiving the player's button taps for moving left and right and another thread that draws all the graphics to the screen.

Problems with threads

Programs with multiple threads can have problems, like the threads of a story in which if proper synchronization does not occur, then things go wrong. What if our soldier went into battle before the battle or war even existed? Weird.

What if we have a variable, `int x`, that represents a key piece of data that three threads of our program use. What happens if one thread gets slightly ahead of itself and makes the data "wrong" for the other two? This problem is the problem of **correctness** caused by multiple threads racing to completion obliviously — because after all, they are just dumb code.

The problem of correctness can be solved by close oversight of the threads and **locking**, locking meaning temporarily preventing execution in one thread to be sure things are working in a synchronized manner. This is kind of like preventing a soldier from boarding a ship to war until the ship has actually docked and the gang plank has been lowered, avoiding an embarrassing splash.

The other problem with programs with multiple threads is the problem of **deadlock**, where one or more threads become locked waiting for the right moment to access `int x`, but that moment never comes, and eventually the entire program grinds to a halt.

You might have noticed that it was the solution to the first problem (correctness) that is the cause of the second problem (deadlock). Now, consider all we have just been discussing and mix it in with the Android activity lifecycle, and it's possible you start to feel a little nauseous with the complexity.

Fortunately, the problem has been solved for us. Just as we use the `Activity` class and override its methods to interact with the lifecycle, we can also use other classes to create and manage our threads. Just as with `Activity`, we only need to know how to use them not how they work.

"So, why tell me all this stuff about threads when I didn't need to know?" you rightly ask. Simply because we will be writing code that looks different and is structured in an unfamiliar manner, if we can:

- Accept that the new concepts we introduce are what we need to work with in order to work with the Android-specific solution to the thread-related problems
- Understand the general concept of a thread, which is the same thing as a story thread that happens almost simultaneously
- Learn the few rules of using a thread

Then, we will have no sweat writing our Java code to create and work within our threads. There are a few different Android classes that handle threads. Different thread classes work best in different situations.

There are many different thread-related classes in the Android API, and we will only cover one in this book. If you want to learn more about threads, then I recommend the book *Asynchronous Android* by Steve Liles, and you can find out more at this link: https://www.packtpub.com/application-development/asynchronous-android.

All we need to remember is that we will be writing parts of our program that will run at *almost* the same time as each other.

 What do I mean by almost? What is actually happening is that the CPU switches between threads in turn. However, this happens so fast that we will not be able to perceive anything but simultaneity.

Let's take a glimpse at what our thread code will look like:

We can declare an object of the type Thread like this:

```
Thread gameThread;
```

Initialize and start it like this:

```
gameThread = new Thread(this);
gameThread.start();
```

We can then use the Java `@override` keyword to change what happens when the operating system allows our `gameThread` object to run its code. Within the overridden `run` method, we call two methods that we will write in our Pong game. The first is `update`, which is where all our calculations, artificial intelligence, and collision detection will go, and then `draw`, where perhaps unsurprisingly, we will draw all our graphics:

```
@override
public void run() {

    // Update the game world based on
    // user input, physics,
    // collision detection and artificial intelligence
    update();

    // Draw all the game objects in their updated locations
    draw();

}
```

When necessary, we can also stop our thread like this:

```
gameThread.join();
```

Now, everything that is in the `run` method is executing in a separate thread, leaving the default or UI thread to listen for touches and system events. We will see how the two threads communicate with each other in the Pong project.

Note that exactly where all these parts of the code will go within our game has not been explained, but it is so much easier to actually show you in a real project.

When we build our retro game, we will see how simple it is to have two sets of code running apparently simultaneously.

So, how do we draw things?

Drawing with canvas and paint

So far, we have been using the Android Studio UI designer to implement all aspects of our interface with which our users interact.

If we want smooth-moving customized graphics, then we need to move away from predefined UI widgets.

We are going to need to start looking at and designing with individual pixels and lines. Fortunately, as you might have guessed, Android has some classes to make this nice and easy for us. We will be learning how to get started with the Canvas and Paint classes.

To achieve this, we will learn about the coordinate system that we use to draw our pixels and lines. Then, we will look at the Paint and Canvas classes themselves.

The Android coordinate system

A pixel is the smallest graphical element we can manipulate using the Paint and Canvas classes. It is essentially a dot. If your device resolution is 1920 x 1080 like the Nexus 5 emulator, then we have 1920 pixels across the longest length of the device and 1080 across the other.

We can therefore think of our screen onto which we will be drawing as a grid. We will draw by plotting points (pixels), lines, shapes, and text using coordinates on this grid.

The coordinate system starts in the top-left corner of the screen.

As an example, take a look at the following line of code:

```
drawPoint(0, 0); // Not actual code
```

In this, we would plot a single pixel in the top-left corner of the screen. Now, look at the following code:

```
drawPoint(1919, 1079); // Not actual code
```

If we use it like that, we would draw a point in the bottom-right corner of one of these high-end devices (while in the landscape position).

We could also draw lines by specifying a start and end coordinate position, a bit like this:

```
drawLine(0,0,1919, 1079); // Not actual code
```

This would draw a line from the top-left corner of the screen to the bottom-right.

Now, you might have noticed some potential problems. First, not all Android devices have such a high resolution; in fact, most are very significantly lower. Even on devices with this high resolution, they will have totally different coordinates when held in landscape or portrait positions. How will we write code that adapts regardless of the screen resolution? We will see the solution soon. First, we will do some basic drawing and ignore this problem.

The aptly named `Canvas` class provides just what you would expect: a virtual canvas to draw our graphics on.

We can make a virtual canvas using the `Canvas` class from any Android UI element. In our demo app, we will draw onto `ImageView`, and when we make our game, we will draw straight onto a special type of view, which will bring some extra advantages, as we will see.

So, to get started, we need a widget to draw on. Assuming there is `ImageView` in the layout, we could do the following to get a reference to it:

```
ImageView ourVIew = (ImageView) findViewById(R.id.imageView);
```

Now, we need a bitmap. A bitmap itself has a coordinate system much like the screen. We are creating a bitmap to turn it into our drawing canvas:

```
Bitmap ourBitmap = Bitmap.createBitmap
    (300,600, Bitmap.Config.ARGB_8888);
```

The previous line of code declares and creates an object of the type `Bitmap`. It will have a size of 300 x 600 pixels. We will keep this in mind when we draw on it shortly.

 The last argument in the `createBitmap` method, `Bitmap.Config.ARGB_8888`, is simply a format. If you want to know more about bitmap formats, you can do so here: `https://en.wikipedia.org/wiki/BMP_file_format`.

Now, we can prepare `Bitmap` for drawing by creating a `Canvas` object with it:

```
Canvas ourCanvas = new Canvas(ourBitmap);
```

Next, we get ourselves an object of the type `Paint`. Literally, we can think of this object as both the brush and paint for our virtual canvas:

```
Paint paint = new Paint();
```

At this point, we are ready to use our `Paint` and `Canvas` objects to do some drawing. The actual code to draw a pixel in the top-left corner of the screen will look like this:

```
ourCanvas.drawPoint(0, 0, paint); // How simple is that?
```

Let's look at a working drawing mini app.

Android Canvas demo app

Let's make an app that uses the `Canvas` and `Paint` classes and do a bit of drawing. This example will be completely static (no animation), so we can clearly see how to use `Canvas` and `Paint` without cluttering up the code with things we will learn later.

In this demo app, we use some conceptually helpful variable names to help us grasp the role that each object is playing. But we will go through the whole thing at the end to make sure we know exactly what is going on at each stage. Of course, you don't have to type all this in; you can open the completed code files from the `Canvas Demo` folder in the `Chapter 28` folder of the download bundle.

Start a new project and call it `Canvas Demo`. Open the `layout_main.xml` file, and edit it to have a single `ImageView` with an ID of `imageView`, as in this code:

```
<RelativeLayout xmlns:android=
  "http://schemas.android.com/apk/res/android"
  xmlns:tools="http://schemas.android.com/tools"
  android:layout_width="match_parent"
  android:layout_height="match_parent"
  android:paddingLeft="@dimen/activity_horizontal_margin"
  android:paddingRight="@dimen/activity_horizontal_margin"
  android:paddingTop="@dimen/activity_vertical_margin"
  android:paddingBottom="@dimen/activity_vertical_margin"
  tools:context="com.gamecodeschool.canvasdemo.app.MainActivity">

  <ImageView
    android:layout_width="match_parent"
    android:layout_height="match_parent"
    android:id="@+id/imageView" />

</RelativeLayout>
```

Now, we can code the `MainActivity` class and do some drawing on our `ImageView`.

Add some `import` directives:

```
import android.graphics.Bitmap;
import android.graphics.Canvas;
import android.graphics.Color;
import android.graphics.Paint;
import android.os.Bundle;
import android.support.v7.app.AppCompatActivity;
import android.view.Menu;
import android.view.MenuItem;
import android.widget.ImageView;
import java.util.Random;

public class MainActivity extends AppCompatActivity {

  @Override
  protected void onCreate(Bundle savedInstanceState) {
    super.onCreate(savedInstanceState);
    setContentView(R.layout.activity_main);

    // All our code will go here
  }
...
```

Set up the `Paint` and `Canvas` classes by adding the following code that we have already discussed. In addition, we call the `drawColor` method to change the background color of the `Canvas` and `setColor` method, which determines the color we will use to draw when we start drawing:

```
@Override
protected void onCreate(Bundle savedInstanceState) {
  super.onCreate(savedInstanceState);
  setContentView(R.layout.activity_main);

  // All our code will go here

  // Get a reference to our ImageView in the layout
  ImageView ourFrame = (ImageView) findViewById(R.id.imageView);

  // Create a bitmap object to use as our canvas
  Bitmap ourBitmap = Bitmap.createBitmap
    (750,1500, Bitmap.Config.ARGB_8888);
```

```
Canvas ourCanvas = new Canvas(ourBitmap);

// A paint object that does our drawing, on our canvas
Paint paint = new Paint();

// Set the background color
ourCanvas.drawColor(Color.BLACK);

// Change the color of the virtual paint brush
paint.setColor(Color.argb(255, 255, 255, 255));


    ...
```

Next, add this code, which loops six hundred times and draws a single pixel each time in a random location, a bit like a star field. This code goes straight after the last code, still in the onCreate method:

```
// Draw a bunch of random points
Random random = new Random();
for (int i = 0; i < 600; i ++) {

  int x = random.nextInt(750);
  int y = random.nextInt(1500);

  ourCanvas.drawPoint(x, y, paint);

}
```

Draw some shapes and a message by adding this code:

```
// Draw a line
ourCanvas.drawLine(0, 0, 750, 1500, paint);

// Change the color of the virtual paint brush
paint.setColor(Color.argb(255, 0, 255, 0));


// Make the text bigger
paint.setTextSize(120f);

// Draw some text
ourCanvas.drawText("Hello Canvas!", 10, 750, paint);

// Draw a circle
ourCanvas.drawCircle(500, 500, 100, paint);
```

```
// Change the color of the virtual paint brush
paint.setColor(Color.argb(255, 0, 0, 255));

// Draw a rectangle
ourCanvas.drawRect(500, 10, 200, 200, paint);

//Now put the canvas in the frame
ourFrame.setImageBitmap(ourBitmap);
```

Run the mini app and gaze in awe at our wondrous graphics. It isn't quite Unreal Engine quality yet, but it's a good first step:

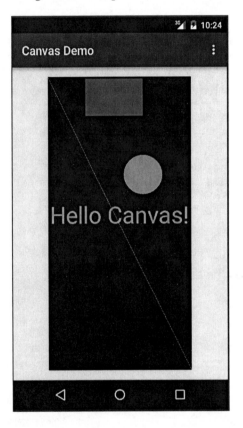

In the previous image, we can see the line, rectangle, circle, and text that we drew. If you are reading this in paper form, the 600 pixels might be quite hard to see.

Now, we still need to get smarter with managing the screen. Also, we need to look into a system that will allow us to rub out and redraw our images at a set interval to create the illusion of movement. We will solve all these problems when we build our Pong game.

The Canvas class, as with so many classes we have seen throughout the book, is a lot more in depth than we have covered here. If you want to learn how to make drawing apps and much more, try the book *Learning Android Canvas* by Nauman Tahir, which can be found at `https://www.packtpub.com/application-development/learning-android-canvas`.

Now, let's take a look at how the player will control the game. After all, we are not going to have any handy button widgets to do this for us.

Handling touches

In our Pong game, we will have no UI buttons, and therefore cannot use the `OnCLickListener` interface and override the `onClick` method. This is not a problem, however. We will just use another interface to suit our situation. We will use `OnTouchListener` and override the `onTouchEvent` method. It works a little bit differently, so let's take a look before we dive into the game code.

We must implement the `OnTouchListener` interface for the activity we want to listen for touches in, like this:

```
public class MainActivity extends Activity
    implements View.OnTouchListener{
```

Then, we can override the `onTouchEvent` method, perhaps a bit like this:

```
@Override
public boolean onTouchEvent(MotionEvent motionEvent) {

    float x = motionEvent.getX();
    float y = motionEvent.getY();

    //do something with the x and y values

    return false;
}
```

The variable x will hold the horizontal value of the position on the screen that was touched, and y will hold the vertical position. It is worth noting that the `motionEvent` object parameter contains lots of information as well as the *x* and *y* location. For example, depending on whether the screen was touched or released, we can make some really useful switch statements with this information, as we will see.

Exactly how we use this to achieve our goals in the squash game requires us to first consider the design of the game.

A simple game engine

Drawing shapes, lines, and pixels is all very well, but how do we make them appear to move? We will be using the same animation trick used in cartoons, movies, and other video games, given as follows:

1. Draw an object

2. Rub it out

3. Draw it in its new position

4. Repeat steps 1 to 3 fast enough to trick the player's brain that the game objects are moving

5. Do all the above while listening for touches on a separate thread

The theory makes it all sound more complicated than it is. Let's make our Pong game and it should all become clear.

Building a simple game of Pong

Create a new project called Pong, and leave all the settings at their defaults.

Adding sound files to the project

Using your operating system's file browser, go to the app/src/main folder of the project and add a new folder called assets.

There are four sound files already made for you in the Chapter 28/Pong/assets folder of the download bundle. Place these four files into the assets directory you just created, or you can use some sound effects you create yourself. The important thing is that their filenames must be beep1.ogg, beep2.ogg, beep3.ogg, and loseLife.ogg.

Coding the ball

Create a new class called Ball. Unsurprisingly, this class will handle everything to do with the ball in the game. We will code it in eight short segments.

First, add the following member variables. The only one that is completely new is the `RectF` object. This is simply an object that holds four `float` values that define the four coordinates of a rectangle. This is perfect for a ball that looks like the primitive graphics from the 1970s. In addition, we have four more separate `float` variables to represent the speed of the ball in the *x* and *y* axes, as well as the width and height of the ball.

Add the member variables to the `Ball` class:

```
public class Ball {

    private RectF mRect;
    private float mXVelocity;
    private float mYVelocity;
    private float mBallWidth;
    private float mBallHeight;

}
```

In the `Ball` constructor method, we initialize the ball's width and height relative to the width of the screen that was passed into the constructor method. Then, we initialize the *x* and *y* speed relative to the screen height. The ball will be one hundredth of the screen width and will travel at one quarter of the screen height per second. We will see how we control this in our thread shortly.

We also initialize our `RectF` object, but don't assign any coordinates yet.

Add the `Ball` constructor method we have just discussed:

```
public Ball(int screenX, int screenY){

    // Make the mBall size relative to the screen resolution
    mBallWidth = screenX / 100;
    mBallHeight = mBallWidth;

    /*
       Start the ball travelling straight up
       at a quarter of the screen height per second
    */
    mYVelocity = screenY / 4;
    mXVelocity = mYVelocity;

    // Initialize the Rect that represents the mBall
    mRect = new RectF();

}
```

Next, we will code a getter method so we can get a hold of the `RectF` (which will represent the location of the ball) from outside the `Ball` class. Add the `getRect` method:

```
// Give access to the Rect
public RectF getRect(){
  return mRect;
}
```

Next, we see the `update` method, not to be confused with the update method we will write in our thread. This update method will be called once every frame of the game.

It updates the `top` and `left` values of the ball based on the velocity member variables (`mXVelocity` and `mYVelocity`) divided by the number of frames per second (`fps`) that the device is managing to run the game at. Then, the other points of `mRect` are updated relative to the top-left and size of the ball.

The effect of this is that regardless of how fast or slow the device's CPU might be, the ball will travel at the same rate. We will soon see how we get **fps (frames per second)** and pass it in to the ball's `update` method.

Add the update method to the `Ball` class:

```
// Change the position each frame
public void update(long fps){
  mRect.left = mRect.left + (mXVelocity / fps);
  mRect.top = mRect.top + (mYVelocity / fps);
  mRect.right = mRect.left + mBallWidth;
  mRect.bottom = mRect.top - mBallHeight;
}
```

Now, we need a few little helper methods that will enable us to easily deal with various situations we will learn about soon. We need to be able to reverse the vertical and horizontal headings, set a new random x velocity and speed up by 10%. The `reverseYVelocity`, `reverseXVelocity`, `setRandomXVelocity`, and `increaseVelocity` methods achieve these things.

Add the four methods we have just discussed to the `Ball` class:

```
// Reverse the vertical heading
public void reverseYVelocity(){
  mYVelocity = -mYVelocity;
}

// Reverse the horizontal heading
public void reverseXVelocity(){
  mXVelocity = -mXVelocity;
```

```
    }

    public void setRandomXVelocity(){
      Random generator = new Random();
      int answer = generator.nextInt(2);

      if(answer == 0){
        reverseXVelocity();
      }
    }

    // Speed up by 10%
    // A score of 25 is quite tough on this setting
    public void increaseVelocity(){
      mXVelocity = mXVelocity + mXVelocity / 10;
      mYVelocity = mYVelocity + mYVelocity / 10;
    }
```

Next, we add three more helper methods—one that clears an obstacle on the *y* axis
(clearObstacleY), another that clears an obstacle on the *x* axis (clearObstacleX),
and one that resets the position of the ball in the bottom-center of the screen (reset).
Each of these methods simply tweaks/repositions the ball. Their usefulness will
become apparent when we see them in action:

```
    public void clearObstacleY(float y){
      mRect.bottom = y;
      mRect.top = y - mBallHeight;
    }

    public void clearObstacleX(float x){
      mRect.left = x;
      mRect.right = x + mBallWidth;
    }

    public void reset(int x, int y){
      mRect.left = x / 2;
      mRect.top = y - 20;
      mRect.right = x / 2 + mBallWidth;
      mRect.bottom = y - 20 - mBallHeight;
    }
```

The ball is ready to start bouncing all over the place, so let's get the paddle coded,
and then we can start on the game engine itself.

Coding the paddle

Create a new class and call it `Paddle`. First, we will add the constructor method. We have `RectF` for holding the paddle's four coordinates. We also have separate `mXcoord` and `mYCoord` float variables, which hold the left and top positions.

We have a float for the speed (`mPaddleSpeed`). Next, we have three `final int` members (`STOPPED`, `LEFT`, and `RIGHT`), which are `public`. We will be able to refer to these values from outside the class to manipulate the paddle's direction.

We also have a private variable (`mPaddleMoving`), which will always be assigned one of those three `public final` values. We begin by setting it to `STOPPED`.

In the `Paddle` class, we want to keep a permanent copy of the screen resolution (size in pixels), so we declare `mScreenX` and `mScreenY`, which we will initialize soon.

Add the `Paddle` members we have just discussed:

```
public class Paddle {

    // RectF is an object that holds four coordinates
    // - just what we need
    private RectF mRect;

    // How long and high our mPaddle will be
    private float mLength;
    private float mHeight;

    // X is the far left of the rectangle which forms our mPaddle
    private float mXCoord;

    // Y is the top coordinate
    private float mYCoord;

    // This will hold the pixels per second speed that
    // the mPaddle will move
    private float mPaddleSpeed;

    // Which ways can the mPaddle move
    public final int STOPPED = 0;
    public final int LEFT = 1;
    public final int RIGHT = 2;

    // Is the mPaddle moving and in which direction
    private int mPaddleMoving = STOPPED;
```

```
// The screen length and width in pixels
private int mScreenX;
private int mScreenY;

}
```

In the constructor, we initialize mScreenX and mScreenY with the passed in x and y values. We initialize the length of the paddle to one-eighth of the screen width and the height to one-twenty-fifth.

We initialize mXCoord and mYCoord to roughly the bottom-center of the screen. We set mPaddleSpeed to the same value as mScreenX, which has the effect of setting the paddle's movement to be able to cover the whole screen in one second. This is not as overpowering as it might first seem.

Add the Paddle constructor we have just discussed:

```
// This is the constructor method
// When we create an object from this class we will pass
// in the screen width and mHeight
public Paddle(int x, int y){

    mScreenX = x;
    mScreenY = y;

    // 1/8 screen width wide
    mLength = mScreenX / 8;

    // 1/25 screen mHeight high
    mHeight = mScreenY / 25;

    // Start mPaddle in roughly the screen center
    mXCoord = mScreenX / 2;
    mYCoord = mScreenY - 20;

    mRect = new RectF(mXCoord, mYCoord, mXCoord + mLength,
      mYCoord + mHeight);

    // How fast is the mPaddle in pixels per second
    mPaddleSpeed = mScreenX;
    // Cover entire screen in 1 second
}
```

Add the public getter to return the `RectF` that represents the paddle's location:

```
// This is a getter method to make the rectangle that
// defines our paddle available in GameView class
public RectF getRect(){
  return mRect;
}
```

The `setMovementState` method receives `int` as a parameter. We will call this method using one of the three `public final int` members: LEFT, RIGHT, or STOPPED. This method will simply set that state to the `mPaddleMoving` member:

```
// This method will be used to change/set
// if the mPaddle is going
// left, right or nowhere

public void setMovementState(int state){
  mPaddleMoving = state;
}
```

The final method for the `Paddle` class is its `update` method. First, it uses a couple of `if` statements to see if it is moving left or right. If it is, it moves the `mXCoord` by the `mPaddleSpeed` divided by the frames per second, just like the ball.

Then, it does two checks to see if the paddle might be moving off the screen. If the paddle is about to disappear off the left-hand side, it prevents it from doing so by setting `mXCoord` to `0`. If it is about to disappear off the right-hand side, it sets `mXCoord` to `mScreenX`, take away the width of the paddle.

Finally, based on the results of all those `if` statements, it updates the values held by the `RectF`, ready for the game engine to make use of them when it calls `getRect`:

```
// This update method will be called from update in GameView
// It determines if the paddle needs to move
// and changes the coordinates
// contained in mRect if necessary
public void update(long fps){
  if(paddleMoving == LEFT){
    mXCoord = mXCoord - mPaddleSpeed / fps;
  }
  if(paddleMoving == RIGHT){
    mXCoord = mXCoord + mPaddleSpeed / fps;
  }

  // Make sure it's not leaving screen
  if(mRect.left < 0){
```

```
      mXCoord = 0;
  }

  if(mRect.right > mScreenX){
    mXCoord = mScreenX -
    // The width of the paddle
    (mRect.right - mRect.left);
  }

  // Update the paddle graphics
  mRect.left = mXCoord;
  mRect.right = mXCoord + mLength;
}
```

Coding MainActivity

Most of the action will take place in the next class we create. We will call that class GameView. So, the job of MainActivity is to communicate with the lifecycle events of the OS and pass on any relevant information to GameView. It needs to instantiate a GameView object as well. Notice in the next code there is indeed an object of the type GameView declared as a member.

In the onCreate method, we use a Display object and the getWindowManager(). getDefaultDisplay() chained methods to initialize it. Then, we declare an object of the type Point. Using the Display object, we can load the screen resolution into point using the getSize method.

We can now call the constructor of GameView to initialize gameView. Notice when we do that we pass in x and y, which is the screen resolution. It is from here that our Paddle and Ball objects will eventually get hold of them.

Finally, in onCreate, we do something that might at first look slightly odd. Look at the call to setContentView. Instead of passing in the XML layout file, we pass in our GameView reference.

This is exactly what we need. GameView will extend a class called SurfaceView, which not only allows us to have a Thread, but also implements onTouchListener and allows us to attach a Canvas object directly to it.

So, GameView, because it extends SurfaceView, is like an all-in-one solution to our thread, touching, and drawing needs, and we simply set it as the view of our entire Activity.

Add the highlighted member variable and code to `onCreate`:

```
// gameView will be the view of the game
// It will also hold the logic of the game
// and respond to screen touches as well
GameView gameView;

@Override
protected void onCreate(Bundle savedInstanceState) {
  super.onCreate(savedInstanceState);

  // Get a Display object to access screen details
  Display display = getWindowManager().getDefaultDisplay();

  // Load the resolution into a Point object
  Point size = new Point();
  display.getSize(size);

  // Initialize gameView and set it as the view
  gameView = new GameView(this, size.x, size.y);
  setContentView(gameView);

}
```

Lastly, in `MainActivity`, we will override the `onResume` and `onPause` methods. In these methods, we will call the `resume` and `pause` methods on `GameView`. In these methods, in the `GameView` class, we will start and stop our thread. This is just what we need because after our `GameView` class is set up, as its constructor is called in `onCreate`, then `onResume` will run and set the thread going as well. Then, when the player quits the app and the OS calls `onPause`, our `pause` method will be called and the thread will be stopped. Otherwise, our ball will still be bouncing and beeping around the screen, perhaps while the player is taking a phone call from his boss.

Add the overridden `onResume` and `onPause` methods to the `MainActivity` class:

```
// This method executes when the player starts the game
@Override
protected void onResume() {
  super.onResume();

  // Tell the gameView resume method to execute
  gameView.resume();
}

// This method executes when the player quits the game
```

```
@Override
protected void onPause() {
  super.onPause();

  // Tell the gameView pause method to execute
  gameView.pause();
}
```

Now, we can code the main class of our game.

Coding SurfaceView

Create a new class called `GameView`, extend `SurfaceView`, and implement `Runnable`.

Now, we will add a whole bunch of members:

- A thread called `mGameThread` that we will start and stop from the `pause` and `resume` methods that we will implement soon. These methods are of course called by the `onResume` and `onPause` methods of the `MainActivity` class.

- `SurfaceHolder` is what we need to allow us to do to our drawing.

- `Volatile boolean mPlaying` will be `true` when the thread is running and `false` otherwise. It will be used to determine whether we enter a `while` loop that will control the whole game loop. We have not seen the `volatile` keyword before, and we use it because `mPlaying` can be accessed from outside and inside the thread.

- We have a `boolean mPaused` variable, which will determine whether the game is currently paused.

- We have a `Paint` and `Canvas` object, which we will use in the same way we did in the Canvas Demo mini app.

- Next, we have a `long` variable, `mFPS`, which will hold the current number of frames per second that our game loop is achieving, and of course this is the value we will be passing in to the `update` methods of `Paddle` and `Ball` to allow them to move by the correct amount.

- Next, we declare `mScreenX` and `mScreenY` to hold the screen resolution, which as we saw is passed into the constructor from `MainActivity` when we instantiate a `GameView` object. We will code that constructor very soon.

- Now, we get to the neat stuff: a `Ball` object called `mBall` and a `Paddle` object called `mPaddle`.

- Next up, we have all the members that will take care of sound effects, including a `SoundPool` and four `int` IDs for sound effects.

- Finally, `mLives` and `mScore` will keep track of the player's score and how many lives he or she has left.

Code the `GameView` class and its members as we have just discussed:

```java
// Notice we implement runnable so we have
// A thread and can override the run method.
class GameView extends SurfaceView implements Runnable {

    // This is our thread
    Thread mGameThread = null;

    // This is new. We need a SurfaceHolder
    // When we use Paint and Canvas in a thread
    // We will see it in action in the draw method soon.
    SurfaceHolder mOurHolder;

    // A boolean which we will set and unset
    // when the game is running- or not
    volatile boolean mPlaying;

    // Game is mPaused at the start
    boolean mPaused = true;

    // A Canvas and a Paint object
    Canvas mCanvas;
    Paint mPaint;

    // This variable tracks the game frame rate
    long mFPS;

    // The size of the screen in pixels
    int mScreenX;
    int mScreenY;

    // The players mPaddle
    Paddle mPaddle;

    // A mBall
    Ball mBall;

    // For sound FX
    SoundPool sp;
    int beep1ID = -1;
    int beep2ID = -1;
    int beep3ID = -1;
    int loseLifeID = -1;
```

```
    // The mScore
    int mScore = 0;

    // Lives
    int mLives = 3;
}
```

The constructor has quite a lot of code, but we have seen much of it before, and what is left is fairly straightforward.

We initialize `mScreenX` and `mScreenY` from the passed in screen resolution.

We initialize `mOurHolder` by calling `getHolder`, and we initialize `mPaint` by calling the default `Paint` constructor.

Next, we instantiate our paddle and ball by calling their constructors and passing in the screen resolution, as is required.

Almost all the rest of the code sets up the sound in exactly the same manner we saw in *Chapter 17, Sound FX and Supporting Different Versions of Android.*

The final line of code calls the `setupAndRestart` method to start a new game, and we will code that method shortly.

Add the `GameView` constructor we have just discussed:

```
/*
   When we call new() on gameView
   This custom constructor runs
*/

public GameView(Context context, int x, int y) {

   /*
      The next line of code asks the
      SurfaceView class to set up our object.
   */
   super(context);

   // Set the screen width and height
   mScreenX = x;
   mScreenY = y;

   // Initialize mOurHolder and mPaint objects
   mOurHolder = getHolder();
   mPaint = new Paint();
```

```java
// A new mPaddle
mPaddle = new Paddle(mScreenX, mScreenY);

// Create a mBall
mBall = new Ball(mScreenX, mScreenY);

/*
  Instantiate our sound pool
  dependent upon which version
  of Android is present
*/

if (Build.VERSION.SDK_INT >= Build.VERSION_CODES.LOLLIPOP) {
  AudioAttributes audioAttributes =
    new AudioAttributes.Builder()
    .setUsage(AudioAttributes.USAGE_MEDIA)
    .setContentType(AudioAttributes.CONTENT_TYPE_SONIFICATION)
    .build();

  sp = new SoundPool.Builder()
    .setMaxStreams(5)
    .setAudioAttributes(audioAttributes)
    .build();

} else {
  sp = new SoundPool(5, AudioManager.STREAM_MUSIC, 0);
}


try{
  // Create objects of the 2 required classes
  AssetManager assetManager = context.getAssets();
  AssetFileDescriptor descriptor;

  // Load our fx in memory ready for use
  descriptor = assetManager.openFd("beep1.ogg");
  beep1ID = sp.load(descriptor, 0);

  descriptor = assetManager.openFd("beep2.ogg");
  beep2ID = sp.load(descriptor, 0);

  descriptor = assetManager.openFd("beep3.ogg");
  beep3ID = sp.load(descriptor, 0);
```

```
        descriptor = assetManager.openFd("loseLife.ogg");
        loseLifeID = sp.load(descriptor, 0);

        descriptor = assetManager.openFd("explode.ogg");
        explodeID = sp.load(descriptor, 0);

    }catch(IOException e){
        // Print an error message to the console
        Log.e("error", "failed to load sound files");
    }

    setupAndRestart();

}
```

Here is the `setupAndRestart` method that we first call from the constructor. We will also call this method at the end of every game to start a new one. The code calls the `reset` method on `ball` to position it for the start of a game and if necessary, resets the `mScore` and `mLives` variables to 0 and 3 respectively.

Add the `setupAndRestart` method to the `GameView` class:

```
public void setupAndRestart(){

    // Put the mBall back to the start
    mBall.reset(mScreenX, mScreenY);

    // if game over reset scores and mLives
    if(mLives == 0) {
        mScore = 0;
        mLives = 3;
    }

}
```

Here, we have our `run` method, which is the code that is running in a thread. We have a `while` loop controlled by the value of our `volatile boolean` called `mPlaying`. This `while` loop wraps all the rest of the code inside the `run` method.

Inside the `while` loop, we get the system time in milliseconds (thousandths of a second) and initialize the `startFrameTime` variable with the result. Then, we check if the game is currently paused `if(!mPaused)`, and if the game isn't paused, we call the `update` method. Note this is the update method of the `GameView` class, not the `Ball` or `Paddle` classes' `update` methods. We will code this method soon.

Next, we call the `draw` method, which will contain all our drawing code. Now, we calculate the time the frame took to execute by getting the current system time again and subtracting `startFrameTime` from the result. We then put the result into `mFPS`, which of course will be passed to the `update` methods of the `Ball` and `Paddle` classes when they are called.

The reason we wrap the last bit of code in `if (timeThisFrame >= 1)` is because if `timeThisFrame` equals zero, trying to divide by zero will crash the app.

Dividing by zero is a bad move in any language and on any platform. If you want to know more, take a look at this article: `https://en.wikipedia.org/wiki/Division_by_zero`.

Code the overridden `run` method we have just discussed:

```java
@Override
public void run() {
  while (mPlaying) {

    // Capture the current time in milliseconds in startFrameTime
    long startFrameTime = System.currentTimeMillis();

    // Update the frame
    // Update the frame
    if(!mPaused){
      update();
    }

    // Draw the frame
    draw();

    /*
      Calculate the FPS this frame
      We can then use the result to
      time animations in the update methods.
    */
    long timeThisFrame = System.currentTimeMillis()
      - startFrameTime;
    if (timeThisFrame >= 1) {
      mFPS = 1000 / timeThisFrame;
    }

  }

}
```

Now, we can code the update method.

Coding the update method

The `update` method is quite long, so we will go through and code it a chunk at a time to make sure everything is explained.

Add the signature and the body of the `update` method, and we will steadily add all the code to it:

```
// Everything that needs to be updated goes in here
// Movement, collision detection etc.
public void update(){

}
```

Call the `update` methods on our ball and paddle to handle any required movement. Add the highlighted code we have just discussed to the `update` method:

```
// Everything that needs to be updated goes in here
// Movement, collision detection etc.
public void update() {

  // Move the mPaddle if required
  mPaddle.update(mFPS);

  mBall.update(mFPS);
}
```

Now that the ball and paddle are in their new positions for this frame, we can run a bunch of tests to see if anything important has happened to our game.

The first test is to see if the ball has hit the paddle. Using the `getRect` methods of both the ball and the paddle, we pass the two returned results into the static `intersects` method of `RectF`. The `intersects` method returns `true` if the ball and the paddle overlap (have touched) each other.

If a collision is detected, execution enters the `if` block and does a number of things:

- Calls `setRandomXVelocity` on the ball to choose a random horizontal direction for when the ball heads back up the screen
- Calls `reverseYVelocity` to start to head back up the screen
- Calls `clearObstacle`, which jumps the ball a few pixels and avoids the possibility of the ball getting stuck on the paddle
- Increments `mScore` to increase the player's score
- Plays a beep sound from `SoundPool`

Add the code we have just discussed to the `update` method:

```
// Check for mBall colliding with mPaddle
if(RectF.intersects(mPaddle.getRect(), mBall.getRect())) {
  mBall.setRandomXVelocity();
  mBall.reverseYVelocity();
  mBall.clearObstacleY(mPaddle.getRect().top - 2);

  mScore++;
  mBall.increaseVelocity();

  sp.play(beep1ID, 1, 1, 0, 0, 1);
}
...
```

Next, we handle what happens if the ball hits the bottom of the screen. The test to see if this has happened works by calculating the position of the underside of the ball (`mBall.getRect.bottom`) and comparing it to the height of the screen in pixels (`mScreenY`).

If a collision has occurred, the following steps happen inside the `if` block:

- Reversing the ball's velocity
- Jumping a few pixels in case the ball gets stuck
- Decrementing `mLives`
- Playing a gloomy sound
- Checking if that was the last life and if it was, pause the game and calling `setupAndRestart`

Add the highlighted code we have just discussed to the `update` method:

```
// Bounce the mBall back when it hits the bottom of screen
if(mBall.getRect().bottom > mScreenY){
  mBall.reverseYVelocity();
  mBall.clearObstacleY(mScreenY - 2);

  // Lose a life
  mLives--;
  sp.play(loseLifeID, 1, 1, 0, 0, 1);

  if(mLives == 0){
    mPaused = true;
    setupAndRestart();
  }
}
```

The next code uses the top of the ball and compares it to zero to see if it has reached the top of the screen. If it has, it just reverses the ball on the *y* axis, clears any potential obstacles, and plays a beep.

Add the highlighted code we have just discussed to the `update` method:

```
// Bounce the mBall back when it hits the top of screen
if(mBall.getRect().top < 0){
  mBall.reverseYVelocity();
  mBall.clearObstacleY(12);

  sp.play(beep2ID, 1, 1, 0, 0, 1);
}
```

The next code uses the left of the ball and compares it to zero to see if it has reached the left of the screen. If it has, it just reverses the ball on the *x* axis, clears any potential obstacles, and plays a beep.

Add the highlighted code we have just discussed to the `update` method:

```
// If the mBall hits left wall bounce
if(mBall.getRect().left < 0){
  mBall.reverseXVelocity();
  mBall.clearObstacleX(2);

  sp.play(beep3ID, 1, 1, 0, 0, 1);
}
```

The next code uses the right of the ball and compares it to `mScreenX` to see if it has reached the right of the screen. If it has, it just reverses the ball on the *x* axis, clears any potential obstacles, and plays a beep.

Add the highlighted code we have just discussed to the `update` method:

```
// If the mBall hits right wall bounce
if(mBall.getRect().right > mScreenX){
  mBall.reverseXVelocity();
  mBall.clearObstacleX(mScreenX - 22);

  sp.play(beep3ID, 1, 1, 0, 0, 1);
}
```

Now, we move on to the `draw` method.

Coding the draw method

The first thing we have to do is attempt to get a lock on the surface to draw on and check if it is valid. This is achieved with the following line of code (don't add it just yet):

```
// Make sure our drawing surface is valid or we crash
  if (mOurHolder.getSurface().isValid()) {

  // Draw everything here

}
```

If the test returns `true`, we are almost ready to draw. We just need this code before we start using our canvas (don't add this yet):

```
// Lock the mCanvas ready to draw
mCanvas = mOurHolder.lockCanvas();
```

Now, we can go mad with `mPaint`. In this order, we:

1. Make sure the surface is valid and lock the canvas, as discussed just now
2. Draw a background
3. Change the brush color
4. Draw the paddle as a rectangle by passing in `getRect` as the argument
5. Draw the ball as a rectangle by calling `getRect` as the argument
6. Change the brush color again
7. Change the size of the text
8. Draw the score and number of lives on the screen
9. Call `mOurHolder.unlockCanvasAndPost(mCanvas)` to finish the drawing process for this frame

Add the `draw` method we have just discussed to the `GameView` class:

```
// Draw the newly updated scene
public void draw() {

    // Make sure our drawing surface is valid or we crash
    if (mOurHolder.getSurface().isValid()) {

      // Draw everything here

      // Lock the mCanvas ready to draw
```

```
    mCanvas = mOurHolder.lockCanvas();

    // Draw the background color
    mCanvas.drawColor(Color.argb(255, 26, 128, 182));

    // Choose the brush color for drawing
    mPaint.setColor(Color.argb(255, 255, 255, 255));

    // Draw the mPaddle
    mCanvas.drawRect(mPaddle.getRect(), mPaint);

    // Draw the mBall
    mCanvas.drawRect(mBall.getRect(), mPaint);


    // Choose the brush color for drawing
    mPaint.setColor(Color.argb(255, 255, 255, 255));

    // Draw the mScore
    mPaint.setTextSize(40);
    mCanvas.drawText("Score: " + mScore +
       "   Lives: " + mLives, 10, 50, mPaint);

    // Draw everything to the screen
    mOurHolder.unlockCanvasAndPost(mCanvas);
  }


}
```

Now, we can implement our pause and resume methods, which stop and start the thread. Of course, these methods are called by the MainActivity class in response to the Activity lifecycle methods:

```
// If the Activity is paused/stopped
// shutdown our thread.
public void pause() {
  mPlaying = false;
  try {
    mGameThread.join();
  } catch (InterruptedException e) {
    Log.e("Error:", "joining thread");
  }


}
```

```
// If the Activity starts/restarts
// start our thread.
public void resume() {
  mPlaying = true;
  mGameThread = new Thread(this);
  mGameThread.start();
}
```

The last major piece of our Pong game is handling the user's touches. To make the controls as easy as possible, we will say that holding anywhere on the right will move the paddle right, and anywhere on the left will move the paddle left.

When the `onTouchEvent` method is called, we `switch` based on the type of event. The first case that we handle is `MotionEvent.ACTION_DOWN`. This occurs when the player touches the screen. We can access the precise location with the `motionEvent.getX` method.

Therefore, in the code that follows, we use the following `if` statement:

```
if(motionEvent.getX() > mScreenX / 2){
```

This determines if the screen has been touched at a position higher than the width of the screen divided by two (the right-hand side). If the preceding statement is `true`, we simply call `paddle.setMovementState(mPaddle.RIGHT)`, and the `Paddle` class will take care of moving correctly the next time `update` is called.

If the previous `if` statement is `false`, then it must have been touched on the left, and we call `paddle.setMovementState(mPaddle.LEFT)`.

We also need to remember to stop the paddle if the player removes their finger from the screen. We can handle this in the `MotionEvent.ACTION_UP` case of the `switch` block.

Add the overridden `onTouchEvent` method:

```
// The SurfaceView class implements onTouchListener
// So we can override this method and detect screen touches.
@Override
public boolean onTouchEvent(MotionEvent motionEvent) {

  switch (motionEvent.getAction() & MotionEvent.ACTION_MASK) {

    // Player has touched the screen
    case MotionEvent.ACTION_DOWN:

      mPaused = false;
```

```
      // Is the touch on the right or left?
      if(motionEvent.getX() > mScreenX / 2){
        mPaddle.setMovementState(mPaddle.RIGHT);
      }
      else{
        mPaddle.setMovementState(mPaddle.LEFT);
      }

      break;

    // Player has removed finger from screen
    case MotionEvent.ACTION_UP:

      mPaddle.setMovementState(mPaddle.STOPPED);
      break;
    }
    return true;
  }
```

If you are wondering why we set `mPaused` to `false` in the `MotionEvent.ACTION_DOWN` case, it is because we pause the game when the player runs out of lives. When the player taps the screen, this will then have the effect of starting it again.

We are nearly there now.

Lock the screen orientation and make it full-screen

We can achieve this by adding the highlighted line to the `AndroidManifest.xml` file:

```
<?xml version="1.0" encoding="utf-8"?>
<manifest xmlns:android=
  "http://schemas.android.com/apk/res/android"
  package="com.gamecodeschool.pong" >

  <application
    android:allowBackup="true"
    android:icon="@mipmap/ic_launcher"
    android:label="@string/app_name"
    android:theme="@style/AppTheme" >
    <activity
      android:name=".MainActivity"
      android:theme="@android:style/Theme.NoTitleBar.Fullscreen"
      android:screenOrientation="landscape"
```

```
        android:label="@string/app_name" >
        <intent-filter>
          <action android:name="android.intent.action.MAIN" />

          <category android:name="android.intent.category.LAUNCHER"

          />
        </intent-filter>
      </activity>
    </application>

  </manifest>
```

And we're ready to play!

Running the game

Apps of this type always work better on a real device if you have one, but they do run OK on the emulator too:

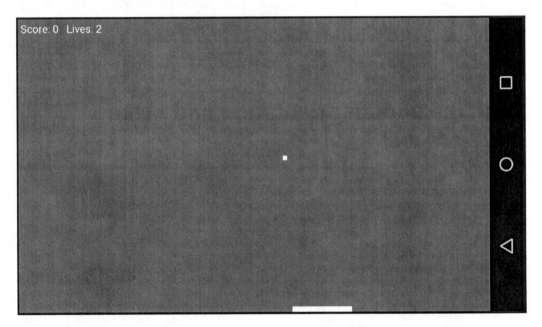

You will probably find the game gets quite challenging around about a score of 15 (or even lower on the emulator).

Pong enhancements

Although our game is quite minimalistic, we already know enough about the Android API to build a home screen and perhaps a settings screen. We could easily implement a small database for high scores, as well.

Summary

In this chapter, we covered a lot of ground—threads, drawing, touches, and basic games. I have already suggested where you can get further information on threads and drawing, so I hope you will forgive me for a shameless plug to one of my other books that focuses on Android games. If you want to build a shooter, a platformer, and a flappy bird-like game and learn how to draw super-fast graphics at sixty frames per second, please take a look at *Android Game Programming by Example* at `https://www.packtpub.com/game-development/android-game-programming-example`.

Now that we can plan and build our own apps of many types, we had better find out how to go about publishing and selling them on the Google Play marketplace.

29
Publishing Apps

This is one of the shortest chapters and there is absolutely nothing technical in it at all. However, it does take a while to complete. In this chapter, we will prepare all the required resources before we can upload our app, as well as export the publishable APK file.

This chapter will cover the following topics:

- Preparing to publish
- Building the publishable APK file
- Publishing the app
- The basics of promoting the app

Preparing to publish

You probably don't want to upload any of the apps from this book, so the first step is to develop an app that you want to publish.

Head over to `https://play.google.com/apps/publish/` and follow the instructions to get a Google Play developer account. This was $25 at the time of writing and is a one-time charge with no limit on the number of apps you can publish.

Creating an app icon

Exactly how to design an icon is beyond the remit of this book. But, simply put, you need to create a nice image for each of the Android screen density categorizations.

This is easier than it sounds. Design one nice app icon in your favorite drawing program and save it as a `.png` file. Then, visit `http://romannurik.github.io/ AndroidAssetStudio/icons-launcher.html`. This will turn your single icon into a complete set of icons for every single screen density.

 Warning! The trade-off for using this service is that the website will collect your e-mail address for their own marketing purposes.

There are many sites that offer a similar free service. Once you have downloaded your `.zip` file from the preceding site, you can simply copy the `res` folder from the download into the `main` folder within the project explorer. All icons at all densities have now been updated.

Preparing the required resources

When we log into Google Play to create a new listing in the store, there is nothing technical to handle, but we do need to prepare quite a few images that we will need to upload.

Prepare upto 8 screenshots for each device type (a phone/tablet/TV/watch) that your app is compatible with. Don't crop or pad these images.

Create a 512 x 512 pixel image that will be used to show off your app icon on the Google Play store. You can prepare your own icon, or the process of creating app icons that we just discussed will have already autogenerated icons for you.

You also need to create three banner graphics, which are as follows:

- 1024 x 500
- 180 x 120
- 320 x 180

These can be screenshots, but it is usually worth taking a little time to create something a bit more special. If you are not artistically minded, you can place a screenshot inside some quite cool device art and then simply add a background image. You can generate some device art at `https://developer.android.com/ distribute/tools/promote/device-art.html`.

Then, just add the title or feature of your app to the background. The following banner was created with no skill at all, just with a pretty background purchased for $10 and the device art tool I just mentioned:

Also, consider creating a video of your app. Recording video of your Android device is nearly impossible unless your device is rooted. I cannot recommend you to root your device; however, there is a tool called **ARC (App Runtime for Chrome)** that enables you to run APK files on your desktop. There is no debugging output, but it can run a demanding app a lot more smoothly than the emulator. It will then be quite simple to use a free, open source desktop capture program such as **OBS (Open Broadcaster Software)** to record your app running within ARC. You can learn more about ARC at `https://developer.chrome.com/apps/getstarted_arc` and about OBS at `https://obsproject.com/`.

Building the publishable APK file

What we are doing in this section is preparing the file that we will upload to Google Play. The format of the file we will create is .apk. This type of file is often referred to as an APK. The actual contents of this file are the compiled class files, all the resources that we've added, and the files and resources that Android Studio has autogenerated. We don't need to concern ourselves with the details, as we just need to follow these steps.

The steps not only create the APK, but they also create a key and sign your app with the key. This process is required and it also protects the ownership of your app:

 Note that this is not the same thing as copy protection/digital rights management.

1. In Android Studio, open the project that you want to publish and navigate to **Build | Generate Signed APK** and a pop-up window will open, as shown:

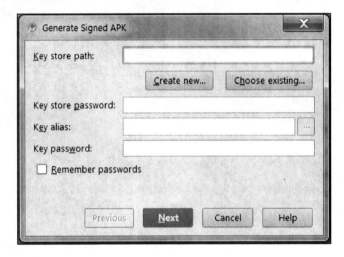

2. In the **Generate Signed APK** window, click on the **Create new** button. After this, you will see the **New Key Store** window, as shown in the following screenshot:

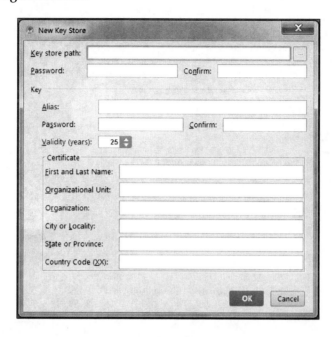

3. In the **Key store path** field, browse to a location on your hard disk where you would like to keep your new key, and enter a name for your key store. If you don't have a preference, simply enter `keys` and click on **OK**.

4. Add a password and then retype it to confirm it.

5. Next, you need to choose an alias and type it into the **Alias** field. You can treat this like a name for your key. It can be any word that you like. Now, enter another password for the key itself and type it again to confirm.

6. Leave **Validity (years)** at its default value of **25**.

7. Now, all you need to do is fill out your personal/business details. This doesn't need to be 100% complete as the only mandatory field is **First and Last Name**.

8. Click on the **OK** button to continue. You will be taken back to the **Generate Signed APK** window with all the fields completed and ready to proceed, as shown in the following window:

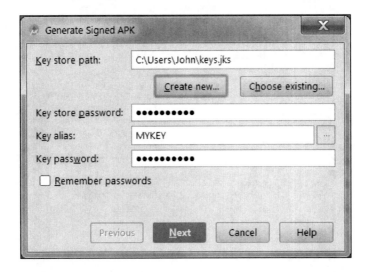

9. Now, click on **Next** to move to the next screen:

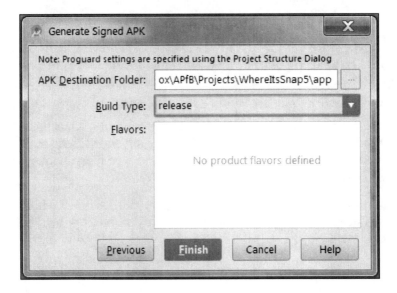

10. Choose where you would like to export your new APK file and select **release** for the **Build Type** field. Click on **Finish** and Android Studio will build the shiny new APK into the location you've specified, ready to be uploaded to the App Store.

Taking a backup of your key store in multiple safe places!

The key store is extremely valuable. If you lose it, you will effectively lose control over your app. For example, if you try to update an app that you have on Google Play, it will need to be signed by the same key. Without it, you would not be able to update it. Think of the chaos if you had lots of users and your app needed a database update, but you had to issue a whole new app because of a lost key store.

As we will need it quite soon, locate the file that has been built and ends in the `.apk` extension.

Publishing the app

Log in to your developer account at `https://play.google.com/apps/publish/`. From the left-hand side of your developer console, make sure that the **All applications** tab is selected, as shown:

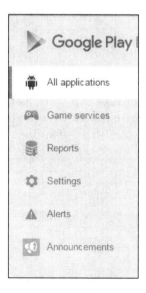

On the top right-hand side corner, click on the **Add new application** button, as shown in the next screenshot:

Now, we have a bit of form filling to do, and you will need all the images from the *Preparing to publish* section that is near the start of the chapter.

In the **ADD NEW APPLICATION** window shown next, choose a default language and type the title of your application:

Now, click on the **Upload APK** button and then the **Upload your first APK** button and browse to the APK file that you built and signed in the *Building the publishable APK file* section. Wait for the file to finish uploading:

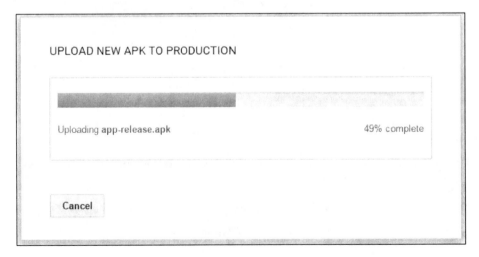

Now, from the inner left-hand side menu, click on **Store Listing**:

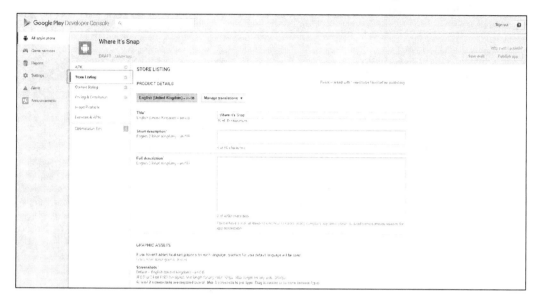

We are faced with a fair bit of form filling here. If, however, you have all your images to hand, you can get through this in about 10 minutes.

Almost all the fields are self-explanatory, and the ones that aren't have helpful tips next to the field entry box. Here are a few hints and tips to make the process smooth and produce a good end result:

- In the **Full description** and **Short description** fields, you enter the text that will be shown to potential users/buyers of your app. Be sure to make the description as enticing and exciting as you can. Mention all the best features in a clear list, but start the description with one sentence that sums up your app and what it does.

- Don't worry about the **New content rating** field as we will cover that in a minute.

- If you haven't built your app for tablet/phone devices, then don't add images in these tabs. If you have, however, make sure that you add a full range of images for each because these are the only images that the users of this type of device will see.

When you have completed the form, click on the **Save draft** button at the top-right corner of the web page.

Now, click on the **Content rating** tab and you can answer questions about your app to get a content rating that is valid (and sometimes varied) across multiple countries.

The last tab you need to complete is the **Pricing and Distribution** tab. Click on this tab and choose the **Paid** or **Free** distribution button. Then, enter a price if you've chosen **Paid**.

Note that if you choose **Free**, you can never change this. You can, however, unpublish it.

If you chose **Paid**, you can click on **Auto-convert prices now** to set up equivalent pricing for all currencies around the world.

In the **DISTRIBUTE IN THESE COUNTRIES** section, you can select countries individually or check the **SELECT ALL COUNTRIES** checkbox, as shown in the next screenshot:

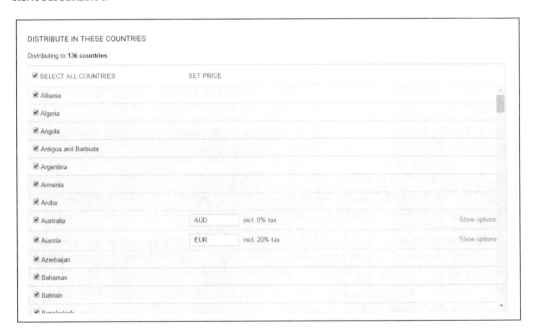

The next six options under the **Device categories** and **User programs** sections in the context of what you have learned in this book should all be left unchecked. Do read the tips to find out more about Android Wear, Android TV, Android Auto, Designed for families, Google Play for work, and Google Play for education, however.

Finally, you must check two boxes to agree with the Google consent guidelines and US export laws.

Click on the **Publish App** button in the top-right corner of the web page and your app will soon be live on Google Play. Congratulations.

Marketing

The temptation at this stage is to sit back and wait for your app to hit the top position in the best-selling apps. This never happens. You can do some things to boost your app, as shown:

- **Improve it**: To make sure that our app achieves its full potential, we need to continuously improve it by squashing bugs, making it run smoother, and making it easier/more intuitive to use.

- **Promote it**: This could be the subject of another book, but there are so many ways in which we can spread the word about our app. We can create a page/profile on all social media sites, for example, Facebook, Twitter, Flickr, and the rest. Add regular updates and announcements. We can create a website to promote our app and promote it in all the ways we would promote any other website. We can add a message in the app itself, asking players to rate it. Perhaps, pop up a message just after they have successfully used a key feature. We can ask everyone we know and everyone who visits our social media/website to rate and leave a review. There are many more ways to promote an app as well. The secret to all of them is this: to keep doing it. For example, don't create a Facebook page and then expect it to grow in popularity on its own. Keep adding to all of your channels of promotion.

- **Add worthwhile features**: There is always something new that you can add to your app. Don't add things for the sake of it. For example, the ability to play Pong in the Where it's snap app is an example of a bad feature, but the ability to draw on or customize a photo might be something your users want.

- **Various campaigns**: You can also run a paid Google Adwords campaign directly from your Google Play developer console.

More to see

Your Google Play developer console is crammed full of features and tools that are worth exploring. Some of these things are straightforward; whereas, others are quite technical. However, all are worth taking at least a quick look:

- The **All Applications** tab: By clicking on this tab, you can view statistics about downloads, ratings, and current installs. Also, see an overview of the number of **ANR** (**Application not responding**) crashes that your app has suffered.

- The **Reports** tab: Through this tab, you can search all your apps and download detailed PDF reports of your app's statistics.

- The **Crashes & ANRs** tab: If you click on one of your applications from the **All Applications** tab, you can then click on **Crashes & ANRs** to view the specific details of crashes that have occurred in a format very similar to what we have seen in the logcat. You can then fix the problem and quickly issue an update.

- The **Optimization tips** tab: If you click on one of your applications from the **All Applications** tab, you can then click on **Optimization tips**, which will display a recommended list of steps that you can take to improve sales of your app. Things such as specific localization steps for your app and support of other form factors will be shown like a to-do list.

- The **User Acquisition** tab: This tab is new and allows you to see how effective your store listing is by showing statistics such as page visitors, installers, and buyers.

Summary

It's been a long journey, and if you've reached this point, you can now pursue a career in building Android apps. Don't run off and build the next Evernote, Runtatstic, or Angry Birds just yet. Take a look at the final short chapter about what you might like to do next.

30
Before You Go

When you first opened this book, the last page probably seemed like a long way off. But it wasn't too tough, I hope.

The point is you are here now, and hopefully, you've built a few of the example apps and learned a decent amount of Java and Android along the way.

The motive behind this chapter is to congratulate you on your fine achievement. You have a working Android development environment and know your way around it. Also, you have a firm grasp of the Java programming language and have seen or developed around 40 apps.

It is worth pointing out, however, that this short chapter probably shouldn't be the end of your journey. With this in mind, let's take a look at what you can do next that might benefit you.

What next

This book has taken a very deliberate path to teach you as many different areas of Android as possible via a route that makes sense to a previously non-programming reader.

It is, therefore, possible to take the main topic from any of the chapters and expand upon it. In some cases, very significantly. Let's look at a few ways in which you can expand your current app building prowess.

Keep reading

To differentiate between reading and studying, here are a few suggestions where some light (fairly light) reading will help increase your knowledge.

GitHub

GitHub allows you to search and browse code that other people have written and see how they have solved problems. This is really useful because by seeing the file structure of classes and then dipping into them, you can often see how to plan your apps from the start, and this will prevent you from starting off on the wrong path. You can even get a GitHub app that allows you to do this from the comfort of your phone or tablet. You can even configure Android Studio to save and share your projects on GitHub. For example, search for "Android Fragment" on the homepage, `https://github.com/`, and you will see more than 1,000 related projects that you can snoop through:

StackOverflow

If you get stuck, have a weird error, or an unexplained crash, often, the best place to turn is Google. Do this and you will be surprised at how often StackOverflow seems to be prominent in the search results—and for good reason.

StackOverflow allows users to post a description of their problem along with sample code so that the community can respond with answers. In my experience, however, it is rarely necessary to post a question because there is almost always somebody who has had the exact problem earlier.

StackOverflow is especially good for bleeding-edge issues. If a new Android Studio version has a bug or a new version of the Android API seems to be not doing what it should, then you can be almost certain that a few thousand other developers around the world are having exactly the same problem as you. Then, a smart coder, often from the Android development team itself, will be there with an answer.

StackOverflow is also good for a bit of light reading. Go to the homepage, `http://stackoverflow.com/`, type `Android` in the search box, and you will see a list of all the latest problems that the StackOverflow community is having:

I am not suggesting that you dive in and start trying to answer them all just yet, but reading the problems and suggestions will teach you a lot. And you will probably find that more often than you expect, you have the solution or at least an idea of the solution. There is at least one question from the previous screenshot that readers of *Chapter 17, Sound FX and Supporting Different Versions of Android* will be able to answer.

Android user forums

Also, it is well worth signing up to Android forums and visiting them occasionally to find out what the hot topics and trends are from a user's perspective. I haven't listed any here because a quick web search is all that is required.

If you're really serious, then you can attend some Android conferences, where you can rub shoulders with thousands of other developers and attend lectures. If this interests you, perform a web search for Droidcon, Android Developer Days, and GDG DevFest.

For further study

You can now read a wider selection of other Android books. I mentioned at the start of this book that there were very few, arguably none at all, books that taught Android programming to readers with no Java experience. That was the reason I wrote this book.

Now that you have a good understanding of OOP and Java , and have also been briefly introduced to app design and patterns, you are well placed to read the Android "beginner" books for people who already know how to program in Java, like you now do.

These books are packed with really good examples that you can build or just read about to reinforce what you have learned in this book. With these, you can use your knowledge in different ways and, of course, learn some completely new stuff too.

I have already mentioned around a dozen books throughout these 30 chapters. It might also be worth reading a few pure Java books as well. It might be hard to believe, having just waded through around all these pages, but there is a whole lot more to Java than there was time to cover here.

I could name a few titles, but the books with the largest number of positive reviews on Amazon tend to be the ones worth exploring.

When you are really confident and want to get your hands dirty with more advanced concepts, Packt Publishing has a range of "Mastering" titles that are worth exploring. With these, however, you can expect a steep learning curve.

Make some apps!

You can ignore everything we talked about in this chapter if you just put this one thing into practice.

 Don't wait until you are an expert before you start making apps!

Start building your dream app, the one with all the features that are going to take Google Play by storm. A simple piece of advice, however, is this: do some planning first—not too much—and then get started.

Have a few smaller and more easily achievable projects on the sidelines. Projects that you will be able to show to friends and family, and projects that explore areas of Android that are new to you. If you are confident about these apps, you could upload them on to Google Play. If you are worried about how they might be received by reviewers, then make them free and put a note in the description about it being "just a prototype" or something similar.

If your experience is anything like mine, you will find that as you read, study, and build apps, you will discover that your dream app can be improved in many ways and you will probably be inspired to redesign it or even start again.

When you do this, I can guarantee that the next time you build it, you will do it in half the time and twice as good, at least!

gamecodeschool.com

I have a website that I hope you will visit sometime. As you can tell from the name, `http://gamecodeschool.com/` focuses on game programming. It does so not just for Android, but for many platforms and covers a number of different programming languages too.

Even if your focus is non-gaming apps, you will find lots of articles and projects that will help your regular coding too. This is especially true if your next app will use graphics, sound, animation, screen touch handling, databases, threads, and so on. This is also true if you want to get started making apps for other platforms or multiple platforms simultaneously.

And if you are new to coding and you want to make games, then the website was made for you.

Goodbye and thank you

I had a lot of fun writing this book. I know that's a cliché, but it's also true. Most importantly though, I hope you've managed to take something from it and are able to use it as a stepping stone for your future in programming.

You are perhaps reading this for a bit of fun or the kudos of releasing an app, a stepping stone to a programming job, or maybe you actually do build that app to take Google Play by storm. Whatever the case, a big thank you from me for buying this book, and I wish you all the luck for your future endeavors.

Index

out of bounds exceptions 309
used, for entering nth dimension 305
used, for handling large amount
    of data 298-300

B

BaseAdapter
about 313
inner classes 317
URL 318, 329
using, with ListView 314-317
basic classes mini app
about 193-196
first class 196, 197
Bfxr
URL 384
bitmap formats
URL 602

C

camel casing 140
camera
used, for capturing images 493, 494
canvas
drawing with 601
capture Fragment, Where in the
    world mini app
coding 500-507
layout, creating 501, 503
testing 508
capturing images mini app
about 494, 495
camera permission, adding to
    manifest 495, 496
camera used 493, 494
capture Fragment, coding 500
MainActivity class, coding 497, 498
simple layout, defining 496
Simple Photo app, running 499, 500
chaining 269, 209
CheckBox widget 250, 251
class
about 188
access, in nutshell 199
code 188

implementation 189
object, declaring 190-193
object, initializing 190
object, using 190
class declaration 46
class use
controlling, access modifiers used 198, 199
code
exploring 45-47
code comments 137, 138
Color class
URL 260
communications interface
coding 546
compiling 1
configuration qualifiers
about 409, 410
summary 412
using 411
constant 209
constructor
about 190
objects, setting up 206, 207
controller 400

D

Dalvik EXecutable (DEX) code 1
Dalvik Virtual Machine (DVM) 2
data
passing, between activities 333, 334
persisting, with SharedPreferences 338-340
database mini app
about 510, 517
class, coding 520-523
database class, coding 520-524
layout, implementing 517, 520
MainActivity, coding 524-527
running 527, 528
decisions
about 150
boolean variable 153
code, indenting 151
else keyword 154-156
making 156, 157
operators 152, 153
Switch Demo app 157, 158

onStop method 413
reference link 413

G

gamecodeschool.com 649
getActivity method 291
GitHub
  about 646
  URL 646
Global Positioning System (GPS) 557, 558
GNSS (Global Navigation
        Satellite System) 557
Google Developers Console 565
Google Maps mini app
  about 564, 565
  API key, acquiring 565-568
  connecting to 565
Google Play services API
  installing 568, 569
  MapsActivity, coding 570
  maps_activity layout, coding 570
  simple map app, running 571
GPS mini app
  about 558, 559
  simple layout, implementing 559, 560
Gradle
  URL 70
gravity
  using 92

H

HAXM (Hardware Acceleration Execution
        Manager) 36

I

image gallery/slider app
  building 459
  layout, implementing 460, 461
  MainActivity class, coding 464, 465
  PagerAdapter class, coding 461-463
  running 465, 466
ImageView image 244, 245
inheritance mini app 217-221

instance 186
integrated development
        environment (IDE) 5
intent class 331, 332
Inter-Fragment communications
  defining 427-429
interpolators
  about 360
  reference link 360

J

Java
  about 3, 59, 136
  and Android, working 1
  animations, controlling 358
  Animations Demo app, wiring up 367-375
  class 3
  code comments 137, 138
  code, structure 133, 134
  code, writing 61, 62
  comments 60
  messages, sending 60
  methods, writing 63, 64
  object 3
  syntax 136, 137
Java array 299
Java code, structure
  about 23
  Android packages 23-25
Java exceptions 347
Java JDK downloads
  URL 8
Java Runtime Environment (JRE) 7
JavaScript Object Notation (JSON) 346
JDK
  about 7
  installing 7-14
JSON data
  URL 353

K

key-value pairs 334

X

Thank you for buying
Android Programming for Beginners

About Packt Publishing

Packt, pronounced 'packed', published its first book, *Mastering phpMyAdmin for Effective MySQL Management*, in April 2004, and subsequently continued to specialize in publishing highly focused books on specific technologies and solutions.

Our books and publications share the experiences of your fellow IT professionals in adapting and customizing today's systems, applications, and frameworks. Our solution-based books give you the knowledge and power to customize the software and technologies you're using to get the job done. Packt books are more specific and less general than the IT books you have seen in the past. Our unique business model allows us to bring you more focused information, giving you more of what you need to know, and less of what you don't.

Packt is a modern yet unique publishing company that focuses on producing quality, cutting-edge books for communities of developers, administrators, and newbies alike. For more information, please visit our website at www.packtpub.com.

About Packt Open Source

In 2010, Packt launched two new brands, Packt Open Source and Packt Enterprise, in order to continue its focus on specialization. This book is part of the Packt Open Source brand, home to books published on software built around open source licenses, and offering information to anybody from advanced developers to budding web designers. The Open Source brand also runs Packt's Open Source Royalty Scheme, by which Packt gives a royalty to each open source project about whose software a book is sold.

Writing for Packt

We welcome all inquiries from people who are interested in authoring. Book proposals should be sent to author@packtpub.com. If your book idea is still at an early stage and you would like to discuss it first before writing a formal book proposal, then please contact us; one of our commissioning editors will get in touch with you.

We're not just looking for published authors; if you have strong technical skills but no writing experience, our experienced editors can help you develop a writing career, or simply get some additional reward for your expertise.

Android Studio Cookbook

ISBN: 978-1-78528-618-6   Paperback: 232 pages

Design, debug, and test your apps using
Android Studio

1. See what Material design is about and how to
   apply it your apps.

2. Explore the possibilities to develop apps that
   works on any type of device.

3. A step-by-step practical guide that will help
   you build improved applications, change their
   look, and debug them.

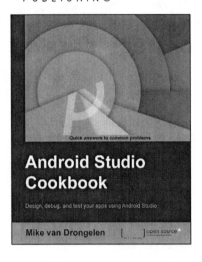

Learning Android Google Maps

ISBN: 978-1-84969-886-3   Paperback: 356 pages

Integrate Google Maps with your Android
application to offer feature-rich and interactive maps

1. Set up the development environment and
   obtain the Google API key to create your first
   map application.

2. Create a cutting edge Google maps application
   by implementing all the concepts learned.

3. A step-by-step tutorial guide that is full of
   pragmatic examples.

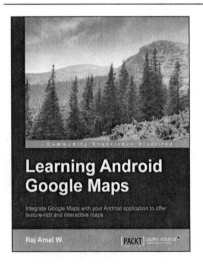

Please check **www.PacktPub.com** for information on our titles